First Footsteps in East Africa

or,

An Exploration of Harar

Richard F. Burton

Edited by Isabel Burton

TWO VOLUMES
BOUND AS ONE

Dover Publications, Inc.
NEW YORK

Published in Canada by General Publishing Company, Ltd., 30 Lesmill Road, Don Mills, Toronto, Ontario.

Published in the United Kingdom by Constable and Company, Ltd.

This Dover edition, first published in 1987, is an unabridged republication in a single volume of the work as published by Tylston and Edwards, London, 1894, as Volumes VI and VII of "The Memorial Edition of the Works of Captain Sir Richard F. Burton, K.C.M.G., F.R.G.S., &c., &c., &c." (Absolute first edition of the work: 1856.) The four color plates of the 1894 edition appear here in black and white. A reference in the "List of Illustrations in Volume I" to a nonexistent illustration has been deleted.

Manufactured in the United States of America
Dover Publications, Inc., 31 East 2nd Street, Mineola, N.Y. 11501

Library of Congress Cataloging-in-Publication Data

Burton, Richard Francis, Sir, 1821–1890.
First footsteps in East Africa, or, An exploration of Harar.

Reprint. Previously published: London : Tylston and Edwards, 1894. (The memorial edition of the works of Captain Sir Richard F. Burton ; v. 6–7)
Includes index.
1. Somalia—Description and travel. 2. Hárer (Ethiopia)—Description. 3. Harari language. I. Burton, Isabel, Lady, 1831–1896. II. Title. III. Title: Exploration of Harar.
DT401.8.B87   1987   963'.2   87-13639
ISBN 0-486-25475-5 (pbk.)

DUTERCQ. DEL.^

HARAR FROM THE COFFE STREAM

FIRST FOOTSTEPS

IN

EAST AFRICA

OR,

AN EXPLORATION OF HARAR

BY

CAPTAIN SIR RICHARD F. BURTON,

K.C.M.G., F.R.G.S., &c., &c., &c.

EDITED BY HIS WIFE,

ISABEL BURTON.

Memorial Edition.

————

IN TWO VOLUMES.
VOLUME I.

CONTENTS

OF

THE FIRST VOLUME.

———

LIST OF ILLUSTRATIONS

IN VOLUME I.

PREFACE

TO

The Memorial Edition.

AFTER Richard Burton left Meccah, he returned up the Red Sea to Egypt, and after a short rest, to Bombay. The East India Company Service had long wished to explore Somali-land in Abyssinia, because Berberah, its chief port, is far better than Aden. As Harar, its capital, was the most difficult place, and no white man had ever succeeded in entering it, the whole country being then inhabited by a most dangerous race to deal with, he obtained leave to go there as a private traveller, the Company agreeing to allow him his pay, but no Government protection. He applied for three other Anglo-Indian Officers (amongst them Lieutenant Speke), to tell off to different employments on the coast. Speke was to go to Bunder Guray to buy horses and camels, Herne was to go to Berberah on another errand, and Stroyan on a third errand was to meet him there, whilst Richard Burton was to do the dangerous part, *i.e.*, plunge into the country, and enter Harar as an Arab merchant. This was one of his most splendid and dangerous expeditions, and the least known, partly because his pilgrimage to Meccah was in every man's mouth, and partly because the excitement aroused by the Crimean War had to a large extent deadened the interest in all personal adventure.

He disappeared into the desert for four months, but this unnoticed, unknown, journey has been of great importance to the Egyptians, to the English, and now to the Italian Army. The way was long and weary, adventurous and dangerous, but at last the " Dreadful City " was sighted, and relying on his good Star and audacity, he walked boldly in, sending his compliments to the Amir, and asking for audience. His diplomacy on this occasion, his capacity for passing as an Arab, and his sound Mohammedan Theology, gave him ten days in the City, where he slept every night in peril of his life.

The journey back was full of peril, the provisions being only five biscuits, a few limes, a few lumps of sugar, and a single skin of water. They passed through a terrible desert, such as Grant Allen describes when relating the journey of Mohammed Ali and Ivan Royle from Eagle City through the desert to Carthage. When Richard however had made up his mind that he would soon become food for the desert beasts, for he had been thirty-six hours without water, could go no further, and was prepared to die the worst of all deaths, a bird flew by him, and plunging down a hundred yards away showed him a charming spring, a little shaft of water about two feet in diameter, in a margin of green; man and beast raced to it, and drank till they could drink no more.

By dodging his enemies he at last reached the coast of Berberah, where he found his three comrades, and where he and the wretched mule were duly provided for, and he says he "fell asleep, conscious of having performed a feat which, like a certain ride to York, will live in local annals for many and many a year."

But he would not " let well alone " ; he wanted to make a new expedition, Nilewards *viâ* Harar, on a large and imposing scale, and he went and came back from Aden with forty-two armed men, established an agency, and a camp in a place where he could have the protection of an English gunboat which brought them ; but unfortunately the Government drew off the gun-boat, and 300 of the natives swarmed round them in the night, and tried to throw the tents down, and trap them like mice. They fought desperately, but Speke received eleven wounds, poor Stroyan was killed, Herne was untouched, and Richard Burton, sabreing his way through the crowd, heard a friendly voice behind him, hesitated for a moment, and received a javelin through both cheeks, carrying away four teeth, and transfixing the palate. He could not draw it out on account of its barb and had to wander up and down on the coast for hours from night to daylight. They all managed to escape to the water's edge, where they hailed a native craft, which was just sailing out, and to whose master and crew Richard fortunately had shown great hospitality. They picked them up and managed to extract the javelin and bind up his jaws till they reached Aden. They were so badly wounded that they had to return to England, and as soon as he recovered, he proceeded to the Crimea.

Every word of this narrative is full of interest, and ought to be especially so at the present moment to the Italian Army, which now occupies the country that was in those days so difficult to enter.

Isabel Burton.

January 25th, 1894.

PREFACE

TO THE

FIRST (1856) EDITION.

AVERSE to writing, as well as to reading, diffuse Prolegomena, the author finds himself compelled to relate, at some length, the circumstances which led to the subject of these pages.

In May 1849, the late Vice-Admiral Sir Charles Malcolm, formerly Superintendent of the Indian Navy, in conjunction with Mr. William John Hamilton, then President of the Royal Geographical Society of Great Britain, solicited the permission of the Court of Directors of the Honourable East India Company to ascertain the productive resources of the unknown Somali Country in East Africa.[1] The answer returned, was to the following effect :—

" If a fit and proper person volunteer to travel in the Somali Country, he goes as a private traveller, the Government giving no more protection to him than they would to an individual totally unconnected with the

------

[1] It occupies the whole of the Eastern Horn, extending from the north of Bab al-Mandeb to several degrees south of Cape Guardafui. In the former direction it is bounded by the Dankali and the Ittu Gallas; in the latter by the Sawahil or Negrotic regions; the Red Sea is its eastern limit, and westward it stretches to within a few miles of Harar.

service. They will allow the officer who obtains permission to go, during his absence on the expedition, to retain all the pay and allowances he may be enjoying when leave was granted: they will supply him with all the instruments required, afford him a passage going and returning, and pay the actual expenses of the journey."

The project lay dormant until March 1850, when Sir Charles Malcolm and Captain Smyth, President of the Royal Geographical Society of Great Britain, waited upon the chairman of the Court of Directors of the Honourable East India Company. He informed them that if they would draw up a statement of what was required, and specify how it could be carried into effect, the document should be forwarded to the Governor-General of India, with a recommendation that, should no objection arise, either from expense or other causes, a fit person should be permitted to explore the Somali Country.

Sir Charles Malcolm then offered the charge of the expedition to Dr. Carter, of Bombay, an officer favourably known to the Indian world by his services on board the "Palinurus" brig whilst employed upon the maritime survey of Eastern Arabia. Dr. Carter at once acceded to the terms proposed by those from whom the project emanated; but his principal object being to compare the geology and botany of the Somali Country with the results of his Arabian travels, he volunteered to traverse only that part of Eastern Africa which lies north of a line drawn from Berberah to Ras Hafun—in fact, the maritime mountains of the Somal. His health not permitting him to be left on shore, he required a cruizer to convey him from place to place, and to preserve his store of presents and provisions. By this means he hoped to land at the most interesting points, and to penetrate here and there from sixty to eighty miles inland, across the region which he undertook to explore.

On the 17th of August, 1850, Sir Charles Malcolm wrote to Dr. Carter in these terms:—"I have communicated with the President of the Royal Geographical Society and others: the feeling is, that though much valuable information could no doubt be gained by skirting the coast (as you propose) both in geology and botany, yet that it does not fulfil the primary and great object of the London Geographical Society, which was, and still is, to have the interior explored." The Vice-Admiral, however, proceeded to say that, under the circumstances of the case, Dr. Carter's plans were approved of, and asked him to confer immediately with Commodore Lushington, then Commander-in-Chief of the Indian Navy.

In May 1851, Vice-Admiral Sir Charles Malcolm died: geographers and travellers lost in him an influential and an energetic friend. During the ten years of his superintendence over the Indian Navy, that service rose, despite the incubus of profound peace, to the highest distinction. He freely permitted the officers under his command to undertake the task of geographical discovery, retaining their rank, pay, and batta, whilst the actual expenses of their journeys were defrayed by contingent bills. All papers and reports submitted to the local government were favourably received, and the successful traveller looked forward to distinction and advancement.

During the decade which elapsed between 1828 and 1838, "officers of the Indian Navy journeyed, as the phrase is, *with their lives in their hands*, through the wildest districts of the East. Of these we name the late Commander J. A. Young, Lieutenants Wellsted, Wyburd, Wood, and Christopher, retired Commander Ormsby, the present Capt. H. B. Lynch C.B., Commanders Felix Jones and W. C. Barker, Lieutenants Cruttenden and Whitelock. Their researches extended from the banks of the Bosphorus to the shores of India.

Of the vast, the immeasurable value of such services,"
to quote the words of the Quarterly Review (No. cxxix.
Dec. 1839), "which able officers thus employed, are in
the mean time rendering to science, to commerce, to
their country, and to the whole civilized world, we need
say nothing :—nothing we could say would be too much."

"In five years, the admirable maps of that coral-
bound gulf—the Red Sea—were complete: the terrors
of the navigation had given place to the confidence
inspired by excellent surveys.   In 1829 the Thetis of ten
guns, under Commander Robert Moresby, convoyed the
first coal ship up the Red Sea, of the coasts of which
this skilful and enterprising seaman made a cursory
survey, from which emanated the subsequent trigonometrical operations which form our present maps.   Two
ships were employed, the 'Benares' and 'Palinurus,' the
former under Commander Elwon, the latter under Commander Moresby.   It remained, however, for the latter
officer to complete the work.   Some idea may be formed
of the perils these officers and men went through, when
we state the 'Benares' was forty-two times aground."

"Robert Moresby, the genius of the Red Sea,
conducted also the survey of the Maldive Islands and
groups known as the Chagos Archipelago.   He narrowly
escaped being a victim to the deleterious climate of his
station, and only left it when no longer capable of working.
A host of young and ardent officers — Christopher,
Young, Powell, Campbell, Jones, Barker, and others—
ably seconded him : death was busy amongst them for
months and so paralyzed by disease were the living, that
the anchors could scarcely be raised for a retreat to the
coast of India.   Renovated by a three months' stay,
occasionally in port, where they were strengthened by
additional numbers, the undaunted remnants from time
to time returned to their task ; and in 1837, gave to the
world a knowledge of those singular groups which

heretofore—though within 150 miles of our coasts—had been a mystery hidden within the dangers that environed them. The beautiful maps of the Red Sea, drafted by the late Commodore Carless,[1] then a lieutenant, will ever remain permanent monuments of Indian Naval Science, and the daring of its officers and men. Those of the Maldive and Chagos groups, executed by Commander then Acting Lieutenant Felix Jones, were, we hear, of such a high order, that they were deemed worthy of special inspection by the Queen."

" While these enlightening operations were in progress, there were others of this profession, no less distinguished, employed on similar discoveries. The coast of Mekran westward from Scinde, was little known, but it soon found a place in the hydrographical offices of India, under Captain, then Lieutenant, Stafford Haines, and his staff, who were engaged on it. The journey to the Oxus, made by Lieut. Wood, Sir A. Burnes's companion in his Lahore and Afghan missions, is a page of history which may not be opened to us again in our own times; while in Lieut. Carless's drafts of the channels of the Indus, we trace those designs, that the sword of Sir Charles Napier only was destined to reveal."

" The ten years prior to that of 1839 were those of fitful repose, such as generally precedes some great outbreak. The repose afforded ample leisure for research,

---

1 In A.D. 1838, Lieut. Carless surveyed the seaboard of the Somali country, from Ras Hafun to Burnt Island ; unfortunately his labours were allowed by Sir Charles Malcolm's successor to lie five years in the obscurity of MS. Meanwhile the steam frigate " Memnon," Capt. Powell commanding, was lost at Ras Assayr ; a Norie's chart, an antiquated document, with an error of from fifteen to twenty miles, being the only map of reference on board. Thus the Indian Government, by the dilatoriness and prejudices of its Superintendent of Marine, sustained an unjustifiable loss of at least 50,000*l*.

and the shores of the island of Socotra, with the south coast of Arabia, were carefully delineated. Besides the excellent maps of these regions, we are indebted to the survey for that unique work on Oman, by the late Lieut. Wellsted of this service, and for valuable notices from the pen of Lieut. Cruttenden.[1]"

" Besides the works we have enumerated, there were others of the same nature, but on a smaller scale, in operation at the same period around our own coasts. The Gulf of Cambay, and the dangerous sands known as the Molucca Banks, were explored and faithfully mapped by Captain Richard Ethersey, assisted by Lieutenant (now Commander) Fell. Bombay Harbour was de-lineated again on a grand scale by Capt. R. Cogan, assisted by Lieut. Peters, now both dead ; and the ink of the Maldive charts had scarcely dried, when the labours of those employed were demanded of the Indian Govern-ment by Her Majesty's authorities at Ceylon, to undertake trigonometrical surveys of that Island, and the dangerous and shallow gulfs on either side of the neck of sand con-necting it with India. They were the present Captains F. F. Powell, and Richard Ethersey, in the Schooner ' Royal Tiger ' and ' Shannon,' assisted by Lieut. (now Commander) Felix Jones, and the late Lieut. Wilmot Christopher, who fell in action before Mooltan. The first of these officers had charge of one of the tenders under Lieut. Powell, and the latter another under Lieut. Ethersey. The maps of the Pamban Pass and the Straits of Manaar were by the hand of Lieut. Felix Jones, who was the draftsman also on this survey: they speak for themselves.[2]"

---

1 In A.D. 1836-38, Lieut. Cruttenden published descriptions of travel, which will be alluded to in a subsequent part of this preface.

2 This "hasty sketch of the scientific labours of the Indian navy," is extracted from an able anonymous pamphlet, un-promisingly headed " Grievances and Present Condition of our Indian Officers."

In 1838 Sir Charles Malcolm was succeeded by Sir Robert Oliver, an " old officer of the old school"—a strict disciplinarian, a faithful and honest servant of Government, but a violent, limited, and prejudiced man. He wanted " sailors," individuals conversant with ropes and rigging, and steeped in knowledge of shot and shakings, he loved the "rule of thumb," he hated " literary razors," and he viewed science with the profoundest contempt. About twenty surveys were ordered to be discontinued as an inauguratory measure, causing the loss of many thousand pounds, independent of such contingencies as the "Memnon."[1] Batta was withheld from the few officers who obtained leave, and the life of weary labour on board ship was systematically made monotonous and uncomfortable : — in local phrase it was described as " many stripes and no stars." Few measures were omitted to heighten the shock of contrast. No notice was taken of papers forwarded to Government, and the man who attempted to distinguish himself by higher views than quarter-deck duties, found himself marked out for the angry Commodore's red-hot displeasure. No place was allowed for charts and plans : valuable original surveys, of which no duplicates existed, lay tossed amongst the brick and mortar with which the Marine Office was being rebuilt. No instruments were provided for ships, even a barometer was not supplied in one case, although duly indented for during five years. Whilst Sir Charles Malcolm ruled the Bombay dockyards, the British name rose high in the Indian, African, and Arabian seas. Each vessel had its presents—guns, pistols, and powder, Abbas, crimson cloth and shawls, watches, telescopes and similar articles—with a suitable

---

[1] In A.D. 1848, the late Mr. Joseph Hume called in the House of Commons for a return of all Indian surveys carried on during the ten previous years. The result proved that no fewer than a score had been suddenly " broken up," by order of Sir Robert Oliver.

stock of which every officer visiting the interior on leave
was supplied. An order from Sir Robert Oliver withdrew presents as well as instruments : with them disappeared the just idea of our faith and greatness as a
nation entertained by the maritime races, who formerly
looked forward to the arrival of our cruizers. Thus the
Indian navy was crushed by neglect and routine into
a mere transport service, remarkable for little beyond
constant quarrels between sea-lieutenants and land-
lieutenants, sailor-officers and soldier-officers, their
" passengers." And thus resulted that dearth of enterprise—alluded to *ex cathedrâ* by a late President of the
Royal Geographical Society of Great Britain—which
now characterizes Western India erst so celebrated for
ardour in adventure.

To return to the subject of East African discovery.
Commodore Lushington and Dr. Carter met in order
to concert some measures for forwarding the plans of
a Somali Expedition. It was resolved to associate
three persons, Drs. Carter and Stocks, and an officer
of the Indian navy : a vessel was also warned for service
on the coast of Africa. This took place in the beginning
of 1851 : presently Commodore Lushington resigned his
command, and the project fell to the ground.

The author of these pages, after his return from
Al-Hijaz to Bombay, conceived the idea of reviving
the Somali Expedition : he proposed to start in the
spring of 1854, and accompanied by two officers, to
penetrate *viâ* Harar and Gananah to Zanzibar. His
plans were favourably received by the Right Hon. Lord
Elphinstone, the enlightened governor of the colony,
and by the local authorities, amongst whom the name
of James Grant Lumsden, then Member of the Council,
will ever suggest the liveliest feelings of gratitude and
affection. But it being judged necessary to refer once
more for permission to the Court of Directors, an official

letter bearing date the 28th April, 1854, was forwarded
from Bombay with a warm recommendation.   Lieut.
Herne of the 1st Bombay European Regiment of Fusil-
eers, an officer skilful in surveying, photography, and
mechanics, together with the writer, obtained leave,
pending the reference, and a free passage to Aden in
Arabia.   On the 23rd August a favourable reply was
despatched by the Court of Directors.

Meanwhile the most painful of events had modified
the original plan.   The third member of the Expedition,
Assistant Surgeon J. Ellerton Stocks, whose brilliant
attainments as a botanist, whose long and enterprising
journeys, and whose eminently practical bent of mind
had twice recommended him for the honours and trials
of African exploration, died suddenly of apoplexy in the
prime of life.   Deeply did his friends lament him for many
reasons: a universal favourite, he left in the social circle
a void never to be filled up, and they mourned the more
that Fate had not granted him the time, as it had given
him the will and the power, to trace a deeper and more
enduring mark upon the iron tablets of Fame.

No longer hoping to carry out his first project, the
writer determined to make the geography and commerce
of the Somali country his principal objects.   He therefore applied to the Bombay Government for the assistance
of Lieut. William Stroyan, I. N., an officer distinguished
by his surveys on the coast of Western India, in Sind,
and on the Panjab Rivers.   It was not without difficulty
that such valuable services were spared for the deadly
purpose of penetrating into Eastern Africa.   All obstacles,
however, were removed by their ceaseless and energetic
efforts, who had fostered the author's plans, and early
in the autumn of 1854, Lieut. Stroyan received leave
to join the Expedition.   At the same time, Lieut. J. H.
Speke, of the 46th Regiment Bengal N. I., who had
spent many years collecting the Fauna of Thibet and

the Himalayan mountains, volunteered to share the hardships of African exploration.

In October 1854, the writer and his companions received at Aden in Arabia the sanction of the Court of Directors. It was his intention to march n a body, using Berberah as a base of operations, westwards to Harar, and thence in a south-easterly direction towards Zanzibar.

But the voice of society at Aden was loud against the expedition. The rough manners, the fierce looks, and the insolent threats of the Somal—the effects of our too peaceful rule—had prepossessed the timid colony at the " Eye of Al-Yaman " with an idea of extreme danger. The Anglo-Saxon spirit suffers, it has been observed, from confinement with any but wooden walls, and the European degenerates rapidly, as do his bull-dogs, his game-cocks, and other pugnacious animals, in the hot, enervating, and unhealthy climates of the East. The writer and his comrades were represented to be. men deliberately going to their death, and the Somal at Aden were not slow in imitating the example of their rulers. The savages had heard of the costly Shoa Mission, its 300 camels and 50 mules, and they longed for another rehearsal of the drama : according to them a vast outlay was absolutely necessary, every village must be feasted, every chief propitiated with magnificent presents, and dollars must be dealt out by handfuls. The Political Resident refused to countenance the scheme proposed, and his objection necessitated a further change of plans.

Accordingly, Lieut. Herne was directed to proceed, after the opening of the annual fair-season, to Berberah, where no danger was apprehended. It was judged that the residence of this officer upon the coast would produce a friendly feeling on the part of the Somal, and, as indeed afterwards proved to be the case, would facilitate the writer's egress from Harar, by terrifying the ruler for the fate of his caravans.[1] Lieut. Herne, who on the 1st of January 1855, was joined by Lieut. Stroyan, resided on the African coast from November to April; he inquired into the commerce, the caravan lines, and the state of the slave trade, visited the maritime mountains, sketched all the places of interest, and made a variety of meteorological and other observations as a prelude to extensive research.

Lieut. Speke was directed to land at Bunder Guray, a small harbour in the "Arz al-Aman," or "Land of Safety," as the windward Somal style their country. His aim was to trace the celebrated Wady Nogal, noting its watershed and other peculiarities, to purchase horses and camels for the future use of the Expedition, and to collect specimens of the reddish earth which, according to the older African travellers, denotes the presence of gold dust.[2] Lieut. Speke started on the 23rd October 1854, and returned, after about three months, to Aden. He had failed, through the rapacity and treachery of his guide, to reach the Wady Nogal. But he had penetrated beyond the maritime chain of hills, and his journal (condensed in the Appendix) proves that he had collected some novel and important information.

Meanwhile the author, assuming the disguise of an Arab merchant, prepared to visit the forbidden city of Harar. He left Aden on the 29th of October 1854, arrived at the capital of the ancient Hadiyah Empire on the 3rd January 1855, and on the 9th of the ensuing February returned in safety to Arabia, with the

---

1 This plan was successfully adopted by Messrs. Antoine and Arnauld d'Abbadie, when travelling in dangerous parts of Abyssinia and the adjacent countries.

2 In A.D. 1660, Vermuyden found gold at Gambia always "on naked and barren hills embedded in a reddish earth." All I got was a big lizard : lost £500.

view of purchasing stores and provisions for a second and a longer journey.[1] What unforeseen circumstance cut short the career of the proposed Expedition, the Postscript of the present volume will show.

The following pages contain the writer's diary, kept during his march to and from Harar. It must be borne in mind that the region traversed on this occasion was previously known only by the vague reports of native travellers. All the Abyssinian discoverers had traversed the Dankali and other northern tribes: the land of the Somal was still a *terra incognita.* Harar, moreover, had never been visited, and few are the cities of the world which in the present age, when men hurry about the earth, have not opened their gates to European ad-venture. The ancient metropolis of a once mighty race, the only permanent settlement in Eastern Africa, the reported seat of Moslem learning, a walled city of stone houses, possessing its independent chief, its peculiar population, its unknown language, and its own coinage, the emporium of the coffee trade, the head-quarters of slavery, the birth-place of the Kat plant,[2] and the great manufactory of cotton-cloths, amply, it appeared, deserved the trouble of exploration. That the writer was successful in his attempt, the following pages will prove. Unfortunately it was found impossible to use

---

1 The writer has not unfrequently been blamed by the critics of Indian papers, for venturing into such dangerous lands with an outfit nearly 1500*l.* in value. In the Somali, as in other countries of Eastern Africa, travellers must carry not only the means of purchasing passage, but also the very necessaries of life. Money being unknown, such bulky articles as cotton-cloth, tobacco, and beads are necessary to provide meat and milk, and he who would eat bread must load his camels with grain. The Somal of course exaggerate the cost of travelling; every chief, however, may demand a small present, and every pauper, as will be seen in the following pages, expects to be fed.

2 It is described at length in Chap. III.

any instruments except a pocket compass, a watch, and a portable thermometer more remarkable for convenience than for correctness. But the way was thus paved for scientific observation: shortly after the author's departure from Harar, the Amir or chief wrote to the Acting Political Resident at Aden, earnestly begging to be supplied with a " Frank physician," and offering protection to any European who might be persuaded to visit his dominions.

The Appendix contains the following papers connected with the movements of the expedition in the year 1854.

1. The diary and observations made by Lieut. Speke, when attempting to reach the Wady Nogal.

2. A sketch of the grammar, and a vocabulary of the Harari tongue. This dialect is little known to European linguists : the only notices of it hitherto published are in Salt's Abyssinia, Appendix I. pp. 6—10; by Balbi Atlas Ethnogr. Tab. xxxix. No. 297; Kielmaier, Ausland, 1840, No. 76; and Dr. Beke (Philological Journal, April 25, 1845).

3. Meteorological observations in the cold season of 1854—55 by Lieuts. Herne, Stroyan, and the Author.

4. A brief description of certain peculiar customs, noticed in Nubia, by Brown and Werne under the name of fibulation.[1]

5. The conclusion is a condensed account of an attempt to reach Harar from Ankobar.[2] On the 14th October 1841, Major Sir William Cornwallis Harris (then Captain in the Bombay Engineers), Chief of the Mission

---

1 [The publishers of the present edition have made diligent search for the MS. of this Appendix, which the publishers of the first edition " found it necessary to omit," but they regret to say that no trace of it can be found.]

2 The author hoped to insert Lieut. Herne's journal, kept at Berberah, and the different places of note in its vicinity ; as yet, however, the paper has not been received.

sent from India to the King of Shoa, advised Lieut. W. Barker, I. N., whose services were imperatively required by Sir Robert Oliver, to return from Abyssinia *via* Harar, " over a road hitherto untrodden by Europeans." As His Majesty Sahalah Selassie had offered friendly letters to the Moslem Amir, Capt. Harris had " no doubt of the success of the enterprise." Although the adventurous explorer was prevented by the idle fears of the Badawin Somal and the rapacity of his guides from visiting the city, his pages, as a narrative of travel, will amply reward perusal. They have been introduced into this volume mainly with the view of putting the reader in possession of all that has hitherto been written and not published, upon the subject of Harar.[1] For the same reason the author has not hesitated to enrich his pages with observations drawn from Lieutenants Cruttenden and Rigby. The former printed in the Transactions of the Bombay Geographical Society two excellent papers : one headed " Report on the Mijjertheyn Tribe of Somallies inhabiting the district forming the North East Point of Africa ; " secondly, a " Memoir on

---

[1] Harar has frequently been described by hearsay ; the following are the principal authorities :—

Rochet (Second Voyage Dans le Pays des Adels, &c. Paris, 1846), page 263.

Sir W. Cornwallis Harris (Highlands of Æthiopia, vol. i. ch. 43, et passim).

Cruttenden (Transactions of the Bombay Geological Society A.D. 1848).

Barker (Report of the probable Position of Harar. Vol. xii. Royal Geographical Society).

M'Queen (Geographical Memoirs of Abyssinia, prefixed to Journals of Rev. Messrs. Isenberg and Krapf).

Christopher (Journal whilst commanding the H. C.'s brig " Tigris," on the East Coast of Africa).

Of these by far the most correct account is that of Lieut. Cruttenden.

the Western or Edoor Tribes, inhabiting the Somali coast of North East Africa ; with the Southern Branches of the family of Darood, resident on the banks of the Webbe Shebayli, commonly called the River Webbe." Lieut. C. P. Rigby, 16th Regiment Bombay N. I., published, also in the Transactions of the Geographical Society of Bombay, an " Outline of the Somali Language, with Vocabulary," which supplied a great lacuna in the dialects of Eastern Africa.

A perusal of the following pages will convince the reader that the extensive country of the Somal is by no means destitute of capabilities. Though partially desert, and thinly populated, it possesses valuable articles of traffic, and its harbours export the produce of the Gurague, Abyssinian, Galla, and other inland races. The natives of the country are essentially commercial: they have lapsed into barbarism by reason of their political condition—the rude equality of the Hottentots, —but they appear to contain material for a moral regeneration. As subjects they offer a favourable contrast to their kindred, the Arabs of Al-Yaman, a race untameable as the wolf, and which, subjugated in turn by Abyssinian, Persian, Egyptian, and Turk, has ever preserved an indomitable spirit of freedom, and eventually succeeded in shaking off the yoke of foreign dominion. For half a generation we have been masters of Aden, filling Southern Arabia with our calicoes and rupees—what is the present state of affairs there ? We are dared by the Badawin to come forth from behind our stone walls and fight like men in the plain,—British *protégés* are slaughtered within the range of our guns —our allies' villages have been burned in sight of Aden—our deserters are welcomed and our fugitive felons protected,—our supplies are cut off, and the garrison is reduced to extreme distress, at the word of a half-naked bandit—the miscreant Bhagi who mur-

dered Captain Mylne in cold blood still roams the hills
unpunished—gross insults are the sole acknowledgments
of our peaceful overtures—the British flag has been
fired upon without return, our cruizers being ordered to
act only on the defensive,—and our forbearance to attack
is universally asserted and believed to arise from mere
cowardice. Such is, and such will be, the character of
the Arab!

The Sublime Porte still preserves her possessions in
the Tahamah, and the regions conterminous to Al-Yaman,
by the stringent measures with which Mohammed
Ali of Egypt opened the robber-haunted Suez road.
Whenever a Turk or a traveller is murdered, a few
squadrons of Irregular Cavalry are ordered out; they
are not too nice upon the subject of retaliation, and
rarely refuse to burn a village or two, or to lay waste
the crops near the scene of outrage.

A civilized people, like ourselves, objects to such
measures for many reasons, of which none is more feeble
than the fear of perpetuating a blood feud with the
Arabs. Our present relations with them are a " very
pretty quarrel," and moreover one which time must
strengthen, cannot efface. By a just, wholesome, and
unsparing severity we may inspire the Badawi with
fear instead of contempt: the veriest visionary would
deride the attempt to animate him with a higher
sentiment.

" Peace," observes a modern sage, " is the dream of
the wise, war is the history of man." To indulge in
such dreams is but questionable wisdom. It was not a
" peace-policy" which gave the Portuguese a seaboard
extending from Cape Non to Macao. By no peace
policy the Osmanlis of a past age pushed their victorious
arms from the deserts of Tartary to Aden, to Delhi, to
Algiers, and to the gates of Vienna. It was no peace
policy which made the Russians seat themselves upon

the shores of the Black, the Baltic, and the Caspian seas: gaining in the space of 150 years, and, despite war, retaining, a territory greater than England and France united. No peace policy enabled the French to absorb region after region in Northern Africa, till the Mediterranean appears doomed to sink into a Gallic lake. The English of a former generation were celebrated for gaining ground in both hemispheres: their broad lands were not won by a peace policy, which, however, in this our day, has on two distinct occasions well nigh lost for them the "gem of the British Empire" —India. The philanthropist and the political economist may fondly hope, by outcry against "territorial aggrandizement," by advocating a compact frontier, by abandoning colonies, and by cultivating "equilibrium," to retain our rank amongst the great nations of the world. Never! The facts of history prove nothing more conclusively than this: a race either progresses or retrogrades, either increases or diminishes: the children of Time, like their sire, cannot stand still.

The occupation of the port of Berberah has been advised for many reasons.

In the first place, Berberah is the true key of the Red Sea, the centre of East African traffic, and the only safe place for shipping upon the western Erythrœan shore, from Suez to Guardafui. Backed by lands capable of cultivation, and by hills covered with pine and other valuable trees, enjoying a comparatively temperate climate, with a regular although thin monsun, this harbour has been coveted by many a foreign conqueror. Circumstances have thrown it as it were into our arms, and, if we refuse the chance, another and a rival nation will not be so blind.

Secondly, we are bound to protect the lives of British subjects upon this coast. In A.D. 1825 the crew of the "Mary Ann" brig was treacherously murdered by the Somal. The consequence of a summary and exemplary punishment[1] was that in August 1843, when the H. E. I. C.'s war-steamer " Memnon " was stranded at Ras Assayr near Cape Guardafui, no outrage was attempted by the barbarians, upon whose barren shores our seamen remained for months labouring at the wreck. In A.D. 1855 the Somal, having forgotten the old lesson, renewed their practices of pillaging and murdering strangers. It is then evident that this people cannot be trusted without supervision, and equally certain that vessels are ever liable to be cast ashore in this part of the Red Sea. But a year ago the French steam corvette, " Le Caïman," was lost within sight of Zayla ; the Badawin Somal, principally Ísa, assembled a fanatic host, which was, however, dispersed before blood had been drawn, by the exertion of the governor and his guards. It remains for us, therefore, to provide against

---

1 In A.D. 1825, the Government of Bombay received intelligence that a brig from the Mauritius had been seized, plundered, and broken up near Berberah, and that part of her crew had been barbarously murdered by the Somal. The " Elphinstone " sloop of war (Capt. Greer commanding) was sent to blockade the coast ; when her guns opened fire, the people fled with their wives and children, and the spot where a horseman was killed by cannon ball is still shown on the plain near the town. Through the intervention of Al-Hajj Sharmarkay, the survivors were recovered ; the Somal bound themselves to abstain from future attacks upon English vessels, and also to refund by annual instalments the full amount of plundered property. For the purpose of enforcing the latter stipulation it was resolved that a vessel of war should remain upon the coast until the whole was liquidated. When attempts at evasion occurred, the traffic was stopped by sending all craft outside the guardship, and forbidding intercourse with the shore. The " Coote" (Capt. Pepper commanding), the " Palinurus " and the " Tigris," in turn with the " Elphinstone," maintained the blockade through the trading seasons till 1833. About 6000*l.* were recovered, and the people were strongly impressed with the fact that we had both the will and the means to keep their plundering propensities within bounds.

such contingencies.   Were one of the Peninsular and Oriental Company's vessels cast by any accident upon this inhospitable shore, in the present state of affairs the lives of the passengers, and the cargo, would be placed in imminent peril.

In advocating the establishment of an armed post at Berberah no stress is laid upon the subject of slavery. To cut off that traffic the possession of the great export harbour is by no means necessary.   Whenever a British cruizer shall receive positive and *bonâ fide* orders to search native craft, and to sell as prizes all that have slaves on board, the trade will receive a death-blow.

Certain measures have been taken during the last annual fair to punish the outrage perpetrated by the Somal at Berberah in A.D. 1855.   The writer on his return to Aden proposed that the several clans implicated in the offence should at once be expelled from British dominions.   This preliminary was carried out by the Acting Political Resident at Aden.   Moreover, it was judged advisable to blockade the Somali coast, from Siyaro to Zayla not included, until, in the first place, Lieut. Stroyan's murderer, and the ruffian who attempted to spear Lieut. Speke in cold blood, should be given up[1]; and secondly, that due compensation for all losses should be made by the plunderers.   The former condition was approved by the Right Honourable the Governor-General of India, who, however, objected it is said, to the money-demand.[2]   At present the H. E. I. C.'s cruizers " Mahi,"

---

1 The writer advised that these men should be hung upon the spot where the outrage was committed, that the bodies should be burned and the ashes cast into the sea, lest by any means the murderers might become martyrs.   This precaution should invariably be adopted when Moslems assassinate Infidels.

2 The reason of the objection is not apparent.   A savage people is imperfectly punished by a few deaths : the fine is the only true way to produce a lasting impression upon their heads and hearts.   Moreover, it is the custom of India and the East generally, and is in reality the only safeguard of a traveller's property.

and "Elphinstone," are blockading the harbour of Berberah, the Somal have offered 15,000 dollars indemnity, and they pretend, as usual, that the murderer has been slain by his tribe.

To conclude. The writer has had the satisfaction of receiving from his comrades assurances that they are willing to accompany him once more in the task of African exploration. The plans of the Frank are now publicly known to the Somali. Should the loss of life, however valuable, be an obstacle to prosecuting them, he must fall in the esteem of the races around him. On the contrary, should he, after duly chastising the offenders, carry out the original plan, he will command the respect of the people, and wipe out the memory of a temporary reverse. At no distant period the project will, it is hoped, be revived. Nothing is required but permission to renew the attempt—an indulgence which will not be refused by a Government raised by energy, enterprise, and perseverance from the ranks of a society of merchants to national wealth and imperial grandeur.

14, St. James's Square,
    10th February, 1856.

TO THE HONOURABLE

JAMES GRANT LUMSDEN,

MEMBER OF COUNCIL, ETC., ETC., BOMBAY.

I HAVE ventured, my dear Lumsden, to address you in, and inscribe to you, these pages. Within your hospitable walls my project of African travel was matured, in the fond hope of submitting, on return, to your friendly criticism, the record of adventures in which you took so warm an interest. Dîs aliter visum! Still I would prove that my thoughts are with you, and thus request you to accept with your wonted *bonhommie* this feeble token of a sincere good will.

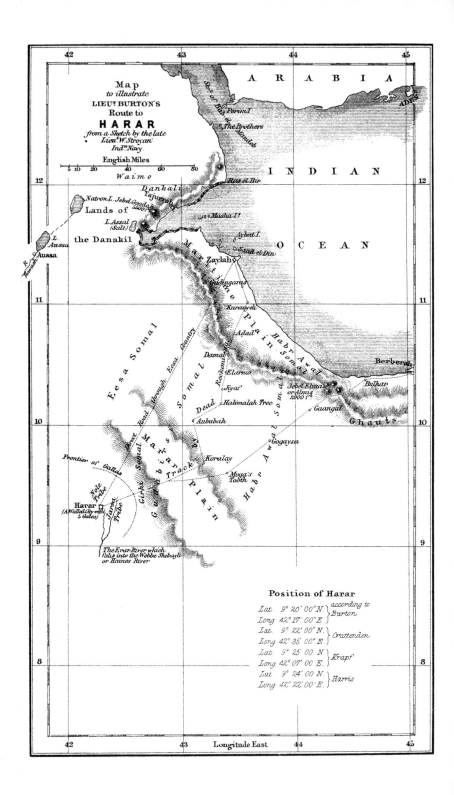

Map
to illustrate
LIEUT BURTON'S
Route to
HARAR
from a Sketch by the late
Lieut. W. Stroyan,
Indn. Navy.

English Miles

5 10 20   40   60   80

ARABIA

ADEN

Perim I.

Str. of Bab el Mandeb

The Brothers

INDIAN

Waimo

Ras el Bir

Dankali

Tajurrah

Natron L. Jebel Goodah
5500 ft.

Lands of

L. Assal
(Salt)

Masha I.

Aybat I.

OCEAN

Saad el Din

L. Aussa

Aussa

R. Hawash

the Danakil

Zaylah

Gudingaras

Kuranyed

Maritime Plain

Habr Awal

Eesa Somal

Somal Country

Road through Eesa Country

Adad

Damal

Kedanneh

Elarmo

Hyas

Berberah

Jebel Elmas
or Almas
2000 ft.

Bulhar

Dead

Halimalah Tree

Aububah

Ghauts

Gaangat

Habr Awal Somal

Gogaysa

Maritime Plain

Frontier of Galla

Nole
Tribe

Harar
(A Walled City with
5 Gates)

Jarsa
Tribe

Gudabirsi

Track

Koralay

Moga's
Tooth

Habr Awal Plain

Harris Road through Eesa Country

Ginhi

The Erar River which
falls into the Webbe Shebayli
or Haines River

Position of Harar

Lat. 9° 20' 00" N.	according to Burton
Long. 42° 17' 00" E.	
Lat. 9° 22' 00" N.	Cruttenden
Long. 42° 35' 00" E.	
Lat. 9° 25' 00 N.	Krapf
Long. 42° 07' 00 E.	
Lat. 9° 24' 00 N.	Harris
Long. 42° 22' 00" E.	

Longitude East

FIRST FOOTSTEPS

IN

EAST AFRICA.

CHAPTER I.

DEPARTURE FROM ADEN.

I DOUBT not there are many who ignore the fact that in
Eastern Africa, scarcely three hundred miles distant from
Aden, there is a counterpart of ill-famed Timbuctoo in
the Far West. The more adventurous Abyssinian travellers, Salt and Stuart, Krapf and Isenberg, Barker and
Rochet—not to mention divers Roman Catholic Mis-
sioners—attempted Harar, but attempted it in vain.
The bigoted ruler and barbarous people threatened death
to the Infidel who ventured within their walls; some
negro Merlin having, it is said, read Decline and Fall
in the first footsteps of the Frank.[1] Of all foreigners the

---

1 "A tradition exists," says Lieut. Cruttenden, "amongst the
people of Harar, that the prosperity of their city depends upon the
exclusion of all travellers not of the Moslem faith, and all Christians
are specially interdicted." These freaks of interdiction are common
to African rulers, who on occasions of war, famine or pestilence,
struck with some superstitious fear, close their gates to strangers.

English were, of course, the most hated and dreaded; at
Harar slavery still holds its head-quarters, and the old
Dragon well knows what to expect from the hand of
St. George. Thus the various travellers who appeared in
beaver and black coats became persuaded that the city
was inaccessible, and Europeans ceased to trouble themselves about Harar.

It is, therefore, a point of honour with me, dear L., to
utilize my title of Haji by entering the city, visiting the
ruler, and returning in safety, after breaking the guardian
spell.

The most auspicious day in the Moslem year for
beginning a journey is, doubtless, the 6th of the month
Safar,[1] on which, quoth the Prophet, Al-Islam emerged
from obscurity. Yet even at Aden we could not avail
ourselves of this lucky time: our delays and difficulties
were a fit prelude for a journey amongst those "Blameless
Ethiopians," with whom no less a personage than august
Jove can dine and depart.[2]

On Sunday, the 29th October, 1854, our manifold
impediments were pronounced complete. Friend S. threw
the slipper of blessing at my back, and about 4 p.m. em-
barking from Maala Bunder, we shook out our "muslin,"
and sailed down the fiery harbour. Passing the guard-
boat, we delivered our permit; before venturing into the
open sea we repeated the Fátihah-prayer in honour of the

---

1 The 6th of Safar in 1854 corresponds with our 28th October.
The Hadis is اذا خرج سته من الصفر خرج امتي من الدفر " when the 6th of
Safar went forth, my faith from the cloud came forth."

2 The Abyssinian law of detaining guests—Pedro Covilhaõ,
the first Portuguese envoy (A.D. 1499), lived and died a prisoner
there—appears to have been the Christian modification of the old
Ethiopic rite of sacrificing strangers.

Shaykh Majid, inventor of the mariners' compass,[1] and evening saw us dancing on the bright clear tide, whose "magic waves," however, murmured after another fashion

---

1 It would be wonderful if Orientals omitted to romance about the origin of such an invention as the Dayrah, or compass. Shaykh Majid is said to have been a Syrian saint, to whom Allah gave the power of looking upon earth as though it were a ball in his hand. Most Moslems agree in assigning this origin to the Dayrah, and the Fatihah in honour of the holy man is still repeated by the pious mariner.

Easterns do not "box the compass" after our fashion: with them each point has its own name, generally derived from some prominent star on the horizon. Of these I subjoin a list as in use amongst the Somal, hoping that it may be useful to Oriental students. The names in hyphens are those given in a paper on the nautical instrument of the Arabs by Jas. Prinseps (Journal of the As. Soc., December, 1836). The learned secretary appears not to have heard the legend of Shaykh Majid, for he alludes to the "Majidi Kitab" or Oriental Ephemeris, without any explanation.

North . . .	Jah, جاه		East . .	Matla, مطلع
N. by E. . . .	Farjad, فرجد		E. by S.	Jauza, جوزا
	(or فرقد)		E.S.E. . .	Tir, تير
N.N.E. . .	Naash, نعش		S.E. by E.	Iklil, اكليل
N.E. by E. .	Nakah, ناقه		S.E.. . .	Akrab, عقرب
N.E. . . .	Ayyuk, عيوق		S.E. by S.	Himarayn, حمارين
N.E. by E. .	Waki, واقع		S.S.E. . .	Suhayl, سهيل
E.N.E. . .	Sumak, سماك		S. by E.	Suntubar, سنتبار
E. by N. . . .	Surayya, ثريا			(or سلبار)

The south is called Al-Kutb (القطب) and the west Al-Maghib (المغيب). The western points are named like the eastern. Northeast, for instance, is Ayyuk al-Matlai; north-west, Ayyuk al-Maghibi. Finally, the Dayrah Jahi is when the magnetic needle points due north. The Dayrah Farjadi (more common in these regions) is when the bar is fixed under Farjad, to allow for variation, which at Berberah is about 4° 50' west.

the siren song which charmed the senses of the old Arabian voyagers.[1]

Suddenly every trace of civilization fell from my companions as if it had been a garment. At Aden, shaven and beturbanded, Arab fashion, now they threw off all dress save the loin cloth, and appeared in their dark morocco. Mohammed filled his mouth with a mixture of coarse Surat tobacco and ashes—the latter article intended, like the Anglo-Indian soldier's chili in his arrack, to "make it bite." Gulad uncovered his head, a member which in Africa is certainly made to go bare, and buttered himself with an unguent redolent of sheep's tail; and Ismail, the rais or captain of our "foyst,"[2] the Sahalah, applied himself to puffing his nicotiana out of a goat's shank-bone. Our crew, consisting of seventy-one men and boys, prepared, as evening fell, a mess of Jowari grain[3] and grease, the recipe of which I spare you, and it was despatched in a style that would have done credit to Kafirs as regards gobbling, bolting, smearing lips, licking fingers, and using ankles as napkins. Then with a light easterly breeze and the ominous cliffs of Little Aden still in sight, we spread our mats on deck and prepared to sleep under the moon.[4]

My companions, however, felt, without perhaps comprehending, the joviality arising from a return to Nature. Every man was forthwith nicknamed, and

---

1 The curious reader will find in the Herodotus of the Arabs, Al-Masudi's "Meadows of gold and mines of gems," a strange tale of the blind billows and the singing waves of Berberah and Jofuni (Cape Guardafui, the classical Aromata).

2 "Foyst" and "buss," are the names applied by old travellers to the half-decked vessels of these seas.

3 Holcus Sorghum, the common grain of Africa and Arabia: the Somali call it Hirad ; the people of Al-Yaman, Ta'am.

4 The Somal being a people of less nervous temperament than the Arabs and Indians, do not fear the moonlight.

pitiless was the raillery upon the venerable subjects of long and short, fat and thin. One sang a war-song, another a love-song, a third some song of the sea, whilst the fourth, an Ísa youth, with the villanous expression of face common to his tribe, gave us a rain measure, such as men chaunt during wet weather. All these effusions were *naïve* and amusing: none, however, could bear English translation without an amount of omission which would change its nature. Each effort of minstrelsy was accompanied by roars of laughter, and led to much manual pleasantry, All swore that they had never spent, intellectually speaking, a more charming *soirée*, and pitied me for being unable to enter thoroughly into the spirit of the dialogue. Truly it is not only the polished European, as was said of a certain travelling notability, that lapses with facility into pristine barbarism.

I will now introduce you to my companions. The managing man is one Mohammed Mahmud,[1] generally called Al-Hammal, or the porter: he is a Havildar, or sergeant in the Aden police, and was entertained for me by Lieut. Dansey, an officer who unfortunately was not "confirmed" in a political appointment at Aden. The Hammal is a bull-necked, round-headed fellow of lymphatic temperament, with a lamp-black skin, regular features, and a pulpy figure—two rarities amongst his countrymen, who compare him to a Banyan. An orphan in early youth, and becoming, to use his own phrase, sick of milk, he ran away from his tribe, the Habr Girhajis, and engaged himself as a coal-trimmer with the slaves on board an Indian war-steamer. After rising in rank to the command of the crew, he became servant and interpreter

---

1 The first name is that of the individual, as the Christian name with us, the second is that of the father; in the Somali country, as in India, they are not connected by the Arab "bin"—son of.

to travellers, visited distant lands—Egypt and Calcutta—
and finally settled as a Faringhi policeman. He cannot
read or write, but he has all the knowledge to be acquired
by fifteen or twenty years' hard "knocking about": he
can make a long speech, and, although he never prays, a
longer prayer; he is an excellent mimic, and delights his
auditors by imitations and descriptions of Indian ceremony, Egyptian dancing, Arab vehemence, Persian
abuse, European vivacity, and Turkish insolence. With
prodigious inventiveness, and a habit of perpetual intrigue, acquired in his travels, he might be called a
"knowing" man, but for the truly Somali weakness of
showing in his countenance all that passes through his
mind. This people can hide nothing : the blank eye, the
contracting brow, the opening nostril and the tremulous
lip, betray, despite themselves, their innermost thoughts.

The second servant whom I bring before you is
Gulad, another policeman at Aden. He is a youth of
good family, belonging to the Ismail Arrah, the royal
clan of the great Habr Girhajis tribe. His father was a
man of property, and his brethren near Berberah, are
wealthy Badawin : yet he ran away from his native
country when seven or eight years old, and became a
servant in the house of a butter merchant at Mocha.
Thence he went to Aden, where he began with private
service, and ended his career in the police. He is one of
those long, live skeletons, common amongst the Somal :
his shoulders are parallel with his ears, his ribs are
straight as a mummy's, his face has not an ounce of flesh
upon it, and his features suggest the idea of some lank
bird : we call him Long Gulad, to which he replies with
the Yaman saying " Length is Honour, even in Wood."
He is brave enough, because he rushes into danger
without reflection; his great defects are weakness of
body and nervousness of temperament, leading in times
of peril to the trembling of hands, the dropping of

caps, and the mismanagement of bullets: besides which, he cannot bear hunger, thirst, or cold.

The third is one Abdi Abokr, also of the Habr Girhajis, a personage whom, from his smattering of learning and his prodigious rascality, we call the Mulla " End of Time."[1] He is a man about forty, very old-looking for his age, with small, deep-set cunning eyes, placed close together, a hook nose, a thin beard, a bulging brow, scattered teeth,[2] and a short scant figure, remarkable only for length of back. His gait is stealthy, like a cat's, and he has a villanous grin. This worthy never prays, and can neither read nor write; but he knows a chapter or two of the Koran, recites audibly a long Ratib or task, morning and evening,[3] whence, together with his store of hashed Hadís (tradition), he derives the title of Widad or hedge-priest. His tongue, primed with the satirical sayings of Abn Zayd al-Halali, and Humayd ibn Mansur,[4] is the terror of men upon whom repartee imposes. His fath r was a wealthy ship-owner in his day; but, cursed with Abdi and another son, the old man has lost all his property, his children have deserted him, and he now depends entirely upon the charity of the Zayla chief. The " End of Time" has squandered considerable sums in travelling far and wide from Harar to Cutch, he has managed everywhere to

---

1 Abdi is an abbreviation of Abdullah; Abokr, a corruption of Abu Bakr. The " End of Time " alludes to the prophesied corruption of the Moslem priesthood in the last epoch of the world.

2 This peculiarity is not uncommon amongst the Somal; it is considered by them a sign of warm temperament.

3 The Moslem should first recite the Farz prayers, or those ordered in the Koran; secondly, the Sunnat or practice of the Prophet; and thirdly the Nafilah or Supererogatory. The Ratib or self-imposed task is the last of all; our Mulla placed it first, because he could chant it upon his mule within hearing of the people.

4 Two modern poets and wits well known in Al-Yaman.

perpetrate some peculiar villany. He is a pleasant companion, and piques himself upon that power of quotation
which in the East makes a polite man. If we be
disposed to hurry, he insinuates that " Patience is of
Heaven, Haste of Hell." When roughly addressed, he
remarks,—

> " There are cures for the hurts of lead and steel,
>   But the wounds of the tongue—they never heal."

If a grain of rice adhere to our beards, he says,
smilingly, "the gazelle is in the garden"; to which we
reply " we will hunt her with the five.[1]" Despite these
merits, I hesitated to engage him, till assured by the
governor of Zayla that he was to be looked upon as a
son, and, moreover, that he would bear with him one of
those state secrets to an influential chief which in this
country are never committed to paper. I found him an
admirable buffoon, skilful in filling pipes and smoking
them ; *au reste*, an individual of " many words and little
work," infinite intrigue, cowardice, cupidity, and endowed
with a truly evil tongue.

The morning sun rose hot upon us, showing Mayyum
and Zubah, the giant staples of the " Gate under the
Pleiades.[2] " Shortly afterwards, we came in sight of the
Barr al-'Ajam (barbarian land), as the Somal call their
country,[3] a low glaring flat of yellow sand, desert and

---

1 That is to say, "we will remove it with the five fingers."
These are euphuisms to avoid speaking broadly and openly of that
venerable feature, the beard.

2 Bab al-Mandab is called as above by Humayd from its astro-
nomical position. Jabal Mayyum is in Africa, Jabal Zubah or
Muayyin, celebrated as the last resting-place of a great saint, Shaykh
Sa'id, is in Arabia.

3 'Ajam probably means all nations not Arab. In Egypt and
Central Asia it is now confined to Persians. On the west of the Red
Sea, it is invariably used to denote the Somali country : thence Bruce
draws the Greek and Latin name of the coast, Azamia, and De Sacy
derives the word " Ajan," which in our maps is applied to the inner
regions of the Eastern Horn, So in Africa, Al-Sham, which probably
means Damascus and Syria, is applied to Al-Hijaz.

heat-reeking, tenanted by the Ísa, and a meet habitat for savages. Such to us, at least, appeared the land of Adel.[1] At midday we descried the Ras al-Bir,—Headland of the Well,—the promontory which terminates the bold Tajurrah range, under which lie the sleeping waters of the Maiden's Sea.[2] During the day we rigged out an awning, and sat in the shade smoking and chatting merrily, for the weather was not much hotter than our English summer seas. Some of the crew tried praying; but prostrations are not easily made on board ship, and Al-Islam, as Umar shrewdly suspected, was not made for a seafaring race. At length the big red sun sank slowly behind the curtain of sky-blue rock, where lies the not yet "combusted" village of Tajurrah.[3] We lay down to rest with the light of day, and had the satisfaction of closing our eyes upon a fair though captious breeze.

On the morning of the 31st October, we entered the Zayla Creek, which gives so much trouble to native craft. We passed, on the right, the low island of

---

1 Adel, according to M. Krapf, derived its name from the Ad Ali, a tribe of the Afar or Danakil nation, erroneously used by Arab synecdoche for the whole race. Mr. Johnston (Travels in Southern Abyssinia, ch. 1) more correctly derives it from Adule, a city which, as proved by the monument which bears its name, existed in the days of Ptolemy Euergetes (B.C. 247—222), had its own dynasty, and boasted of a conquerer who overcame the Troglodytes, Sabæans, Homerites, &c., and pushed his conquests as far as the frontier of Egypt. Mr. Johnston, however, incorrectly translates Barr al-'Ajam "land of fire," and seems to confound Avalites and Adulis.

2 Bahr al-Banattin, the Bay of Tajurrah.

3 A certain German missionary, well known in this part of the world, exasperated by the seizure of a few dollars and a claim to the *droit d'aubaine*, advised the authorities of Aden to threaten the "combustion" of Tajurrah. The measure would have been equally unjust and unwise. A traveller, even a layman, is bound to put up peacefully with such trifles; and to threaten "combustion" without being prepared to carry out the threat is the readiest way to secure contempt.

Masha, belonging to the " City of the Slave Merchant,"
—Tajurrah—and on the left two similar patches of
seagirt sand, called Aybat and Sa'ad al-Din. These
places supply Zayla, in the Kharif or hot season,[1] with
thousands of gulls' eggs—a great luxury. At noon we
sighted our destination. Zayla is the normal African.
port—a strip of sulphur-yellow sand, with a deep blue
dome above, and a foreground of the darkest indigo.
The buildings, raised by refraction, rose high, and
apparently from the bosom of the deep. After hearing
the worst accounts of it, I was pleasantly disappointed
by the spectacle of white-washed houses and minarets,
peering above a long low line of brown wall, flanked
with round towers.

As we slowly threaded the intricate coral reefs of
the port, a bark came scudding up to us ; it tacked, and
the crew proceeded to give news in roaring tones.
Friendship between the Amir of Harar and the governor
of Zayla had been broken ; the road through the Isa
Somal had been closed by the murder of Mas'ud, a
favourite slave and adopted son of Sharmarkay ; all
strangers had been expelled the city for some misconduct
by the Harar chief ; moreover, small-pox was raging
there with such violence that the Galla peasantry would
allow neither ingress nor egress.[2] I had the pleasure of

---

1 The Kharif in most parts of the Oriental world corresponds with
our autumn.   In Eastern Africa it invariably signifies the hot season
preceding the monsoon rains.

2 The circumstances of Mas'ud's murder were truly African.
The slave caravans from Abyssinia to Tajurrah were usually escorted
by the Rer Guleni, a clan of the great Ísa tribe, and they monopo-
lized the profits of the road.   Summoned to share their gains with
their kinsmen generally, they refused, upon which the other clans
rose about August, 1854, and cut off the road.   A large caravan was
travelling down in two bodies, each of nearly 300 slaves, the Ísa
attacked the first division, carried off the wives and female slaves,

C.BRANDARD

THE "HAMMAL".

reflecting for some time, dear L., upon the amount of responsibility incurred by using the phrase " I will"; and the only consolation that suggested itself was the stale assurance that

> " Things at the worst most surely mend."

No craft larger than a canoe can ride near Zayla. After bumping once or twice against the coral reefs, it was considered advisable for our good ship, the Sahalah, to cast anchor. My companions caused me to dress, put me with my pipe and other necessaries into a cock-boat, and, wading through the water, shoved it to shore. Lastly, at Bab al-Sahil, the Seaward or Northern Gate, they proceeded to array themselves in the bravery of clean Tobes and long daggers strapped round the waist ; each man also slung his targe to his left arm, and in his right hand grasped lance and javelin. At the gate we were received by a tall black spearman with a " Ho there ! to the governor "; and a crowd of idlers gathered to inspect the strangers. Marshalled by the warder, we traversed the dusty roads—streets they could not be called—of the old Arab town, ran the gauntlet of a gaping mob, and finally entering a mat door, found ourselves in the presence of the governor.

I had met Sharmarkay at Aden, where he received from the authorities strong injunctions concerning my personal safety : the character of a Moslem merchant, however, requiring us to appear strangers, an introduction by our master of ceremonies, the Hammal, followed my entrance. Sharmarkay was living in an

---

whom they sold for ten dollars a head, and savagely mutilated upwards of 100 wretched boys. This event caused the Tajurrah line to be permanently closed. The Rer Guleni in wrath, at once murdered Mas'ud, a peaceful traveller, because Inna Handun, his Abban or protector, was of the party who had attacked their protégés : they came upon him suddenly as he was purchasing some article, and stabbed him in the back, before he could defend himself.

apartment by no means splendid, preferring an Arish or kind of cow-house—as the Anglo-Indian Nabobs do the bungalow

> " with mat half hung,
> The walls of plaster and the floors of · · · ·,"

—to all his substantial double-storied houses. The ground was wet and comfortless; a part of the reed walls was lined with cots bearing mattresses and silk-covered pillows, a cross between a diwán and a couch : the only ornaments were a few weapons, and a necklace of gaudy beads suspended near the door. I was placed upon the principal seat : on the right were the governor and the Hammal ; whilst the lowest portion of the room was occupied by Mohammed Sharmarkay, the son and heir. The rest of the company squatted upon chairs, or rather stools, of peculiar construction. Nothing could be duller than this *assemblée* : pipes and coffee are here unknown ; and there is nothing in the East to act substitute for them.[1]

The governor of Zayla, Al-Hajj Sharmarkay bin Ali Salih, is rather a remarkable man. He is sixteenth, according to his own account, in descent from Ishak al-Hazrami,[2] the saintly founder of the great Girhajis and

---

1 In Zayla there is not a single coffee-house. The settled Somal care little for the Arab beverage, and the Badawin's reasons for avoiding it are not bad. " If we drink coffee once," say they, " we shall want it again, and then where are we to get it ?" The Abyssinian Christians, probably to distinguish themselves from Moslems, object to coffee as well as to tobacco. The Gallas, on the the other hand, eat it : the powdered bean is mixed with butter, and on forays a lump about the size of a billiard-ball is preferred to a substantial meal when the latter cannot be obtained.

2 The following genealogical table was given to me by Mohammed Sharmarkay :—
1. Ishak (ibn Ahmad ibn Abdillah).
1. Girhajis (his eldest son).
3. Sa'id (the eldest son ; Da'ud being the second).

Awal tribes. His enemies derive him from a less illustrious stock ; and the fairness of his complexion favours
the report that his grandfather Salih was an Abyssinian
slave. Originally the Nacoda or captain of a native
craft, he has raised himself, chiefly by British influence,
to the chieftainship of his tribe.[1] As early as May, 1825,
he received from Captain Bagnold, then our resident at
Mocha, a testimonial and a reward, for a severe sword
wound in the left arm, received whilst defending the
lives of English seamen.[2] He afterwards went to
Bombay, where he was treated with consideration; and
about fifteen years ago he succeeded the Sayyid Mohammed al-Barr as governor of Zayla and its dependencies,
under the Ottoman Pasha in Western Arabia.

---

4. Arrah (also the eldest ; Ili, *i.e.*, Ali, being the second).
5. Musa (the third son : the eldest was Ismail ; then, in succession, Ishak, Misa, Mikahil, Gambah, Dandan, &c.).

6. Ibrahim.	12. Ali.
7. Fikih (*i.e.* Fakih).	13. Awaz.
8. Adan (*i.e.* Adam.)	14. Salih.
9. Mohammed.	15. Ali.
10. Hamid.	16. Sharmarkay.
11. Jibril (*i.e.* Jibrail).	

The last is a peculiarly Somali name, meaning " one who sees
no harm "—Shar-ma-arkay.

1 Not the hereditary chieftainship of the Habr Girhajis, which
belongs to a particular clan.

2 The following is a copy of the document :—
" This Testimonial,
together with an Honorary Dress, is presented by the British
Resident at Mocha to Nagoda Shurmakey Ally Sumaulley, in token
of esteem and regard for his humane and gallant conduct at the
Port of Burburra, on the coast of Africa, April 10, 1825, in saving
the lives of Captain William Lingard, chief officer of the Brig Mary
Anne, when that vessel was attacked and plundered by the natives.
The said Nagoda is therefore strongly recommended to the notice
and good offices of Europeans in general, but particularly so to all
English gentlemen visiting these seas."

The Hajj Sharmarkay in his youth was a man of valour: he could not read or write; but he carried in battle four spears,[1] and his sword-cut was recognizable. He is now a man about sixty years old, at least six feet two inches in stature, large-limbed, and raw-boned: his leanness is hidden by long wide robes. He shaves his head and upper lip Sháfe'i-fashion, and his beard is represented by a ragged tuft of red-stained hair on each side of his chin. A visit to Aden and a doctor cost him one eye, and the other is now white with age. His dress is that of an Arab, and he always carries with him a broad-bladed, silver-hilted sword. Despite his years, he is a strong, active, and energetic man, ever looking to the "main chance." With one foot in the grave, he meditates nothing but the conquest of Harar and Berberah, which, making him master of the seaboard, would soon extend his power as in days of old even to Abyssinia.[2] To hear his projects, you would fancy them the

---

1 Two spears being the usual number: the difficulty of three or four would mainly consist in their management during action.

2 In July, 1855, the Hajj Sharmarkay was deposed by the Turkish Pasha of Hodaydah, ostensibly for failing to keep some road open, or, according to others, for assisting to plunder a caravan belonging to the Dankali tribe. It was reported that he had been made a prisoner, and the Political Resident at Aden saw the propriety of politely asking the Turkish authorities to "be easy" upon the old man. In consequence of this representation, he was afterwards allowed, on paying a fine of 3000 dollars, to retire to Aden.

I deeply regret that the Hajj should have lost his government. He has ever clung to the English party, even in sore temptation. A few year ago, the late M. Rochet (*soi-disant* d'Hericourt), French agent at Jeddah, paying treble its value, bought from Mohammed Sharmarkay, in the absence of the Hajj, a large stone house, in order to secure a footing at Zayla. The old man broke off the bargain on his return, knowing how easily an Agency becomes a Fort, and preferring a considerable loss to the presence of dangerous friends.

offspring of a brain in the prime of youth: in order to carry them out he would even assist in suppressing the profitable slave-trade.[1]

After half an hour's visit I was led by the Hajj through the streets of Zayla,[2] to one of his substantial

---

1 During my residence at Zayla few slaves were imported, owing to the main road having been closed. In former years the market was abundantly stocked; the numbers annually shipped to Mocha, Hodaydah, Jeddah, and Berberah, varied from 600 to 1000. The Hajj received as duty one gold " Kirsh," or about three-fourths of a dollar, per head.

2 Zayla, called Audal or Auzal by the Somal, is a town about the size of Suez, built for 3000 or 4000 inhabitants, and containing a dozen large whitewashed stone houses, and upwards of 200 Arish or thatched huts, each surrounded by a fence of wattle and matting. The situation is a low and level spit of sand, which high tides make almost an island. There is no harbour: a vessel of 250 tons cannot approach within a mile of the landing-place; the open roadstead is exposed to the terrible north wind, and when gales blow from the west and south, it is almost unapproachable. Every ebb leaves a sandy flat, extending half a mile seaward from the town; the reefy anchorage is difficult of entrance after sunset, and the coralline bottom renders wading painful.

The shape of this once celebrated town is a tolerably regular parallelogram, of which the long sides run from east to west. The walls, without guns or embrasures, are built, like the houses, of coralline rubble and mud, in places dilapidated. There are five gates. The Bab al-Sahil and the Bab al-Jadd (a new postern) open upon the sea from the northern wall. At the Ashurbara, in the southern part of the enceinte, the Badawin encamp, and above it the governor holds his Durbar. The Bab Abd al-Kadir derives its name from a saint buried outside and eastward of the city, and the Bab al-Saghir is pierced in the western wall.

The public edifices are six mosques, including the Jami, or cathedral, for Friday prayer: these buildings have queer little crenelles on whitewashed walls, and a kind of elevated summerhouse to represent the minaret. Near one of them are remains of a circular Turkish Munar, manifestly of modern construction. There is no Mahkamah or Kazi's court: that dignitary transacts business at his own house, and the Festival prayers are recited near the

houses of coralline and mud plastered over with glaring
whitewash.   The ground floor is a kind of warehouse
full of bales and boxes, scales and buyers.   A flight of
steep steps leads into a long room with shutters to
exclude the light, floored with tamped earth, full of

Saint's Tomb outside the eastern gate.   The north-east angle of the
town is occupied by a large graveyard with the usual deleterious
consequences.

The climate of Zayla is cooler than that of Aden, and the site
being open all around, it is not so unhealthy.   Much spare room is
enclosed by the town walls : evaporation and Nature's scavengers
act succedanea for sewerage.

Zayla commands the adjacent harbour of Tajurrah, and is by
position the northern port of Aussa (the ancient capital of Adel), of
Harar, and of southern Abyssinia : the feuds of the rulers have,
however, transferred the main trade to Berberah.   It sends caravans northwards to Dankali, and south-westwards, through the Isa
and Gudabirsi tribes as far as Ifat and Gurague.   It is visited by
Cafilas from Abyssinia, and by the different races of Badawin, extending from the hills to the seaboard.   The exports are valuable—
slaves, ivory, hides, honey, antelope horns, clarified butter, and
gums : the coast abounds in sponge, coral, and small pearls, which
Arab divers collect in the fair season.   In the harbour I found
about twenty native craft, large and small : of these, ten belonged
to the governor.   They trade with Berberah, Arabia, and Western
India, and are navigated by "Rajput" or Hindu pilots.

Provisions at Zayla are cheap ; a family of six persons live well
for about 30*l.* per annum.   The general food is mutton : a large
sheep costs one dollar, a small one half the price ; camels' meat,
beef, and in winter kid, abound.   Fish is rare, and fowls are not
commonly eaten.   Holcus, when dear, sells at forty pounds per
dollar, at seventy pounds when cheap.   It is usually levigated with
slab and roller, and made into sour cakes.   Some, however, prefer
the Arab form " balilah," boiled and mixed with ghi.   Wheat and
rice are imported : the price varies from forty to sixty pounds the
Riyal or dollar.   Of the former grain the people make a sweet cake
called Sabaya, resembling the Fatirah of Egypt : a favourite dish
also is " harisah "—flesh, rice flour, and boiled wheat, all finely
pounded and mixed together.   Milk is not procurable during the
hot weather ; after rain every house is full of it ; the Badawin bring
it in skins and sell it for a nominal sum.

"evening flyers,[1]" and destitute of furniture. Parallel
to it are three smaller apartments; and above is a
terraced roof, where they who fear not the dew and the
land breeze sleep.[2] I found a room duly prepared; the
ground was spread with mats, and cushions against the
walls denoted the Diwan: for me was placed a Kursi or
cot, covered with fine Persian rugs and gaudy silk and
satin pillows. The Hajj installed us with ceremony,
and insisted, despite my remonstrances, upon occupying
the floor whilst I sat on the raised seat. After ushering
in supper, he considerately remarked that travelling is
fatiguing, and left us to sleep.

The well-known sounds of Al-Islam returned from
memory. Again the melodious chant of the Muezzin—

Besides a large floating population, Zayla contains about 1500
souls. They are comparatively a fine race of people, and suffer
from little but fever and an occasional ophthalmia. Their greatest
hardship is the want of the pure element; the Hissi or well, is about
four miles distant from the town, and all the pits within the walls
supply brackish or bitter water, fit only for external use. This is
probably the reason why vegetables are unknown, and why a horse,
a mule, or even a dog, is not to be found in the place.

1 "Fid-mer," or the evening flyer, is the Somali name for a
bat. These little animals are not disturbed in houses, because they
keep off flies and mosquitoes, the plagues of the Somali country.
Flies abound in the very jungles wherever cows have been, and
settle in swarms upon the traveller. Before the monsoon their bite
is painful, especially that of the small green species; and there is a
red variety called "Diksi as," whose venom, according to the
people, causes them to vomit. The latter abounds in Gulays and
the hill ranges of the Berberah country: it is innocuous during the
cold season. The mosquito bites bring on, according to the same
authority, deadly fevers: the superstition probably arises from the
fact that mosquitoes and fevers become formidable about the same
time.

2 Such a building at Zayla would cost at most 500 dollars. At
Aden, 2000 rupees, or nearly double the sum, would be paid for a
matted shed, which excludes neither sun, nor wind, nor rain.

no evening bell can compare with it for solemnity and beauty—and in the neighbouring mosque, the loudly-intoned Amin and Allaho Akbar—far superior to any organ—rang in my ear. The evening gun of camp was represented by the Nakyarah, or kettle-drum, sounded about seven P.M. at the southern gate; and at ten a second drumming warned the paterfamilias that it was time for home, and thieves, and lovers—that it was the hour for bastinado. Nightfall was ushered in by the song, the dance, and the marriage festival—here no permission is required for "native music in the lines"—and muffled figures flitted mysteriously through the dark alleys.

.   .   .   .

After a peep through the open window, I fell asleep, feeling once more at home.

CHAPTER II.

LIFE IN ZAYLA.

I WILL not weary you, dear L., with descriptions of twenty-six quiet, similar, uninteresting days—days of sleep, and pipes, and coffee—spent at Zayla, whilst a route was traced out, guides were propitiated, camels were bought, mules sent for, and all the wearisome pre-liminaries of African travel were gone through. But a *journée* in the Somali country may be a novelty to you: its events shall be succinctly depicted.

With earliest dawn we arise, thankful to escape from mosquitoes and close air. We repair to the terrace where devotions are supposed to be performed, and busy ourselves in watching our neighbours. Two in particular engage my attention: sisters by different mothers. The daughter of an Indian woman is a young person of fast propensities—her chocolate-coloured skin, long hair, and parrot-like profile[1] are much admired by the *élégants* of Zayla; and she coquettes by combing, dancing, singing, and slapping the slave-girls, whenever an adorer may be looking. We sober-minded men, seeing her, quote the well-known lines—

---

1 This style of profile—highly oval, with the chin and brow receding—is very conspicuous in Eastern Africa, where the face, slightly prognathous, projects below the nose.

" Sans justice a king is a cloud without rain ;
    Sans goodness a sage is a field without grain ;
    Sans manners a youth is a horse taking rein ;
    Sans lore an old man is a waterless plain ;
    And bread without salt is a woman sans shame."

The other is a matron of Abyssinian descent, as her skin, scarcely darker that a gipsy's, her long and bright blue fillet, and her gaudily-fringed dress, denote. She tattoos her face[1]: a livid line extends from her front hair to the tip of her nose ; between her eyebrows is an ornament representing a *fleur-de-lis*, and various beauty-spots adorn the corners of her mouth and the flats of her countenance. She passes her day superintending the slave-girls, and weaving mats,[2] the worsted work of this part of the world. We soon made acquaintance, as far as an exchange of salams. I regret, however, to say that there was some scandal about my charming neighbour; and that more than once she was detected making signals to distant persons with her hands.[3]

At 6 a.m. we descend to breakfast, which usually consists of sour grain cakes and roast mutton—at this hour a fine trial of health and cleanly living. A napkin is passed under my chin, as if I were a small child, and a sound scolding is administered when appetite appears deficient. Visitors are always asked to join us: we squat on the uncarpeted floor, round a circular stool, eat

---

1 Gall-nuts form the base of the tattooing dye. It is worked in with a needle, when it becomes permanent : applied with a pen, it requires to be renewed about once a fortnight.

2 Mats are the staple manufacture in Eastern, as in many parts of Western, Africa. The material is sometimes Daum or other palm : there are, however, many plants in more common use ; they are made of every variety in shape and colour, and are dyed red, black, and yellow — madder from Tajurrah and alum being the the matter principally used.

3 When woman addresses woman she always uses her voice.

hard, and never stop to drink. The appetite of Africa astonishes us ; we dispose of six ounces here for every one in Arabia—probably the effect of sweet water, after the briny produce of the " Eye of Yaman." We conclude this early breakfast with coffee and pipes, and generally return, after it, to the work of sleep.

Then, provided with some sanctified Arabic book, I prepare for the reception of visitors. They come in by dozens — no man having apparently any business to occupy him—doff their slippers at the door, enter wrapped up in their Tobes or togas,[1] and deposit their spears, point-upwards, in the corner ; those who have swords—the mark of respectability in Eastern Africa— place them at their feet. They shake the full hand (I was reproved for offering the fingers only); and when politely disposed, the inferior wraps his fist in the hem of his garment. They have nothing corresponding with

---

1 The Tobe, or Abyssinian " Quarry," is the general garment of Africa from Zayla to Bornou. In the Somali country it is a cotton sheet eight cubits long, and two breadths sewn together. An article of various uses, like the Highland plaid, it is worn in many ways ; sometimes the right arm is bared ; in cold weather the whole person is muffled up, and in summer it is allowed to fall below the waist. Generally it is passed behind the back, rests upon the left shoulder, is carried forward over the breast, surrounds the body, and ends hanging on the left shoulder, where it displays a gaudy silk fringe of red and yellow. This is the man's Tobe. The woman's dress is of similar material, but differently worn : the edges are knotted generally over the right, sometimes over the left shoulder ; it is girdled round the waist, below which hangs a lappet, which in cold weather can be brought like a hood over the head. Though highly becoming, and picturesque as the Roman toga, the Somali Tobe is by no means the most decorous of dresses: women in the towns often prefer the Arab costume—a short-sleeved robe extending to the knee, and a Futah or loin-cloth underneath.

As regards the word Tobe, it signifies, in Arabic, a garment generally : the Somal call it " Maro," and the half Tobe a " Shukkah."

the European idea of manners ; they degrade all
ceremony by the epithet Shughl al-banat, or " girls'
work," and pique themselves upon downrightness of
manner—a favourite mask, by-the-by, for savage cunning
to assume. But they are equally free from affectation,
shyness, and vulgarity ; and, after all, no manners are
preferable to bad manners.

Sometimes we are visited at this hour by Mohammed
Sharmarkay, eldest son of the old governor. He is in
age about thirty, a fine tall figure, slender but well knit,
beardless and of light complexion, with large eyes, and a
length of neck which a lady might covet. His only de-
tracting feature is a slight projection of the oral region,
that unmistakeable proof of African blood. His movements have the grace of strength and suppleness : he is a
good jumper, runs well, throws the spear admirably, and
is a tolerable shot. Having received a liberal education
at Mocha, he is held a learned man by his fellow-countrymen. Like his father he despises presents, looking higher ;
with some trouble I persuaded him to accept a common
map of Asia, and a revolver. His chief interest was concentrated in books: he borrowed my Abu Kasim to copy,[1]
and was never tired of talking about the religious sciences:
he had weakened his eyes by hard reading, and a couple
of blisters were sufficient to win his gratitude. Mohammed is now the eldest son[2]; he appears determined to
keep up the family name, having already married ten
wives: the issue however, two infant sons, were murdered
by the Ísa Badawin. Whenever he meets his father in

---

[1] Abu Kasim of Gaza, a well-known commentator upon Abu
Shuja'a of Isfahan, who wrote a text-book of the Shafe'i school.

[2] The Hajj had seven sons, three of whom died in infancy. Al
and Mahmud, the latter a fine young man, fell victims to small pox :
Mohammed is now the eldest, and the youngest is a child called
Ahmad, left for education at Mocha. The Hajj has also two
daughters, married to Badawi Somal.

the morning, he kisses his hand, and receives a salute upon the forehead. He aspires to the government of Zayla, and looks forward more reasonably than the Hajj to the day when the possession of Berberah will pour gold into his coffers. He shows none of his father's "softness": he advocates the bastinado, and, to keep his people at a distance, he has married an Arab wife, who allows no adult to enter the doors. The Somal, Spaniard-like, remark, "He is one of ourselves, though a little richer"; but when times change and luck returns, they are not unlikely to find themselves mistaken.

Amongst other visitors, we have the Amir al-Bahr, or Port Captain, and the Nakib al-Askar (*Commandant de place*), Mohammed Umar al-Hamumi. This is one of those Hazramaut adventurers so common in all the countries bordering upon Arabia: they are the Swiss of the East, a people equally brave and hardy, frugal and faithful, as long as pay is regular. Feared by the soft Indians and Africans for their hardness and determination, the common proverb concerning them is, "If you meet a viper and a Hazrami, spare the viper." Natives of a poor and rugged region, they wander far and wide, preferring every country to their own; and it is generally said that the sun rises not upon a land that does not contain a man from Hazramaut.[1] This commander of an army of forty men[2] often read out to us from the Kitab al-Anwar (the

---

1 It is related that a Hazrami, flying from his fellow-countrymen, reached a town upon the confines of China. He was about to take refuge in a mosque, but entering, he stumbled over the threshold. "Ya Amud al-Din"—"O Pillar of the Faith!" exclaimed a voice from the darkness, calling upon the patron saint of Hazramaut to save a Moslem from falling. "May the Pillar of the Faith break thy head!" exclaimed the unpatriotic traveller, at once rising to resume his vain peregrinations.

2 Mercenaries from Mocha, Hazramaut, and Bir Hamid, near Aden: they are armed with matchlock, sword, and dagger; and each receives from the governor a monthly stipend of two dollars and a half.

Book of Lights) the tale of Abu Jahl, that Judas of Al-Islam made ridiculous.   Sometimes comes the Sayyid Mohammed al-Barr, a stout personage, formerly governor of Zayla, and still highly respected by the people on account of his pure pedigree.   With him is the Fakih Adan, a *savan* of ignoble origin.[1]   When they appear the con-

---

[1] The system of caste, which prevails in Al-Yaman, though not in the northern parts of Arabia, is general throughout the Somali country.   The principal families of outcasts are the following :—

The Yabir correspond with the Dushan of Southern Arabia : the males are usually jesters to the chiefs, and both sexes take certain parts at festivals, marriages, and circumcisions.   The number is said to be small, amounting to about 100 families in the northern Somali country.

The Tomal or Handad, the blacksmiths, originally of Aydur race, have become vile by intermarriage with serviles.   They must now wed maidens of their own class, and live apart from the community : their magical practices are feared by the people—the connection of wits and witchcraft is obvious—and all private quarrels are traced to them.   It has been observed that the blacksmith has ever been looked upon with awe by barbarians on the same principle that made Vulcan a deity.   In Abyssinia all artisans are Budah, sorcerers, especially the blacksmith, and he is a social outcast as amongst the Somal; even in Al-Hijaz, a land, unlike Al-Yaman, opposed to distinctions amongst Moslems, the Khalawiyah, who work in metal, are considered vile.   Throughout the rest of Al-Islam, the blacksmith is respected as   reading in the path of David, the father of the craft.

The word "Tomal," opposed to Somal, is indigenous.   "Handad" is palpably a corruption of the Arabic "Haddad," ironworker.

The Midgan, "one-hand," corresponds with the Khadim of Al-Yaman: he is called Rami, or "archer," by the Arabs.   There are three distinct tribes of this people, who are numerous in the Somali country: the best genealogists cannot trace their origin, though some are silly enough to derive them, like the Akhdam, from Shimr.   All, however, agree in expelling the Midgan rom the gentle blood of Somali land, and his position has been compared to that of Freedman amongst the Romans.   These people take service under the different chiefs, who sometimes entertained great numbers to aid in forays and frays; they do not, however, confine themselves to one craft.   Many Midgans employ themselves in hunting and agriculture.

versation becomes intensely intellectual: sometimes we dispute religion, sometimes politics, at others history and other humanities. Yet, it is not easy to talk history with a people who confound Miriam and Mary, or politics to those whose only idea of a king is a robber on a large scale, or religion to men who measure excellence by forbidden

The Mountain Kaf.

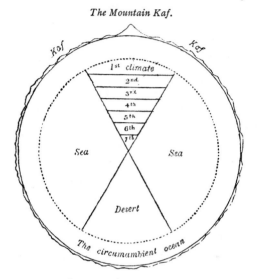

meats, or geography to those who represent the earth in this guise. Yet, though few of our ideas are in common,

---

Instead of spear and shield, they carry bows and a quiver full of diminutive arrows, barbed and poisoned with the Waba—a weapon used from Faizoghli to the Cape of Good Hope. Like the Veddah of Ceylon, the Midgan is a poor shot, and scarcely strong enough to draw his stiff bow. He is accused of maliciousness; and the twanging of his string will put to flight a whole village. The poison is greatly feared: it causes, say the people, the hair and nails to drop off, and kills a man in half an hour. The only treatment known is instant excision of the part; and this is done the more frequently, because here, as in other parts of Africa, such *stigmates* are deemed ornamental.

In appearance the Midgan is dark and somewhat stunted; he is known to the people by peculiarities of countenance and accent.

there are many words; the verbosity of these anti-Laconic Oriental dialects[1] renders at least half the subject intelligible to the most opposite thinkers. When the society is wholly Somal, I write Arabic, copy some useful book, or extract from it, as Bentley advised, what is fit to quote. When Arabs are present, I usually read out a tale from "The Thousand and One Nights," that wonderful work, so often translated, so much turned over, and so little understood at home. The most familiar of books in England, next to the Bible, it is one of the least known, the reason being that about one-fifth is utterly unfit for translation; and the most sanguine Orientalist would not dare to render literally more than three-quarters of the remainder. Consequently, the reader loses the contrast— the very essence of the book—between its brilliancy and dulness, its moral putrefaction, and such pearls as—

> " Cast the seed of good works on the least fit soil,
> Good is never wasted, however it may be laid out."

And in a page or two after such divine sentiment, the ladies of Baghdad sit in the porter's lap, and indulge in a facetiousness which would have killed Pietro Aretino before his time.

Often I am visited by the Topchi-Bashi, or master of the ordnance—half-a-dozen honey-combed guns—a wild fellow, Bashi Buzuk in the Hijaz and commandant of artillery at Zayla. He shaves my head on Fridays, and on other days tells me wild stories about his service in the Holy Land; how Kurdi Usman slew his son-in-law, Ibn Rumi, and how Turkchih Bilmaz would have

---

[1] The reason why Europeans fail to explain their thoughts to Orientals generally is that they transfer the Laconism of Western Eastern tongues. We for instance say, "Fetch the book I gave you last night." This in Hindustani, to choose a well-known tongue, must be smothered with words thus, " What book was by me given to you yesterday by night, that book bringing to me, come!"

murdered Mohammed Ali in his bed.[1] Sometimes the room is filled with Arabs, Sayyids, merchants, and others settled in the place : I saw nothing amongst them to justify the oft-quoted saw, " Koraysh pride and Zayla's boastfulness." More generally the assembly is one of the Somal, who talk in their own tongue, laugh, yell, stretch their legs, and lie like cattle upon the floor, smoking the common Hukkah, which stands in the centre, industriously cleaning their teeth with sticks, and eating snuff like Swedes. Meanwhile, I occupy the Kursi or couch, sometimes muttering from a book to excite respect, or reading aloud for general information, or telling fortunes by palmistry, or drawing out a horoscope.

It argues " peculiarity," I own, to enjoy such a life. In the first place there is no woman's society : Al-Islam seems purposely to have loosened the ties between the sexes in order to strengthen the bonds which connect man and man.[2] Secondly, your house is by no means your castle. You must open your doors to your friend at all hours ; if when inside it suit him to sing, sing he will ; and until you learn solitude in a crowd, or the art of concentration, you are apt to become *ennuyé* and irritable. You must abandon your prejudices, and for a time cast off all European prepossessions in favour of Indian politeness, Persian polish, Arab courtesy, or Turkish dignity.

" They are as free as Nature e'er made man;"

---

1 I have alluded to these subjects in a previous work upon the subject of Meccah and Al-Madinah.

2 This is one of the stock complaints against the Moslem scheme. Yet is it not practically the case with ourselves? In European society, the best are generally those who prefer the companionship of their own sex; the " ladies' man " and the woman who avoids women are rarely choice specimens.

and he who objects to having his head shaved in public, to seeing his friends combing their locks in his sitting-room, to having his property unceremoniously handled, or to being addressed familiarly by a perfect stranger, had better avoid Somali-land.

You will doubtless, dear L., convict me, by my own sentiments, of being an " amateur barbarian." You must, however, remember that I visited Africa fresh from Aden, with its dull routine of meaningless parades and tiresome courts-martial, where society is broken by ridiculous distinctions of staff-men and regimental-men, Madras-men and Bombay-men, " European " officers, and " black " officers ; where literature is confined to acquiring the art of explaining yourself in the jargons of half-naked savages; where the business of life is comprised in ignoble official squabbles, dislikes, disapprobations, and " references to superior authority " ; where social intercourse is crushed by " gup," gossip, and the scandal of small colonial circles; where—pleasant predicament for those who really love women's society!— it is scarcely possible to address fair dame, preserving at the same time her reputation and your own, and if seen with her twice, all " camp " will swear it is an " affair " : where, briefly, the march of mind is at a dead halt, and the march of matter is in double-quick time to the hospital or sick-quarters. Then the fatal struggle for Name, and the painful necessity of doing the most with the smallest materials for a reputation ! In Europe there are a thousand grades of celebrity, from statesmanship to taxidermy; all, therefore, co-exist without rivalry. Whereas, in these small colonies, there is but one fame, and as that leads directly to rupees and rank, no man willingly accords it to his neighbour. And, finally, such semi-civilized life abounds in a weary ceremoniousness. It is highly improper to smoke outside your bungalow. You shall pay your visits at 11 A.M., when the glass

stands at 120°. You shall be generally shunned if you
omit your waistcoat, no matter what the weather be.
And if you venture to object to these Median laws— as
I am now doing—you elicit a chorus of disapproval, and
acquire some evil name.

About 11 A.M., when the fresh water arrives from
the Hissi or wells, the Hajj sends us dinner, mutton
stews of exceeding greasiness, boiled rice, maize cakes,
sometimes fish, and generally curds or milk. We all sit
round a primitive form of the Round Table, and I doubt
that King Arthur's knights ever proved doughtier
trenchermen than do my companions. We then rise to
pipes and coffee, after which, excluding visitors, my
attendants apply themselves to a siesta, I to my journal
and studies.

At 2 P.M. there is a loud clamour at the door : if it
be not opened in time, we are asked if we have a Nazarene inside. Enters a crowd of visitors, anxious to pass
the afternoon. We proceed with a copy of the forenoon
till the sun declines, when it is time to escape the flies,
to repair to the terrace for fresh air, or to dress for a
walk. Generally our direction is through the town eastwards, to a plain of dilapidated graves and salt sand,
peopled only by land-crabs. At the extremity near the
sea is a little mosque of wattle-work : we sit there under
the shade, and play a rude form of draughts, called
Shantarah, or at Shahh, a modification of the former.[1]

---

1 The Shantarah board is thus made, with twenty-five points
technically called houses. The players have twelve counters a-piece,

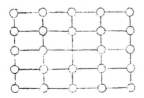

More often, eschewing these effeminacies, we shoot at
a mark, throw the javelin, leap, or engage in some
gymnastic exercise. The favourite Somali weapons are
the spear, dagger, and war-club ; the bow and poisoned
arrows are peculiar to the servile class, who know

> " the dreadful art
> To taint with deadly drugs the barbed dart;"

and the people despise, at the same time that they fear

---

and each places two at a time upon any of the unoccupied angles,
till all except the centre are filled up. The player who did not begin
the game must now move a man ; his object is to inclose one of his
adversary's between two of his own, in which case he removes it,
and is entitled to continue moving till he can no longer take. It is a
game of some skill, and perpetual practice enables the Somal to play
it as the Persians do backgammon, with great art and little reflection. The game is called Kurkabod when, as in our draughts, the
piece passing over one of the adversary's takes it.

Shahh is another favourite game. The board is made thus,

and the pieces as at Shantarah are twelve in number. The object is
to place three men in line—as the German Mühle and the Afghan
" Kitar "—when any one of the adversary's pieces may be removed.

Children usually prefer the game called indifferently Togantog
and Saddikiya. A double line of five or six holes is made in the
ground, four counters are placed in each, and when in the course of
play four men meet in the same hole, one of the adversary's is
removed. It resembles the Bornou game, played with beans and
holes in the sand. Citizens and the more civilized are fond of
" Bakkis," which, as its name denotes, is a corruption of the well-
known Indian Pachisi. None but the travelled knows chess, and the
Damal (draughts) and Tavola (backgammon) of the Turks.

firearms, declaring them to be cowardly weapons[1] with which the poltroon can slay the bravest.

The Somali spear is a form of the Cape Assegai. A long, thin, pliant and knotty shaft of the Dibi, Diktab, and Makari trees, is dried, polished, and greased with rancid butter : it is generally of a dull yellow colour, and some-times bound, as in Arabia, with brass wire for ornament. Care is applied to make the rod straight, or the missile flies crooked ; it is garnished with an iron button at the head, and a long, thin, tapering head of coarse bad iron,[2] made at Berberah and other places by the Tomal. The length of the shaft may be four feet eight inches ; the blade varies from twenty to twenty-six inches, and the whole weapon is about seven feet long. Some polish the entire spear-head, others only its socket or ferule ; com-monly, however, it is all blackened by heating it to redness, and rubbing it with cow's horn. In the towns, one of these weapons is carried ; on a journey and in battle two, as amongst the Tíbús—a small javelin for throwing and a large spear reserved for the thrust. Some warriors, especially amongst the Ísa, prefer a coarse heavy lance, which never leaves the hand. The Somali spear is held in various ways : generally the thumb and forefinger grasp the third nearest to the head, and the shaft resting

---

1 The same objection against "villanous saltpetre" was made by ourselves in times of old : the French knights called gunpowder the Grave of Honour. This is natural enough, the bravest weapon being generally the shortest—that which places a man hand to hand with his opponent. Some of the Kafir tribes have discontinued throwing the Assegai, and enter battle wielding it as a pike. Usually, also, the shorter the weapon is, the more fatal are the conflicts in which it is employed. The old French "Briquet," the Afghan "Charay," and the Goorka "Kukkri," exemplify this fact in the history of arms.

2 In the latter point it differs from the Assegai, which is worked by the Kafirs to the finest temper.

upon the palm is made to quiver. In action, the javelin is rarely thrown at a greater distance than six or seven feet, and the heavier weapon is used for " jobbing." Stripped to his waist, the thrower runs forward with all the action of a Kafir, whilst the attacked bounds about and crouches to receive it upon the round targe, which it cannot pierce. He then returns the compliment, at the same time endeavouring to break the weapon thrown at him by jumping and stamping upon it. The harmless missiles being exhausted, both combatants draw their daggers, grapple with the left hand, and with the right dig hard and swift at each other's necks and shoulders. When matters come to this point the duel is soon decided, and the victor, howling his slogan, pushes away from his front the dying enemy, and rushes off to find another opponent. A puerile weapon during the day when a steady man can easily avoid it, the spear is terrible in night attacks or in the "bush," whence it can be hurled unseen. For practice we plant a pair of slippers upright in the ground, at the distance of twelve yards, and a skilful spearman hits the mark once in every three throws.

The Somali dagger is an iron blade abont eighteen inches long by two in breadth, pointed and sharp at both edges. The handle is of buffalo or other horn, with a double scoop to fit the grasp; and at the hilt is a conical ornament of zinc. It is worn strapped round the waist by a thong sewed to the sheath, and long enough to encircle the body twice: the point is to the right, and the handle projects on the left. When in town, the Somal wear their daggers under the Tobe: in battle, the strap is girt over the cloth to prevent the latter being lost. They always stab from above: this is as it should be, a thrust with a short weapon "underhand" may be stopped, if the adversary have strength enough to hold the stabber's forearm. The thrust is parried with the shield, and the wound is rarely mortal except in the back: from the great length of the blade, the least movement of the man attacked causes it to fall upon the shoulder-blade.

The "Budd," or Somali club, resembles the Kafir "Tonga." It is a knobstick about a cubit long, made of some hard wood: the head is rounded on the inside, and the outside is cut to an edge. In quarrels it is considered a harmless weapon, and is often thrown at the opponent and wielded viciously enough where the spear point would carefully be directed at the buckler. The Gashan or shield is a round targe about eighteen inches in diameter; some of the Badawin make it much larger. Rhinoceros' skin being rare, the usual material is common bull's hide, or, preferably, that of the Oryx, called by the Arabs, Wa'al, and by the Somal, Ba'id. The shields are prettily cut, and are always protected when new with a covering of canvass. The boss in the centre easily turns a spear, and the strongest throw has very little effect even upon the thinnest portion. When not used, the Gashan is slung upon the left forearm: during battle, the handle, which is in the middle, is grasped by the left hand, and held out at a distance from the body.

We are sometimes joined in our exercises by the Arab mercenaries, who are far more skilful than the Somal. The latter are unacquainted with the sword, and cannot defend themselves against it with the targe; they know little of dagger practice, and were beaten at their own weapon, the javelin, by the children of Bir Hamid. Though unable to jump for the honour of the turband, I soon acquired the reputation of being the strongest man in Zayla: this is perhaps the easiest way of winning respect from a barbarous people, who honour body, and degrade mind to mere cunning.

When tired of exercise we proceed round the walls to the Ashurbara or Southern Gate. Here boys play at "hockey" with sticks and stones energetically as in

England: they are fine manly specimens of the race, but noisy and impudent, like all young savages. At two years of age they hold out their right hand for sweetmeats, and if refused become insolent. The citizens amuse themselves with the ball,[1] at which they play roughly as Scotch linkers: they are divided into two parties, bachelors and married men; accidents often occur, and no player wears any but the scantiest clothing, otherwise he would retire from the conflict in rags. The victors sing and dance about the town for hours, brandishing their spears, shouting their slogans, boasting of ideal victories—the Abyssinian Donfatu, or war vaunt,—and advancing in death-triumph with frantic gestures: a battle won would be celebrated with less circumstance in Europe. This is the effect of no occupation—the *primum mobile* of the Indian prince's kite-flying and all the puerilities of the pompous East.

We usually find an encampment of Badawin outside the gate. Their tents are worse than any gipsy's, low, smoky, and of the rudest construction. These people are a spectacle of savageness. Their huge heads of shock hair, dyed red and dripping with butter, are garnished with a Firin, or long three-pronged comb, a stick, which acts as scratcher when the owner does not wish to grease his fingers, and sometimes with the ominous ostrich feather, showing that the wearer has " killed his man "; a soiled and ragged cotton cloth covers their shoulders, and a similar article is wrapped round their loins.[2] All wear coarse sandals, and appear in the

---

1 It is called by the Arabs, Kubabah, by the Somal Goasa. Johnston (Travels in Southern Abyssinia, chap. 8) has described the game ; he errs, however, in supposing it peculiar to the Dankali tribes.

2 This is in fact the pilgrim dress of Al-Islam ; its wide diffusion to the eastward, as well as west of the Red Sea, proves its antiquity as a popular dress.

bravery of targe, spear and dagger. Some of the women would be pretty did they not resemble the men in their scowling, Satanic expression of countenance : they are decidedly *en deshabille*, but a black skin always appears a garb. The cantonment is surrounded by asses, camels and a troupe of native Flibertigibbets, who dance and jump in astonishment whenever they see me : " The white man ! the white man ! " they shriek ; " run away, run away, or we shall be eaten[1] ! " On one occasion, however, my *amour propre* was decidedly flattered by the attentions of a small black girl, apparently four or five years old, who followed me through the streets ejaculating " Wa Wanaksan ! "—" O fine ! " The Badawin, despite their fierce scowls, appear good-natured ; the women flock out of the huts to stare and laugh, the men to look and wonder. I happened once to remark, " Lo, we come forth to look at them and they look at us ; we gaze at their complexion and they gaze at ours ! " A Badawi who understood Arabic translated this speech to the others, and it excited great merriment. In the mining counties of civilized England, where the " genial brick-bat " is thrown at the passing stranger, or in enlightened Scotland, where hair a few inches too long or a pair of mustachioes justifies " mobbing," it would have been impossible for me to have mingled as I did with these wild people.

We must return before sunset, when the gates are locked and the keys are carried to the Hajj, a vain precaution, when a donkey could clear half a dozen places in the town wall. The call to evening prayers sounds as we enter : none of my companions prays,[2] but all when

---

1 I often regretted having neglected the precaution of a bottle of walnut-juice—a white colour is decidedly too conspicuous in this part of the East.

2 The strict rule of the Moslem faith is this : if a man neglect to pray, he is solemnly warned to repent. Should he simply refuse,

asked reply in the phrase which an Englishman hates,
" Inshallah Bukra "—" if Allah please, to-morrow ! "—
and they have the decency not to appear in public at the
hours of devotion. The Somal, like most Africans, are
of a somewhat irreverent turn of mind.[1] When re-
proached with gambling, and asked why they persist in
the forbidden pleasure, they simply answer, " Because we
like." One night, encamped among the Ísa, I was
disturbed by a female voice indulging in the loudest
lamentations : an elderly lady, it appears, was suffering
from tooth-ache, and the refrain of her groans was, " O
Allah, may thy teeth ache like mine ! O Allah, may
thy gums be sore as mine are ! " A well-known and
characteristic tale is told of the Jirad Hirsi, now chief
of the Berteri tribe. Once meeting a party of unarmed

---

without, however, disbelieving in prayer, he is to be put to death,
and receive Moslem burial; in the other contingency, he is not
bathed, prayed for, or interred in holy ground. This severe order,
however, lies in general abeyance.

1 " Tuarick grandiloquence," says Richardson (vol. i. p. 207),
" savours of blasphemy, *e.g.*, the lands, rocks, and mountains of
Ghat do not belong to God but to the Azghar." Equally irreverent
are the Kafirs of the Cape. They have proved themselves good men
in wit as well as in war ; yet, like the old Greenlanders and some of the
Burmese tribes, they are apparently unable to believe in the existence of the Supreme. A favourite question to the missionaries was
this, " Is your God white or black ? " If the European, startled by
the question, hesitated for a moment, they would leave him with
open signs of disgust at having been made the victims of a hoax.

The assertion generally passes current that the idea of an
Omnipotent Being is familiar to all people, even the most barbarous.
My limited experience argues the contrary. Savages begin with
fetishism and demon-worship, they proceed to physiolatry (the
religion of the Vedas) and Sabæism : the deity is the last and highest
pinnacle of the spiritual temple, not placed there except by a comparatively civilized race of high development, which leads them
to study and speculate upon cosmical and psychical themes. This
progression is admirably wrought out in Professor Max Müller's
" Rig Veda Sanhita."

pilgrims, he asked them why they had left their weapons at home: they replied in the usual phrase, "Nahnu mutawakkilin"—"we are trusters (in Allah)." That evening, having feasted them hospitably, the chief returned hurriedly to the hut, declaring that his soothsayer ordered him at once to sacrifice a pilgrim, and begging the horror-struck auditors to choose the victim. They cast lots and gave over one of their number: the Jirad placed him in another hut, dyed his dagger with sheep's blood, and returned to say that he must have a second life. The unhappy pilgrims rose *en masse*, and fled so wildly that the chief, with all the cavalry of the desert, found difficulty in recovering them. He dismissed them with liberal presents, and not a few jibes about their trustfulness in Allah. The wilder Badawin will inquire where Allah is to be found: when asked the object of the question, they reply, "If the Ísa could but catch him, they would spear him upon the spot—who but he lays waste their homes and kills their cattle and wives?" Yet, conjoined to this truly savage incapability of conceiving the idea of a Supreme Being, they believe in the most ridiculous exaggerations: many will not affront a common pilgrim, for fear of being killed by a glance or a word.

Our supper, also provided by the hospitable Hajj, is the counterpart of the midday dinner. After it we repair to the roof, to enjoy the prospect of the far Tajurrah hills and the white moonbeams sleeping upon the nearer sea. The evening star hangs like a diamond upon the still horizon: around the moon a pink zone of light mist, shading off into turquoise blue, and a delicate green like chrysopraz, invests the heavens with a peculiar charm. The scene is truly suggestive: behind us, purpling in the night-air and silvered by the radiance from above, lie the wolds and mountains tenanted by the fiercest of savages; their shadowy mysterious forms exciting vague alarms in the traveller's breast.   Sweet as the harp of David, the night-breeze and the music of the water come up from the sea : but the ripple and the rustling sound alternate with the hyena's laugh, the jackal's cry, and the wild dog's lengthened howl.

Or, the weather becoming cold, we remain below, and Mohammed Umar returns to read out more " Book of Lights," or some pathetic ode.   I will quote in free translation the following production of the celebrated poet Abd al-Rahman al-Burai, as a perfect specimen of melancholy Arab imagery :

" No exile is the exile to the latter end of earth,
    The exile is the exile to the coffin and the tomb !

" He hath claims on the dwellers in the places of their birth
    Whoso wandereth the world, for he lacketh him a home.

" Then blamer, blame me not, were my heart within thy breast,
    The sigh would take the place of thy laughter and thy scorn.

" Let me weep for the sin that debars my soul of rest,
    The tear may yet avail,—all in vain I may not mourn !¹

" Woe ! woe to thee, Flesh !—with a purer spirit, now
    The death-day were a hope, and the judgment-hour a joy !

" One morn I woke in pain, with a pallor on my brow,
    As though the dreaded Angel was descending to destroy :

" They brought to me a leech, saying, ' Heal him lest he die ! '
    On that day, by Allah, were his drugs a poor deceit !

" They stripped me and bathed me, and closed the glazing eye,
    And dispersed unto prayers, and to haggle for my sheet.

---

    1 The Moslem corpse is partly sentient in the tomb, reminding the reader of Tennyson :

        " I thought the dead had peace, but it is not so ;
            To have no peace in the grave, is that not sad ? "

" The prayers without a bow[1] they prayed over me that day,
Brought nigh to me the bier, and disposèd me within.

" Four bare upon their shoulders this tenement of clay,
Friend and kinsman in procession bore the dust of friend and kin.

" They threw upon me mould of the tomb, and went their way—
A guest, 'twould seem, had flitted from the dwellings of the tribe !

" My gold and my treasures each a share they bore away,
Without thanks, without praise, with a jest and with a jibe.

" My gold and my treasures each a share they bore away,
On me they left the weight !—with me they left the sin !

" That night within the grave without hoard or child I lay,
No spouse, no friend were there, no comrade and no kin.

" The wife of my youth soon another husband found—
A stranger sat at home on the hearthstone of my sire.

" My son became a slave, though not purchasèd nor bound,
The hireling of a stranger, who begrudged him his hire.

" Such, alas, is human life ! such the horror of his death !
Man grows like a grass, like a god he sees no end.

" Be wise, then, ere too late, brother ! praise with every breath
The Hand that can chastise, the Arm that can defend :

" And bless thou the Prophet, the averter of our ills,
While the lightning flasheth bright o'er the ocean and the hills."

At this hour my companions become imaginative and superstitious. One Salimayn, a black slave from the

---

1 The prayers for the dead have no Ruka'at, or bow, as in other orisons.

Sawahil,[1] now secretary to the Hajj, reads our fortunes in the rosary. The "fal,[2]" as it is called, acts a prominent part in Somali life. Some men are celebrated for accuracy of prediction; and in times of danger, when the human mind is ever open to the "fooleries of faith," perpetual reference is made to their art. The worldly-wise Salimayn, I observed, never sent away a questioner with an ill-omened reply, but he also regularly insisted upon the efficacy of sacrifice and almsgiving, which, as they would assuredly be neglected, afforded him an excuse in case of accident. Then we had a recital of the tales common to Africa, and perhaps to all the world. In modern France, as in ancient Italy, "versipelles" become wolves and hide themselves in the woods: in Persia they change themselves into bears, and in Bornou and Shoa assume the shapes of lions, hyenas, and leopards.[3] The origin of this metamorphic superstition is easily trace-

---

1 The general Moslem name for the African coast from the Somali seaboard southwards to the Mozambique, inhabited by negroid and negrotic races.

2 The Moslem rosary consists of ninety-nine beads divided into sets of thirty-three each by some peculiar sign, as a bit of red coral. The consulter, beginning at a chance place, counts up to the mark: if the number of beads be odd, he sets down a single dot, if even, two. This is done four times, when a figure is produced as in the margin. Of these there are sixteen, each having its peculiar name and properties. The art is merely Geomancy in its rudest shape; a mode of vaticination which, from its wide diffusion, must be of high antiquity. The Arabs call it Al-Raml, and ascribe its present form to the Imam Ja'afar al-Sadik; amongst them it is a ponderous study, connected as usual with astrology. Napoleon's "Book of Fate" is a specimen of the old Eastern superstition presented to Europe in a modern and simple form.

3 In this country, as in Western and Southern Africa, the leopard, not the wolf, is the shepherd's scourge.

able like man's fetishism or demonology, to his fears; a Badawi, for instance, becomes dreadful by the reputation of sorcery: bears and hyenas are equally terrible; and the two objects of horror are easily connected. Curious to say, individuals having this power were pointed out to me, and people pretended to discover it in their countenances: at Zayla I was shown a Badawi, by name, Farih Badaun, who notably became a hyena at times, for the purpose of tasting human blood.[1] About forty years ago, three brothers, Kayna, Fardayna, and Sollan, were killed on Gulays near Berberah for the crime of metamorphosis. The charge is usually substantiated either by the bestial tail remaining appended to a part of the human shape which the owner has forgotten to rub against the magic tree, or by some peculiar wound which the beast received and the man retained. Kindred to this superstition is the belief that many of the Badawin have learned the languages of birds and beasts. Another widely-diffused fancy is that of the Aksar,[2] which in this pastoral land becomes a kind of wood: wonderful tales are told of battered milk-pails which, by means of some peg accidently cut in the jungle, have been found full of silver, or have acquired the qualities of cornucopiæ. It is supposed that a red heifer always breaks her fast upon the wonderful plant, consequently much time and trouble have been expended by the Somal in watching the morning proceedings of red heifers. At other times we hear fearful tales of old women who, like the Jigar Khwar of Persia, feed upon man's liver; they are fond of destroying young children; even adults are not ashamed of defending themselves with talismans. In this country the

---

1 Popular superstition in Abyssinia attributes the same power to the Felashas or Jews.

2 Our Elixir, a corruption of the Arabic Al-Iksir.

crone is called Bida'a or Kumayyo, words signifying a witch: the worst is she that destroys her own progeny. No wound is visible in this vampyre's victim: generally he names his witch, and his friends beat her to death unless she heal him: many are thus martyred; and in Somali land scant notice is taken of such a peccadillo as murdering an old woman. The sex indeed has by no means a good name: here, as elsewhere, those who degrade it are the first to abuse it for degradation. At Zayla almost all quarrels are connected with women; the old bewitch in one way, the young in another, and both are equally maligned. "Wit in a woman," exclaims one man, "is a habit of running away in a dromedary." "Allah," declares another, "made woman of a crooked rib; he who would straighten her, breaketh her." Perhaps, however, by these generalisms of abuse the sex gains: they prevent personal and individual details; and no society of French gentlemen avoids mentioning in public the name of a woman more scrupulously than do the misogynist Moslems.

After a conversazione of two hours my visitors depart, and we lose no time—for we must rise at cock-crow—in spreading our mats round the common room. You would admire the Somali pillow,[1] a dwarf pedestal of carved wood, with a curve upon which the greasy poll and its elaborate *frisure* repose. Like the Abyssinian article, it resembles the head-rest of ancient Egypt in all points, except that it is not worked with Typhons and other horrors to drive away dreadful dreams. Sometimes the sound of the kettledrum, the song, and the clapping of hands, summon us at a later hour than usual to a dance. The performance is complicated, and, as usual with the trivialities easily learned in early youth, it is uncommonly

---

[1] In the Somali tongue its name is Barki: they make a stool of similar shape, and call it Barjimo

difficult to a stranger. Each dance has its own song and
measure, and, contrary to the custom of Al-Islam, the
sexes perform together. They begin by clapping the
hands and stamping where they stand; to this succeed
advancing, retiring, wheeling about, jumping about, and
the other peculiarities of the Jim Crow school. The
principal measures are those of Ugadayn and Batar;
these are again divided and subdivided. I fancy that
the description of Dileho, Jibwhayn, and Hobala would
be as entertaining and instructive to you, dear L., as
Polka, Gavotte, and Mazurka would be to a Somali.

On Friday—our Sunday—a drunken crier goes
about the town, threatening the bastinado to all who
neglect their five prayers. At half-past eleven a kettle-
drum sounds a summons to the Jami or Cathedral. It
is an old barn rudely plastered with whitewash; posts or
columns of artless masonry support the low roof, and the
smallness of the windows, or rather air-holes, renders
its dreary length unpleasantly hot. There is no pulpit;
the only ornament is a rude representation of the Meccan
Mosque, nailed like a pot-house print to the wall; and
the sole articles of furniture are ragged mats and old
boxes containing tattered chapters of the Koran in
greasy bindings. I enter with a servant carrying a
prayer carpet, encounter the stare of 300 pairs of eyes,
belonging to parallel rows of squatters, recite the
customary two-bow prayer in honour of the mosque,
placing sword and rosary before me, and then, taking up
a Koran, read the Cow Chapter (No. 18) loud and twang-
ingly. At the Zohr or midday hour, the Mu'ezzin inside
the mosque, standing before the Khatib, or preacher,
repeats the call to prayer, which the congregation,
sitting upon their shins and feet, intone after him. This
ended, all present stand up, and recite every man for
himself a two-bow prayer of Sunnat or Example, concluding with the blessing on the Prophet and the Salam

over each shoulder to all brother Believers. The Khatib
then ascends his hole in the wall, which serves for pulpit,
and thence addresses us with " The peace be upon you,
and the mercy of Allah, and his benediction ;" to which
we respond through the Mu'ezzin, " And upon you be
peace, and Allah's mercy !" After sundry other religious
formulas and their replies, concluding with a second call
to prayer, our preacher rises, and in a voice with which
Sir Hudibras was wont

" To blaspheme custard through the nose,"

preaches Al-Wa'az,[1] or the advice sermon. He sits down
for a few minutes, and then, rising again, recites Al-
Na'at, or the Praise of the Prophet and his Companions.
These are the two heads into which the Moslem discourse is divided ; unfortunately, however, there is no
application. Our preacher, who is also Kazi or Judge,
makes several blunders in his Arabic, and he reads his
sermons, a thing never done in Al-Islam, except by the
modicè docti. The discourse over, our clerk, who is, if
possible, worse than the curate, repeats the form of call
termed Al-Ikamah : then entering the Mihrab, or niche,
he recites the two-bow Friday litany, with, and in front
of, the congregation. I remarked no peculiarity in the
style of praying, except that all followed the practice of
the Shafe'is in Al-Yaman—raising the hands for a
moment, instead of letting them depend along the thighs,
between the Ruka'at or bow and the Sujdah or prostra-
tion. This public prayer concluded, many people leave
the mosque ; a few remain for more prolonged devotions.

There is a queer kind of family likeness between
this scene and that of a village church in some quiet nook

---

[1] Specimens of these discourses have been given by Mr. Lane,
Mod. Egypt, chap. 3. It is useless to offer others, as all bear the
closest resemblance.

of rural England. Old Sharmarkay, the squire, attended by his son, takes his place close to the pulpit; and although the *Honoratioren* have no padded and cushioned pews they comport themselves very much as if they had. Recognitions of the most distant description are allowed before the service commences: looking around is strictly forbidden during prayers; but all do not regard the prohibition, especially when a new moustache enters. Leaving the church, men shake hands, stand for a moment to exchange friendly gossip, or address a few words to the preacher, and then walk home to dinner. There are many salient points of difference. No bonnets appear in public: the squire, after prayers, gives alms to the poor, and departs escorted by two dozen matchlock-men, who perseveringly fire their shotted guns, as in Ireland, blunderbusses.[1]

---

1 So in the last century the Highland piper played before the Laird every Sunday on his way to the Kirk, which he circled three times; performing the family march, which implied defiance to all enemies of the clan. In Ireland, in the early part of the present century, gentlemen went to church with a brace of bull-dogs or a brass blunderbuss, *the* article to clear a staircase.

CHAPTER III.

EXCURSIONS NEAR ZAYLA.

WE determined on the 9th of November to visit the island of Sa'ad al-Din, the larger of the two patches of ground which lie about two miles north of the town. Reaching our destination, after an hour's lively sail, we passed through a thick belt of underwood tenanted by swarms of midges, with a damp chill air crying fever, and a fetor of decayed vegetation smelling death. To this succeeded a barren flat of silt and sand, white with salt and ragged with salsolaceous stubble, reeking with heat, and covered with old vegetation. Here, says local tradition, was the ancient site of Zayla,[1] built by Arabs from Al-Yaman. The legend runs that when Sa'ad al-Din was besieged and slain by David, king of Ethiopia, the wells dried up and the island sank. Something doubtless occurred which rendered a removal advisable: the sons of the Moslem hero fled to Ahmad bin al-Ashraf, Prince of Sana'a, offering their allegiance if he would build fortifications for them and aid them against the Christians of Abyssinia. The consequence was a walled circuit upon

---

1 Bruce describes Zayla as " a small island, on the very coast of Adel." To reconcile discrepancy, he adopts the usual clumsy expedient of supposing two cities of the same name, one situated seven degrees south of the other. Salt corrects the error, but does not seem to have heard of old Zayla's insular position.

the present site of Zayla ; of its old locality almost may be said "*perière ruinæ.*"

During my stay with Sharmarkay I made many inquiries about historical works, and the Kazi ; Mohammed Khatib, a Harar man of the Hawiyah tribe, was at last persuaded to send his Daftar, or office papers for my inspection. They formed a kind of parish register of births, deaths, marriages, divorces, and manumissions. From them it appeared that in A.H. 1081 (A.D. 1670-71) the Shanabila Sayyids were Kazis of Zayla and retained the office for 138 years. It passed two generations ago into the hands of Mohammed Musa, a Hawiyah, and the present Kazi is his nephew.

The origin of Zayla, or as it is locally called, "Audal," is lost in the fogs of Phœnician fable. The Avalites[1] of the Periplus and Pliny, it was in earliest ages dependent upon the kingdom of Axum.[2] About the seventh century, when the Southern Arabs penetrated into the heart of Abyssinia,[3] it became the great factory

---

1 The inhabitants were termed Avalitæ, and the Bay, "Sinus Avaliticus." Some modern travellers have confounded it with Adule or Adulis, the port of Axum, founded by fugitive Egyptian slaves. The latter however, lies further north: D'Anville places it at Arkiko, Salt at Zula (or Azule), near the head of Annesley Bay.

2 The Arabs were probably the earliest colonists of this coast. Even the Sawahil people retain a tradition that their forefathers originated in the south of Arabia.

3 To the present day the district of Gozi is peopled by Mohammedans called Arablet, "whose progenitors," according to Harris, "are said by tradition to have been left there prior to the reign of Nagasi, first king of Shoa. Hossain, Wahabit, and Abdool Kurreem, generals probably detached from the victorious army of Graan (Mohammed Gragne), are represented to have come from Mecca, and to have taken possession of the country—the legend assigning to the first of these warriors as his capital, the populous village of Medina, which is conspicuous on a cone among the mountains, shortly after entering the valley of Robi."

of the eastern coast, and rose to its height of splendour. Taki al-Din Makrizi[1] includes, under the name of Zayla, a territory of forty-three days' march by forty and divides it into seven great provinces, speaking about fifty languages, and ruled by Amirs, subject to the Hati (Hatze) of Abyssinia.

In the fourteenth century it became celebrated by its wars with the kings of Abyssinia: sustaining severe defeats the Moslems retired upon their harbour, which after an obstinate defence fell into the hands of the Christians. The land was laid waste, the mosques were converted into churches, and the Abyssinians returned to their mountains laden with booty. About A.D. 1400, Sa'ad al-Din, the heroic prince of Zayla, was besieged in his city by the Hatze David the Second: slain by a spear-thrust, he left his people powerless in the hands of their enemies, till his sons, Sabr al-Din, Ali, Mansur, and Jamal al-Din retrieved the cause of Al-Islam.

Ibn Batutah, a voyager of the fourteenth century, thus describes the place: " I then went from Aden by sea, and after four days came to the city of Zayla. This is a settlement of the Berbers,[2] a people of Sudan, of the Shafi'a sect. Their country is a desert of two months' extent; the first part is termed Zayla, the last Makdashu. The greatest number of the inhabitants, however, are of the Rafizah sect.[3] Their food is mostly camels' flesh and fish.[4]

---

1 Historia Regum Islamiticorum in Abyssinia, Lugd. Bat. 1790.

2 The affinity between the Somal and the Berbers of Northern Africa, and their descent from Cana'an, son of Ham, has been learnedly advanced and refuted by several Moslem authors. The theory appears to have arisen from a mistake ; Berberah, the great emporium of the Somali country, being confounded with the Berbers of Nubia.

3 Probably Za'idi from Al-Yaman. At present the people of Zayla are all orthodox Sunnites.

4 Fish, as will be seen in these pages, is no longer a favourite article of diet.

The stench of the country is extreme, as is also its filth, from the stink of the fish and the blood of camels which are slaughtered in its streets."

About A.D. 1500 the Turks conquered Al-Yaman, and the lawless Janissaries, " who lived upon the very bowels of commerce,[1] " drove the peaceable Arab merchants to the opposite shore. The trade of India, flying from the same enemy, took refuge in Adel, amongst its partners.[2]

The Turks of Arabia, though they were blind to the cause, were sensible to the great influx of wealth into the opposite kingdoms. They took possession, therefore, o Zayla, which they made a den of thieves, established there what they called a custom-house,[3] and, by means of that post and galleys cruising in the narrow straits of Bab al-Mandab, they laid the Indian trade to Adel under heavy contributions that might indemnify them for the great desertion their violence and injustice had occasioned in Arabia.

This step threatened the very existence both of Adel and Abyssinia ; and considering the vigorous government of the one, and the weak politics and prejudices of the other, it is more than probable that the Turks would

---

1 Bruce, book 3.

2 Hence the origin of the trade between Africa and Cutch, which continues uninterrupted to the present time. Adel, Arabia and India, as Bruce remarks, were three partners in one trade, who mutually exported their produce to Europe, Asia, and Africa, at that time the whole known world.

3 The Turks, under a show of protecting commerce, established these posts in their different ports. But they soon made it appear that the end proposed was only to ascertain who were the subjects from whom they could levy the most enormous extortions. Jeddah, Zabid, and Mocha, the places of consequence nearest to Abyssinia on the Arabian coast, Suakin, a seaport town on the very barriers of Abyssinia, in the immediate way of their caravan to Cairo on the African side, were each under the command of a Turkish Pasha, and garrisoned by Turkish troops sent thither from Constantinople by the Emperors Salim and Sulayman.

have subdued both, had they not in India, their chief object, met the Portuguese strongly established.

Bartema, travelling in A.D. 1503, treats in his 15th chapter of " Zeila in Æthiopia and the great fruitlessness thereof, and of certain strange beasts seen there."

" In this city is great frequentation of merchandise, as in a most famous mart. There is marvellous abundance of gold and iron, and an innumerable number of black slaves sold for small prices; these are taken in war by the Mahomedans out of Æthiopia, of the kingdom of Presbyter Johannes, or Preciosus Johannes, which some also call the king of Jacobins or Abyssins, being a Christian; and are carried away from thence into Persia, Arabia Felix, Babylonia of Nilus or Alcair, and Meccah. In this city justice and good laws are observed.[1] . . . . . It hath an innumerable multitude of merchants; the walls are greatly decayed, and the haven rude and despicable. The King or Sultan of the city is a Mahomedan, and entertaineth in wages a great multitude of footmen and horsemen. They are greatly given to war, and wear only one loose single vesture: they are of dark ash colour, inclining to black."

---

1 Bartema's account of its productions is as follows: " The soil beareth wheat and hath abundance of flesh and divers other commodious things. It hath also oil, not of olives, but of some other thing, I know not what. There is also plenty of honey and wax; there are likewise certain sheep having their tails of the weight of sixteen pounds, and exceeding fat; the head and neck are black, and all the rest white. There are also sheep altogether white, and having tails of a cubit long, and hanging down like a great cluster of grapes, and have also great laps of skin hanging down from their throats, as have bulls and oxen, hanging down almost to the ground. There are also certain kind with horns like unto harts' horns; these are wild, and when they be taken are given to the Sultan of that city as a kingly present. I saw there also certain kind having only one horn in the midst of the forehead, as hath the unicorn, and about a span of length, but the horn bendeth backward: they are of bright shining red colour. But they that have harts' horns are inclining to black colour. Living is there good and cheap."

In July, 1516, Zayla, described as then the " great market of those parts," was taken, and the town burned by a Portuguese armament, under Lopez Suarez Alberguiera, and Berberah would have shared the same fate had not the fleet been dispersed by storms. When the Turks were compelled to retire from Southern Arabia, it became subject to the Prince of Sana'a, who gave it in perpetuity to the family of a Sana'ani merchant.

The kingdom of Al-Yaman falling into decay, Zayla passed under the authority of the Sherif of Mocha, who, though receiving no part of the revenue, had yet the power of displacing the Governor. By him it was farmed out to the Hajj Sharmarkay, who paid annually to Sayyid Mohammed al-Barr, at Mocha, the sum of 750 crowns, and reserved all that he could collect above that sum for himself. In A.D. 1848 Zayla was taken from the family Al-Barr, and farmed out to Sharmarkay by the Turkish Governor of Mocha and Hodaydah.

The extant remains at Sa'ad al-Din are principally those of water-courses, rude lines of coralline, stretching across the plain towards wells, now lost,[1] and diminutive tanks, made apparently to collect rain water. One of these latter is a work of some art—a long sunken vault, with a pointed arch projecting a few feet above the surface of the ground; outside, it is of rough stone, the interior is carefully coated with fine lime, and from the roof long stalactites depend. Near it is a cemetery : the graves are, for the most part, provided with large slabs of close black basalt, planted in the ground edgeways, and in the shape of a small oblong. The material was most probably brought from the mountains near Tajurrah : at another part of the island I found it in the shape of a

---

1 The people have a tradition that a well of sweet water exists unseen in some part of the island. When Sa'ad al-Din was besieged in Zayla by the Hatzi David, the host of Al-Islam suffered severely for the want of the fresh element.

gigantic mill-stone, half imbedded in the loose sand.
Near the cemetery we observed a mound of rough stones
surrounding an upright pole ; this is the tomb of Shaykh
Sa'ad al-Din, formerly the hero, now the favourite patron
saint of Zayla—still popularly venerated, as was proved
by the remains of votive banquets, broken bones, dried
garbage, and stones blackened by the fire.

After wandering through the island, which contained
not a human being save a party of Somal boatmen cutting firewood for Aden, and having massacred a number
of large fishing hawks and small sea-birds, to astonish
the natives our companions, we returned to the landing-
place. Here an awning had been spread ; the goat destined for our dinner—I have long since conquered all
dislike, dear L., to seeing dinner perambulating—had
been boiled and disposed in hunches upon small
mountains of rice, and jars of sweet water stood in the
air to cool. After feeding, regardless of Quartana and
her weird sisterhood, we all lay down for siesta in the
light sea-breeze. Our slumbers were heavy, as the
Zayla people say is ever the case at Sa'ad al-Din, and
the sun had declined low ere we awoke. The tide was
out, and we waded a quarter of a mile to the boat,
amongst giant crabs who showed grisly claws, sharp
coralline, and sea-weed so thick as to become almost
a mat. You must believe me when I tell you that in
the shallower parts the sun was painfully hot, even to
my well-tried feet. We picked up a few specimens of
fine sponge, and coral, white and red, which, if collected,
might be valuable to Zayla, and, our pic-nic concluded,
we returned home.

On the 14th November we left the town to meet a
caravan of the Danakil,[1] and to visit the tomb of the

---

1 The singular is Dankali, the plural Danakil : both words are
Arabic, the vernacular name being " Afar " or " Afer," the Somal
" Afar nimun." The word is pronounced like the Latin " Afer," an
African.

great saint Abu Zarbay. The former approached in a straggling line of asses, and about fifty camels laden with cows' hides, ivories and one Abyssinian slave-girl. The men were wild as ourang-outangs, and the women fit only to flog cattle: their animals were small, meagre-looking, and loosely made; the asses of the Badawin, however, are far superior to those of Zayla, and the camels are, comparatively speaking, well bred.[1] In a few minutes the beasts were unloaded, the Gurgis or wigwams pitched, and all was prepared for repose. A caravan so extensive being an unusual event—small parties carrying only grain come in once or twice a week—the citizens abandoned even their favourite game of ball, with an eye to speculation. We stood at " Government House," over the Ashurbara Gate, to see the Badawin, and we quizzed (as Town men might denounce a tie or scoff at a boot) the huge round shields and the uncouth spears of

---

[1] Occasionally at Zayla—where all animals are expensive—Dankali camels may be bought: though small, they resist hardship and fatigue better than the other kinds. A fair price would be about ten dollars. The Somal divide their animals into two kinds, Gel Ad and Ayyun. The former is of white colour, loose and weak, but valuable, I was told by Lieut. Speke, in districts where little water is found: the Ayyun is darker and stronger ; its price averages about a quarter more than the Gel Ad.

To the Arabian traveller nothing can be more annoying than these Somali camels. They must be fed four hours during the day, otherwise they cannot march. They die from change of food or sudden removal to another country. Their backs are ever being galled, and, with all precautions, a month's march lays them up for three times that period. They are never used for riding except in cases of sickness or accidents.

The Somali ass is generally speaking a miserable animal. Lieut. Speke, however, reports that on the windward coast it is not to be despised. At Harar I found a tolerable breed, superior in appearance but inferior in size to the thorough-bred little animals at Aden. They are never ridden; their principal duty is that of carrying water-skins to and from the wells.

these provincials. Presently they entered the streets, where we witnessed their frantic dance in presence of the Hajj and other authorities. This is the wild men's way of expressing their satisfaction that Fate has enabled them to convoy the caravan through all the dangers of the desert.

The Shaykh Ibrahim Abu Zarbay[1] lies under a whitewashed dome close to the Ashurbara Gate of Zayla : an inscription cut in wood over the doorway informs us that the building dates from A.H. 1155= A.D. 1741-2. It is now dilapidated, the lintel is falling in, the walls are decaying, and the cupola, which is rudely built, with primitive gradients—each step supported as in Kashmír and other parts of India, by wooden beams —threatens the heads of the pious. The building is divided into two compartments, forming a Mosque and a Mazar or place of pious visitation : in the latter are five tombs, the two largest covered with common chintz stuff of glaring colours. Ibrahim was one of the forty-four Hasrami saints who landed at Berberah, sat in solemn conclave upon Auliya Kumbo or Holy Hill, and thence dispersed far and wide for the purpose of propagandism. He travelled to Harar about A.D. 1430,[2] converted many to Al-Islam, and left there an honoured memory. His name is immortalised in Al-Yaman by the introduction of Al-Kat.[3]

---

1 He is generally called Abu Zerbin, more rarely Abu Zarbayn, and Abu Zarbay. I have preferred the latter orthography upon the authority of the Shaykh Jami, most learned of the Somal.

2 In the same year (A.D. 1429-30) the Shaykh al-Shazili, buried under a dome at Mocha, introduced coffee into Arabia.

3 The following is an extract from the Pharmaceutical Journal, vol. xii. No. v. Nov. 1, 1852. Notes upon the drugs observed at Aden, Arabia, by James Vaughan, Esq., M.R.C.S.E., Assist. Surg., B.A., Civil and Port. Surg., Aden, Arabia.

"Kât قات, the name of the drug which is brought into Aden from the interior, and largely used, especially by the Arabs, as a

Tired of the town, I persuaded the Hajj to send me with an escort to the Hissi or well. At daybreak I set out with four Arab matchlock men, and taking a direction nearly due west, waded and walked over an alluvial plain flooded by every high tide. On our way we passed lines

---

pleasurable excitant. It is generally imported in small camel-loads, consisting of a number of parcels, each containing about forty slender twigs with the leaves attached, and carefully wrapped so as to prevent as much as possible exposure to the atmosphere. The leaves form the edible part, and these, when chewed, are said to produce great hilarity of spirits and an agreeable state of wakefulness. Some estimate may be formed of the strong predilection which the Arabs have for this from the quantity used in Aden alone, which averages about 280 camel-loads annually. The market price is one and a quarter rupees per parcel, and the exclusive privilege of selling it is farmed by the government for 1500 rupees per year. Forskäl found the plant growing on the mountain of Al-Yaman, and has enumerated it as a new genus in the class Pentandria, under the name of Catha. He notices two species, and distinguishes them as *Catha edulis* and *Catha spinosa*. According to his account it is cultivated on the same ground as coffee, and is planted from cuttings. Besides the effects above stated, the Arabs, he tells us, believe the land where it grows to be secure from the inroads of plague; and that a twig of the Kât carried in the bosom is a certain safeguard against infection. The learned botanist observes, with respect to these supposed virtues, 'Gustus foliorum tamen virtutum tantam indicare non videtur.' Like coffee, Kât, from its acknowledged stimulating effects, has been a fertile theme for the exercise of Mohamedan casuistry, and names of renown are ranged on both sides of the question, whether the use of Kât does or does not contravene the injunction of the Koran, Thou shalt not drink wine or anything intoxicating. The succeeding notes borrowed chiefly from De Sacy's researches, may be deemed worthy of insertion here.

" Sheikh Abdool Kader Ansari Jezeri, a learned Mahomedan author, in his treatise on the use of coffee, quotes the following from the writings of Fakr ood Deen Mekki :—' It is said that the first who introduced coffee was the illustrious saint Aboo Abdallah Mahomed Dhabhani ibn Said; but we have learned by the testimony of many persons that the use of coffee in Yemen, its origin, and first introduction into that country are due to the learned Ali Shadeli ibn Omar, one

of donkeys and camels carrying water skins from the town; they were under guard like ourselves, and the sturdy dames that drove them indulged in many a loud joke at our expense. After walking about four miles we arrived at what is called the Takhushshah—the sandy

---

of the disciples of the learned doctor Nasr ood Deen, who is regarded as one of the chiefs among the order Shadeli, and whose worth attests the high degree of spirituality to which they had attained. Previous to that time they made coffee of the vegetable substance called Cafta, which is the same leaf known under the name of Kât, and not of Boon (the coffee berry) nor any preparation of Boon. The use of this beverage extended in course of time as far as Aden, but in the days of Mahomed Dhabhani the vegetable substance from which it was prepared disappeared from Aden. Then it was that the Sheikh advised those who had become his disciples to try the drink made from the Boon, which was found to produce the same effect as the Kât, inducing sleeplessness, and that it was attended with less expense and trouble. The use of coffee has been kept up from that time to the present.'

" D'Herbelot states that the beverage called Calmat al Catiat or Caftah, was prohibited in Yemen in consequence of its effects upon the brain. On the other hand a synod of learned Mussulmans is said to have decreed that as beverages of Kât and Cafta do not impair the health or impede the observance of religious duties, but only increase hilarity and good-humour, it was lawful to use them, as also the drink made from the boon or coffee-berry. I am not aware that Kât is used in Aden in any other way than for mastication. From what I have heard, however, I believe that a decoction resembling tea is made from the leaf by the Arabs in the interior; and one who is well acquainted with our familiar beverage assures me that the effects are not unlike those produced by strong green tea, with this advantage in favour of Kât, that the excitement is always of a pleasing and agreeable kind.[1]

---

[1] " Mr. Vaughan has transmitted two specimens called Tubbare Kàt and Muktaree Kàt, from the districts in which they are produced: the latter fetches the lower price. Catha edulis *Forsk.*, Nat. Ord. Celastraceæ, is figured in Dr. Lindley's Vegetable Kingdom, p. 588 (Lond. 1846). But there is a still more complete representation of the plant under the name of Catha Forskalii *Richard*, in a work published under the auspices of the

bed of a torrent nearly a mile broad,[1] covered with a thin coat of caked mud: in the centre is a line of pits from three to four feet deep, with turbid water at the bottom. Around them were several frame-works of four upright sticks connected by horizontal bars, and on these were stretched goats'-skins, forming the cattle trough of the Somali country. About the well stood troops of camels, whose Ísa proprietors scowled fiercely at us, and stalked over the plain with their long, heavy spears: for protection against these people, the citizens have erected a kind of round tower, with a ladder for a staircase. Near it are some large tamarisks and the wild henna of the Somali country, which supplies a sweet-smelling flower, but is valueless as a dye. A thick hedge of thorn-

---

French Government, entitled, 'Voyage en Abyssinie éxecuté pendant les années 1839-43, par une commission scientifique composée de MM. Théophile Lefebvre, Lieut. du Vaisseau, A. Petit et Martin-Dillon, docteurs médecins, naturalistes du Museum, Vignaud dessinateur.' The botanical portion of this work, by M. Achille Richard, is regarded either as a distinct publication under the title of Tentamen Floræ Abyssinicæ, or as a part of the Voyage en Abyssinie. M. Richard enters into some of the particulars relative to the synonyms of the plant, from which it appears that Vahl referred Forskäl's genus Catha to the Linnæan genus Celastrus, changing the name of Catha edulis to Celastrus edulis. Hochstetter applied the name of Celastrus edulis to an Abyssinian species (Celastrus obscurus *Richard*), which he imagined identical with Forskäl's Catha edulis, while of the real Catha edulis *Forsk.* he formed a new genus and species under the name of Trigonotheca serrata *Hochs.* Nat. Ord. Hippocrateaceæ. I quote the following references from the Tentamen Floræ Abyssinicæ, vol. i. p. 134: 'Catha Forskalii *Nob.* Catha No. 4. Forsk. loc. cit. (Flor. Ægypt. Arab. p. 63). Trigonotheca serrata *Hochs.* in pl. Schimp. Abyss. sect. ii. No. 649. Celastrus edulis *Vahl, Ecl.* 1, 21.' Although in the Flora Ægyptiaco-Arabica of Forskäl no specific name is applied to the Catha at p. 63, it is enumerated as Catha edulis at p. 107. The reference to Celastrus edulis is not contained in the Eclogæ Americanæ of Vahl, but in the author's Symbolæ Botanicæ (Hanuiæ, 1790, fol.) pars i. p. 21. (Daniel Hanbury signed).

1 This is probably the " River of Zayla," alluded to by Ibn Sa'id and others. Like all similar features in the low country, it is a mere surface drain.

trees surrounds the only cultivated ground near Zayla :
as Ibn Sa'id declared in old times, "the people have no
gardens, and know nothing of fruits." The variety and
the luxuriance of growth, however, prove that industry is
the sole desideratum. I remarked the castor-plant—no
one knows its name or nature[1]—the Rayhan or Basil, the
Kadi, a species of aloe, whose strongly-scented flowers
the Arabs of Al-Yaman are fond of wearing in their turbands.[2] Of vegetables, there were cucumbers, egg-plants,
and the edible hibiscus; the only fruit was a small kind
of water-melon.

After enjoying a walk through the garden and a bath
at the well, I started, gun in hand, towards the jungly
plain that stretches towards the sea. It abounds in
hares, and in a large description of spur-fowl[3]; the
beautiful little sand antelope, scarcely bigger than an
English rabbit,[4] bounded over the bushes, its thin legs

---

1 In the upper country I found a large variety growing wild in
the Fiumaras. The Badawin named it Buamado, but ignored its
virtues.

2 This ornament is called Mushgur.

3 A large brown bird with black legs, not unlike the domestic
fowl. The Arabs call it Dijajat al-Barr, (the wild hen): the Somal
"digarin," a word also applied to the Guinea fowl, which it
resembles in its short strong flight and habit of running. Owing
to the Badawi prejudice against eating birds, it is found in large
coveys all over the country.

4 It has been described by Salt and others. The Somal call it
Sagaro, the Arabs Ghazalah: it is found throughout the land generally in pairs, and is fond of ravines under the hills, beds of torrents
and patches of desert vegetation. It is easily killed by a single pellet
of shot striking the neck. The Somal catch it by a loop of strong
twine hung round a gap in a circuit of thorn hedge, or they run
it down on foot, an operation requiring half a day on account of
its fleetness, which enables it to escape the jackal and wild dog.
When caught it utters piercing cries. Some Badawin do not eat the
flesh: generally, however, it is considered a delicacy, and the skulls
and bones of these little animals lie strewed around the kraals.

being scarcely perceptible during the spring. I was afraid to fire with ball, the place being full of Badawin huts, herds, and dogs, and the vicinity of man made the animals too wild for small shot. In revenge, I did considerable havoc amongst the spur-fowl, who proved equally good for sport and the pot, besides knocking over a number of old crows, whose gall the Arab soldiers wanted for collyrium.[1] Beyond us lay Warabalay or Hyænas' hill[2]: we did not visit it, as all its tenants had been driven away by the migration of the Nomads.

---

1 The Somal hold the destruction of the " Tuka " next in the religious merit to that of the snake. They have a tradition that the crow, originally white, became black for his sins. When the Prophet and Abu Bakr were concealed in the cave, the pigeon hid there from their pursuers : the crow, on the contrary, sat screaming " ghar! ghar! " (the cave ! the cave !) upon which Mohammed ordered him into eternal mourning, and ever to repeat the traitorous words.

There are several species of crows in this part of Africa. Besides the large-beaked bird of the Harar Hills, I found the common European variety, with, however, the breast feathers white tipped in small semicircles as far as the abdomen. The little " king crow " of India is common : its bright red eye and purplish plume render it a conspicuous object as it perches upon the tall camel's back or clings to waving plants.

2 The Waraba or Durwa is, according to Mr. Blyth, the distinguished naturalist, now Curator of the Asiatic Society's Museum at Calcutta, the Canis pictus seu venaticus (Lycaon pictus or Wilde Honde of the Cape Boers). It seems to be the Chien Sauvage or Cynhyène (Cynhyæna venatica) of the French traveller M. Delegorgue, who in his " Voyage dans l'Afrique Australe," minutely and diffusely describes it. Mr. Gordon Cumming suppose sit to form the connecting link between the wolf and the hyæna. This animal swarms throughout the Somali country, prowls about the camps all night, dogs travellers, and devours everything he can find, at times pulling down children and camels, and when violently pressed by hunger, men. The Somal declare the Waraba to be a hermaphrodite ; so the ancients supposed the hyæna to be of both sexes—an error arising from the peculiar appearance of an orifice situated near two glands which secrete an unctuous fluid.

Returning, we breakfasted in the garden, and rain coming on, we walked out to enjoy the Oriental luxury of a wetting. Ali Iskandar, an old Arab mercenary, afforded us infinite amusement: a little opium made him half crazy, when his sarcastic pleasantries never ceased. We then brought out the guns, and being joined by the other escort, proceeded to a trial of skill. The Arabs planted a bone about 200 paces from us—a long distance for a people who seldom fire beyond fifty yards; moreover, the wind blew the flash strongly in their faces. Some shot two or three dozen times wide of the mark and were derided accordingly : one man hit the bone ; he at once stopped practice, as the wise in such matters will do, and shook hands with all the party. He afterwards showed that his success on this occasion had been accidental; but he was a staunch old sportsman, remarkable, as the Arab Badawin generally are, for his skill and perseverance in stalking. Having no rifle, I remained a spectator. My revolvers excited abundant attention, though none would be persuaded to touch them. The largest, which, fitted with a stock, became an excellent carbine, was at once named Abu Sittah (the Father of Six) and the Shaytan or Devil: the pocket pistol became the Malunah or Accursed, and the distance to which it carried ball made every man wonder. The Arabs had antiquated matchlocks, mostly worn away to paper thinness at the mouth: as usual they fired with the right elbow raised to the level of the ear, and the left hand grasping the barrel, where with us the breech would be. Hassan Turki had one of those fine old Shishkhanah rifles formerly made at Damascus and Sana'a : it carried a two-ounce ball with perfect correctness, but was so badly mounted in its block-butt, shaped like a Dutch cheese, that it always required a rest.

On our return home we met a party of Ísa girls, who derided my colour and doubted the fact of my being a Moslem. The Arabs declared me to be a Shaykh of Shaykhs, and translated to the prettiest of the party an impromptu proposal of marriage. She showed but little coyness, and stated her price to be an Audulli or necklace,[1] a couple of Tobes—she asked one too many—a few handfuls of beads,[2] and a small present for her papa. She promised, naïvely enough, to call next day and inspect the goods : the publicity of the town did not deter her, but the shamefacedness of my two companions prevented our meeting again. Arrived at Zayla after a sunny walk, the Arab escort loaded their guns, formed a line for me to pass along, fired a salute, and entered to coffee and sweetmeats.

On the 24th of November I had an opportunity of seeing what a timid people are these Somal of the towns, who, as has been well remarked, are, like the settled Arabs, the worst specimens of their race. Three Ísa Badawin appeared before the southern gate, slaughtered a cow,

---

1 Men wear for ornament round the neck a bright red leather thong, upon which are strung in front two square bits of true or imitation amber or honey stone : this "Makkawi," however, is seldom seen amongst the Badawin. The Audulli or woman's necklace is a more elaborate affair of amber, glass beads, generally coloured, and coral : every matron who can afford it possesses at least one of these ornaments. Both sexes carry round the necks or hang above the right elbow, a talisman against danger and disease, either in a silver box or more generally sewn up in a small case of red morocco. The Badawin are fond of attaching a tooth-stick to the neck thong.

2 Beads are useful in the Somali country as presents, and to pay for trifling purchases : like tobacco they serve for small change. The kind preferred by women and children is the "binnur," large and small white porcelain : the others are the red, white, green, and spotted twisted beads, round and oblong. Before entering a district the traveller should ascertain what may be the especial variety. Some kind are greedily sought for in one place, and in another rejected with disdain.

buried its head, and sent for permission to visit one of
their number who had been imprisoned by the Hajj for
the murder of his son Mas'ud. The place was at once
thrown into confusion, the gates were locked, and the
walls manned with Arab matchlock men: my three
followers armed themselves, and I was summoned to the
fray. Some declared that the Badawin were "doing[1]"
the town; other that they were the van of a giant host
coming to ravish, sack, and slay: it turned out that
these Badawin had preceded their comrades, who were
bringing in, as the price of blood,[2] an Abyssinian slave,
seven camels, seven cows, a white mule, and a small
black mare. The prisoner was visited by his brother,
who volunteered to share his confinement, and the
meeting was described as most pathetic: partly from
mental organization and partly from the peculiarities of

---

1 The Somali word " Făl " properly means " to do "; "to bewitch," is its secondary sense.

2 The price of blood in the Somali country is the highest
sanctioned by Al-Islam. It must be remembered that amongst the
pagan Arabs, the Koraysh "diyat," was twenty she-camels. Abd al-
Muttalib, grandfather of Mohammed, sacrificed 100 animals to
ransom the life of his son, forfeited by a rash vow, and from that
time the greater became the legal number. The Somal usually
demand 100 she-camels, or 300 sheep and a few cows ; here, as in
Arabia, the sum is made up by all the near relations of the slayer ; 30
of the animals may be aged, and 30 under age, but the rest must be
sound and good. Many tribes take less—from strangers 100 sheep, a
cow, and a camel; but after the equivalent is paid, the murderer or one
of his clan, contrary to the spirit of Al-Islam, is generally killed by the
kindred or tribe of the slain. When blood is shed in the same tribe,
the full reparation, if accepted by the relatives, is always exacted;
this serves the purpose of preventing fratricidal strife, for in such
a nation of murderers, only the Diyat prevents the taking of life.

Blood money, however is seldom accepted unless the murdered
man has been slain with a lawful weapon. Those who kill with the
Dankalah, a poisonous juice rubbed upon meat, are always put to
death by the members of their own tribe.

society the only real tie acknowledged by these people is that which connects male kinsmen. The Hajj, after speaking big, had the weakness to let the murderer depart alive; this measure like peace-policy in general, is the best and surest way to encourage bloodshed and mutilation. But a few months before, an Ísa Badawi enticed out of the gate a boy about fifteen, and slaughtered him for the sake of wearing the feather. His relations were directed to receive the Diyat or blood fine, and the wretch was allowed to depart unhurt—a silly clemency!

You must not suppose, dear L., that I yielded myself willingly to the weary necessity of a month at Zayla. But how explain to you the obstacles thrown in our way by African indolence, petty intrigue, and interminable suspicion ? Four months before leaving Aden I had taken the precaution of meeting the Hajj, requesting him to select for us an Abban,[1] or protector, and to provide

---

1 The Abban or protector of the Somali country is the Mogasa of the Gallas, the Akh of Al-Hijaz, the Ghafir of the Sinaitic Peninsula, and the Rabi'a of Eastern Arabia. It must be observed, however, that the word denotes the protégé as well as the protector ; in the latter sense it is the polite address to a Somali, as Ya Abbanah, O Protectress, would be to his wife.

The Abban acts at once as broker, escort, agent, and interpreter, and the institution may be considered the earliest form of transit dues. In all sales he receives a certain percentage, his food and lodging are provided at the expense of his employer, and he not unfrequently exacts small presents from his kindred. In return he is bound to arrange all differences, and even to fight the battles of his client against his fellow-countrymen. Should an Abban be slain, his tribe is bound to take up the cause and to make good the losses of their protégé. Al-Ta'abanah, the office, being one of " name," the eastern synonym for our honour, as well as of lucre, causes frequent quarrels, which become exceedingly rancorous.

According to the laws of the country, the Abban is master of the life and property of his client. The traveller's success will depend mainly upon his selection: if inferior in rank, the protector can neither forward nor defend him ; if timid, he will impede advance;

camels and mules; two months before starting I had advanced to him the money required in a country where nothing can be done without a whole or partial prepayment. The protector was to be procured anywhere, the cattle at Tajurrah, scarcely a day's sail from Zayla: when I arrived nothing was forthcoming. I at once begged the governor to exert himself; he politely promised to start a messenger that hour, and he delayed doing so for ten days. An easterly wind set in and gave the crew an excuse for wasting another fortnight.[1] Travellers are an irritable genus: I stormed and fretted at the delays, to show earnestness of purpose. All the effect was a paroxysm of talking. The Hajj and his son treated me, like a spoilt child, to a double allowance of food and milk: they warned me that the small-pox was depopulating Harar, that the road swarmed with brigands, and that the Amir or prince was certain destruction,—I contented myself with determining that both were true Oriental hyperbolists, and fell into more frequent fits of passion. The old man could not comprehend my secret. "If the English," he privately remarked, "wish to take Harar, let them send me 500 soldiers; if not, I can give

---

and if avaricious, he will, by means of his relatives, effectually stop the journey by absorbing the means of prosecuting it. The best precaution against disappointment would be the registering Abbans at Aden; every donkey boy will offer himself as a protector, but only the chiefs of tribes should be provided with certificates. During my last visit to Africa, I proposed that English officers visiting the country should be provided with servants, not protectors, the former, however, to be paid like the latter; all the people recognized the propriety of the step.

In the following pages occur manifold details concerning the complicated subject, Al-Ta'abanah.

[1] Future travellers would do well either to send before them a trusty servant with orders to buy cattle; or, what would be better, though a little more expensive, to take with them from Aden all the animals required.

all information concerning it." When convinced of my determination to travel, he applied his mind to calculating the benefit which might be derived from the event, and, as the following pages will show, he was not without success.

Towards the end of November, four camels were procured, an Abban was engaged, we hired two women cooks and a fourth servant; my baggage was reformed, the cloth and tobacco being sewn up in matting, and made to fit the camels' sides[1]; sandals were cut out for walking, letters were written, messages of dreary length —too important to be set down in black and white—were solemnly entrusted to us, palavers were held, and affairs began to wear the semblance of departure. The Hajj strongly recommended us to one of the principal families of the Gudabirsi tribe, who would pass us on to their brother-in-law Adan, the Jirad or prince of the Girhi; and he, in due time, to his kinsman the Amir of Harar. The chain was commenced by placing us under the protection of one Raghi, a petty Ísa chief of the Mummasan clan. By the good aid of the Hajj and our sweetmeats, he was persuaded, for the moderate consideration of ten Tobes,[2] to accompany us to the frontier

---

1 The Somal use as camel saddles the mats which compose their huts; these lying loose upon the animal's back, cause, by slipping backwards and forwards, the loss of many a precious hour, and in wet weather become half a load. The more civilized make up of canvass or "gunny bags" stuffed with hay and provided with cross bars, a rude pack saddle, which is admirably calculated to gall the animal's back. Future travellers would do well to purchase camel-saddles at Aden, where they are cheap and well made.

2 He received four cloths of Cutch canvass, and six others of coarse American sheeting. At Zayla these articles are double the Aden value, which would be about thirteen rupees or twenty-six shillings; in the bush the price is quadrupled. Before leaving us the Abban received at least double the original hire. Besides small

of his clan, distant about fifty miles, to introduce us to the Gudabirsi, and to provide us with three men as servants, and a suitable escort, a score or so, in dangerous places. He began with us in an extravagant manner, declaring that nothing but " name " induced him to undertake the perilous task; that he had left his flocks and herds at a season of uncommon risk, and that all his relations must receive a certain honorarium. But having paid at least three pounds for a few days of his society, we declined such liberality, and my companions, I believe, declared that it would be "next time":—on all such occasions I make a point of leaving the room, since for one thing given, at least five are promised on oath. Raghi warned us seriously to prepare for dangers and disasters, and this seemed to be the general opinion of Zayla, whose timid citizens determined that we were tired of our lives. The cold had driven the Nomads from the hills to the warm maritime plains,[1] we should therefore traverse a populous region ; and, as the End of Time aptly observed, " Man eats you up, the Desert does not." Moreover this year the Ayyal Nuh Ismail, a clan of the Habr Awal tribe, is " out," and has been successful against the Ísa, who generally are the better men. They sweep the country in Kaum or Commandos,[2]

---

presents of cloth, dates, tobacco and rice to his friends, he had six cubits of Sa'uda Wilayati or English indigo-dyed calico for women's fillets, and two of Sa'uda Kashshi, a Cutch imitation, a Shukkah or half Tobe for his daughter, and a sheep for himself, together with a large bundle of tobacco.

1 When the pastures are exhausted and the monsún sets in, the Badawin return to their cool mountains ; like the Iliyat of Persia, they have their regular Kishlakh and Yaylakh.

2 " Kaum " is the Arabic, " All " the Somali, term for these raids.

numbering from twenty to two hundred troopers, armed
with assegai, dagger, and shield, and carrying a water-
skin and dried meat for a three days' ride, sufficient to
scour the length of the low land. The honest fellows
are not so anxious to plunder as to ennoble themselves
by taking life: every man hangs to his saddle bow an
ostrich[1] feather—emblem of truth—and the moment his
javelin has drawn blood, he sticks it into his tufty poll
with as much satisfaction as we feel when attaching a
medal to our shell-jackets. It is by no means necessary
to slay the foe in fair combat: Spartan-like, treachery is
preferred to stand-up fighting; and you may measure
their ideas of honour, by the fact that women are
murdered in cold-blood, as by the Amazulus, with
the hope that the unborn child may prove a male.
The hero carries home the trophy of his prowess,[2] and

---

1 Amongst the old Egyptians the ostrich feather was the symbol
of truth. The Somal call it " Bal," the Arabs " Rish "; it is
universally used here as the sign and symbol of victory. Generally
the white feather only is stuck in the hair; the Isa are not
particular in using black when they can procure no other. All the
clans wear it in the back hair, but each has its own rules; some
make it a standard decoration, others discard it after the first few
days. The learned have an aversion to the custom, stigmatizing it
as pagan and idolatrous; the vulgar look upon it as the highest
mark of honour.

2 This is an ancient practice in Asia as well as in Africa. The
Egyptian temples show heaps of trophies placed before the monarchs
as eyes or heads were presented in Persia. Thus in 1 Sam. xviii.
25, David brings the spoils of 200 Philistines, and shows them in
full tale to the king, that he might be the king's son-in-law. Any
work upon the subject of Abyssinia (Bruce, book 7, chap. 8), or the
late Afghan war, will prove that the custom of mutilation, opposed
as it is both to Christianity and to Al-Islam, is still practised in
the case of hated enemies and infidels; and De Bey remarks of the
Cape Kafirs, " Victores cæsis excidunt τα αιδοια, quæ exsiccata regi
afferunt."

his wife, springing from her tent, utters a long shrill
scream of joy, a preliminary to boasting of her man's
valour, and bitterly taunting the other possessors of
noirs fainéants : the derided ladies abuse their lords with
peculiar virulence, and the lords fall into paroxysms of
envy, hatred, and malice. During my short stay at
Zayla six or seven murders were committed close to the
walls : the Abban brought news, a few hours before our
departure, that two Ísas had been slaughtered by the
Habr Awal. The Ísa and Dankali also have a blood
feud, which causes perpetual loss of life. But a short
time ago six men of these two tribes were travelling
together, when suddenly the last but one received from
the hindermost a deadly spear-thrust in the back. The
wounded man had the presence of mind to plunge his
dagger in the side of the wayfarer who preceded him,
thus dying as the people say, in company. One of these
events throws the country into confusion, for the *vendetta*
is rancorous and bloody, as in ancient Germany or
in modern Corsica. Our Abban enlarged upon the unpleasant necessity of travelling all night towards the
hills, and lying *perdu* during the day. The most
dangerous times are dawn and evening-tide : the
troopers spare their horses during the heat, and themselves during the dew-fall. Whenever, in the desert—
where, says the proverb, all men are enemies—you sight
a fellow-creature from afar, you wave the right arm
violently up and down, shouting, " War Joga ! War
Joga !"—stand still ! stand still ! If they halt, you send
a parliamentary to within speaking distance. Should
they advance,[1] you fire, taking especial care not to
miss ; when two saddles are emptied the rest are sure
to decamp.

1 When attacking cattle, the plundering party endeavour with
shouts and noise to disperse the herds, whilst the assailants huddle
them together, and attempt to face the danger in parties.

I had given the Abban orders to be in readiness—
my patience being thoroughly exhausted—on Sunday,
the 26th of November, and determined to walk the whole
way, rather than waste another day waiting for cattle.
As the case had become hopeless, a vessel was descried
standing straight from Tajurrah, and, suddenly as could
happen in the Arabian Nights, four fine mules, saddled
and bridled, Abyssinian fashion, appeared at the door.[1]

---

1 For the cheapest I paid twenty-three, for the dearest twenty-
six dollars, besides a Riyal upon each, under the names of custom
dues and carriage. The Hajj had doubtless exaggerated the price,
but all were good animals, and the traveller has no right to complain,
except when he pays dear for a bad article.

CHAPTER IV.

Before leaving Zayla, I must not neglect a short description of its inhabitants, and the remarkable Somal races around it.[1]

Eastern Africa, like Arabia, presents a population composed of three markedly distinct races.

1. The Aborigines, such as the Negroes, the Bushmen, Hottentots, and other races, having such physiological peculiarities as the steatopyge, the tablier, and other developments described, in 1815, by the great Cuvier.

2. The almost pure Caucasian of the northern regions, west of Egypt: their immigration comes within the range of comparatively modern history.

3. The half-castes in Eastern Africa are represented principally by the Abyssinians, Gallas, (Hamites), Somal Sawahili, and Kafirs. The first-named people derive their descent from Menelek, son of Solomon by the Queen of Sheba: it is evident from their features and figures—too well known to require description—that they are descended from Semitic as well as Negrotic (Nigro-Hamitic) progenitors.[2]

---

1 The ancients reckoned in Africa, (1) Libians, (2) Æthiopians. Herodotus added to these (3) Greeks, (4) Phœnicians.

2 Eusebius declares that the Abyssinians migrated from Asia to Africa whilst the Hebrews were in Egypt (circ. A. M. 2345); and Syncellus places the event about the age of the Judges.

About the origin of the Gallas there is a diversity of opinion.[1] Some declare them to be Meccan Arabs, who settled on the western coast of the Red Sea at a remote epoch : according to the Abyssinians, however, and there is little to find fault with in their theory, the Gallas are descended from a princess of their nation, who was given in marriage to a slave from the country south of Gurague. She bare seven sons, who became mighty robbers and founders of tribes : their progenitors obtained the name of Gallas, after the river Gala, in Gurague, where they gained a decisive victory over their kinsmen the Abyssins.[2] A variety of ethnologic and physiological reasons —into which space and subject prevent my entering—argue the Kafirs of the Cape to be a northern people, pushed southwards by some, to us, as yet, unknown cause. The origin of the Somal is a matter of modern history.

" Barbarah " (Berberah),[3] according to the Kamus,

---

1 Moslems, ever fond of philological fable, thus derive the word Galla. When Ullabu, the chief, was summoned by Mohammed to Islamize, the messenger returned to report that " he said *no*,"—Kál lá pronounced Gál lá—which impious refusal, said the Prophet, should from that time become the name of the race.

2 Others have derived them from Metcha, Karaiyo, and Tulema, three sons of an Æthiopian Emperor by a female slave. They have, according to some travellers, a prophecy that one day they will march to the east and north, and conquer the inheritance of their Jewish ancestors. Mr. Johnston asserts that the word Galla is " merely another form of *Calla*, which in the ancient Persian, Sanscrit, Celtic, and their modern derivative languages, under modified, but not changed terms, is expressive of blackness." The Gallas, however, are not a black people.

3 The Aden stone has been supposed to name the " Berbers," who must have been Gallas from the vicinity of Berberah. A certain amount of doubt still hangs on the interpretation : the Rev. Mr. Forster and Dr. Bird being the principal contrasts.

Rev. Mr. Forster.	*Dr. Bird.*
" We assailed with cries of hatred and rage the Abyssinians and Berbers.	" He, the Syrian philosopher in Abadan, Bishop of Cape Aden, who inscribed this in the desert, blesses the institution of the faith."
" We rode forth wrathfully against this refuse of mankind."	

is " a well known town in El Maghrib, and a race located between El Zanj—Zanzibar and the Negrotic coast—and El Habash[1]: they are descended from the Himyar chiefs Sanháj (Sinhagia) (صنهاج) and Sumámah (ثمامه), and they arrived at the epoch of the conquest of Africa by the king Afríkús (Scipio Africanus ?)." A few details upon the subjects of mutilation and excision prove these to have been the progenitors of the Somal,[2] who are nothing but a slice of the great Gala nation Islamized and Semiticized by repeated immigrations from Arabia. In the Kamus we also read that Samal (سمل) is the name of the father of a tribe, so called because he *thrust out* (سمل, samala) his brother's eye.[3] The Shaykh Jami, a celebrated genealogist, informed me that in A.H. 666 = A.D. 1266-7, the Sayyid Yusuf al-Baghdadi visited the port of Siyaro near Berberah, then occupied by an infidel magician, who passed through mountains by the power of his gramarye: the saint summoned to his aid Mohammed bin Yunis al-Siddiki, of Bayt al-Fakih in Arabia, and by their united prayers a hill closed upon

---

1 This word is generally translated Abyssinia; Oriental geographers, however, use it in a more extended sense. The Turks have held possessions in " Habash," in Abyssinia never.

2 The same words are repeated in the Infak al-Maysur fi Tarikh bilad al-Takrur (Appendix to Denham and Clapperton's Travels, No. xii.), again confounding the Berbers and the Somal. Afrikus, according to that author, was a king of Al-Yaman who expelled the Berbers from Syria !

3 The learned Somal invariably spell their national name with an initial Sin, and disregard the derivation from Saumal (صومل), which would allude to the hardihood of the wild people. An intelligent modern traveller derives " Somali " from the Abyssinian " Soumahe," or heathens, and asserts that it corresponds with the Arabic word Kafir or unbeliever, the name by which Edrisi, the Arabian geographer, knew and described the inhabitants of the Affah (Afar) coast, to the east of the Straits of Bab al-Mandib. Such derivation is, however, unadvisable.

the pagan. Deformed by fable, the foundation of the tale is fact: the numerous descendants of the holy men still pay an annual fine, by way of blood-money to the family of the infidel chief. The last and most important Arab immigration took place about fifteen generations or 450 years ago, when the Sharif Ishak bin Ahmad,[1] left his native country Hazramaut, and, with forty-four saints, before mentioned, landed on Makhar—the windward coast extending from Karam Harbour to Cape Guardafui. At the town of Met, near Burnt Island, where his tomb still exists, he became the father of all the gentle blood and the only certain descent in the Somali country: by Magaden, a free woman, he had Jirhajis, Awal, and Arab; and by a slave or slaves, Jailah, Sambur, and Rambad. Hence the great clans, Habr Jirhajis and Awal, who prefer the matronymic— Habr signifying a mother—since, according to their dictum, no man knows who may be his sire.[2] These increased and multiplied by connection and affiliation to such an extent that about A.D. 1500 they drove their progenitors, the Galla, from Berberah, and gradually encroached upon them, till they entrenched themselves in the Highlands of Harar.

The old and pagan genealogies still known to the Somal, are Dirr, Aydur, Darud, and, according to some, Hawiyah. Dirr and Aydur, of whom nothing is certainly known but the name,[3] are the progenitors of the northern

---

1 According to others he was the son of Abdullah. The written genealogies of the Somal were, it is said, stolen by the Sharifs of al-Yaman, who feared to leave with the wild people documents that prove the nobility of their descent.

2 The salient doubt suggested by this genealogy is the barbarous nature of the names. A noble Arab would not call his children Jirhajis, Awal, and Rambad.

3 Lieut. Cruttenden applies the term Edoor (Aydur) to the descendants of Ishak, the children of Jirhajis, Awal, and Jailah.

Somal, the Ísa, Gudabirsi, Ishak, and Bursuk tribes. Darud Jabarti[1] bin Ismail bin Akil (or Ukayl) is supposed by his descendants to have been a noble Arab from Al-Hijaz, who, obliged to flee his country, was wrecked on the north-east coast of Africa, where he married a daughter of the Hawiyah tribe : rival races declare him to have been a Galla slave, who, stealing the Prophet's slippers,[2] was dismissed with the words, Inná-*tarad*-ná-hu (verily we have rejected him) : hence his name Tarud (طارود) or Darud, the Rejected.[3] The etymological part of the story is, doubtless, fabulous ; it expresses however, the popular belief that the founder of the eastward or windward tribes, now extending over the seaboard from Bundir Jadid to Ras Hafun, and southward from the sea to the Webbes,[4] was a man of ignoble origin. The children of Darud are now divided into two great bodies : "Harti" is the family name of the Dulbahanta, Ogadayn, Warsangali and Mijjarthayn, who call themselves sons of Harti bin Kombo bin Kabl Ullah bin Darud : the other Darud tribes not included under that appellation are the Girhi, Berteri, Marayhan, and Bahabr Ali. The

---

His informants and mine differ, therefore, *toto cælo*. According to some, Dirr was the father of Aydur ; others make Dirr (it has been written Tir and Durr) to have been the name of the Galla family into which Shaykh Ishak married.

1 Some travellers make Jabarti or Ghiberti to signify " slaves," from the Abyssinian Guebra ; others, " Strong in the Faith " (Al-Islam). Bruce applies it to the Moslems of Abyssinia ; it is still used, though rarely, by the Somal, who in these times generally designate by it the Sawahili or Negroid Moslems.

2 The same scandalous story is told of the venerable patron saint of Aden, the Sharif Haydrus.

3 Darud bin Ismail's tomb is near the Yubbay Tug in the windward mountains ; an account of it will be found in Lieut. Speke's diary.

4 The two rivers Shabayli and Juba.

Hawiyah are doubtless of ancient and pagan origin ; they call all Somal except themselves Hashiyah, and thus claim to be equivalent to the rest of the nation. Some attempt, as usual, to establish a holy origin, deriving themselves like the Shaykhash from the Caliph Abu Bakr : the antiquity, and consequently the pagan origin of the Hawiyah are proved by its present widely scattered state ; it is a powerful tribe in the Mijjarthayn country, and yet is found in the hills of Harar.

The Somal, therefore, by their own traditions, as well as their strongly-marked physical peculiarities, their customs, and their geographical position, may be determined to be a half-caste tribe, an offshoot of the great Galla race, approximated, like the originally Negro-Egyptian, to the Caucasian type by a steady influx of pure Asiatic blood.

In personal appearance the race is not unprepossessing. The crinal hair is hard and wiry, growing, like that of a half-caste West Indian, in stiff ringlets which sprout in tufts from the scalp, and, attaining a moderate length, which they rarely surpass, hang down. A few elders, savans, and the wealthy, who can afford the luxury of a turband, shave the head. More generally, each filament is duly picked out with the comb or a wooden scratcher like a knitting-needle, and the mass made to resemble a child's " pudding," an old bob-wig, a mop, a counsellor's peruke, or an old-fashioned coachman's wig—there are a hundred ways of dressing the head. The Badawin, true specimens of the " greasy African race," wear locks dripping with rancid butter, and accuse their citizen brethren of being more like birds than men. The colouring matter of the hair, naturally a bluish-black, is removed by a mixture of quicklime and water, or in the desert by a *lessive* of ashes[1]: this makes it a dull

---

[1] Curious to say this mixture does not destroy the hair ; it would soon render a European bald. Some of the Somal have

yellowish-white, which is converted into red permanently by henna, temporarily by ochreish earth kneaded with water. The ridiculous Somali peruke of crimsoned sheepskin—almost as barbarous an article as the Welsh —is apparently a foreign invention: I rarely saw one in the low country, although the hill tribes about Harar sometimes wear a black or white " scratch-wig.[1]" The head is rather long than round, and generally of the amiable variety, it is gracefully put on the shoulders, belongs equally to Africa and Arabia, and would be exceedingly weak but for the beauty of the brow. As far as the mouth, the face, with the exception of high cheek-bones, is good ; the contour of the forehead ennobles it ; the eyes are large and well-formed, and the upper features are frequently handsome and expressive. The jaw, however, is almost invariably prognathous and African ; the broad, turned-out lips betray approximation to the Negro ; and the chin projects to the detriment of the facial angle. The beard is represented by a few tufts ; it is rare to see anything equal to even the Arab development : the long and ample eyebrows admired by the people are uncommon, and the mustachioes are short and thin, often twisted outwards in two dwarf curls. The mouth is coarse as well as thick-lipped ; the teeth rarely project as in the Negro, but they are not good : the habit of perpetually chewing coarse Surat tobacco stains them,[2] the gums become black and mottled, and the use of ashes with the quid discolours the lips. The skin, amongst the tribes inhabiting the hot regions, is smooth, black, and glossy ; as the altitude increases it becomes lighter, and about Harar it is generally of a *café*

---

applied it to their beards ; the result has been the breaking and falling off of the filaments.

1 Second-hand lawyers' wigs were exported to Guinea.

2 Few Somal except the citizens smoke, on account of the expense, all, however, use the Takhzinah or quid.

au lait colour. The Badawin are fond of raising beauty marks in the shape of ghastly seams, and the thickness of the epidermis favours the size of these *stigmates*. The male figure is tall and somewhat ungainly. In only one instance I observed an approach to the steatopyge, making the shape to resemble the letter S ; but the shoulders are high, the trunk is straight, the thighs fall off, the shin bones bow slightly forwards, and the feet, like the hands, are coarse, large, and flat. Yet with their hair, of a light straw colour, decked with the light waving feather, and their coal-black complexions set off by that most graceful of garments the clean white Tobe,[1] the contrasts are decidedly effective.

In mind the Somal are peculiar as in body. They are a people of most susceptible character, and withal uncommonly hard to please. They dislike the Arabs, fear and abhor the Turks, have a horror of Franks, and despise all other Asiatics who with them come under the general name of Hindí (Indians). The latter are abused on all occasions for cowardice, and a want of generosity, which has given rise to the following piquant epigram :

> " Ask not thy want from the Hindi :
> Impossible to find liberality in the Hindi !
> Had there been one liberal man in Al-Hind,
> Allah had raised up a prophet in Al-Hind ! "

They have all the levity and instability of the Negro character ; light-minded as the Abyssinians—described by Gobat as constant in nothing but inconstancy— soft, merry, and affectionate souls, they pass without any apparent transition into a state of fury, when

---

1 The best description of the dress is that of Fénélon : " Leurs habits sont aisés à faire, car en ce doux climat on ne porte qu'une pièce d'étoffe fine et légère, qui n'est point taillée, et que chacun met à longs plis autour de son corps pour la modestie ; lui donnant la forme qu'il veut."

they are capable of terrible atrocities. At Aden they appear happier than in their native country. There I have often seen a man clapping his hands and dancing, child-like, alone to relieve the exuberance of his spirits : here they become as the Mongols and other pastoral people, a melancholy race, who will sit for hours upon a bank gazing at the moon, or croning some old ditty under the trees. This state is doubtless increased by the perpetual presence of danger and the uncertainty of life, which make them think of other things than dancing and singing. Much learning seems to make them mad ; like the half-crazy Fakíhs of the Sahara in Northern Africa, the Widad, or priest, is generally unfitted for the affairs of this world, and the Hafiz or Koran-reciter, is almost idiotic. As regards courage, they are no exception to the generality of savage races. They have none of the recklessness standing in lieu of creed which characterizes the civilized man. In their great battles a score is considered a heavy loss ; usually they will run after the fall of half a dozen : amongst a Kraal full of braves who boast a hundred murders, not a single maimed or wounded man will be seen, whereas in an Arabian camp half the male population will bear the marks of lead and steel. The bravest will shirk fighting if he has forgotten his shield: the sight of a lion and the sound of a gun elicit screams of terror, and their Kaum or forays much resemble the style of tactics rendered obsolete by the Great Turenne, when the tactician's chief aim was not to fall in with his enemy. Yet they are by no means deficient in the wily valour of wild men : two or three will murder a sleeper bravely enough ; and when the passions of rival tribes, between whom there has been a blood feud for ages, are violently excited, they will use with asperity the dagger and spear. Their massacres are fearful. In February, 1847, a small sept, the Ayyal Yunis, being expelled from Berberah, settled at the roadstead of Bulhar, where a few merchants, principally Indian and Arab, joined them. The men were in the habit of leaving their women and children, sick and aged, at the encampment inland, whilst, descending to the beach, they carried on their trade. One day, as they were thus employed, unsuspicious of danger, a foraging party of about 2,500 Ísas attacked the camp: men, women, and children were indiscriminately put to the spear, and the plunderers returned to their villages in safety, laden with an immense amount of booty. At present, a man armed with a revolver would be a terror to the country; the day, however, will come when the matchlock will supersede the assegai, and then the harmless spearman in his strong mountains will become, like the Arab, a formidable foe. Travelling among the Badawin, I found them kind and hospitable. A pinch of snuff or a handful of tobacco sufficed to win every heart, and a few yards of coarse cotton cloth supplied all our wants. I was petted like a child, forced to drink milk and to eat mutton; girls were offered to me in marriage; the people begged me to settle amongst them, to head their predatory expeditions, free them from lions, and kill their elephants; and often a man has exclaimed in pitying accents, " What hath brought thee, delicate as thou art, to sit with us on the cowhide in this cold under a tree ? " Of course they were beggars, princes and paupers, lairds and loons, being all equally unfortunate; the Arabs have named the country Bilad Wa Issi—the " Land of Give me Something "—but their wants were easily satisfied, and the open hand always made a friend.

The Somal hold mainly to the Shafe'i school of Al-Islam : their principal peculiarity is that of not reciting prayers over the dead even in the towns. The marriage ceremony is simple : the price of the bride and the feast being duly arranged, the formula is recited by some priest or pilgrim. I have often been requested to officiate on these occasions, and the End of Time has done it by irreverently reciting the Fatihah over the happy pair.[1] The Somal, as usual among the heterogeneous mass amalgamated by Al-Islam, have a diversity of superstitions attesting their pagan origin. Such, for instance, are their oaths by stones, their reverence of cairns and holy trees, and their ordeals of fire and water, the Bolungo of Western Africa. A man accused of murder or theft walks down a trench full of live charcoal and about a spear's length, or he draws out of the flames a smith's anvil heated to redness: some prefer picking four or five cowries from a large pot full of boiling water. The member used is at once rolled up in the intestines of a sheep and not inspected for a whole day. They have traditionary seers called Tawuli, like the Greegree-men of Western Africa, who, by inspecting the fat and bones of slaughtered cattle, " do medicine," predict rains, battles, and diseases of animals. This class is of both sexes: they never pray or bathe, and are therefore considered always impure ; thus, being feared, they are greatly respected by the vulgar. Their predictions are delivered in a rude rhyme, often put for importance into the mouth of some deceased seer. During the three months called Rajalo[2] the Koran is not read over graves, and no marriage ever takes place. The reason of this peculiarity is stated to be imitation of their ancestor Ishak, who happened not to contract a matrimonial alliance at such epoch : it is, however, a manifest remnant of the pagan's auspicious and inauspicious months. Thus they sacrifice she-camels in the month

---

1 Equivalent to reading out the Church Catechism at an English wedding.

2 Certain months of the lunar year. In 1854, the third Rajalo, corresponding with Rabia the Second, began on the 21st of December.

Sabuh, and keep holy with feasts and bonfires the Dubshid or New Year's Day.[1] At certain unlucky periods when the moon is in ill-omened asterisms those who die are placed in bundles of matting upon a tree, the idea being that if buried a loss would result to the tribe.[2]

Though superstitious, the Somal are not bigoted like the Arabs, with the exception of those who, wishing to become learned, visit Al-Yaman or Al-Hijaz, and catch the complaint. Nominal Mohammedans, Al-Islam hangs so lightly upon them, that apparently they care little for making it binding upon others.

The Somali language is no longer unknown to Europe. It is strange that a dialect which has no written character should so abound in poetry and eloquence. There are thousands of songs, some local, others general, upon all conceivable subjects, such as camel loading, drawing water, and elephant hunting; every man of education knows a variety of them. The rhyme is imperfect, being generally formed by the syllable "ay" (pronounced as in our word "hay"), which gives the verse a monotonous regularity; but, assisted by a tolerably regular alliteration

---

1 The word literally means, " lighting of fire." It corresponds with the Nayruz of Yaman, a palpable derivation, as the word itself proves, from the old Guebre conquerors. In Arabia New Year's Day is called Ras al-Sanah, and is not celebrated by any peculiar solemnities. The ancient religion of the Afar coast was Sabæism, probably derived from the Berbers or shepherds—according to Bruce the first faith of the East, and the only religion of Eastern Africa. The Somal still retain a tradition that the " Furs," or ancient Guebres, once ruled the land.

2 Their names also are generally derived from their pagan ancestors: a list of the most common may be interesting to ethnologists. Men are called Rírásh, Igah, Beuh, Fáhí, Samattar, Fárih, Madar, Rághe, Dubayr, Irik, Diddar, Awálah, and Alyán. Women's names are Ayblá, Ayyo, Aurálá, Ambar, Zahabo, Ashkaro, Alká, Asobá, Gelo, Gobe, Mayrán and Samawedá.

and cadence, it can never be mistaken for prose, even
without the song which invariably accompanies it.   The
country teems with "poets, poetasters, poetitos, poet-
accios:" every man has his recognized position in literature as accurately defined as though he had been reviewed
in a century of magazines—the fine ear of this people[1]
causing them to take the greatest pleasure in harmonious
sounds and poetical expressions, whereas a false quantity
or a prosaic phrase excite their violent indignation.
Many of these compositions are so idiomatic that Arabs
settled for years amongst the Somal cannot understand
them though perfectly acquainted with the conversational
style.   Every chief in the country must have a panegyric
to be sung by his clan, and the great patronize light
literature by keeping a poet.   The amatory is of course
the favourite theme: sometimes it appears in dialogue,
the rudest form, we are told, of the Drama.   The subjects
are frequently pastoral: the lover for instance invites his
mistress to walk with him towards the well in Lahelo,
the Arcadia of the land ; he compares her legs to the tall
straight Libi tree, and imprecates the direst curses on her
head if she refuse to drink with him the milk of his
favourite camel.   There are a few celebrated ethical
compositions, in which the father lavishes upon his son
all the treasures of Somali good advice, long as the som-
niferous sermons of Mentor to the insipid son of Ulysses.
Sometimes a black Tyrtæus breaks into a wild lament for
the loss of warriors or territory ; he taunts the clan with
cowardice, reminds them of their slain kindred, better
men than themselves, whose spirits cannot rest unavenged
in their gory graves, and urges a furious onslaught upon
the exulting victor.

---

1 It is proved by the facility with which they pick up languages,
Western as well as Eastern, by mere ear and memory.

And now, dear L., I will attempt to gratify your just curiosity concerning *the* sex in Eastern Africa.

The Somali matron is distinguished—externally—from the maiden by a fillet of blue network or indigo-dyed cotton, which, covering the head and containing the hair, hangs down to the neck. Virgins wear their locks long, parted in the middle, and plaited in a multitude of hard thin pigtails : on certain festivals they twine flowers and plaster the head like Kaffir women, with a red ochre—the *coiffure* has the merit of originality. With massive rounded features, large flat craniums, long big eyes, broad brows, heavy chins, rich brown complexions, and round faces, they greatly resemble the stony beauties of Egypt —the models of the land ere Persia, Greece, and Rome reformed the profile and bleached the skin. They are of the Venus Kallipyga order of beauty: the feature is scarcely ever seen amongst young girls, but after the first child it becomes remarkable to a stranger. The Arabs have not failed to make it a matter of jibe.

> " 'Tis a wonderful fact that your hips swell
> Like boiled rice or a skin blown out,"

sings a satirical Yamani : the Somal retort by comparing the lank haunches of their neighbours to those of tadpoles or young frogs. One of their peculiar charms is a soft, low, and plaintive voice, derived from their African progenitors. Always an excellent thing in woman, here it has an undefinable charm. I have often lain awake for hours listening to the conversation of the Badawi girls, whose accents sounded in my ears rather like music than mere utterance.

In muscular strength and endurance the women of the Somal are far superior to their lords : at home they are engaged all day in domestic affairs, and tending the cattle ; on journeys their manifold duties are to load and

drive the camels, to look after the ropes, and, if necessary, to make them; to pitch the hut, to bring water
and firewood, and to cook. Both sexes are equally
temperate from necessity ; the mead and the millet-beer,
so common among the Abyssinians and the Danakil, are
entirely unknown to the Somal of the plains. As regard
their morals, I regret to say that the traveller does not
find them in the golden state which Teetotal doctrines
lead him to expect. After much wandering, we are
almost tempted to believe the bad doctrine that morality
is a matter of geography ; that nations and races have,
like individuals, a pet vice, and that by restraining one
you only exasperate another. As a general rule Somali
women prefer *amourettes* with strangers, following the
well-known Arab proverb, " The new comer filleth the
eye." In cases of scandal, the woman's tribe revenges
its honour upon the man. Should a wife disappear with
a fellow-clansman, and her husband accord divorce, no
penal measures are taken, but she suffers in reputation,
and her female friends do not spare her. Generally, the
Somali women are of cold temperament, the result of
artificial as well as natural causes : like the Kafirs, they
are very prolific, but peculiarly bad mothers, neither
loved nor respected by their children. The fair sex lasts
longer in Eastern Africa than in India and Arabia : at
thirty, however, charms are on the wane, and when old
age comes on they are no exceptions to the hideous
decrepitude of the East.

The Somal, when they can afford it, marry between
the ages of fifteen and twenty. Connections between
tribes are common, and entitle the stranger to immunity
from the blood-feud: men of family refuse, however, to
ally themselves with the servile castes. Contrary to the
Arab custom, none of these people will marry cousins;
at the same time a man will give his daughter to his
uncle, and take to wife, like the Jews and Gallas, a

brother's relict. Some clans, the Habr Yunis for instance, refuse maidens of the same or even of a consanguineous family. This is probably a political device to preserve nationality and provide against a common enemy. The bride, as usual in the East, is rarely consulted, but frequent *tête à têtes* at the well and in the bush when tending cattle effectually obviate this inconvenience: her relatives settle the marriage portion, which varies from a cloth and a bead necklace to fifty sheep or thirty dollars, and dowries are unknown. In the towns marriage ceremonies are celebrated with feasting and music. On first entering the nuptial hut, the bridegroom draws forth his horsewhip and inflicts memorable chastisement upon the fair person of his bride, with the view of taming any lurking propensity to shrewishness.[1] This is carrying out with a will the Arab proverb,

" The slave girl from her capture, the wife from her wedding."

During the space of a week the spouse remains with his espoused, scarcely ever venturing out of the hut; his friends avoid him, and no lesser event than a plundering party or dollars to gain, would justify any intrusion. If the correctness of the wife be doubted, the husband on the morning after marriage digs a hole before his door and veils it with matting, or he rends the skirt of his Tobe, or he tears open some new hut-covering: this disgraces the woman's family. Polygamy is indispensable in a country where children are the principal wealth.[2] The chiefs, arrived at manhood, immediately

---

1 So the old Muscovites, we are told, always began married life with a sound flogging.

2 I would not advise polygamy amongst highly civilized races, where the sexes are nearly equal, and where reproduction becomes a minor duty. Monogamy is the growth of civilization: a plurality of wives is the natural condition of man in thinly-populated countries, where he who has the largest family is the greatest benefactor of his kind.

marry four wives: they divorce the old and unfruitful, and, as amongst the Kafirs, allow themselves an un-limited number in peculiar cases, especially when many of the sons have fallen. Daughters, as usual in Oriental countries, do not "count" as part of the family: they are, however, utilized by the father, who disposes of them to those who can increase his wealth and im-portance. Divorce is exceedingly common, for the men are liable to sudden fits of disgust. There is little cere-mony in contracting marriage with any but maidens. I have heard a man propose after half an hour's acquain-tance, and the fair one's reply was generally the question direct concerning "settlements." Old men frequently marry young girls, but then the portion is high and the *ménage à trois* common.

The Somal know none of the exaggerated and chivalrous ideas by which passion becomes refined affection amongst the Arab Badawin and the sons of civilization, nor did I ever hear of an African abandoning the spear and the sex to become a Darwaysh. Their "Hudhudu," however, reminds the traveller of the Abyssinian "eye-love," the Afghan's "Namzad-bazi," and the Semite's "Ishkuzri," which for want of a better expression we translate "Platonic love."[1] This meeting of the sexes, however, is allowed in Africa by male relatives; in Arabia and Central Asia it provokes their direst indignation. Curious to say, throughout the Somali country, kissing is entirely unknown.

Children are carried on their mothers' backs or laid sprawling upon the ground for the first two years:[2] they

---

[1] The old French term "la petite oie" explains it better. Some trace of the custom may be found in the Kafir's Slambuka or Schlabonka, for a description of which I must refer to the traveller Delegorgue.

The Somal ignore the Kafir custom during lactation.

are circumcised at the age of seven or eight, provided with a small spear, and allowed to run about naked till the age of puberty. They learn by conversation, not books, eat as much as they can beg, borrow and steal, and grow up healthy, strong, and well proportioned according to their race.

As in Al-Islam generally, so here, a man cannot make a will. The property of the deceased is divided amongst his children—the daughters receiving a small portion, if any, of it. When a man dies without issue, his goods and chattels are seized upon by his nearest male relatives; one of them generally marries the widow, or she is sent back to her family. Relicts, as a rule receive no legacies.

You will have remarked, dear L., that the people of Zayla are by no means industrious. They depend for support upon the Desert: the Badawi becomes the Nazil or guest of the townsmen, and he is bound to receive a little tobacco, a few beads, a bit of coarse cotton cloth, or, on great occasions, a penny looking-glass and a cheap German razor, in return for his slaves, ivories, hides, gums, milk, and grain. Any violation of the tie is severely punished by the Governor, and it can be dissolved only by the formula of triple divorce: of course the wild men are hopelessly cheated,[1] and their citizen brethren live in plenty and indolence. After the early breakfast, the male portion of the community leave their houses on business, that is to say, to chat, visit, and *flaner* about the streets and mosques.[2] They return to dinner and the siesta,

---

1 The citizens have learned the Asiatic art of bargaining under a cloth. Both parties sit opposite each other, holding hands : if the little finger for instance be clasped, it means 6, 60, or 600 dollars, according to the value of the article for sale; if the ring finger, 7, 70, or 700, and so on.

2 So, according to M. Krapf, the Suaheli of Eastern Africa wastes his morning hours in running from house to house, to his

after which they issue forth again, and do not come home till night.   Friday is always an idle day, festivals are frequent, and there is no work during weddings and mournings.   The women begin after dawn to plait mats and superintend the slaves, who are sprinkling the house with water, grinding grain for breakfast, cooking, and breaking up firewood; to judge, however, from the amount of chatting and laughter, there appears to be far less work than play.

In these small places it is easy to observe the mechanism of a government which, *en grand*, becomes that of Delhi, Teheran, and Constantinople.   The Governor farms the place from the Porte; he may do what he pleases as long as he pays his rent with punctuality and provides presents and *douceurs* for the Pasha of Mocha. He punishes the petty offences of theft, quarrels, and arson by fines, the bastinado, the stocks, or confinement in an Arish or thatch-hut: the latter is a severe penalty, as the prisoner must provide himself with food.   In cases of murder, he either refers to Mocha or he carries out the Kisas—*lex talionis*—by delivering the slayer to the relatives of the slain.   The Kazi has the administration of the Shariat or religious law: he cannot, however, pronounce sentence without the Governor's permission; and generally his powers are confined to questions of divorce, alimony, manumission, the wound mulct, and similar cases which come within Koranic jurisdiction.   Thus the religious code is ancillary and often opposed to "Al-Jabr"—"the tyranny"—the popular designation of what we call Civil Law.[1]   Yet is Al-Jabr, despite its name,

---

friends or superiors, *ku amkia* (as he calls it), to make his morning salutations.   A worse than Asiatic idleness is the curse of this part of the world.

[1] Diwan al-Jabr, for instance, is a civil court, opposed to the Mahkamah or the Kazi's tribunal.

generally preferred by the worldly wise. The Governor contents himself with a moderate bribe, the Kazi is insatiable : the former may possibly allow you to escape unplundered, the latter assuredly will not. This I believe to be the history of religious jurisdiction in most parts of the world.

CHAPTER V.

FROM ZAYLA TO THE HILLS.

Two routes connect Zayla with Harar; the south-western or direct line numbers ten long or twenty short stages [1] : the first eight through the Ísa country, and the last two among the Nole Gallas, who own the rule of "Waday," a Makad or chief of Christian persuasion. The Hajj objected to this way, on account of his recent blood-feud with the Rer Guleni. He preferred for me the more winding road which passes south, along the coast, through the Ísa Badawin dependent upon Zayla, to the nearest hills, and thence strikes south-westwards among the Gudabirsi and Girhi Somal, who extend within sight of Harar. I cannot but suspect that in selecting this route the good Sharmarkay served another

---

[1] By this route the Mukattib or courier travels on foot from Zayla to Harar in five days at the most. The Somal reckon their journeys by the Gadi or march, the Arab "Hamlah," which varies from four to five hours. They begin before dawn and halt at about 11 A.M., the time of the morning meal. When a second march is made they load at 3 P.M. and advance till dark; thus fifteen miles would be the average of fast travelling. In places of danger they will cover twenty-six or twenty-seven miles of ground without halting to eat or rest: nothing less, however, than regard for "dear life" can engender such activity. Generally two or three hours' work per diem is considered sufficient; and, where provisions abound, halts are long and frequent.

purpose besides my safety. Petty feuds between the chiefs had long " closed the path," and perhaps the Somal were not unwilling that British cloth and tobacco should re-open it.

Early in the morning of the 27th of November, 1854, the mules and all the paraphernalia of travel stood ready at the door. The five camels were forced to kneel, growling angrily the while, by repeated jerks at the halter : their forelegs were duly tied or stood upon till they had shifted themselves into a comfortable position, and their noses were held down by the bystanders whenever, grasshopper-like, they attempted to spring up. Whilst spreading the saddle-mats, our women, to charm away remembrance of chafed hump and bruised sides, sang with vigour the " Song of Travel ":

" O caravan-men, we deceive ye not, we have laden the camels !
 Old women on the journey are kenned by their sleeping !
 (O camel) can'st sniff the cock-boat and the sea ?
 Allah guard thee from the Mikahil and their Midgans ! "[1]

As they arose from squat it was always necessary to adjust their little mountains of small packages by violently " heaving up " one side—an operation never failing to elicit a vicious grunt, a curve of the neck, and an attempt to bite. One camel was especially savage ; it is said that on his return to Zayla, he broke a Badawi girl's neck. Another, a diminutive but hardy little brute of Donkali breed, conducted himself so uproariously that he at once obtained the name of Al-Harami, or the Ruffian.

About 3 P.M., accompanied by the Hajj, his amiable son Mohammed, and a party of Arab matchlock-men,

---

[1] The Mikahil is a clan of the Habr Awal tribe living nea Berberah, and celebrated for their bloodthirsty and butcherin propensities, Many of the Midgan or serviles (a term explaine ̇ Chap. II.) are domesticated amongst them.

who escorted me as a token of especial respect, I issued from the Ashurbara Gate, through the usual staring crowds, and took the way of the wilderness. After half a mile's march, we exchanged affectionate adieus, received much prudent advice about keeping watch and ward at night, recited the Fatihah with upraised palms, and with many promises to write frequently and to meet soon, shook hands and parted. The soldiers gave me a last volley, to which I replied with the " Father of Six."

You see, dear L., how travelling maketh man *banal*. It is the natural consequence of being forced to find in every corner where Fate drops you for a month, a " friend of the soul" and a "moon-faced beauty." With Orientals generally you *must* be on extreme terms, as in Hibernia, either an angel of light or, that failing, a goblin damned. In East Africa especially, English phlegm, shyness, or pride, will bar every heart and raise every hand against you,[1] whereas what M. Rochet calls " a certain *rondeur* of manner " is a specific for winning affection. You should walk up to your man, clasp his fist, pat his back, speak some unintelligible words to him —if, as is the plan of prudence, you ignore the language —laugh a loud guffaw, sit by his side, and begin pipes and coffee. He then proceeds to utilize you, to beg in one country for your interest, and in another for your tobacco. You gently but decidedly thrust that subject out of the way, and choose what is most interesting to yourself. As might be expected, he will at times revert to his own concerns; your superior obstinacy will oppose effectual passive resistance to all such efforts; by degrees the episodes diminish in frequency and duration : at last they cease altogether. The man is now your own.

You will bear in mind, if you please, that I am a

---

[1] So the Abyssinian chief informed M. Krapf, that he loved the French, but could not endure us—simply the effect of manner.

Moslem merchant, a character not to be confounded with the notable individuals seen on 'Change. Mercator in the East is a compound of tradesman, divine and T. G. Usually of gentle birth, he is everywhere welcomed and respected ; and he bears in his mind and manner that, if Allah please, he may become prime minister a month after he has sold you a yard of cloth. Commerce appears to be an accident, not an essential, with him ; yet he is by no means deficient in acumen. He is a grave and reverend signior, with rosary in hand and Koran on lip, is generally a pilgrim, talks at dreary length about Holy Places, writes a pretty hand, has read and can recite much poetry, is master of his religion, demeans himself with respectability, is perfect in all points of ceremony and politeness, and feels equally at home whether sultan or slave sit upon his counter. He has a wife and children in his own country, where he intends to spend the remnant of his days ; but "the world is uncertain "—" Fate descends, and man's eye seeth it not "—" the earth is a charnel house " : briefly his many wise old saws give him a kind of theoretical consciousness that his bones may moulder in other places than his fatherland.

To describe my little caravan. Foremost struts Raghi, our Ísa guide, in all the bravery of Abbanship. He is bare-headed and clothed in Tobe and slippers: a long, heavy, horn-hilted dagger is strapped round his waist, outside his dress ; in his right hand he grasps a ponderous wire-bound spear, which he uses as a staff, and the left forearm supports a round targe of battered hide. Being a man of education, he bears on one shoulder a Musalla or prayer carpet of tanned leather, the article used throughout the Somali country ; slung over the other is a Wesi or wicker bottle containing water for religious ablution. He is accompanied by some men who carry a little stock of town goods and drive a camel colt, which by-the-by they manage to lose before mid-night.

My other attendants must now be introduced to you, as they are to be for the next two months companions of our journey.

First in the list are the fair Samaweda Yusuf, and Aybla Farih,[1] buxom dames about thirty years old, who presently secured the classical nicknames of Shahrázád, and Dunyazad. They look each like three average women rolled into one, and emphatically belong to that race for which the article of feminine attire called, I believe, a "bussle" would be quite superfluous. Wonderful, truly, is their endurance of fatigue! During the march they carry pipe and tobacco, lead and flog the camels, adjust the burdens, and will never be induced to ride, in sickness or in health. At the halt they unload the cattle, dispose the parcels in a semicircle, pitch over them the Gurgi or mat tent, cook our food, boil tea and coffee, and make themselves generally useful. They bivouack outside our abode, modesty not permitting the sexes to mingle, and in the severest cold wear no clothing but a head fillet and an old Tobe. They have curious soft voices, which contrast agreeably with the harsh organs of the males. At first they were ashamed to see me; but that feeling soon wore off, and presently they enlivened the way with pleasantries far more naïve than refined. To relieve their greatest fatigue, nothing seems necessary but the " Jogsi"[2]: they lie at full length, prone, stand upon each other's backs trampling and kneading with the

---

1 The first is the name of the individual; the second is that of her father.

2 This delicate operation is called by the Arabs, Da'asah (whence the "Doseh ceremony" at Cairo). It is used over most parts of the Eastern World as a remedy for sickness and fatigue, and is generally preferred to Takbis or Dugmo, the common style of shampooing, which, say many Easterns, loosens the skin.

toes, and rise like giants much refreshed. Always attendant upon these dames is Yusuf, a Zayla lad, who, being one-eyed, was pitilessly named by my companions, the "Kalandar;" he prays frequently, is strict in his morals, and has conceived, like Mrs. Brownrigg, so exalted an idea of discipline, that, but for our influence, he certainly would have beaten the two female 'prentices to death. They hate him therefore, and he knows it.

Immediately behind Raghi and his party walk Shahrázád and Dunyazad, the former leading the head camel, the latter using my chibúk stick as a staff. She has been at Aden, and sorely suspects me; her little black eyes never meet mine; and frequently, with affected confusion, she turns her sable cheek the clean contrary way. Strung together by their tails, and soundly beaten when disposed to lag, the five camels pace steadily along under their burdens—bales of Wilayati or American sheeting, Duwwarah or Cutch canvass, with indigo-dyed stuff slung along the animals' sides, and neatly sewn up in a case of matting to keep off dust and rain—a cow's hide, which serves as a couch, covering the whole. They carry a load of "Mushakkar" (bad Mocha dates) for the Somal, with a parcel of better quality for ourselves, and a half hundredweight of coarse Surat tobacco;[1] besides which we have a box of beads, and

---

1 The Somal, from habit, enjoy no other variety; they even shewed disgust at my Latakia. Tobacco is grown in some places by the Gudabirsi and other tribes; but it is rare and bad. Without this article it would be impossible to progress in East Africa; every man asks for a handful, and many will not return milk for what they expect to receive as a gift. Their importunity reminds the traveller of the Galloway beggars some generations ago:—" They are for the most part great chewers of tobacco, and are so addicted to it, that they will ask for a piece thereof from a stranger as he is riding on his way; and therefore let not a traveller want an ounce or two of roll tobacco in his pocket, and for an inch or two thereof he need not fear the want of a guide by day or night."

another of trinkets, mosaic-gold earrings, necklaces, watches and similar nick-nacks. Our private provisions are represented by about 300 lbs. of rice—here the traveller's staff of life—a large pot full of "Kawurmah,"[1] dates, salt,[2] clarified butter, tea, coffee, sugar, a box of biscuits in case of famine, "Halwá" or Arab sweetmeats to be used when driving hard bargains, and a little turmeric for seasoning. A simple *batterie de cuisine*, and sundry skins full of potable water,[3] dangle from chance rope-ends : and last but not the least important, is a heavy box[4] of ammunition sufficient for a three months' sporting tour.[5] In the rear of the caravan trudges a

---

[1] Flesh boiled in large slices, sun-dried, broken to pieces and fried in ghí.

[2] The Bahr Assal or Salt Lake, near Tajurrah, annually sends into the interior thousands of little matted parcels containing this necessary. Inland, the Badawin will rub a piece upon the tongue before eating, or pass about a lump, as the Dutch did with sugar in the last war ; at Harar a donkey load is the price of a slave ; and the Abyssinians say of a *millionaire*, " he eateth salt."

[3] The element found upon the maritime plain is salt or brackish. There is nothing concerning which the African traveller should be so particular as water; bitter with nitre, and full of organic matter, it causes all those dysenteric diseases which have made research in this part of the world a Upas tree to the discoverer. Pocket filters are invaluable. The water of wells should be boiled and passed through charcoal ; and even then it might be mixed to a good purpose with a few drops of proof spirit. The Somal generally carry their stores in large wickerwork pails. I preferred skins, as more portable and less likely to taint the water.

[4] Here as in Arabia, boxes should be avoided, the Badawin always believed them to contain treasures. Day after day I have been obliged to display the contents to crowds of savages, who amused themselves by lifting up the case with loud cries of " hoo ! hoo !! hoo !!! " (the popular exclamation of astonishment), and by speculating upon the probable amount of dollars contained therein.

[5] The following list of my expenses may perhaps be useful to future travellers. It must be observed that, had the whole out-

Badawi woman driving a donkey—the proper "tail" in
these regions, where camels start if followed by a horse
or mule.   An ill-fated sheep, a parting present from the
Hajj, races and frisks about the Kafilah.   It became so
tame that the Somal received an order not to "cut" it;
one day, however, I found myself dining, and that pet
lamb was the *menu*.

By the side of the camels ride my three attendants,
the pink of Somali fashion.   Their frizzled wigs are
radiant with grease; their Tobes are splendidly white,
with borders dazzlingly red; their new shields are covered
with canvas cloth; and their two spears, poised over the
right shoulder, are freshly scraped, oiled, blackened, and
polished.   They have added my spare rifle and guns to
the camel-load; such weapons are well enough at Aden,
in Somali-land men would deride the outlandish tool!
I told them that in my country women use bows and
arrows, moreover that lancers are generally considered
a corps of non-combatants; in vain! they adhered as
strongly—so mighty a thing is prejudice—to their partiality
for bows, arrows, and lances.   Their horsemanship is

---

fit been purchased at Aden, a considerable saving would have
resulted:

	Cos. Rs.
Passage money from Aden to Zayl - - -	33
Presents at Zayla - - - - -	100
Price of four mules with saddles and bridles - -	225
Price of four camels - - - -	88
Provisions (tobacco, rice, dates, &c.) for three months	428
Price of 150 Tobes - - - - -	357
Nine pieces of indigo-dyed cotton - - -	16
Minor expenses (cowhides for camels, mats for tents, presents to Arabs, a box of beads, three handsome Abyssinian Tobes bought for chiefs) - -	166
Expenses at Berberah, and passage back to Aden -	77

Total Cos. Rs.   1490=£149

peculiar, they balance themselves upon little Abyssinian saddles, extending the leg and raising the heel in the Louis Quinze style of equitation, and the stirrup is an iron ring admitting only the big toe. I follow them mounting a fine white mule, which with its gaudily *galonné* Arab pad and wrapper cloth, has a certain dignity of look; a double-barrelled gun lies across my lap; and a rude pair of holsters, the work of Hasen Turki, contains my Colt's six-shooters.

Marching in this order, which was to serve as a model, we travelled due south along the coast, over a hard, stoneless, and alluvial plain, here dry, there muddy (where the tide reaches), across boggy creeks, broad water-courses, and warty flats of black mould powdered with nitrous salt, and bristling with the salsolaceous vegetation familiar to the Arab voyager. Such is the general forma-tion of the plain between the mountains and the sea, whose breadth, in a direct line, may measure from forty-five to forty-eight miles. Near the first zone of hills, or sub-Ghauts, it produces a thicker vegetation; thorns and acacias of different kinds appear in clumps; and ground broken with ridges and ravines announces the junction. After the monsún this plain is covered with rich grass. At other seasons it affords but a scanty supply of " aqueous matter " resembling bilge-water. The land belongs to the Mummasan clan of the Ísa: how these " Kurrah-jog " or " sun-dwellers," as the Badawin are called by the burgher Somal, can exist here in summer, is a mystery. My arms were peeled even in the month of December; and my companions, panting with the heat, like the Atlantes of Herodotus, poured forth reproaches upon the rising sun. The townspeople, when forced to hurry across it in the hotter season, cover themselves during the day with Tobes wetted every half hour in sea water; yet they are sometimes killed by the fatal thirst which the Samún engenders. Even the Badawin are now longing for rain ; a few weeks' drought destroys half their herds.

Early in the afternoon our Abban and a woman halted for a few minutes, performed their ablutions, and prayed with a certain display : satisfied apparently, with the result, they never repeated the exercise. About sunset we passed, on the right, clumps of trees overgrowing a water called "Warabod," the Hyena's Well; this is the first Marhalah or halting-place usually made by travellers to the interior. Hence there is a direct path leading south-south-west, by six short marches, to the hills. Our Abban, however, was determined that we should not so easily escape his kraal. Half an hour afterwards we passed by the second station, "Hangagarri," a well near the sea : frequent lights twinkling through the darkening air informed us that we were in the midst of the Ísa. At 8 P.M., we reached "Gagab," the third Marhalah, where the camels, casting themselves upon the ground, imperatively demanded a halt. Raghi was urgent for an advance, declaring that already he could sight the watch-fires of his Rer or tribe :[1] but the animals carried the point against him. They were presently unloaded and turned out to graze, and the lariats of the mules, who are addicted to running away, were fastened to stones for want of pegs.[2] Then lighting a fire, we sat down to a homely supper of dates.

The air was fresh and clear, and the night breeze was delicious after the steamy breath of day. The weary confinement of walls made the splendid expanse a luxury

---

[1] I shall frequently use Somali terms, not to display my scanty knowledge of the dialect, but because they perchance may prove serviceable to my successors.

[2] The Somal always "side-line" their horses and mules with stout stiff leathern thongs provided with loops and wooden buttons; we found them upon the whole safer than lariats or tethers.

to the sight, whilst the tumbling of the surf upon the near shore, and the music of the jackal, predisposed to sweet sleep. We now felt that at length the die was cast. Placing my pistols by my side, with my rifle-butt for a pillow, and its barrel as a bed-fellow, I sought repose with none of that apprehension which even the most stout-hearted traveller knows before the start. It is the difference between fancy and reality, between anxiety and certainty: to men gifted with any imaginative powers the anticipation must ever be worse than the event. Thus it happens, that he who feels a thrill of fear before engaging in a peril, exchanges it for a throb of exultation when he finds himself hand to hand with the danger.

The " End of Time " volunteered to keep watch that night. When the early dawn glimmered he aroused us, and blew up the smouldering fire, whilst our women proceeded to load the camels. We pursued our way over hard alluvial soil to sand, and thence passed into a growth of stiff yellow grass not unlike a stubble in English September. Day broke upon a Somali Arcadia, whose sole flaws were salt water and Samun. Whistling shepherds[1] carried in their arms the younglings of the herds, or, spear in hand, drove to pasture long regular lines of camels, that waved their vulture-like heads, and arched their necks to bite in play their neighbours' faces, humps, and hind thighs. They were led by a patriarch, to whose throat hung a Kor or wooden bell, the preventa-

---

1 Arabs hate " Al-Sifr " or whistling, which they hold to be the chit-chat of the Jinns. Some say that the musician's mouth is not to be purified for forty days ; others that Satan, touching a man's person, causes him to produce the offensive sound. The Hijazis objected to Burckhardt that he could not help talking to devils, and walking about the room like an unquiet spirit. The Somali has no such prejudice. Like the Kafir of the Cape, he passes his day whistling to his flocks and herds ; moreover, he makes signals by changing the note, and is skilful in imitating the song of birds.

tive for straggling: and most of them were followed (for winter is the breeding season) by colts in every stage of infancy.[1] Patches of sheep, with snowy skins, and jetty faces, flecked the yellow plain; and herds of goats resembling deer were driven by hide-clad children to the bush. Women, in similar attire, accompanied them, some chewing the inner bark of trees, others spinning yarn of a white creeper called Sagsug for ropes and tent mats. The boys carried shepherds' crooks,[2] and bore their watering pails,[3] foolscap fashion, upon their heads. Sometimes they led the ram, around whose neck a cord of white leather was bound for luck; at other times they frisked with the dog, an animal by no means contemptible in the eyes of the Badawin.[4] As they advanced, the graceful little sand antelopes bounded away over the bushes; and above them, soaring high in the cloudless skies, were flights of vultures and huge percnopters, unerring indicators of man's habitation in Somali-land.[5]

A net-work of paths showed that we were approaching a populous place; and presently men swarmed forth from their hive-shaped tents, testifying their satisfaction

---

1 In this country camels foal either in the Gugi (monsun), or during the cold season immediately after the autumnal rains.

2 The shepherd's staff is a straight stick about six feet long, with a crook at one end, and at the other a fork to act as a rake.

3 These utensils will be described in a future chapter.

4 The settled Somal have a holy horror of dogs, and, Wahhabi-like, treat man's faithful slave most cruelly. The wild people are more humane; they pay two ewes for a good colley, and demand a two-year-old sheep as "diyat" or blood-money for the animal, if killed.

5 Vultures and percnopters lie upon the wing waiting for the garbage of the kraals; consequently they are rare near the cow-villages, where animals are not often killed.

at our arrival, the hostile Habr Awal having threatened to "eat them up." We rode cautiously, as is customary, amongst the yeaning she-camels, who are injured by a sudden start, and about 8 A.M. arrived at our guide's kraal, the fourth station, called "Gudingaras," or the low place where the Garas tree grows. The encampment lay south-east (165°) of, and about twenty miles from, Zayla.

Raghi disappeared, and the Badawin flocked out to gaze upon us as we approached the kraal. Meanwhile Shahrazad and Dunyazad fetched tent-sticks from the village, disposed our luggage so as to form a wall, rigged out a wigwam, spread our beds in the shade, and called aloud for sweet and sour milk. I heard frequently muttered by the red-headed spearmen the ominous term "Faranj[1]"; and although there was no danger, it was deemed advisable to make an impression without delay. Presently they began to deride our weapons: the Hammal requested them to put up one of their shields as a mark; they laughed aloud but shirked compliance. At last a large brown, bare-necked vulture settled on the ground at twenty paces' distance. The Somal hate the "Gurgur," because he kills the dying and devours the dead on the battle-field : a bullet put through the bird's body caused a cry of wonder, and some ran after the lead as it span whistling over the ridge. Then loading with swan shot which these Badawin had never seen, I knocked over a second vulture flying. Fresh screams followed the marvellous feat; the women exclaimed, "Lo! he bringeth down the birds from heaven;" and one old man, putting his forefinger in his mouth, praised Allah and prayed to

---

1 They apply this term to all but themselves ; an Indian trader who had travelled to Harar, complained to me that he had always been called a Frank by the Badawin in consequence of his wearing Shalwar, or drawers.

be defended from such a calamity. The effect was such
that I determined always to carry a barrel loaded with
shot as the best answer for all who might object to
" Faranj."

We spent our day in the hut after the normal
manner, with a crowd of woolly-headed Badawin squatting perseveringly opposite our quarters, spear in hand,
with eyes fixed upon every gesture. Before noon the
door-mat was let down—a precaution also adopted whenever box or package was opened—we drank milk and
ate rice with " a kitchen " of Kawurmah. About midday the crowd retired to sleep ; my companions followed
their example, and I took the opportunity of sketching
and jotting down notes.[1] Early in the afternoon the
Badawin returned, and resumed their mute form of
pleading for tobacco : each man, as he received a handful, rose slowly from his hams and went his way. The
senior who disliked the gun was importunate for a charm
to cure his sick camel : having obtained it, he blessed us in
a set speech, which lasted at least half an hour, and concluded with spitting upon the whole party for good luck.[2]
It is always well to encourage these Nestors ; they are
regarded with the greatest reverence by the tribes, who
believe that

> " old experience doth attain
> To something like prophetic strain ; "

---

1 Generally it is not dangerous to write before these Badawin,
as they only suspect account-keeping, and none but the educated
recognizes a sketch. The traveller, however, must be on his guard :
in the remotest villages he will meet Somal who have returned to
savage life after visiting the sea-board, Arabia, and possibly India
or Egypt.

2 I have often observed this ceremony performed upon a new
turband or other article of attire ; possibly it may be intended as a
mark of contempt, assumed to blind the evil eye.

and they can either do great good or cause much petty annoyance.

In the evening I took my gun, and, accompanied by the End of Time, went out to search for venison : the plain, however, was full of men and cattle, and its wilder denizens had migrated. During our walk we visited the tomb of an Ísa brave. It was about ten feet long, heaped up with granite pebbles, bits of black basalt, and stones of calcareous lime : two upright slabs denoted the position of the head and feet, and upon these hung the deceased's milk-pails, much the worse for sun and wind. Round the grave was a thin fence of thorns : opposite the single narrow entrance were three blocks of stone planted in line, and showing the number of enemies slain by the brave.[1] Beyond these trophies, a thorn roofing, supported by four bare poles, served to shade the relatives, when they meet to sit, feast, weep, and pray.

The Badawin funerals and tombs are equally simple. They have no favourite cemeteries as in Sind and other Moslem and pastoral lands : men are buried where they die, and the rarity of the graves scattered about the country excited my astonishment. The corpse is soon interred. These people, like most barbarians, have a horror of death and all that reminds them of it : on several occasions I have been begged to throw away a hut-stick, that had been used to dig a grave. The bier is a rude framework of poles bound with ropes of hide. Some tie up the body and plant it in a sitting posture, to save themselves the trouble of excavating deep : this perhaps may account for the circular tombs seen in many parts of the country. Usually the corpse is thrust into a long hole, covered with wood and matting, and

---

1 Such is the general form of the Somali grave. Sometimes wo stumps of wood take the place of the upright stones at the head and foot, and around one grave I counted twenty trophies.

heaped over with earth and thorns, half-protected by an oval mass of loose stones, and abandoned to the jackals and hyenas.

We halted a day at Gudingaras, wishing to see the migration of a tribe. Before dawn, on the 30th November, the Somali Stentor proclaimed from the ridge-top, " Fetch your camels!—Load your goods!— We march!" About 8 A.M. we started in the rear. The spectacle was novel to me. Some 150 spearmen, assisted by their families, were driving before them divisions which, in total, might amount to 200 cows, 7000 camels, and 11,000 or 12,000 sheep and goats. Only three wore the Bal or feather, which denotes the brave; several, however, had the other decoration—an ivory armlet.[1] Assisted by the boys, whose heads were shaved in a cristated fashion truly ridiculous, and large pariah dogs with bushy tails, they drove the beasts and carried the colts, belaboured runaway calves, and held up the hind legs of struggling sheep. The sick, of whom there were many—dysentery being at the time prevalent —were carried upon camels with their legs protruding in front from under the hide-cover. Many of the dromedaries showed the Habr Awal brand:[2] laden with hutting materials and domestic furniture, they were led by the maidens : the matrons followed, bearing their progeny upon their backs, bundled in the shoulder-lappets of cloth or hide. The smaller girls, who, in addition to

---

1 Some braves wear above the right elbow an ivory armlet called Fol or Aj : in the south this denotes the elephant-slayer. Other Ísa clans assert their warriorhood by small disks of white stone, fashioned like rings, and fitted upon the little finger of the left hand. Others bind a bit of red cloth round the brow.

2 It is sufficient for a Badawi to look at the general appearance of an animal; he at once recognizes the breed. Each clan, however, in this part of Eastern Africa has its own mark.

the boys' crest, wore a circlet of curly hair round the
head, carried the weakling lambs and kids, or aided their
mammas in transporting the baby. Apparently in great
fear of the " All " or Commando, the Badawin anxiously
inquired if I had my " fire " with me,[1] and begged us to
take the post of honour—the van. As our little party
pricked forward, the camels started in alarm, and we
were surprised to find that this tribe did not know the
difference between horses and mules. Whenever the
boys lost time in sport or quarrel, they were threatened
by their fathers with the jaws of that ogre, the white
stranger ; and the women exclaimed, as they saw us
approach, " Here comes the old man who knows knowledge[2] ! "

Having skirted the sea for two hours, I rode off with
the End of Time to inspect the Dihh Silil,[3] a fiumara
which runs from the western hills north-eastwards to the
sea. Its course is marked by a long line of graceful
tamarisks, whose vivid green looked doubly bright set
off by tawny stubble and amethyst-blue sky. These
freshets are the Edens of Adel. The banks are charm-
ingly wooded with acacias of many varieties, some
thorned like the fabled Zakkum, others parachute-
shaped, and planted in impenetrable thickets : huge
white creepers, snake-shaped, enclasp giant trees, or
connect with their cordage the higher boughs, or depend
like cables from the lower branches to the ground.
Luxuriant parasites abound : here they form domes of

---

1 They found no better word than " fire " to denote the gun.

2 " Oddai," an old man, corresponds with the Arab Shaykh in
etymology. The Somal, however, give the name to men of all ages
after marriage.

3 The " Dihh " is the Arab " Wady,"—a fiumara or freshet.
" Webbe " (Obbay, Abbai, &c.) is a large river ; " Durdur," a running
stream.

flashing green, there they surround with verdure decayed trunks, and not unfrequently cluster into sylvan bowers, under which—grateful sight!—appears succulent grass. From the thinner thorns the bell-shaped nests of the Loxia depend, waving in the breeze, and the wood resounds with the cries of bright-winged choristers. The torrent-beds are of the clearest and finest white sand, glittering with gold-coloured mica, and varied with nodules of clear and milky quartz, red porphyry, and granites of many hues. Sometimes the centre is occupied by an islet of torn trees and stones rolled in heaps, supporting a clump of thick jujube or tall acacia, whilst the lower parts of the beds are overgrown with long lines of lively green colocynth.[1] Here are usually the wells, surrounded by heaps of thorns, from which the leaves have been browsed off, and dwarf sticks that support the water-hide. When the flocks and herds are absent, troops of gazelles may be seen daintily pacing the yielding surface; snake trails streak the sand, and at night the fiercer kind of animals, lions, leopards, and elephants, take their turn. In Somali-land the well is no place of social meeting; no man lingers to chat near it, no woman visits it, and the traveller fears to pitch hut where torrents descend, and where enemies, human and bestial, meet.

We sat under a tree watching the tribe defile across the water-course: then remounting, after a ride of two miles, we reached a ground called Kuranyali,[2] upon which the wigwams of the Nomads were already rising. The parched and treeless stubble lies about eight miles

---

1 I saw these Dihhs only in the dry season ; at times the torrent must be violent, cutting ten or twelve feet deep into the plain.

2 The name is derived from Kuranyo, an ant : it means the "place of ants," and is so called from the abundance of a tree which attracts them.

from and 145° S.E. of Gudingaras ; both places are supplied by Angagarri, a well near the sea, which is so
distant that cattle, to return before nightfall, must start
early in the morning.

My attendants had pitched the Gurgi or hut : the
Hammal and Long Gulad were, however, sulky on
account of my absence, and the Kalandar appeared disposed to be mutinous. The End of Time, who never lost
an opportunity to make mischief, whispered in my ear,
" Despise thy wife, thy son, and thy slave, or they
despise thee ! " The old saw was not wanted, however,
to procure for them a sound scolding. Nothing is worse
for the Eastern traveller than the habit of " sending
to Coventry : " it does away with all manner of discipline.

We halted that day at Kuranyali, preparing water
and milk for two long marches over the desert to the
hills. Being near the shore, the air was cloudy, although
men prayed for a shower in vain : about midday the
pleasant sea-breeze fanned our cheeks, and the plain was
thronged with tall pillars of white sand.[1]

The heat forbade egress, and our wigwam was
crowded with hungry visitors. Raghi, urged thereto by
his tribe, became importunate, now for tobacco, then for
rice, now for dates, then for provisions in general. No
wonder that the Prophet made his Paradise for the Poor
a mere place of eating and drinking. The half-famished
Badawin, Somal or Arab, think of nothing beyond the
stomach—their dreams know no higher vision of bliss
than mere repletion. A single article of diet, milk or
flesh, palling upon man's palate, they will greedily suck
the stones of eaten dates : yet Abyssinian like, they are
squeamish and fastidious as regards food. They despise
the excellent fish with which Nature has so plentifully

---

1 The Arabs call these pillars " Devils," the Somal " Sigo."

stocked their seas.[1] " Speak not to me with that mouth which eateth fish ! " is a favourite insult amongst the Badawin. If you touch a bird or a fowl of any description, you will be despised even by the starving beggar. You must not eat marrow or the flesh about the sheep's thigh-bone, especially when travelling, and the kidneys are called a woman's dish. None but the Northern Somal will touch the hares which abound in the country, and many refuse the sand antelope and other kinds of game, not asserting that the meat is unlawful, but simply alleging a disgust. Those who chew coffee berries are careful not to place an even number in their mouths, and camel's milk is never heated, for fear of bewitching the animal.[2] The Somali, however, differs in one point from his kinsman the Arab : the latter prides himself upon his temperance ; the former, like the North American Indian, measures manhood by appetite. A " Son of the Somal" is taught, as soon as his teeth are cut, to devour two pounds of the toughest mutton, and ask for more : if his powers of deglutition fail, he is derided as degenerate.

On the next day (Friday, December 1st) we informed the Abban that we intended starting early in the afternoon, and therefore warned him to hold himself and his escort, together with the water and milk necessary for our march, in readiness. He promised compliance and disappeared. About 3 P.M. the Badawin, armed as usual with spear and shield, began to gather round the hut,

---

1 The Cape Kafirs have the same prejudice against fish, comparing its flesh to that of serpents. In some points their squeamishness resembles that of the Somal : he, for instance, who tastes the Rhinoceros Simus is at once dubbed " Om Fogazan " or outcast.

2 This superstition may have arisen from the peculiarity that the camel's milk, however fresh, if placed upon the fire, breaks like some cow's milk.

and—nothing in this country can be done without that
terrible " palaver ! "—the speechifying presently commenced.   Raghi, in a lengthy harangue hoped that the
tribe would afford us all necessary supplies and assist us
in the arduous undertaking.   His words elicited no hear,
hear ! there was an evident unwillingness on the part
of the wild men to let us, or rather our cloth and tobacco,
depart.   One remarked, with surly emphasis, that he
had " seen no good and eaten no Bori[1] from that
caravan, why should he aid it ? "   When we asked the
applauding hearers what they had done for us, they
rejoined by inquiring whose the land was ?   Another
smitten by the fair Shahrazad's bulky charms, had
proposed matrimony, and offered as dowry a milch
camel : she " temporised," not daring to return a
positive refusal, and the suitor betrayed a certain
Hibernian *velleïté* to consider consent an unimportant
part of the ceremony.   The mules had been sent to the
well, with orders to return before noon : at 4 P.M. they
were not visible.   I then left the hut, and, sitting on a
cow's-hide in the sun, ordered my men to begin loading,
despite the remonstrances of the Abban and the interference of about fifty Badawin.   As we persisted, they
waxed surlier, and declared all which was ours became
theirs, to whom the land belonged : we did not deny the
claim, but simply threatened sorcery-death, by wild
beasts and foraging parties, to their " camels, children
and women."   This brought them to their senses, the
usual effect of such threats ; and presently arose the
senior who had spat upon us for luck's sake.   With his
toothless jaws he mumbled a vehement speech, and
warned the tribe that it was not good to detain such
strangers : they lent ready ears to the words of Nestor,

---

1 " Bori " in Southern Arabia popularly means a water-pipe :
here it is used for tobacco.

saying, " Let us obey him, he is near his end ! " The
mules arrived, but when I looked for the escort, none
was forthcoming. At Zayla it was agreed that twenty
men should protect us across the desert, which is the
very passage of plunder ; now, however, five or six
paupers offered to accompany us for a few miles. We
politely declined troubling them, but insisted upon the
attendance of our Abban and three of his kindred: as
some of the Badawin still opposed us, our aged friend
once more arose, and by copious abuse finally silenced
them. We took leave of him with many thanks and
handfuls of tobacco, in return for which he blessed us
with fervour. Then, mounting our mules, we set out,
followed for at least a mile by a long tail of howling
boys, who, ignorant of clothing, except a string of white
beads round the neck, but armed with dwarf spears,
bows, and arrows, showed all the impudence of baboons.
They derided the End of Time's equitation till I feared
a scene ; sailor-like, he prided himself upon graceful
horsemanship, and the imps were touching his tenderest
point.

Hitherto, for the Abban's convenience, we had
skirted the sea, far out of the direct road: now we were
to strike south-westwards into the interior. At 6 P. M.
we started across a " Goban "[1] which eternal summer
gilds with a dull ochreish yellow, towards a thin blue
strip of hill on the far horizon. The Somal have no
superstitious dread of night and its horrors, like Arabs
and Abyssinians: our Abban, however, showed a whole-

---

1 " Goban " is the low maritime plain lying below the " Bor "
or Ghauts, and opposed to Ogú, the table-land above. " Ban " is
an elevated grassy prairie, where few trees grow; " Dir," a small
jungle, called Haija by the Arabs ; and Khain is a forest or thick
bush. " Bor," is a mountain, rock, or hill: a stony precipice is
called " Jar," and the high clay banks of a ravine " Gebi."

some mundane fear of plundering parties, scorpions, and snakes.[1] I had been careful to fasten round my ankles the twists of black wool called by the Arabs Za'al,[2] and universally used in Al-Yaman: a stock of garlic and opium, here held to be specifics, fortified the courage of the party, whose fears were not wholly ideal, for, in the course of the night, Shahrazad nearly trod upon a viper.

At first the plain was a network of holes, the habi-

---

1 Snakes are rare in the cities, but abound in the wilds of Eastern Africa, and are dangerous to night travellers, though seldom seen by day. To kill a serpent is considered by the Badawin almost as meritorious as to slay an Infidel. The Somal have many names for the reptile tribe. The Subhanyo, a kind of whipsnake, and a large yellow rock snake called Got, are little feared. The Abesi (in Arabic Al-Hayyah—the Cobra) is so venomous that it kills the camel; the Mas or Hanash, and a long black snake called Jilbis, are considered equally dangerous. Serpents are in Somali-land the subject of many superstitions. One horn of the Cerastes, for instance, contains a deadly poison: the other, pounded and drawn across the eye, makes man a seer and reveals to him the treasures of the earth. There is a flying snake which hoards precious stones, and is attended by a hundred guards: a Somali horseman once, it is said, carried away a jewel; he was pursued by a reptile army, and although he escaped to his tribe, the importunity of the former proprietors was so great that the plunder was eventually restored to them. Centipedes are little feared; their venom leads to inconveniences more ridiculous than dangerous. Scorpions, especially the large yellow variety, are formidable in hot weather: I can speak of the sting from experience. The first symptom is a sensation of nausea, and the pain shoots up after a few minutes to the groin, causing a swelling accompanied by burning and throbbing, which last about twelve hours. The Somal bandage above the wound and wait patiently till the effect subsides.

2 These are tightened in case of accident, and act as superior ligatures. I should, however, advise every traveller in these regions to provide himself with a pneumatic pump, and not to place his trust in Za'al, garlic, or opium.

tations of the Jir Ad,[1] a field rat with ruddy back and white belly, the Mullah or Parson, a smooth-skinned lizard, and the Dabagalla, a ground squirrel with a brilliant and glossy coat. As it became dark arose a cheerful moon, exciting the howlings of the hyenas, the barkings of their attendant jackals,[2] and the chattered oaths of the Hidinhitu bird.[3] Dotted here and there over the misty landscape, appeared dark clumps of a tree called " Kullan," a thorn with an edible berry not unlike the jujube, and banks of silvery mist veiled the far horizon from the sight.

We marched rapidly and in silence, stopping every quarter of an hour to raise the camels' loads as they slipped on one side. I had now an opportunity of seeing how feeble a race is the Somali. My companions

---

1 The grey rat is called by the Somal " Baradublay " : in Eastern Africa it is a minor plague, after India and Arabia, where, neglecting to sleep in boots, I have sometimes been lamed for a week by their venomous bites.

2 In this country the jackal attends not upon the lion, but the Waraba. His morning cry is taken as an omen of good or evil according to the note.

3 Of this bird, a red and long-legged plover, the Somal tell the following legend. Originally her diet was meat, and her society birds of prey : one night, however, her companions having devoured all the provisions whilst she slept, she swore never to fly with friends, never to eat flesh, and never to rest during the hours of darkness. When she sees anything in the dark she repeats her oaths, and, according to the Somal, keeps careful watch all night. There is a larger variety of this bird, which, purblind during daytime, rises from under the traveller's feet with loud cries. The Somal have superstitions similar to that above noticed about several kinds of birds. When the cry of the " Galu " (so called from his note Gal! Gal! come in! come in!) is heard over a kraal, the people say, " Let us leave this place, the Galu hath spoken ! " At night they listen for the Fin, also an ill-omened bird : when a man declares " the Fin did not sleep last night," it is considered advisable to shift ground.

on the line of march wondered at my being able to carry a gun; they could scarcely support, even whilst riding, the weight of their spears, and preferred sitting upon them to spare their shoulders. At times they were obliged to walk because the saddles cut them, then they remounted because their legs were tired; briefly, an English boy of fourteen would have shown more bottom than the sturdiest. This cannot arise from poor diet, for the citizens, who live generously, are yet weaker than the Badawin; it is a peculiarity of race. When fatigued they become reckless and impatient of thirst: on this occasion, though want of water stared us in the face, one skin of the three was allowed to fall upon the road and burst, and the contents of the second were drunk before we halted.

At 11 P.M., after marching twelve miles in direct line, we bivouacked upon the plain. The night breeze from the hills had set in, and my attendants chattered with cold: Long Gulad in particular became stiff as a mummy. Raghi was clamorous against a fire, which might betray our whereabouts in the " Bush Inn." But after such a march the pipe was a necessity, and the point was carried against him.

After a sound sleep under the moon, we rose at 5 A.M. and loaded the camels. It was a raw morning. A large nimbus rising from the east obscured the sun, the line of blue sea was raised like a ridge by refraction, and the hills, towards which we were journeying, now showed distinct falls and folds. Troops of Dera or gazelles, herding like goats, stood, stared at us, turned their white tails, faced away, broke into a long trot, and bounded over the plain as we approached. A few ostriches appeared, but they were too shy even for bullet.[1] At

---

1 Throughout this country ostriches are exceedingly wild: the Rev. Mr. Erhardt, of the Mombas Mission, informs me that they are

8 P.M. we crossed one of the numerous drains which intersect this desert—" Biya Hablod," or the Girls' Water, a fiumara running from south-west to east and north-east. Although dry, it abounded in the Marar, a tree bearing yellowish red berries full of viscous juice like green gum—edible but not nice—and the brighter vegetation showed that water was near the surface. About two hours afterwards, as the sun became oppressive, we unloaded in a water-course, called by my companions Adad or the Acacia Gum:[1] the distance was about twenty-five miles, and the direction S.W. 225° of Kuranyali.

We spread our couches of cowhide in the midst of a green mass of tamarisk under a tall Kud tree, a bright-leaved thorn, with balls of golden gum clinging to its boughs, dry berries scattered in its shade, and armies of ants marching to and from its trunk. All slept upon the soft white sand, with arms under their hands, for our spoor across the desert was now unmistakeable. At midday, rice was boiled for us by the indefatigable women, and at 3 P.M. we resumed our march towards the hills, which had exchanged their shadowy blue for a coat of pronounced brown. Journeying onwards, we reached the Barragid fiumara, and presently exchanged the plain for rolling ground covered with the remains of an extinct race, and probably alluded to by Al-Makrizi when he records that the Moslems of Adel had erected,

---

equally so farther south. The Somal stalk them during the day with camels, and kill them with poisoned arrows. It is said that about 3 P.M. the birds leave their feeding places, and traverse long distances to roost : the people assert that they are blind at night, and rise up under the pursuer's feet.

1 Several Acacias afford gums, which the Badawin eat greedily to strengthen themselves. The town's people declare that the food produces nothing but flatulence.

throughout the country, a vast number of mosques and oratories for Friday and festival prayers. Places of worship appeared in the shape of parallelograms, un-hewed stones piled upon the ground, with a semicircular niche in the direction of Meccah. The tombs, different from the heaped form now in fashion, closely resembled the older erections in the island of Sa'ad al-Din, near Zayla—oblong slabs planted deep in the soil. We also observed hollow rings of rough blocks, circles measuring about a cubit in diameter: I had not time to excavate them and the End of Time could only inform me that they belonged to the " Awwalin," or olden inhabitants.

At 7 P.M., as evening was closing in, we came upon the fresh trail of a large Habr Awal calvacade. The celebrated footprint seen by Robinson Crusoe affected him not more powerfully than did this " daaseh " my companions. The voice of song suddenly became mute. The women drove the camels hurriedly, and all huddled together, except Raghi, who kept well to the front ready for a run. Whistling with anger, I asked my attendants what had slain them : the End of Time, in a hollow voice, replied, " Verily, O pilgrim, whoso seeth the track, seeth the foe ! " and he quoted in tones of terror those dreary lines—

> " Man is but a handful of dust,
> And life is a violent storm."

We certainly were a small party to contend against 200 horsemen—nine men and two women : moreover all except the Hammal and Long Gulad would infallibly have fled at the first charge.

Presently we sighted the trails of sheep and goats, showing the proximity of a village : their freshness was ascertained by my companions after an eager scrutiny in the moon's bright beams. About half an hour after-wards, rough ravines with sharp and thorny descents warned us that we had exchanged the dangerous plain for a place of safety where horsemen rarely venture. Raghi, not admiring the " open," hurried us onward, in hope of reaching some kraal. At 8 P. M., however, seeing the poor women lamed with thorns, and the camels casting themselves upon the ground, I resolved to halt. Despite all objections, we lighted a fire, finished our store of bad milk—the water had long ago been exhausted—and lay down in the cold, clear air, covering ourselves with hides and holding our weapons.

At 6 A. M. we resumed our ride over rough stony ground, the thorns tearing our feet and naked legs, and the camels slipping over the rounded waste of drift pebbles. The Badawin, with ears applied to the earth, listened for a village, but heard none. Suddenly we saw two strangers, and presently we came upon an Ísa kraal. It was situated in a deep ravine, called Damal, backed by a broad and hollow fiumara at the foot of the hills, running from west to east, and surrounded by lofty trees, upon which brown kites, black vultures, and percnopters like flakes of snow were mewing. We had marched over a winding path about eleven miles from, and in a south-west direction (205°) of, Adad. Painful thoughts suggested themselves: in consequence of wandering southwards, only six had been taken off thirty stages by the labours of seven days.

As usual in Eastern Africa, we did not enter the kraal uninvited, but unloosed and pitched the wigwam under a tree outside. Presently the elders appeared bringing, with soft speeches, sweet water, new milk, fat sheep and goats, for which they demanded a Tobe of Cutch canvas. We passed with them a quiet luxurious day of coffee and pipes, fresh cream and roasted mutton: after the plain-heats we enjoyed the cool breeze of the hills, the cloudy sky, and the verdure of the glades, made doubly green by comparison with the parched stubbles below.

The Ísa, here mixed with the Gudabirsi, have little power: we found them poor and proportionally importunate. The men, wild-looking as open mouths, staring eyes, and tangled hair could make them, gazed with extreme eagerness upon my scarlet blanket: for very shame they did not beg it, but the inviting texture was pulled and fingered by the greasy multitude. We closed the hut whenever a valuable was produced, but eager eyes peeped through every cranny, till the End of Time ejaculated " Praised be Allah[1]! " and quoted the Arab saying, " Show not the Somali thy door, and if he find it, block it up! " The women and children were clad in chocolate-coloured hides, fringed at the tops: to gratify them I shot a few hawks, and was rewarded with loud exclamations—" Allah preserve thy hand! "—" May thy skill never fail thee before the foe! " A crone seeing me smoke, inquired if the fire did not burn; I handed my pipe, which nearly choked her, and she ran away from a steaming kettle, thinking it a weapon. As my companions observed, there was not a " Miskal of sense in a Maund of heads: " yet the people looked upon my sun-burnt skin with a favour they denied to the " lime-white face."

I was anxious to proceed in the afternoon, but Raghi had arrived at the frontier of his tribe: he had blood to settle amongst the Gudabirsi, and without a protector he could not enter their lands. At night we slept armed on account of the lions that infest the hills, and our huts were surrounded with a thorn fence—a precaution here first adopted, and never afterwards neglected. Early on the morning of the 4th of December heavy clouds rolled down from the mountains,

---

1 " Subhan' Allah! " an exclamation of pettishness or displeasure.

and a Scotch mist deepened into a shower: our new Abban had not arrived, and the hut-mats, saturated with rain, had become too heavy for the camels to carry.

In the forenoon the Ísa kraal, loading their asses,[1] set out towards the plain. This migration presented no new features, except that several sick and decrepid were barbarously left behind, for lions and hyænas to devour.[2] To deceive "warhawks" who might be on the look-out, the migrators set fire to logs of wood and masses of sheep's earth, which, even in rain, will smoke and smoulder for weeks.

About midday arrived the two Gudabirsi who intended escorting us to the village of our Abbans. The elder, Rirash, was a black-skinned, wild-looking fellow, with a shock head of hair and a deep scowl which belied his good temper and warm heart: the other was a dun-faced youth betrothed to Raghi's daughter. They both belonged to the Mahadasan clan, and commenced operations by an obstinate attempt to lead us far out of our way eastwards. The pretext was the defenceless state of their flocks and herds, the real reason an itching for cloth and tobacco. We resisted manfully this time, nerved by the memory of wasted days, and, despite their declarations of Absi,[3] we determined upon making westward for the hills.

At 2 P.M. the caravan started along the fiumara course in rear of the deserted kraal, and after an hour's ascent Rirash informed us that a well was near. The Hammal and I, taking two water skins, urged our mules

---

1 The hills not abounding in camels, like the maritime regions, asses become the principal means of transport.

2 This barbarous practice is generally carried out in cases of small-pox where contagion is feared.

3 Fear—danger; it is a word which haunts the traveller in Somali-land.

over stones and thorny ground : presently we arrived at
a rocky ravine, where, surrounded by brambles, rude
walls, and tough frame works, lay the wells—three or
four holes sunk ten feet deep in the limestone. Whilst
we bathed in the sulphureous spring, which at once dis-
coloured my silver ring, Rirash, baling up the water in
his shield, filled the bags and bound them to the saddles.
In haste we rejoined the caravan, which we found about
sunset, halted by the vain fears of the guides. The
ridge upon which they stood was a mass of old mosques
and graves, showing that in former days a thick population tenanted these hills : from the summit appeared
distant herds of kine and white flocks scattered like
patches of mountain quartz. Riding in advance, we
traversed the stony ridge, fell into another ravine, and
soon saw signs of human life. A shepherd descried us
from afar and ran away reckless of property : causing
the End of Time to roll his head with dignity, and to
ejaculate, " Of a truth said the Prophet of Allah, 'fear is
divided.'" Presently we fell in with a village, from
which the people rushed out, some exclaiming, " Lo ! let
us look at the kings !" others, " Come, see the white
man, he is governor of Zayla !" I objected to such
dignity, principally on account of its price : my companions, however, were inexorable ; they would be Salatin
—kings—and my colour was against claims to low
degree. This fairness, and the Arab dress, made me at
different times the ruler of Aden, the chief of Zayla, the
Hajj's son, a boy, an old woman, a man painted white, a
warrior in silver armour, a merchant, a pilgrim, a hedge-
priest, Ahmad the Indian, a Turk, an Egyptian, a
Frenchman, a Banyan, a shariff, and lastly a Calamity
sent down from heaven to weary out the lives of the
Somal : every kraal had some conjecture of its own, and
each fresh theory was received by my companions with
roars of laughter.

As the Gudabirsi pursued us with shouts for tobacco and cries of wonder, I dispersed them with a gun-shot: the women and children fled precipitately from the horrid sound, and the men, covering their heads with their shields, threw themselves face foremost upon the ground. Pursuing the fiumara course, we passed a number of kraals, whose inhabitants were equally vociferous : out of one came a Zayla man, who informed us that the Gudabirsi Abbans, to whom we bore Sharmarkay's letter of introduction, were encamped within three days' march. It was reported, however, that a quarrel had broken out between them and the Jirad Adan, their brother-in-law; no pleasant news!—in Africa, under such circumstances, it is customary for friends to detain, and for foes to oppose, the traveller. We rode stoutly on, till the air darkened and the moon tipped the distant hill peaks with a dim mysterious light. I then called a halt: we unloaded on the banks of the Darkaynlay fiumara, so called from a tree which contains a fiery milk, fenced ourselves in—taking care to avoid being trampled upon by startled camels during our sleep, by securing them in a separate but neighbouring inclosure—spread our couches, ate our frugal suppers, and lost no time in falling asleep. We had travelled five hours that day, but the path was winding, and our progress in a straight line was at most eight miles.

And now, dear L., being about to quit the land of the Ísa, I will sketch the tribe.

The Ísa, probably the most powerful branch of the Somali nation, extends northwards to the Wayma family of the Dankali ; southwards to the Gudabirsi, and midway between Zayla and Berberah ; eastwards it is bounded by the sea, and westwards by the Gallas around Harar. It derives itself from Dirr and Aydur, without, however, knowing aught beyond the ancestral names, and is twitted with paganism by its enemies. This tribe, said to number 100,000 shields, is divided into numerous clans :[1] these again split up into minor septs[2] which plunder, and sometimes murder, one another in time of peace.

A fierce and turbulent race of republicans, the Ísa own nominal allegiance to a Ugaz or chief residing in the Hadagali hills.   He is generally called "Roblay"— Prince Rainy—the name or rather title being one of good omen, for a drought here, like a dinner in Europe, justifies the change of a dynasty.   Every kraal has its Oddai (shaykh or head man,) after whose name the settlement, as in Sind and other pastoral lands, is called. He is obeyed only when his orders suit the taste of King Demos, is always superior to his fellows in wealth of cattle, sometimes in talent and eloquence, and in deliberations he is assisted by the Wail or Akil—the Pítzo-council of Southern Africa — elders obeyed on account of their age.   Despite, however, this apparatus

---

1 The Somali Tol or Tul corresponds with the Arabic Kabilah, a tribe ; under it is the Kola or Jilib (Ar. Fakhizah), a clan.   " Gob," is synonymous with the Arabic Kabail, " men of family," opposed to " Gum," the caste-less.   In the following pages I shall speak of the Somali *nation*, the Ísa tribe, the Rer Musa *clan*, and the Rer Galan *sept*, though by no means sure that such verbal graduation is generally recognized.

2 The Ísa, for instance, are divided into—

1. Rer Wardik (the royal clan).	6. Rer Hurroni.
2. Rer Abdullah.	7. Rer Urwena.
3. Rer Musa.	8. Rer Furlabah.
4. Rer Mummasan.	9. Rer Gada.
5. Rer Gulani.	10. Rer Ali Addah.

These are again subdivided : the Rer Musa (numbering half the Ísa), split up, for instance, into—

1. Rer Galan.	4. Rer Dubbah.
2. Rer Harlah.	5. Rer Kul.
3. Rer Gadishah.	6. Rer Gedi.

of rule, the Badawin have lost none of the characteristics recorded in the Periplus : they are still " uncivilized and under no restraint." Every free-born man holds himself equal to his ruler, and allows no royalties or prerogatives to abridge his birthright of liberty.[1] Yet I have observed, that with all their passion for independence, the Somal, when subject to strict rule as at Zayla and Harar, are both apt to discipline and subservient to command.

In character, the Ísa are childish and docile, cunning, and deficient in judgment, kind and fickle, good-humoured and irascible, warm-hearted, and infamous for cruelty and treachery. Even the protector will slay his *protégé*, and citizens married to Ísa girls send their wives to buy goats and sheep from, but will not trust themselves amongst, their connections. " Traitorous as an Ísa," is a proverb at Zayla, where the people tell you that these Badawin with the left hand offer a bowl of milk, and stab with the right. " Conscience," I may observe, does not exist in Eastern Africa, and " Repentance " expresses regret for missed opportunities of mortal crime. Robbery constitutes an honourable man : murder—the more atrocious the midnight crime the better—makes the hero. Honour consists in taking human life : hyæna-like, the Badawin cannot be trusted where blood may be shed. Glory is the having done all manner of harm. Yet the Ísa have their good points : they are not noted liars, and will rarely perjure themselves : they look down upon petty pilfering without violence, and they are generous and hospitable compared with the other Somal. Personally,

---

1 Traces of this turbulent equality may be found amongst the Kafirs in general meetings of the tribe, on the occasion of harvest home, when the chief who at other times destroys hundreds by a gesture, is abused and treated with contempt by the youngest warrior.

I had no reason to complain of them. They were importunate beggars, but a pinch of snuff or a handful of tobacco always made us friends: they begged me to settle amongst them, they offered me sundry wives and —the Somali Badawi, unlike the Arab, readily affiliates strangers to his tribe—they declared that after a few days' residence, I should become one of themselves.

In appearance, the Ísa are distinguished from other Somal by blackness, ugliness of feature, and premature baldness of the temples; they also shave, or rather scrape off with their daggers, the hair high up the nape of the neck. The locks are dyed dun, frizzled, and greased; the Widads or learned men remove them, and none but paupers leave them in their natural state; the mustachioes are clipped close, the straggling whisker is carefully plucked, and the pile—erroneously considered impure— is removed either by vellication, or by passing the limbs through the fire. The eyes of the Badawin, also, are less prominent than those of the citizens: the brow projects in pent-house fashion, and the organ, exposed to bright light, and accustomed to gaze at distant objects, acquires more concentration and power. I have seen amongst them handsome profiles, and some of the girls have fine figures with piquant, if not pretty, features.

Flocks and herds form the true wealth of the Ísa. According to them, sheep and goats are of silver, and the cow of gold: they compare camels to the rock, and believe, like most Moslems, the horse to have been created from the wind. Their diet depends upon the season. In hot weather, when forage and milk dry up, the flocks are slaughtered, and supply excellent mutton ; during the monsun, men become fat, by drinking all day long the produce of their cattle. In the latter article of diet, the Ísa are delicate and curious: they prefer cow's milk, then the goat's, and lastly the ewe's, which the Arab loves best : the first is drunk fresh, and the two latter clotted, whilst the camel's is slightly soured. The townspeople use camel's milk medicinally: according to the Badawin, he who lives on this beverage, and eats the meat for forty-four consecutive days, acquires the animal's strength. It has perhaps less " body " than any other milk, and is deliciously sweet shortly after foaling: presently it loses flavour, and nothing can be more nauseous than the produce of an old camel. The Somal have a name for cream—" Laban "—but they make no use of the article, churning it with the rest of the milk. They have no buffaloes, they shudder at the Tartar idea of mare's-milk, like the Arabs they hold the name Labban[1] a disgrace, and they make it a point of honour not to draw supplies from their cattle during the day.

The life led by these wild people is necessarily monotonous. They rest but little—from 11 P.M. till dawn—and never sleep in the bush for fear of plundering parties. Few begin the day with prayer as Moslems should: for the most part they apply themselves to counting and milking their cattle. The animals, all of which have names,[2] come when called to the pail, and supply the family with a morning meal. Then the warriors, grasping their spears, and sometimes the young women armed only with staves, drive their herds to pasture: the matrons and children, spinning or rope-making, tend the flocks, and the kraal is abandoned to the very young, the old, and the sick. The herdsmen wander about, watching the cattle and tasting nothing but the pure element or a pinch of coarse tobacco. Sometimes they play at Shahh, Shantarah, and other games, of which they are passionately fond: with a board formed of lines traced in the sand, and bits of dry wood

---

1 " Milk-seller."

2 For instance, Anfarr, the " Spotted ; " Tarren, " Wheatflour ; " &c., &c.

or camel's earth acting pieces, they spend hour after hour, every looker-on vociferating his opinion, and catching at the men, till apparently the two players are those least interested in the game. Or, to drive off sleep, they sit whistling to their flocks, or they perform upon the Florimo, a reed pipe generally made at Harar, which has a plaintive sound uncommonly pleasing.[1] In the evening the kraal again resounds with lowing and bleating : the camel's milk is all drunk, the cow's and goat's reserved for butter and ghi, which the women prepare ; the numbers are once more counted, and the animals are carefully penned up for the night. This simple life is varied by an occasional birth and marriage, dance and foray, disease and murder. Their maladies are few and simple ;[2] death generally comes by the spear, and the

---

1 It is used by the northern people, the Abyssinians, Gallas, Adail, Ísa and Gudabirsi ; the southern Somal ignore it.

2 The most dangerous disease is small-pox, which history traces to Eastern Abyssinia, where it still becomes at times a violent epidemic, sweeping off its thousands. The patient, if a man of note, is placed upon the sand, and fed with rice and millet bread till he recovers or dies. The chicken-pox kills many infants; they are treated by bathing in the fresh blood of a sheep, covered with the skin, and exposed to the sun. Smoke and glare, dirt and flies, cold winds and naked extremities, cause ophthalmia, especially in the hills, this disease rarely blinds any save the citizens, and no remedy is known. Dysentery is cured by rice and sour milk, patients also drink clarified cow's butter; and in bad cases the stomach is cauterised, fire and disease, according to the Somal, never co-existing. Hæmorrhoids, when dry, are reduced by a stick, used as a bougie and allowed to remain *in loco* all night. Sometimes the part affected is cupped with a horn and knife, or a leech performs excision. The diet is camels' or goats' flesh and milk ; clarified butter and Bussorah dates —rice and mutton are carefully avoided. For a certain local disease, they use Senna or colocynth, anoint the body with sulphur boiled in ghi, and expose it to the sun, or they leave the patient all night in the dew ; abstinence and perspiration generally effect a cure. For the minor form, the afflicted drink the melted fat of a sheep's tail.

Badawi is naturally long lived.   I have seen Macrobians
hale and strong, preserving their powers and faculties in
spite of eighty and ninety years.

Consumption is a family complaint, and therefore considered incurable ; to use the Somali expression, they address the patient with
" Allah have mercy upon thee ! " not with " Allah cure thee ! "

There are leeches who have secret simples for curing wounds.
Generally the blood is squeezed out, the place is washed with water,
the lips are sewn up and a dressing of astringent leaves is applied.
They have splints for fractures, and they can reduce disloca-
tions. A medical friend at Aden partially dislocated his knee,
which half-a-dozen of the faculty insisted upon treating as a sprain.
Of all his tortures none was more severe than that inflicted by my
Somali visitors. They would look at him, distinguish the complaint,
ask him how long he had been invalided, and hearing the reply—four
months—would break into exclamations of wonder. " In our
country," they cried, " when a man falls, two pull his body and two
his legs, then they tie sticks round it, give him plenty of camel's milk,
and he is well in a month ; " a speech which made friend S. groan in
spirit.

Firing and clarified butter are the farrier's panaceas. Camels
are cured by sheep's head broth, asses by chopping one ear, mules
by cutting off the tail, and horses by ghi or a drench of melted fat.

CHAPTER VI.

FROM THE ZAYLA HILLS TO THE MARAR PRAIRIE.

I HAVE now, dear L., quitted the maritime plain or
first zone, to enter the Ghauts, that threshold of the Æthiopian highlands which, beginning at Tajurrah, sweeps
in semicircle round the bay of Zayla, and falls about
Berberah into the range of mountains which fringes the
bold Somali coast. This chain has been inhabited,
within History's memory, by three distinct races—the
Gallas, the ancient Moslems of Adel, and by the modern
Somal. As usual, however, in the East, it has no
general vernacular name.[1]

The aspect of these Ghauts is picturesque. The
primitive base consists of micaceous granite, with veins
of porphyry and dykes of the purest white quartz:
above lie strata of sandstone and lime, here dun, there
yellow, or of a dull grey, often curiously contorted and
washed clear of vegetable soil by the heavy monsun.
On these heights, which are mostly conoid with rounded
tops, joined by ridges and saddlebacks, various kinds of
Acacia cast a pallid and sickly green, like the olive tree
upon the hills of Provence. They are barren in the cold

---

1 Every hill and peak, ravine and valley, will be known by some
striking epithet: as Borad, the White Hill; Libahlay, the Lions'
Mountain ; and so forth. Comprehensive names are not adapted to
social wants of uncivilized men.

season, and the Nomads migrate to the plains: when the
monsun covers them with rich pastures, the people
revisit their deserted kraals. The kloofs or ravines are
the most remarkable features of this country: in some
places the sides rise perpendicularly, like gigantic walls,
the breadth varying from one hundred yards to half a
mile; in others cliffs and scaurs, sapped at their founda-
tions, encumber the bed, and not unfrequently a broad
band of white sand stretches between two fringes of
emerald green, delightful to look upon after the bare and
ghastly basalt of Southern Arabia. The Jujube grows
to a height already betraying signs of African luxuriance:
through its foliage flit birds, gaudy-coloured as king-
fishers, of vivid red, yellow, and changing-green. I
remarked a long-tailed jay called Gobiyan or Fat,[1]
russet-hued ringdoves, the modest honey-bird, corn
quails, canary-coloured finches, sparrows gay as those
of Surinam, humming-birds with a plume of metallic
lustre, and especially a white-eyed kind of maina, called
by the Somal, Shimbir Load, or the cow-bird. The
Armo-creeper,[2] with large fleshy leaves, pale green, red,
or crimson, and clusters of bright berries like purple
grapes, forms a conspicuous ornament in the valleys.
There is a great variety of the Cactus tribe, some
growing to the height of thirty and thirty-five feet:
of these one was particularly pointed out to me. The
vulgar Somal call it Guraato, the more learned Shajarat

---

1 The Arabs call it Kakatua, and consider it a species of parrot.
The name Cacatoes, is given by the Cape Boers, according to Delegorgue, to the Coliphymus Concolor. The Gobiyan resembles in
shape and flight our magpie; it has a crest and a brown coat with
patches of white, and a noisy note like a frog. It is very cunning
and seldom affords a second shot.

2 The berries of the Armo are eaten by children, and its leaves,
which never dry up, by the people in times of famine; they must be
boiled or the acrid juice will excoriate the mouth.

al-Zakkum : it is the mandrake of these regions, and the round excrescences upon the summits of its fleshy arms are supposed to resemble men's heads and faces.

On Tuesday, the 5th December, we arose at 6 A.M., after a night so dewy that our clothes were drenched, and we began to ascend the Wady Darkaynlay, which winds from east to south. After an hour's march appeared a small cairn of rough stones, called Siyaro, or Mazar,[1] to which each person, in token of honour, added his quotum. The Abban opined that Auliya or holy men had sat there, but the End of Time more sagaciously conjectured that it was the site of some Galla idol or superstitious rite. Presently we came upon the Hills of the White Ant,[2] a characteristic feature in this part of Africa. Here the land has the appearance of a Turkish cemetery on a grand scale : there it seems like a city in ruins : in some places the pillars are truncated into a resemblance to bee-hives, in others they cluster together, suggesting the idea of a portico : whilst many of them, veiled by trees, and overrun with gay creepers, look like the remains of sylvan altars. Generally the hills are conical, and vary in height from four to twelve feet : they are counted by hundreds, and the Somal account for the number by declaring that the insects abandon their home when dry, and commence building another. The older erections are worn away, by wind and rain, to a thin tapering spire, and are frequently hollowed out and arched beneath by rats and ground squirrels. The substance, fine yellow mud, glued by the secretions of the ant, is hard to break : it is pierced sieve-like, by a net-work of tiny shafts. I saw these hills for the first time in the Wady Darkaynlay :

---

1 Siyaro is the Somali corruption of the Arabic Ziyárat, which, synonymous with Mazar, means a place of pious visitation.

2 The Somal call the insect Abor, and its hill Dundumo.

in the interior they are larger and longer than near the maritime regions.

We travelled up the fiumara in a southerly direction till 8 A.M., when the guides led us away from the bed. They anticipated meeting Gudabirsis: pallid with fear, they also trembled with cold and hunger. Anxious consultations were held. One man, Ali—surnamed "Doso," because he did nothing but eat, drink and stand over the fire—determined to leave us: as, however, he had received a tobe for pay, we put a veto upon that proceeding. After a march of two hours, over ground so winding that we had not covered more than three miles, our guides halted under a tree, near a deserted kraal, at a place called Al-Armo, the "Armo-creeper water," or more facetiously Dabadaláshay: from Damal it bore S.W. 190°. One of our Badawin, mounting a mule, rode forward to gather intelligence, and bring back a skin full of water. I asked the End of Time what they expected to hear: he replied with the proverb "News liveth!" The Somal Badawin have a passion for knowing how the world wags. In some of the more desert regions the whole population will follow the wanderer. No traveller ever passes a kraal without planting spear in the ground, and demanding answers to a lengthened string of queries: rather than miss intelligence he will inquire of a woman. Thus it is that news flies through the country. Among the wild Gudabirsi the Russian war was a topic of interest, and at Harar I heard of a violent storm which had damaged the shipping in Bombay Harbour, but a few weeks after the event.

The Badawi returned with an empty skin but a full budget. I will offer you, dear L., a specimen of the "palaver[1]" which is supposed to prove the aphorism that

---

[1] The corrupted Portuguese word used by African travellers; in the Western regions it is called Kelder, and the Arabs term it "Kalam."

all barbarians are orators. Demosthenes leisurely dismounts, advances, stands for a moment cross-legged—the favourite posture in this region—supporting each hand with a spear planted in the ground : thence he slips to squat, looks around, ejects saliva, shifts his quid to behind his ear, places his weapons before him, takes up a bit of stick, and traces lines which he carefully smooths away— it being ill-omened to mark the earth. The listeners sit gravely in a semicircle upon their heels, with their spears, from whose bright heads flashes a ring of troubled light, planted upright, and look steadfastly on his countenance over the upper edges of their shields, with eyes apparently planted, like those of the Blemmyes, in their breasts. When the moment for delivery is come, the head man inquires, " What is the news ? " The informant would communicate the important fact that he has been to the well: he proceeds as follows, noting emphasis by raising his voice, at times about six notes, and often violently striking at the ground in front.

" It is good news, if Allah please ! "

" Wa Sidda ! "—Even so ! respond the listeners, intoning or rather groaning the response.

" I mounted mule this morning."

" Even so ! "

" I departed from ye riding."

" Even so ! "

" *There !* " (with a scream and pointing out the direction with a stick).

" Even so ! "

" *There* I went."

" Even so ! "

" I threaded the wood."

" Even so ! "

" I traversed the sands."

" Even so ! "

" I feared nothing."

" Even so ! "

" At last I came upon cattle tracks."

" Hoo ! hoo!! hoo!!!" (An ominous pause follows this exclamation of astonishment.)

" They were fresh."

" Even so ! "

" So were the earths."

" Even so ! "

" I distinguished the feet of women."

" Even so ! "

" But there were no camels."

" Even so ! "

" At last I saw sticks "—

" Even so ! "

" Stones "—

" Even so ! "

" Water "—

" Even so ! "

" A well ! ! ! "

Then follows the palaver, wherein, as occasionally happens further West, he distinguishes himself who can rivet the attention of the audience for at least an hour without saying anything in particular. The advantage of *their* circumlocution, however, is that by considering a subject in every possible light and phase as regards its cause and effect, antecedents, actualities, and consequences, they are prepared for any emergency which, without the palaver, might come upon them unawares.

Although the thermometer showed summer heat, the air was cloudy and raw blasts poured down from the mountains. At half past 3 P.M. our camels were lazily loaded, and we followed the course of the fiumara, which runs to the W. and S.W. After half an hour's progress, we arrived at the gully in which are the wells, and the guides halted because they descried half-a-dozen youths and boys bathing and washing their Tobes. All,

cattle as well as men, were sadly thirsty : many of us
had been chewing pebbles during the morning, yet,
afraid of demands for tobacco, the Badawin would have
pursued the march without water had I not forced them
to halt. We found three holes in the sand ; one was
dry, a second foul, and the third contained a scanty
supply of the pure element from twenty to twenty-five
feet below the surface. A youth stood in the water and
filled a wicker-pail, which he tossed to a companion
perched against the side half way up : the latter in his
turn hove it to a third, who, catching it at the brink,
threw the contents, by this time half wasted, into the
skin cattle trough. We halted about half an hour to
refresh man and beast, and then resumed our way up
the Wady, quitting it where a short cut avoids the
frequent windings of the bed. This operation saved
but little time ; the ground was stony, the rough ascents
fatigued the camels, and our legs and feet were lacerated
by the spear-like thorns. Here, the ground was overgrown with aloes,[1] sometimes six feet high with pink and
" pale Pomona green " leaves, bending in the line of
beauty towards the ground, graceful in form as the
capitals of Corinthian columns, and crowned with gay-
coloured bells, but barbarously supplied with woody
thorns and strong serrated edges. There the Hig, an
aloetic plant with a point so hard and sharp that horses
cannot cross ground where it grows, stood in bunches
like the largest and stiffest of rushes.[2] Senna sprang

---

[1] Three species of the Dar or Aloe grow everywhere in the
higher regions of the Somali country. The first is called Dar Main,
the inside of its peeled leaf is chewed when water cannot be procured.
The Dar Murodi or Elephant's aloe is larger and useless : the Dar
Digwen or Long-eared resembles that of Socotra.

[2] The Hig is called " Salab " by the Arabs, who use its long
tough fibre for ropes. Patches of this plant situated on moist
ground at the foot of hills, are favourite places with sand antelope,
spur-fowl and other game.

spontaneously on the banks, and the gigantic Ushr or Asclepias shed its bloom upon the stones and pebbles of the bed. My attendants occupied themselves with gathering the edible pod of an Acacia called Kura,[1] whilst I observed the view. Frequent ant-hills gave an appearance of habitation to a desert still covered with the mosques and tombs of old Adel; and the shape of the country had gradually changed, basins and broad slopes now replacing the thickly crowded conoid peaks of the lower regions.

As the sun sank towards the west, Long Gulad complained bitterly of the raw breeze from the hills. We passed many villages, distinguished by the barking of dogs and the bleating of flocks, on their way to the field: the unhappy Raghi, however, who had now become our *protégé*, would neither venture into a settlement, nor bivouac amongst the lions. He hurried us forwards till we arrived at a hollow called Gud, "the Hole," which supplied us with the protection of a deserted kraal, where our camels, half-starved and knocked-up by an eight miles' march, were speedily unloaded. Whilst pitching the tent, we were visited by some Gudabirsi, who attempted to seize our Abban, alleging that he owed them a cow. We replied doughtily, that he was under our sandals: as they continued to speak in a high tone, a pistol was discharged over their heads, after which they cringed like dogs. A blazing fire, a warm supper, dry beds, broad jests, and funny stories, soon restored the flagging spirits of our party. Towards night the moon dispersed the thick mists which, gathering into clouds, threatened rain, and the cold sensibly diminished: there was little dew, and we

---

1 The Damel or pod has a sweetish taste, not unlike that of a withered pea; pounded and mixed with milk or ghi, it is relished by the Badawin when vegetable food is scarce.

should have slept comfortably had not our hungry mules hobbled as they were, hopped about the kraal and fought till dawn.

On the 6th December, we arose late to avoid the cold morning air, and at 7 A.M. set out over rough ground, hoping to ascend the Ghauts that day. After creeping about two miles, the camels unable to proceed, threw themselves upon the earth, and we unwillingly called a halt at Jiyaf, a basin below the Dobo[1] fiumara. Here, white flocks dotting the hills, and the scavengers of the air warned us that we were in the vicinity of villages. Our wigwam was soon full of fair-faced Gudabirsi, mostly Loajira[2] or cow-herd boys, who, according to the custom of their class, wore their Tobes bound scarf-like round their necks. They begged us to visit their village, and offered a heifer for each lion shot on Mount Libahlay: unhappily we could not afford time. These youths were followed by men and women bringing milk, sheep, and goats, for which, grass being rare, they asked exorbitant prices—eighteen cubits of Cutch canvas for a lamb, and two of blue cotton for a bottle of ghi. Amongst them was the first really pretty face seen by me in the Somali country. The head was well formed, and gracefully placed upon a long thin neck and narrow shoulders; the hair, brow, and nose were unexceptionable, there was an arch look in the eyes of jet and pearl, and a suspicion of African protuberance about the lips, which gave the countenance an exceeding *naïveté.* Her skin was a warm, rich nut-brown, an especial charm in these regions, and her movements had that grace which suggests perfect symmetry of limb. The poor girl's costume, a coif for the back

---

1 Dobo in the Somali tongue signifies mud or clay.

2 The Loajira (from "Loh," a cow) is a neatherd; the "Geljira" is the man who drives camels.

hair, a cloth imperfectly covering the bosom, and a
petticoat of hides, made no great mystery of forms:
equally rude were her ornaments ; an armlet and
pewter earrings, the work of some blacksmith, a necklace of white porcelain beads, and sundry talismans
in cases of tarnished and blackened leather. As a
tribute to her prettiness I gave her some cloth, tobacco,
and a bit of salt, which was rapidly becoming valuable :
her husband stood by, and, although the preference was
marked, he displayed neither anger nor jealousy. She
showed her gratitude by bringing us milk, and by
assisting us to start next morning. In the evening we
hired three fresh camels[1] to carry our goods up the
ascent, and killed some antelopes which, in a stew,
were not contemptible. The End of Time insisted
upon firing a gun to frighten away the lions, who make
night hideous with their growls, but never put in an
appearance.

The morning cold greatly increased, and we did not
start till 8 A.M. After half an hour's march up the bed of a
fiumara, leading apparently to a *cul de sac* of lofty rocks in
the hills, we quitted it for a rude zig-zag winding along its
left side, amongst bushes, thorn trees and huge rocks. The
walls of the opposite bank were strikingly perpendicular!
in some places stratified, in others solid and polished by
the course of stream and cascade. The principal material
was a granite, so coarse, that the composing mica, quartz,
and felspar separated into detached pieces as large as a
man's thumb; micaceous grit, which glittered in the
sunbeams, and various sandstones, abounded. The road
caused us some trouble ; the camels' loads were always
slipping from their mats; I found it necessary to dismount

---

1 For these we paid twenty-four cubits of canvas, and two of
blue cotton ; equivalent to about three shillings.

from my mule, and, sitting down, we were stung by the
large black ants which infest these hills.[1]

About half way up, we passed two cairns, and added
to them our mite like good Somal. After two hours of hard
work the summit of this primitive pass was attained, and
sixty minutes more saw us on the plateau above the hills—
the second zone of East Africa. Behind us lay the plains,
of which we vainly sought a view : the broken ground at
the foot of the mountains is broad, and mists veiled the
reeking expanse of the low country.[2] The plateau in
front of us was a wide extent of rolling ground, rising
slightly towards the west ; its colour was brown with a
threadbare coat of verdure, and at the bottom of each
rugged slope ran a stony water-course trending from south-
west to north-east. The mass of tangled aloes, ragged
thorn, and prim-looking poison trees,[3] must once have been

---

1 The natives call them Jana ; they are about three-fourths of
an inch long, and armed with stings that prick like thorns and burn
violently for a few minutes.

2 Near Berberah, where the descents are more rapid, such
panoramas are common.

3 This is the celebrated Wăbá, which produces the Somali
Wăbáyo, a poison applied to darts and arrows. It is a round stiff
evergreen, not unlike a bay, seldom taller than twenty feet,
affecting hill sides and torrent banks, growing in clumps that look
black by the side of the Acacias ; thornless, with a laurel-coloured
leaf, which cattle will not touch, unless forced by famine, pretty
bunches of pinkish-white flowers, and edible berries black and
ripening to red. The bark is thin, the wood yellow, compact,
exceedingly tough and hard, the root somewhat like liquorice ; the
latter is prepared by trituration and other processes, and the
produce is a poison in substance and colour resembling pitch.
Travellers have erroneously supposed the arrow poison of
Eastern Africa to be the sap of a Euphorbium. The following
" observations accompanying a substance procured near Aden, and
used by the Somalis to poison their arrows," by F. S. Arnott, Esq.,
M.D., will be read with interest.

populous; tombs and houses of the early Moslems covered with ruin the hills and ridges.

About noon, we arrived at a spot called the Kafir's Grave. It is a square enceinte of rude stones about one

---

" In February 1853, Dr. Arnott had forwarded to him a watery extract prepared from the root of a tree, described as ' Wabie,' a toxicodendron from the Somali country on the Habr Gerhajis range of the Goolies mountains. The tree grows to the height of twenty feet. The poison is obtained by boiling the root in water, until it attains the consistency of an inspissated juice. When cool the barb of the arrow is anointed with the juice, which is regarded as a virulent poison, and it renders a wound tainted therewith incurable. Dr. Arnott was informed that death usually took place within an hour; that the hairs and nails dropped off after death, and it was believed that the application of heat assisted its poisonous qualities. He could not, however, ascertain the quantity made use of by the Somalis, and doubted if the point of an arrow would convey a sufficient quantity to produce such immediate effects. He had tested its powers in some other experiments, besides the ones detailed, and although it failed in several instances, yet he was led to the conclusion that it was a very powerful narcotic irritant poison. He had not, however, observed the local effect said to be produced upon the point of insertion."

" The following trials were described :—

" 1. A little was inserted into the inside of the ear of a sickly sheep, and death occurred in two hours.

" 2. A little was inserted into the inside of the ear of a healthy sheep, and death occurred in two hours preceded by convulsions.

" 3. Five grains were given to a dog ; vomiting took place after an hour, and death in three or four hours.

" 4. One grain was swallowed by a fowl, but no effect produced.

" 5. Three grains were given to a sheep, but without producing any effect.

" 6. A small quantity was inserted into the ear and shoulder of a dog, but no effect was produced.

" 7. Upon the same dog two days after, the same quantity was inserted into the thigh ; death occurred in less than two hours.

" 8. Seven grains were given to a sheep without any effect whatever.

hundred yards each side ; and legends say that one Misr, a Galla chief, when dying, ordered the place to be filled seven times with she-camels destined for his Ahan or funeral feast.   This is the fourth stage upon the direct

---

" 9. To a dog five grains were administered, but it was rejected by vomiting ; this was again repeated on the following day, with the same result.   On the same day four grains were inserted into a wound upon the same dog ; it produced violent effects in ten, and death in thirty-five minutes.

" 10. To a sheep two grains in solution were given without any effect being produced.   The post-mortem appearances observed were, absence of all traces of inflammation, collapse of the lungs, and distension of the cavities of the heart."

Further experiments of the Somali arrow poisoned by R. Haines, M.B., assistant surgeon (from Transactions of the Medical and Physical Society of Bombay.   No. 2, new series 1853-1854).

" Having while at Ahmednuggur received from the secretary a small quantity of Somali arrow poison, alluded to by Mr. Vaughan in his notes on articles of the Materia Medica, and published in the last volume of the Society's Transactions, and called ' Wabie,' the following experiments were made with it :—

" September 17th.   1. A small healthy rabbit was taken, and the skin over the hip being divided, a piece of the poisonous extract about the size of a corn of wheat was inserted into the cellular tissue beneath : thirty minutes afterwards, seems disinclined to move, breathing quicker, passed * * : one hour, again passed * * * followed by * * * ; has eaten a little : one hour and a half, appears quite to have recovered from his uneasiness, and has become as lively as before.   (This rabbit was made use of three days afterwards for the third experiment.)

" 2. A full-grown rabbit.   Some of the poison being dissolved in water a portion of the solution corresponding to about fifteen grains was injected into an opening in the peritoneum, so large a quantity being used, in consequence of the apparent absence of effect in the former case : five minutes, he appears to be in pain, squeaking occasionally ; slight convulsive retractions of the head and neck begin to take place, passed a small quantity of * * : ten minutes, the spasms are becoming more frequent, but are neither violent nor prolonged, respiration scarcely preceptible ; he now fell

road from Zayla to Harar: we had wasted ten days, and the want of grass and water made us anxious about our animals. The camels could scarcely walk, and my mule's spine rose high beneath the Arab pad:—such are

---

on his side: twelve minutes, several severe general convulsions came on, and at the end of another minute he was quite dead, the pulsation being for the last minute quite imperceptible. The chest was instantly opened, but there was no movement of the heart whatever.

"September 20th. 3. The rabbit used for the first experiment was taken and an attempt was made to inject a little filtered solution into the jugular vein, which failed from the large size of the nozzle of the syringe; a good deal of blood was lost. A portion of the solution corresponding to about two grains and a half of the poison was then injected into a small opening made in the pleura. Nine minutes afterwards: symptoms precisely resembling those in number two began to appear. Fourteen minutes: convulsions more violent; fell on his side. Sixteen minutes, died.

"4. A portion of the poison, as much as could be applied, was smeared over the square iron head of an arrow, and allowed to dry. The arrow was then shot into the buttock of a goat with sufficient force to carry the head out of sight; twenty minutes afterwards, no effect whatever having followed, the arrow was extracted. The poison had become softened and was wiped completely off two of the sides, and partly off the two other sides. The animal appeared to suffer very little pain from the wound; it was kept for a fortnight, and then died, but not apparently from any cause connected with the wound. In fact it was previously diseased. Unfortunately the seat of the wound was not then examined, but a few days previously it appeared to have healed of itself. In the rabbit of the former experiment, three days after the insertion of the poison in the wound, the latter was closed with a dry coagulum and presented no marks of inflammation around it.

"5. Two good-sized village dogs being secured, to each after several hours' fasting, were given about five grains enveloped in meat. The smaller one chewed it a long time, and frothed much at the mouth. He appeared to swallow very little of it, but the larger one ate the whole up without difficulty. After more than two hours no effect whatever being perceptible in either animal, they were shot to get rid of them. These experiments, though not altogether complete, certainly establish the fact that it is a poison of no very great activity.

the effects of Jílál,[1] the worst of travelling seasons in Eastern Africa.

The quantity made use of in the second experiment was too great to allow a fair deduction to be made as to its properties. When a fourth to a sixth of the quantity was employed in the third experiment the same effects followed, but with rather less rapidity; death resulting in the one case in ten, in the other in sixteen minutes, although the death in the latter case was perhaps hastened by the loss of blood. The symptoms more resemble those produced by nux vomica than by any other agent. No apparent drowsiness, spasms, slight at first, beginning in the neck, increasing in intensity, extending over the whole body, and finally stopping respiration and with it the action of the heart. Experiments first and fourth show that a moderate quantity, such as may be introduced on the point of an arrow, produced no sensible effect either on a goat or a rabbit, and it could scarcely be supposed that it would have more on a man than on the latter animal; and the fifth experiment proves that a full dose taken into the stomach produces no result within a reasonable time.

" The extract appeared to have been very carelessly prepared. It contained much earthy matter, and even small stones, and a large proportion of what seemed to be oxidized extractive matter also was left undisturbed when it was treated with water: probably it was not a good specimen. It seems, however, to keep well, and shows no disposition to become mouldy."

1 The Somal divide their year into four seasons:—

1. Gugi (monsun, from " Gug," rain) begins in April, is violent for forty-four days and subsides in August. Many roads may be traversed at this season, which are death in times of drought ; the country becomes " Barwáko " (in Arabic, Rakha, a place of plenty), forage and water abound, the air is temperate, and the light showers enliven the traveller.

2. Hagá is the hot season after the monsun, and corresponding with our autumn : the country suffers from the Fora, a violent dusty Samun, which is allayed by a fall of rain called Karan.

3. Dáir, the beginning of the cold season, opens the sea to shipping. The rain which then falls is called Diarti or Hais : it comes with a west-south-west wind from the hills of Harar.

4. Jílál is the dry season from December to April. The country then becomes Abar (in Arabic, Jahr), a place of famine : the Nomads migrate to the low plains, where pasture is procurable. Some reckon as a fifth season, Kalíl, or the heats between Jílál and the monsun.

At 1 P.M. we unloaded under a sycamore tree, called, after a Galla chieftain,[1] "Halimalah," and giving its name to the surrounding valley. This ancient of the forest is more than half decayed, several huge limbs lie stretched upon the ground, whence, for reverence, no one removes them : upon the trunk, or rather trunks, for it bifurcates, are marks deeply cut by a former race, and Time has hollowed in the larger stem an arbour capable of containing half-a-dozen men. This holy tree was, according to the Somal, a place of prayer for the infidel, and its ancient honours are not departed. Here, probably to commemorate the westward progress of the tribe, the Gudabirsi Ugaz or chief has the white canvas turband bound about his brows, and hence rides forth to witness the equestrian games in the Harawwah Valley. As everyone who passes by, visits the Halimalah tree, foraging parties of the Northern Ísa and the Jibril Abokr (a clan of the Habr Awal) frequently meet, and the traveller wends his way in fear and trembling.

The thermometer showed an altitude of 3,350 feet : under the tree's cool shade, the climate reminded me of Southern Italy in winter. I found a butter-cup, and heard a wood-pecker[2] tapping on the hollow trunk, a reminiscence of English glades. The Abban and his men urged an advance in the afternoon. But my health had suffered from the bad water of the coast, and the camels were faint with fatigue : we therefore dismissed the hired beasts, carried our property into a deserted kraal, and, lighting a fire, prepared to "make all snug"

---

1 According to Bruce this tree flourishes everywhere on the low hot plains between the Red Sea and the Abyssinian hills. The Gallas revere it and plant it over sacerdotal graves. It suggests the Fetish trees of Western Africa, and the Hiero-Sykaminon of Egypt.

2 There are two species of this bird, both called by the Somal, "Daudaulay" from their tapping.

for the night. The Badawin, chattering with cold, stood
closer to the comfortable blaze than ever did paterfamilias in England: they smoked their faces, toasted
their hands, broiled their backs with intense enjoyment,
and waved their legs to and fro through the flame to
singe away the pile, which at this season grows long.
The End of Time, who was surly, compared them to
demons, and quoted the Arab's saying:—" Allah never
bless smooth man, or hairy woman!"

On the 8th of December, at 8 A.M., we travelled
slowly up the Halimalah Valley, whose clayey surface
glistened with mica and quartz pebbles from the hills.
All the trees are thorny except the Sycamore and the
Asclepias. The Gub, or Jujube, grows luxuriantly in
thickets: its dried wood is used by women to fumigate
their hair[1]: the Kedi, a tree like the porcupine—all
spikes—supplies the Badawin with hatchet-handles. I
was shown the Abol with its edible gum, and a kind of
Acacia, here called Galol. Its bark dyes cloth a dull
red, and the thorn issues from a bulb which, when
young and soft, is eaten by the Somal, when old it
becomes woody, and hard as a nut. At 9 A.M. we
crossed the Lesser Abbaso, a fiumara with high banks
of stiff clay and filled with large rolled stones: issuing
from it, we traversed a thorny path over ascending
ground between higher hills, and covered with large
boulders and step-like layers of grit. Here appeared
several Gudabirsi tombs, heaps of stones or pebbles,
surrounded by a fence of thorns, or an enceinte of loose
blocks: in the latter, slabs are used to make such houses
as children would build in play, to denote the number
of establishments left by the deceased. The new grave
is known by the conical milk-pails surmounting the stick

---

1 The limbs are perfumed with the " Hedi," and " Karanli,"
products of the Ugadayn or southern country.

at the head of the corpse, upon the neighbouring tree is thrown the mat which bore the dead man to his last home, and hard by are the blackened stones upon which his funeral feast was cooked. At 11 A.M. we reached the Greater Abbaso, a fiumara about 100 yards wide, fringed with lovely verdure and full of the antelope called Gurnuk : its watershed was, as usual in this region, from west and south-west to east and north-east. About noon we halted, having travelled eight miles from the Holy Tree.

At half past three reloading we followed the course of the Abbaso Valley, the most beautiful spot we had yet seen. The presence of mankind, however, was denoted by the cut branches of thorn encumbering the bed : we remarked too, the tracks of lions pursued by hunters, and the frequent streaks of serpents, sometimes five inches in diameter. Towards evening our party closed up in fear, thinking that they saw spears glancing through the trees : I treated their alarm lightly, but the next day proved that it was not wholly imaginary. At sunset we met a shepherd who swore upon the stone[1] to bring us milk in exchange for tobacco, and presently, after a five miles' march, we halted in a deserted kraal on the left bank of a fiumara. Clouds gathered black upon the hill tops, and a comfortless blast, threatening rain, warned us not to delay pitching the Gurgi. A large fire was lighted, and several guns were discharged to frighten away the lions that infest this place. Twice during the night our

---

[1] This great oath suggests the litholatry of the Arabs, derived from the Abyssinian and Galla Sabæans ; it is regarded by the Ísa and Gudabirsi Badawin as even more binding than the popular religious adjurations. When a suspected person denies his guilt, the judge places a stone before him saying " Tabo ! " (feel !) ; the liar will seldom dare to touch it. Sometimes a Somali will take up a stone and say " Dagáhá," (it is a stone), he may then generally be believed.

camels started up and rushed round their thorn ring in
alarm.

Late in the morning of Saturday, the 9th December,
I set out accompanied by Rirash and the End of Time,
to visit some ruins a little way distant from the direct road.
After an hour's ride we turned away from the Abbaso
Fiumara and entered a basin among the hills distant
about sixteen miles from the Holy Tree. This is the site
of Darbiyah Kola—Kola's Fort—so called from its
Galla queen. It is said that this city and its neighbour
Aububah fought like certain cats in Kilkenny till both
were "eaten up": the Gudabirsi fix the event at the
period when their forefathers still inhabited Bulhar on
the coast—about 300 years ago. If the date be correct, the
substantial ruins have fought a stern fight with time.
Remnants of houses cumber the soil, and the carefully built
wells are filled with rubbish : the palace was pointed out
to me with its walls of stone and clay intersected by layers
of wood work. The mosque is a large roofless building
containing twelve square pillars of rude masonry, and
the Mihrab, or prayer niche, is denoted by a circular arch
of tolerable construction. But the voice of the Muezzin
is hushed for ever, and creepers now twine round the ruined
fane. The scene was still and dreary as the grave; for a
mile and a half in length all was ruins—ruins—ruins.

Leaving this dead city, we rode towards the south-
west between two rugged hills of which the loftiest summit
is called Wanauli. As usual they are rich in thorns : the
tall "Wadi" affords a gum useful to cloth-dyers, and
the leaves of the lofty Wumba are considered, after the
Daum-palm, the best material for mats. On the ground
appeared the blue flowers of the "Man" or "Himbah,"[1]
a shrub resembling a potato : it bears a gay yellow apple
full of brown seeds which is not eaten by the Somal. My
companions made me taste some of the Karir berries,

---

1 The wild egg-plant, known all over Zanzibar and the East coast.

which in colour and flavour resemble red currants : the leaves are used as a dressing to ulcers. Topping the ridge we stood for a few minutes to observe the view before us. Beneath our feet lay a long grassy plain—the sight must have gladdened the hearts of our starving mules!—and for the first time in Africa horses appeared grazing free amongst the bushes. A little further off lay the Aylonda valley studded with graves, and dark with verdure. Beyond it stretched the Wady Harawwah, a long gloomy hollow in the general level. The background was a bold sweep of blue hill, the second gradient of the Harar line, and on its summit closing the western horizon lay a golden streak—the Marar Prairie. Already I felt at the end of my journey.

About noon, reaching a kraal, whence but that morning our Gudabirsi Abbans had driven off their kine, we sat under a tree and with a pistol reported arrival. Presently the elders came out and welcomed their old acquaintance the End of Time as a distinguished guest. He eagerly inquired about the reported quarrel between the Abbans and their brother-in-law the Jirad Adan. When assured that it was the offspring of Somali imagination, he rolled his head, and with dignity remarked, " What man shutteth to us, that Allah openeth ! " We complimented each other gravely upon the purity of our intentions—amongst Moslems a condition of success—and not despising second causes, lost no time in sending a horseman for the Abbans. Presently some warriors came out and inquired if we were of the Caravan that was travelling last evening up a valley with laden camels. On our answering in the affirmative, they laughingly declared that a commando of twelve horsemen had followed us with the intention of a sham-attack. This is favourite sport with the Badawin. When however the traveller shows fright, the feint is apt to turn out a fact. On one occasion a party of Arab merchants, not understanding the "fun of the thing," shot two Somal: the tribe had the justice to acquit the strangers, mulcting them, however, a few yards of cloth for the families of the deceased. In reply I fired a pistol unexpectedly over the heads of my new hosts, and improved the occasion of their terror by deprecating any practical facetiousness in future.

We passed the day under a tree: the camels escorted by my two attendants, and the women, did not arrive till sunset, having occupied about eight hours in marching as many miles. Fearing lions, we pitched inside the kraal, despite crying children, scolding wives, cattle rushing about, barking dogs, flies and ticks, filth and confinement. I will now attempt a description of a village in Eastern Africa.

The Rer or Kraal[1] is a line of scattered huts on plains where thorns are rare, beasts of prey scarce, and raids not expected. In the hills it is surrounded by a strong fence to prevent cattle straying : this, when danger induces caution, is doubled and trebled. Yet the lion will sometimes break through it, and the leopard clears it, prey in mouth, with a bound. The abattis has usually four entrances which are choked up with heaps of bushes at night. The interior space is partitioned off by dwarf hedges into rings, which contain and separate the different species of cattle. Sometimes there is an outer compartment adjoining the exterior fence, set apart for the camels ; usually they are placed in the centre of the kraal. Horses being most valuable are side-lined and tethered close to the owner's hut, and rude bowers of brush and fire wood protect the weaklings of the flocks from the heat of the sun and the inclement night breeze.

At intervals around and inside the outer abattis are built the Gurgi or wigwams—hemispheric huts like old bee-hives about five feet high by six in diameter : they

---

1 Kariyah is the Arabic word.

are even smaller in the warm regions, but they increase in size as the elevation of the country renders climate less genial. The material is a framework of "Digo," or sticks bent and hardened in the fire : to build the hut, these are planted in the ground, tied together with cords, and covered with mats of two different kinds : the Aus composed of small bundles of grass neatly joined, is hard and smooth ; the Kibid has a long pile and is used as couch as well as roof. The single entrance in front is provided with one of these articles which serves as a curtain; hides are spread upon the top during the monsun, and little heaps of earth are sometimes raised outside to keep out wind and rain.

The furniture is simple as the building. Three stones and a hole form the fireplace, near which sleep the children, kids, and lambs : there being no chimney, the interior is black with soot. The cow-skin couches are suspended during the day, like arms and other articles which suffer from rats and white ants, by loops of cords to the sides. The principal ornaments are basket-work bottles, gaily adorned with beads, cowries, and stained leather. Pottery being here unknown, the Badawin twist the fibres of the root into various shapes, and make them water-tight with the powdered bark of another tree.[1] The Han is a large wicker-work bucket, mounted in a framework of sticks, and used to contain water on journeys. The Guraf (a word derived from the Arabic "Ghurfah") is a conical-shaped vessel, used to bale out the contents of a well. The Del, or milk-pail, is shaped like two cones joined at the base by lateral thongs, the upper and smaller half acting as cup and cover. And finally the Wesi, or water bottle, contains the traveller's store for drinking and religious ablution.

---

1 In the northern country the water-proofing matter is, according to travellers, the juice of the Quolquol, a species of Euphorbia.

When the kraal is to be removed, the huts and furniture are placed upon the camels, and the hedges and earth are sometimes set on fire, to purify the place and deceive enemies. Throughout the country black circles of cinders or thorn diversify the hill sides, and show an extensive population. Travellers always seek deserted kraals for security of encampment. As they swarm with vermin by night and flies by day,[1] I frequently made strong objections to these favourite localities: the utmost conceded to me was a fresh enclosure added by a smaller hedge to the outside abattis of the more populous cow-kraals.

On the 10th December we halted: the bad water, the noonday sun of 107°, and the cold mornings—51° being the average—had seriously affected my health. All the population flocked to see me, darkening the hut with nodding wigs and staring faces : and—Gudabirsi are polite knaves—apologized for the intrusion. Men, women, and children appeared in crowds, bringing milk and ghi, meat and water, several of the elders remembered having seen me at Berberah,[2] and the blear-eyed maidens, who were in no wise shy, insisted upon admiring the white stranger.

Feeling somewhat restored by repose, I started the next day, "with a tail on" to inspect the ruins of Aububah. After a rough ride over stony ground we arrived at a grassy hollow, near a line of hills, and dismounted to visit the Shaykh Aububah's remains.

---

1 The flies are always most troublesome where cows have been; kraals of goats and camels are comparatively free from the nuisance.

2 Some years ago a French lady landed at Berberah : her white face, according to the End of Time, made every man hate his wife, and every wife hate herself. I know not who the fair dame was : her charms and black silk dress, however, have made a lasting impression upon the Somali heart ; from the coast to Harar she is still remembered with rapture.

He rests under a little conical dome of brick, clay and wood, similar in construction to that of Zayla : it is falling to pieces, and the adjoining mosque, long roofless, is overgrown with trees, that rustle melancholy sounds in the light joyous breeze. Creeping in by a dwarf door or rather hole, my Gudabirsi guides showed me a bright object forming the key of the arch: as it shone they suspected silver, and the End of Time whispered a sacrilegious plan for purloining it. Inside the vault were three graves apparently empty, and upon the dark sunken floor lay several rounded stones, resembling cannon balls, and used as weights by the more civilised Somal. Thence we proceeded to the battle-field, a broad sheet of sandstone, apparently dinted by the hoofs of mules and horses : on this ground, which, according to my guides, was in olden days soft and yielding, took place the great action between Aububah and Darbiyah Kola. A second mosque was found with walls in tolerable repair, but, like the rest of the place, roofless. Long Gulad ascended the broken staircase of a small square minaret, and delivered a most ignorant and Badawi-like Azan or call to prayer. Passing by the shells of houses, we concluded our morning's work with a visit to the large graveyard. Apparently it did not contain the bones of Moslems : long lines of stones pointed westward, and one tomb was covered with a coating of hard mortar, in whose sculptured edge my benighted friends detected magical inscriptions. I heard of another city called Ahammad in the neighbouring hills, but did not visit it. These are all remains of Galla settlements, which the ignorance and exaggeration of the Somal fill with "writings" and splendid edifices.

Returning home we found that our Gudabirsi Badawin had at length obeyed the summons. The six sons of a noted chief, Ali Addah or White Ali, by three different mothers, Beuh, Igah, Khayri, Nur, Ismail and Yunis, all advanced towards me as I dismounted, gave the hand of friendship, and welcomed me to their homes.   With the exception of the first-named, a hard-featured man at least forty years old, the brothers were good-looking youths, with clear brown skins, regular features, and graceful figures.   They entered the Gurgi when invited, but refused to eat, saying, that they came for honour not for food.   The Hajj Sharmarkay's introductory letter was read aloud to their extreme delight, and at their solicitation, I perused it a second and a third time ; then having dismissed, with sundry small presents, the two Abbans Raghi and Rirash, I wrote a flattering account of them to the Hajj, and entrusted it to certain citizens who were returning in caravan Zayla-wards, after a commercial tour in the interior.

Before they departed, there was a feast after the Homeric fashion.   A sheep was " cut," disembowelled, dismembered, tossed into one of our huge cauldrons, and devoured within the hour: the almost live food[1] was washed down with huge draughts of milk.   The feasters resembled Wordsworth's cows, " forty feeding like one": in the left hand they held the meat to their teeth, and cut off the slice in possession with long daggers perilously close, were their noses longer and their mouths less obtrusive.   During the dinner I escaped from the place of flies, and retired to a favourite tree.   Here the End of Time seeing me still in pain, insisted upon trying a Somali medicine.   He cut two pieces of dry wood, scooped a hole in the shorter, and sharpened the longer, applied point to socket, which he sprinkled with a little sand, placed his

---

1 The Abyssinian Brindo of omophagean fame is not eaten by the Somal, who always boil, broil, or sun-dry their flesh. They have, however, no idea of keeping it, whereas the more civilized citizens of Harar hang their meat till tender.

foot upon the "female stick," and rubbed the other between his palms till smoke and char appeared. He then cauterized my stomach vigorously in six different places, quoting a tradition, "the End of Physic is Fire."

On Tuesday the 12th December, I vainly requested the two sons of White Ali, who had constituted themselves our guides, to mount their horses : they feared to fatigue the valuable animals at a season when grass is rare and dry. I was disappointed by seeing the boasted " Faras"[1] of the Somal, in the shape of ponies hardly thirteen hands high. The head is pretty, the eyes are well opened, and the ears are small; the form also is good, but the original Arab breed has degenerated in the new climate. They are soft, docile and—like all other animals in this part of the world—timid: the habit of climbing rocks makes them sure-footed, and they show the remains of blood when forced to fatigue. The Gudabirsi will seldom sell these horses, the great safeguard against their conterminous tribes, the Ísa and Girhi, who are all infantry: a village seldom contains more than six or eight, and the lowest value would be ten cows or twenty Tobes.[2] Careful of his beast when at rest, the Somali Badawi in the saddle is rough and cruel: whatever beauty the animal may possess in youth, completely disappears before the fifth year, and few are without spavin, or sprained back-sinews. In some parts of the country,[3] " to ride

---

1 Whilst other animals have indigenous names, the horse throughout the Somali country retains the Arab appellation " Faras." This proves that the Somal, like their progenitors, the Gallas, originally had no cavalry. The Gudabirsi tribe has but lately mounted itself by making purchases of the Habr Girhajis and the Habr Awal herds.

2 The milch cow is here worth two Tobes or about six shillings.

3 Particularly amongst the windward tribes visited by Lieut. Cruttenden, from whom I borrow this description.

violently to your hut two or three times before finally dismounting, is considered a great compliment, and the same ceremony is observed on leaving.   Springing into the saddle (if he has one), with the aid of his spear, the Somali cavalier first endeavours to infuse a little spirit into his half-starved hack by persuading him to accomplish a few plunges and capers : then, his heels raining a hurricane of blows against the animal's ribs, and occasionally using his spear-point as a spur, away he gallops, and after a short circuit, in which he endeavours to show himself to the best advantage, returns to his starting point at full speed, when the heavy Arab bit brings up the blown horse with a shock that half breaks his jaw and fills his mouth with blood.   The affection of the true Arab for his horse is proverbial: the cruelty of the Somali to his, may I think be considered equally so."   The Badawin practise horse-racing, and run for bets, which are contested with ardour : on solemn occasions, they have rude equestrian games, in which they display themselves and their animals.   The Gudabirsi, and indeed most of the Somal, sit loosely upon their horses.   Their saddle is a demi-pique, a high-backed wooden frame, like the Egyptian fellah's : two light splinters leave a clear space for the spine, and the tree is tightly bound with wet thongs : a sheepskin shabracque is loosely spread over it, and the drawf iron stirrup admits only the big toe, as these people fear a stirrup which, if the horse fall, would entangle the foot.   Their bits are cruelly severe ; a solid iron ring, as in the Arab bridle embracing the lower jaw takes the place of a curb chain.   Some of the head-stalls, made at Berberah, are prettily made of cut leather and bright steel ornaments like diminutive quoits.   The whip is a hard hide handle, plated with zinc, and armed with a single short broad thong.

With the two sons of White Ali and the End of Time, at 8 A.M., on the 12th December, I rode forward,

leaving the jaded camels in charge of my companions and
the women. We crossed the plain in a south-westerly
direction, and after traversing rolling ground, we came to
a ridge, which commanded an extensive view. Behind
lay the Wanauli Hills, already purple in the distance.
On our left was a mass of cones, each dignified by its own
name; no one, it is said, can ascend them, which
probably means that it would be a fatiguing walk. Here
are the visitation-places of three celebrated saints, Amud,
Sau, and Shaykh Sharlagamadi, or the "Hidden from
Evil." To the north-west I was shown some blue
peaks tenanted by the Ísa Somal. In front, backed by
the dark hills of Harar, lay the Harawwah valley. The
breadth is about fifteen miles : it runs from south-west to
north-east, between the Highlands of the Girhi and the
rolling ground of the Gudabirsi Somal, as far, it is said,
as the Dankali country. Of old this luxuriant waste
belonged to the former tribe; about twelve years ago it
was taken from them by the Gudabirsi, who carried off
at the same time thirty cows, forty camels, and between
three and four hundred sheep and goats.

Large herds tended by spearmen and grazing about
the bush, warned us that we were approaching the kraal
in which the sons of White Ali were camped ; at half-
past 10 A.M., after riding eight miles, we reached the
place which occupies the lower slope of the Northern
Hills that enclose the Harawwah valley. We spread
our hides under a tree, and were soon surrounded by
Badawin, who brought milk, sun-dried beef, ghi and
honey in one of the painted wooden bowls exported
from Cutch. After breakfast, at which the End of
Time distinguished himself by dipping his meat into
honey, we went out gun in hand towards the bush. It
swarmed with sand-antelope and Gurnuk: the ground-
squirrels haunted every ant-hill, hoopoos and spur-fowls
paced among the thickets, in the trees we heard the

frequent cry of the Gobiyan and the bird facetiously termed from its cry " Dobo-dogon-guswen," and the bright-coloured eagle, the Abodi or Bakiyyah,[1] lay on wing high in the cloudless air. When tired of killing we returned to our cow-hides, and sat in conversation with the Badawin. They boasted of the skill with which they used the shield, and seemed not to understand the efficiency of a sword-parry: to illustrate the novel idea I gave a stick to the best man, provided myself in the same way, and allowed him to cut at me. After repeated failures he received a sounding blow upon the least bony portion of his person: the crowd laughed long and loud, and the pretending "knight-at-arms" retired in confusion.

Darkness fell, but no caravan appeared: it had been delayed by a runaway mule—perhaps by the desire to restrain my vagrant propensities—and did not arrive till midnight. My hosts cleared a Gurgi for our reception, brought us milk, and extended their hospitality to the full limits of even savage complaisance.

Expecting to march on the 13th December soon after dawn, I summoned Beuh and his brethren to the hut, reminding him that the Hajj had promised me an escort without delay to the village of the Jirad Adan. To my instances they replied that, although they were most

---

1 This beautiful bird, with a black and crimson plume, and wings lined with silver, soars high and seldom descends except at night: its shyness prevented my shooting a specimen. The Abodi devours small deer and birds: the female lays a single egg in a large loose nest on the summit of a tall tree, and she abandons her home when the hand of man has violated it. The Somal have many superstitions connected with this eagle: if it touch a child the latter dies, unless protected by the talismanic virtues of the " Hajar Abodi," a stone found in the bird's body. As it frequently swoops upon children carrying meat, the belief has doubtlessly frequently fulfilled itself.

anxious to oblige, the arrival of Mudah the eldest son rendered a consultation necessary; and retiring to the woods, sat in palaver from 8 A.M. to past noon. At last they came to a resolution which could not be shaken. They would not trust one of their number in the Jirad's country; a horseman however, should carry a letter inviting the Girhi chief to visit his brothers-in-law. I was assured that Adan would not drink water before mounting to meet us: but, fear is reciprocal, there was evidently bad blood between them, and already a knowledge of Somali customs caused me to suspect the result of our mission. However, a letter was written reminding the Jirad of " the word spoken under the tree," and containing in case of recusance, a threat to cut off the salt well at which his cows are periodically driven to drink. Then came the bargain for safe conduct. After much haggling, especially on the part of the handsome Igah, they agreed to receive twenty Tobes, three bundles of tobacco, and fourteen cubits of indigo-dyed cotton. In addition to this I offered as a bribe one of my handsome Abyssinian shirts with a fine silk fringe, made at Aden, to be received by the man Beuh on the day of entering the Jirad's village.

I arose early in the next morning, having been promised by the Abbans grand sport in the Harawwah valley. The Somal had already divided the elephants' spoils: they were to claim the hero's feather, I was to receive two-thirds of the ivory—nothing remained to be done but the killing. After sundry pretences and prayers for delay, Beuh saddled his hack, the Hammal mounted one mule, a stout-hearted Badawi called Fahi took a second, and we started to find the herds. The End of Time lagged in the rear: the reflection that a mule cannot outrun an elephant, made him look so ineffably miserable, that I sent him back to the kraal. "Dost thou believe me to be a coward, O Pilgrim?" thereupon exclaimed

the Mullah, waxing bold in the very joy of his heart.
" Of a truth I do! " was my reply.   Nothing abashed, he
hammered his mule with heel, and departed ejaculating,
" What hath man but a single life? and he who throweth
it away, what is he but a fool?"   Then we advanced with
cocked guns, Beuh singing, Boanerges-like, the Song of
the Elephant.

In the Somali country, as amongst the Kafirs, after
murdering a man or boy, the death of an elephant is considered *the* act of heroism: most tribes wear for it the hair-
feather and the ivory bracelet.   Some hunters, like the
Bushmen of the Cape,[1] kill the Titan of the forests with
barbed darts carrying Waba-poison.   The general way of
hunting resembles that of the Abyssinian Agageers
described by Bruce.   One man mounts a white pony, and
galloping before the elephant, induces him, as he readily
does—firearms being unknown—to charge and "chivy."
The rider directs his course along, and close to, some
bush, where a comrade is concealed; and the latter, as
the animal passes at speed, cuts the back sinew of the
hind leg, where in the human subject the tendon Achilles
would be, with a sharp broad and heavy knife.[2]   This
wound at first occasions little inconvenience: presently
the elephant, fancying, it is supposed, that a thorn has
stuck in his foot, stamps violently, and rubs the scratch
till the sinew is fairly divided.   The animal, thus disabled,

---

1 The Bushman creeps close to the beast and wounds it in the
leg or stomach with a diminutive dart covered with a couch of black
poison: if a drop of blood appear, death results from the almost
unfelt wound.

2 So the Veddahs of Ceylon are said to have destroyed the
elephant by shooting a tiny arrow into the sole of the foot.   The
Kafirs attack it in bodies armed with sharp and broad-head
" Omkondo " or assegai: at last, one finds the opportunity of
cutting deep into the hind back sinew, and so disables the animal.

is left to perish wretchedly of hunger and thirst: the tail, as amongst the Kafirs, is cut off to serve as trophy, and the ivories are removed when loosened by decomposition. In this part of Africa the elephant is never tamed.[1]

For six hours we rode the breadth of the Harawwah Valley: it was covered with wild vegetation, and surface-drains, that carry off the surplus of the hills enclosing it. In some places the torrent beds had cut twenty feet into the soil. The banks were fringed with milk-bush and Asclepias, the Armo-creeper, a variety of thorns, and especially the yellow-berried Jujube : here numberless birds followed bright-winged butterflies, and the "Shaykhs of the Blind," as the people call the black fly, settled in swarms upon our hands and faces as we rode by. The higher ground was overgrown with a kind of cactus, which here becomes a tree, forming shady avenues. Its quadrangular fleshy branches of emerald green, sometimes forty feet high, support upon their summits large round bunches of a bright crimson berry : when the plantation is close, domes of extreme beauty appear scattered over the surface of the country. This " Hassadin " abounds in burning milk, and the Somal look downwards when passing under its branches : the elephant is said to love it, and in many places the trees were torn to pieces by hungry trunks. The nearest approaches to game were the last year's earths ; likely places, however, shady trees and green thorns near water, were by no means uncommon. When we reached the valley's southern wall, Beuh informed us that we might ride all day, if we pleased, with the same result.

---

1 The traveller Delegorgue asserts that the Boers induce the young elephant to accompany them, by rubbing upon its trunk the hand wetted with the perspiration of the huntsman's brow, and that the calf, deceived by the similarity of smell, believes that it is with its dam. The fact is, that the orphan elephant, like the bison, follows man because it fears to be left alone.

At Zayla I had been informed that elephants are "thick as sand" in Harawwah : even the Gudabirsi, when at a distance, declared that they fed there like sheep, and, after our failure, swore that they had killed thirty but last year. The animals were probably in the high Harirah Valley, and would be driven downwards by the cold at a later period: some future Gordon Cumming may therefore succeed where the Hajj Abdullah notably failed.

On the 15th December I persuaded the valiant Beuh, with his two brothers and his bluff cousin Fahi, to cross the valley with us. After recovering a mule which had strayed five miles back to the well, and composing sundry quarrels between Shahrazad, whose swains had detained her from camel-loading, and the Kalandar whose one eye flashed with indignation at her conduct, we set out in a southerly direction. An hour's march brought us to an open space surrounded by thin thorn forest: in the centre is an ancient grave, about which are performed the equestrian games when the turband of the Ugaz has been bound under the Holy Tree. Shepherds issued from the bush to stare at us as we passed, and stretched forth the hand for " Bori" : the maidens tripped forwards exclaiming, " Come, girls, let us look at this prodigy ! " and they never withheld an answer if civilly addressed. Many of them were grown up, and not a few were old maids, the result of the tribe's isolation ; for here, as in Somaliland generally, the union of cousins is abhorred. The ground of the valley is a stiff clay, sprinkled with pebbles of primitive formation : the hills are mere rocks, and the torrent banks with strata of small stones, showed a water-mark varying from ten to fifteen feet in height : in these fiumaras we saw frequent traces of the Adler-game, deer and hog. At 1 P.M. our camels and mules were watered at wells in a broad wady called Jannah-Gaban or the Little Garden ;

its course, I was told, lies northwards through the
Harawwah Valley to the Odla and Waruf, two
depressions, in the Wayma country near Tajurrah.
About half an hour afterwards we arrived at a deserted
sheepfold distant six miles from our last station. After
unloading we repaired to a neighbouring well, and found
the water so hard that it raised lumps like nettle stings
in the bather's skin. The only remedy for the evil is an
unguent of oil or butter, a precaution which should never
be neglected by the African traveller. At first the
sensation of grease annoys, after a few days it is
forgotten, and at last the " pat of butter " is expected
as pleasantly as the pipe or the cup of coffee. It
prevents the skin from chaps and sores, obviates the
evil effects of heat, cold, and wet, and neutralizes the
Proteus-like malaria poison. The Somal never fail to
anoint themselves when they can afford ghi, and the
Badawi is at the summit of his bliss, when sitting in
the blazing sun, or—heat acts upon these people as upon
serpents—with his back opposite a roaring fire, he is
being smeared, rubbed, and kneaded by a companion.

My guides, fearing lions and hyenas, would pass the
night inside a foul sheepfold: I was not without difficulty
persuaded to join them. At eight next morning we set
out through an uninteresting thorn-bush towards one of
those Têtes or isolated hills which form admirable bench-
marks in the Somali country. " Koralay," a term corresponding with our Saddle-back, exactly describes its
shape : pommel and crupper, in the shape of two huge
granite boulders, were all complete, and between them
was a depression for a seat. As day advanced the
temperature changed from 50° to a maximum of 121°.
After marching about five miles, we halted in a broad
watercourse called Gallajab, the " Plentiful Water ":
there we bathed, and dined on an excellent camel which
had broken its leg by falling from a bank.

Resuming our march at 5 P.M., we travelled over
ascending ground which must be most fertile after rain:
formerly it belonged to the Girhi, and the Gudabirsi
boasted loudly of their conquest.   After an hour's march
we reached the base of Koralay, upon whose lower slopes
appeared a pair of the antelopes called Alakud[1]: they
are tame, easily shot, and eagerly eaten by the Badawin.
Another hour of slow travelling brought us to a broad
fiumara with high banks of stiff clay thickly wooded and
showing a water-mark eighteen feet above the sand.
The guides named these wells Agjogsi, probably a generic
term signifying that water is standing close by.   Crossing the fiumara we ascended a hill, and found upon the
summit a large kraal alive with heads of kine.   The
inhabitants flocked out to stare at us and the women
uttered cries of wonder.   I advanced towards the
prettiest, and fired my rifle by way of salute over her
head.   The people delighted exclaimed, Mod! Mod!—
" Honour to thee!"—and we replied with shouts of Kulli-
ban—" May heaven aid ye!"[2]   At 5 P.M., after five
miles' march, the camels were unloaded in a deserted
kraal whose high fence denoted danger of wild beasts.
The cowherds bade us beware of lions: but a day before
a girl had been dragged out of her hut, and Moslem
burial could be given to only one of her legs.   A
Badawi named Uddao, whom we hired as mule-keeper,
was ordered to spend the night singing, and, as is
customary with Somali watchmen, to address and

---

1 An antelope, about five hands high with small horns, which
inhabits the high ranges of the mountains, generally in couples,
resembles the musk deer, and is by no means shy, seldom flying till
close pressed; when running it hops awkwardly upon the toes and
never goes far.

2 These are solemn words used in the equestrian games of the
Somal.

answer himself dialogue-wise with a different voice, in order to persuade thieves that several men are on the alert. He was a spectacle of wildness as he sat before the blazing fire—his joy by day, his companion and protector in the shades, the only step made by him in advance of his brethren the Cynocephali.

We were detained four days at Agjogsi by the non-appearance of the Jirad Adan : this delay gave me an opportunity of ascending to the summit of Koralay the Saddleback, which lay about a mile north of our encampment. As we threaded the rocks and hollows of the side we came upon dens strewed with cows' bones, and proving by a fresh taint that the tenants had lately quitted them. In this country the lion is seldom seen unless surprised asleep in his lair of thicket : during my journey, although at times the roaring was heard all night, I saw but one. The people have a superstition that the king of beasts will not attack a single traveller, because such a person, they say, slew the mother of all the lions ; except in darkness or during violent storms, which excite the fiercer carnivors, he is a timid animal, much less feared by the people than the angry and agile leopard. Unable to run with rapidity when pressed by hunger, he pursues a party of travellers as stealthily as a cat, and arrived within distance, springs, strikes down the hindermost, and carries him away to the bush.

From the summit of Koralay, we had a fair view of the surrounding country. At least forty kraals, many of them deserted, lay within the range of sight. On all sides except the north-west and south-east was a mass of sombre rock and granite hill : the course of the valleys between the several ranges was denoted by a lively green, and the plains scattered in patches over the landscape shone with dull yellow, the effect of clay and stubble, whilst a light mist encased the prospect in a circlet of blue and silver. Here the End of Time conceived the jocose idea of crowing me king of the country. With loud cries of Buh! Buh! Buh! he showered leaves of a gum tree and a little water from a prayer bottle over my head, and then with all solemnity bound on the turband.[1] It is perhaps fortunate that this facetiousness was not witnessed: a crowd of Badawin assembled below the hill, suspecting as usual some magical practices, and had they known the truth, our journey might have ended abruptly. Descending, I found porcupines' quills in abundance,[2] and shot a rock pigeon called Elal-jog— the "Dweller at wells." At the foot a "Baune" or Hyrax Abyssinicus, resembling the Coney of Palestine,[3] was observed at its favourite pastime of sunning itself upon the rocks.

On the evening of the 20th December the mounted messenger returned, after a six hours' hard ride, bringing back unopened the letter addressed by me to the Jirad, and a private message for their sister to the sons of White Ali, advising them not to advance. Ensued terrible palavers. It appeared that the Jirad was upon the point of mounting horse, when his subjects swore him to remain and settle a dispute with the Amir of Harar. Our Abbans, however, withdrew their hired camels, positively refused to accompany us, and Beuh privily informed the End of Time that I had acquired through

---

1 Sometimes milk is poured over the head, as gold and silver in the Nuzziranah of India. These ceremonies are usually performed by low-caste men; the free-born object to act in them.

2 The Somal call it Hiddik or Anukub; the quills are used as head scratchers, and are exported to Aden for sale.

3 It appears to be the Ashkoko of the Amharas, identified by Bruce with the Saphan of the Hebrews. This coney lives in chinks and holes of rocks: it was never seen by me on the plains. The Arabs eat it, the Somal generally do not.

the land the evil reputation of killing everything, from an elephant to a bird in the air. One of the younger brethren, indeed, declared that we were the forerunners of good, and if the Jirad harmed a hair of our heads, he would slaughter every Girhi under the sun. We had, however, learned properly to appreciate such vaunts, and the End of Time drily answered that their sayings were honey but their doings myrrh. Being a low-caste and a shameless tribe, they did not reply to our reproaches. At last, a manœuvre was successful: Beuh and his brethren, who squatted like sulky children in different places, were dismissed with thanks—we proposed placing ourselves under the safeguard of Jirad Hirsi, the Berteri chief. This would have thrown the protection-price, originally intended for their brother-in-law, into the hands of a rival, and had the effect of altering their resolve. Presently we were visited by two Widad or hedge-priests, Ao Samattar and Ao Nur,[1] both half-witted fellows, but active and kind-hearted. The former wore a dirty turband, the latter a Zabid cap, a wicker-work calotte, composed of the palm leaf's mid-rib: they carried dressed goatskins, as prayer carpets, over their right shoulders dangled huge wooden ink bottles with Lauh or wooden tablets for writing talismans,[2] and from the left hung a greasy bag, containing a tattered copy of the Koran and a small MS. of prayers. They read tolerably, but did not understand Arabic, and I presented them with cheap Bombay lithographs of the Holy Book. The number of these idlers increased as we approached Harar, the Alma Mater of Somali-land:

---

1 The prefix appears to be a kind of title appropriated by saints and divines.

2 These charms are washed off and drunk by the people: an economical proceeding where paper is scarce.

—the people seldom listen to their advice, but on this occasion Ao Samattar succeeded in persuading the valiant Beuh that the danger was visionary. Soon afterwards rode up to our kraal three cavaliers, who proved to be sons of Adam, the future Ugaz of the Gudabirsi tribe : this chief had fully recognized the benefits of reopening to commerce a highway closed by their petty feuds, and sent to say that, in consequence of his esteem for the Hajj Sharmarkay, if the sons of White Ali feared to escort us, he in person would do the deed. Thereupon Beuh became a " Gesi " or hero, as the End of Time ironically called him : he sent back his brethren with their horses and camels, and valorously prepared to act as our escort. I tauntingly asked him what he now thought of the danger. For all reply he repeated the words, which the Badawin—who, like the Arabs, have a holy horror of towns—had been dinning daily into my ears, " They will spoil that white skin of thine at Harar ! "

At 3 P.M., on the 21st December, we started in a westerly direction through a gap in the hills, and presently turned to the south-west, over rapidly rising ground, thickly inhabited, and covered with flocks and herds. About 5 P.M., after marching two miles, we raised our wigwam outside a populous kraal, a sheep was provided by the hospitality of Ao Samattar, and we sat deep into the night enjoying a genial blaze.

Early the next morning we had hoped to advance : water, however, was wanting, and a small caravan was slowly gathering;—these details delayed us till 4 P.M. Our line lay westward, over rising ground, towards a conspicuous conical hill called Konti. Nothing could be worse for camels than the rough ridges at the foot of the mountain, full of thickets, cut by deep Fiumaras, and abounding in dangerous watercourses : the burdens slipped now backwards then forwards, sometimes the load was almost dragged off by thorns, and at last we were obliged to leave one animal to follow slowly in the rear. After creeping on two miles, we bivouacked in a deserted cow-kraal—*sub dio*, as it was warm under the hills. That evening our party was increased by a Gudabirsi maiden in search of a husband: she was surlily received by Shahrazad and Dunyazad, but we insisted upon her being fed, and superintended the operation. Her style of eating was peculiar; she licked up the rice from the hollow of her hand. Next morning she was carried away in our absence, greatly against her will, by some kinsmen who had followed her.

And now, bidding adieu to the Gudabirsi, I wil briefly sketch the tribe.

The Gudabirsi, or Gudabursi, derive themselves from Dir and Aydur, thus claiming affinity with the Ísa; others declare their tribe to be an offshoot from the Bahgoba clan of the Habr Awal, originally settled near Jabal Almis, and Bulhar, on the sea-shore. The Somal unhesitatingly stigmatize them as a bastard and ignoble race: a noted genealogist once informed me, that they were little better than Midgans or serviles. Their ancestors' mother, it is said, could not name the father of her child: some proposed to slay it, others advocated its preservation, saying, "Perhaps we shall increase by it." Hence the name of the tribe.[1]

The Gudabirsi are such inveterate liars that I could fix them no number between 3,000 and 10,000. They own the rough and rolling ground diversified with thorny hill and grassy vale, above the first or seaward range of mountains ; and they have extended their lands by conquest towards Harar, being now bounded in that direction

---

1 " Birsan," in Somali, meaning to increase.

by the Marar Prairie. As usual, they are subdivided into a multitude of clans.[1]

In appearance the Gudabirsi are decidedly superior to their limitrophes the Ísa. I have seen handsome faces amongst the men as well as the women. Some approach closely to the Caucasian type: one old man, with olive-coloured skin, bald brow, and white hair curling round his temples, and occiput, exactly resembled an Anglo-Indian veteran. Generally, however, the prognathous mouth betrays an African origin, and chewing tobacco mixed with ashes stains the teeth, blackens the gums, and mottles the lips. The complexion is the Abyssinian *café au lait*, contrasting strongly with the sooty skins of the coast; and the hair, plentifully anointed with rancid butter, hangs from the head in lank corkscrews the colour of a Russian pointer's coat. The figure is rather squat, but broad and well set.

The Gudabirsi are as turbulent and unmanageable, though not so bloodthirsty, as the Ísa. Their late chief, Ugaz Roblay of the Bayt Samattar sept, left children who could not hold their own: the turband was at once claimed by a rival branch, the Rer Abdillah, and a civil war ensued. The lovers of legitimacy will rejoice to

---

1 The Ayyal Yunis, the principal clan, contains four septs, viz. :—

1. Jibril Yunis.	3. Ali Yunis.
2. Nur Yunis.	4. Adan Yunis.

The other chief clans are—

1. Mikahil Dera.	7. Basannah.
2. Rer Ugaz.	8. Bahabr Hasan.
3. Jibrain.	9. Abdillah Mikahil.
4. Rer Mohammed Asa	10. Hasan Mikahil.
5. Musa Fin.	11. Eyah Mikahil.
6. Rer Abokr	12. Hasan Waraba.

hear that when I left the country, Galla, son of the former Prince Rainy, was likely to come to his own again.

The stranger's life is comparatively safe amongst this tribe: as long as he feeds and fees them, he may even walk about unarmed. They are, however, liars even amongst the Somal, Bobadils amongst boasters, inveterate thieves, and importunate beggars. The smooth-spoken fellows seldom betray emotion except when cloth or tobacco is concerned ; " dissimulation is as natural to them as breathing," and I have called one of their chiefs a " dog " without exciting his indignation.

The commerce of these wild regions is at present in a depressed state: were the roads safe, traffic with the coast would be considerable. The profit on hides, for instance, at Aden, would be at least cent. per cent. : the way, however, is dangerous, and detention is frequent, consequently the gain will not remunerate for risk and loss of time. No operation can be undertaken in a hurry, consequently demand cannot readily be supplied. What Laing applies to Western, may be repeated of Eastern Africa : " the endeavour to accelerate an undertaking is almost certain to occasion its failure." Nowhere is patience more wanted, in order to perform perfect work.

The wealth of the Gudabirsi consists principally in cattle, peltries, hides, gums, and ghi. The asses are dun-coloured, small, and weak ; the camels large, loose, and lazy; the cows are pretty animals, with small humps, long horns resembling the Damara cattle, and in the grazing season with plump, well-rounded limbs ; there is also a bigger breed, not unlike that of Tuscany. The standard is the Tobe of coarse canvas ; worth about three shillings at Aden, here it doubles in value. The price of a good camel varies from six to eight cloths ; one Tobe buys a two-year-old heifer, three, a cow between three and four years old. A ewe costs half a cloth : the goat, although the flesh is according to the Somal nutritive, whilst " mutton is disease," is a little cheaper than the sheep.   Hides and peltries are usually collected at and exported from Harar ; on the coast they are rubbed over with salt, and in this state carried to Aden. Cows' skins fetch a quarter of a dollar, or about one shilling in cloth, and two dollars are the extreme price for the Kurjah or score of goats' skins.   The people of the interior have a rude way of tanning[1] ; they macerate the hide, dress, and stain it of a deep calf-skin colour with the bark of a tree called Jirmah, and lastly the leather is softened with the hand.   The principal gum is the Adad or Acacia Arabica : foreign merchants purchase it for about half a dollar per Farasilah of twenty pounds : cow's and sheep's butter may fetch a dollar's worth of cloth for the measure of thirty-two pounds.   This great article of commerce is good and pure in the country, whereas at Berberah, the Habr Awal adulterate it, previous to exportation, with melted sheeps' tails.

The principal wants of the country which we have traversed are coarse cotton cloth, Surat tobacco, beads, and indigo-dyed stuffs for women's coifs.   The people would also be grateful for any improvement in their breed of horses, and when at Aden I thought of taking with me some old Arab stallions as presents to chiefs.   Fortunately the project fell to the ground : a strange horse of unusual size and beauty, in these regions, would be stolen at the end of the first march.

---

1 The best prayer-skins are made at Ogadayn ; there they cost about half a dollar each.

CHAPTER VII.

FROM THE MARAR PRAIRIE TO HARAR.

EARLY on the 23rd December assembled the caravan, which we were destined to escort across the Marar Prairie. Upon this neutral ground the Ísa, Berteri, and Habr Awal meet to rob and plunder unhappy travellers. The Somal shuddered at the sight of a wayfarer, who rushed into our encampment *in cuerpo*, having barely run away with his life. Not that our caravan carried much to lose—a few hides and pots of clarified butter, to be exchanged for the Holcus grain of the Girhi cultivators—still the smallest contributions are thankfully received by these plunderers. Our material consisted of four or five half-starved camels, about fifty donkeys with ears cropped as a mark, and their eternal accompaniments in Somali land, old women. The latter seemed to be selected for age, hideousness, and strength: all day they bore their babes smothered in hides upon their backs, and they carried heavy burdens apparently without fatigue. Amongst them was a Badawi widow, known by her " Wer," a strip of the inner bark of a tree tied round the greasy fillet.[1] We were accompanied by three Widads,

---

1 It is worn for a year, during which modest women will not marry. Some tribes confine the symbol to widowhood, others extend it to all male relations; a strip of white cotton, or even a white fillet, instead of the usual blue cloth, is used by the more civilized.

provided with all the instruments of their craft, and uncommonly tiresome companions. They recited Koran *à tort et à travers:* at every moment they proposed Fatihahs, the name of Allah was perpetually upon their lips, and they discussed questions of divinity, like Gil Blas and his friends, with a violence bordering upon frenzy. One of them was celebrated for his skill in the "Fal," or Omens: he was constantly consulted by my companions, and informed them that we had nought to fear except from wild beasts. The prediction was a good hit: I must own however, that it was not communicated to me before fulfilment.

At half past six A.M., we began our march over rough and rising ground, a network of thorns and watercourses, and presently entered a stony gap between two ranges of hills. On our right was a conical peak, bearing the remains of buildings upon its summit. Here, said Abtidon, a wild Gudabirsi hired to look after our mules, rests the venerable Shaykh Samawai. Of old, a number of wells existed in the gaps between the hills: these have disappeared with those who drank of them.

Presently we entered the Barr or Prairie of Marar, one of the long strips of plain which diversify the Somali country. Its breadth, bounded on the east by the rolling ground over which we had passed, on the west by Gurays, a range of cones offshooting from the highlands of Harar, is about twenty-seven miles, the general course is north and south: in the former direction, it belongs to the Ísa: in the latter may be seen the peaks of Kadau and Madir, the property of the Habr Awal tribes; and along these ranges it extends, I was told, towards Ogadayn. The surface of the plain is gently rolling ground: the black earth, filled with the holes of small beasts, would be most productive, and the outer coat is an expanse of tall, waving, sunburnt grass, so unbroken, that from a distance it resembles the nap of yellow velvet. In the frequent

Wadys, which carry off the surplus rain of the hills, scrub and thorn trees grow in dense thickets, and the grass is temptingly green. Yet the land lies fallow: water and fuel are scarce at a distance from the hills, and the wildest Badawi dare not front the danger of foraging parties, the fatal heats of day, and the killing colds of night. On the edges of the plain, however, are frequent vestiges of deserted kraals.

About mid-day, we crossed a depression in the centre, where Acacias supplied us with gum for luncheon, and sheltered flocks of antelope. I endeavoured to shoot the white-tailed Sig, and the large dun Oryx; but the *brouhaha* of the caravan prevented execution. Shortly afterwards we came upon patches of holcus, which had grown wild, from seeds scattered by travellers. This was the first sight of grain that gladdened my eyes since I left Bombay: the grave of the First Murderer never knew a Triptolemus,[1] and Zayla is a barren flat of sand. My companions eagerly devoured the pith of this African "sweet cane," despite its ill reputation for causing fever. I followed their example, and found it almost as good as bad sugar. The Badawin loaded their spare asses with the bitter gourd, called Ubbah; externally it resembles the water melon, and becomes, when shaped, dried, and smoked, the wickerwork of the Somal, and the pottery of more civilized people.

Towards evening, as the setting sun sank slowly behind the distant western hills, the colour of the Prairie changed from glaring yellow to a golden hue, mantled with a purple flush inexpressibly lovely. The animals of the waste began to appear. Shy lynxes[2] and jackals

---

1 Cain is said to repose under Jabal Shamsan at Aden—an appropriate sepulchre.

2 This beast, called by the Somal Jambel, closely resembles the Sind species. It is generally found in the plains and prairies.

fattened by many sheeps' tails,[1] warned my companions
that fierce beasts were nigh, ominous anecdotes were
whispered, and I was told that a caravan had lately lost
nine asses by lions.   As night came on, the Badawi
Kafilah, being lightly loaded, preceded us, and our tired
camels lagged far behind.   We were riding in rear to
prevent straggling, when suddenly my mule, the hindermost, pricked his ears uneasily, and attempted to turn his
head.   Looking backwards, I distinguished the form of
a large animal following us with quick and stealthy
strides.   My companions would not fire, thinking it was a
man : at last a rifle-ball, pinging through the air—the
moon was too young for correct shooting—put to flight a
huge lion.   The terror excited by this sort of an adventure
was comical to look upon : the valiant Beuh, who,
according to himself, had made his *preuves* in a score of
foughten fields, threw his arms in the air, wildly shouting
Libah ! Libah!!—the lion ! the lion ! !—and nothing else
was talked of that evening.

The ghostly western hills seemed to recede as we
advanced over the endless rolling plain.   Presently the
ground became broken and stony, the mules stumbled in
deep holes, and the camels could scarcely crawl along.
As we advanced, our Widads, who poor devils! had been
" roasted " by the women all day on account of their
poverty, began to recite the Koran with might, in
gratitude for having escaped many perils.   Night deepening, our attention was rivetted by a strange spectacle ; a
broad sheet of bright blaze, reminding me of Hanno's
fiery river, swept apparently down a hill, and, according to

---

1 In the Somali country, as in Kafirland, the Duwao or jackal
is peculiarly bold and fierce. Disdaining garbage, he carries off lambs
and kids, and fastens upon a favourite *friandise*, the sheep's tail: the
victim runs away in terror, and unless the jackal be driven off by
dogs, leaves a delicate piece of fat behind it.

my companions, threatened the whole prairie. These accidents are common : a huntsman burns a tree for honey, or cooks his food in the dry grass, the wind rises and the flames spread far and wide. On this occasion no accident occurred; the hills, however, smoked like a Solfatara for two days.

About 9 P.M. we heard voices, and I was told to discharge my rifle lest the kraal be closed to us; in due time we reached a long, low, dark line of sixty or seventy huts, disposed in a circle, so as to form a fence, with a few bushes—thorns being hereabouts rare—in the gaps between the abodes. The people, a mixture of Girhi and Gudabirsi Badawin, swarmed out to gratify their curiosity, but we were in no humour for long conversations. Our luggage was speedily disposed in a heap near the kraal, the mules and camels were tethered for the night, then, supperless and shivering with cold, we crept under our mats and fell asleep. That day we had ridden nearly fifteen hours; our halting place lay about thirty miles from, and 240° south-west of, Koralay.

After another delay, and a second vain message to the Jirad Adan, about noon appeared that dignitary's sixth wife, sister to the valiant Beuh. Her arrival disconcerted my companions, who were too proud to be protected by a woman. " Dahabo," however, relieved their anxiety by informing us that the Jirad had sent his eldest son Shirwa, as escort. This princess was a gipsy-looking dame, coarsely-dressed, about thirty years old, with a gay leer, a jaunty demeanour, and the reputation of being "fast"; she showed little shamefacedness when I saluted her, and received with noisy joy the appropriate present of a new and handsome Tobe. About 4 P.M. returned our second messenger, bearing with him are proving message from the Jirad, for not visiting him without delay ; in token of sincerity, he forwarded his baton, a knobstick about two feet long, painted in rings of Cutch colours, red, black, and yellow alternately, and garnished on the summit with a ball of similar material.

At dawn on the 26th December, mounted upon a little pony, came Shirwa, heir presumptive to the Jirad Adan's knobstick. His father had sent him to us three days before, but he feared the Gudabirsi as much as the Gudabirsi feared him, and he probably hung about our camp till certain that it was safe to enter. We received him politely, and he in acknowledgment positively declared that Beuh should not return before eating honey in his cottage. Our Abban's heroism now became infectious. Even the End of Time, whose hot valour had long since fallen below zero, was inspired by the occasion, and recited, as usual with him in places and at times of extreme safety, the Arabs' warrior lines—

"I have crossed the steed since my eyes saw light,
 I have fronted death till he feared my sight,
 And the cleaving of helm and the riving of mail
 Were the dreams of my youth—are my manhood's delight."

As we had finished loading, a mule's bridle was missed. Shirwa ordered instant restitution to his father's stranger, on the ground that all the property now belonged to the Jirad ; and we, by no means idle, fiercely threatened to bewitch the kraal. The article was presently found hard by, on a hedge. This was the first and last case of theft which occurred to us in the Somali country ;—I have travelled through most civilized lands, and have lost more.

At 8 A.M. we marched towards the north-west, along the southern base of the Gurays hills, and soon arrived at the skirt of the prairie, where a well-trodden path warned us that we were about to quit the desert. After advancing six miles in line we turned to the right, and recited a Fatihah over a heap of rough stones, where, shadowed by venerable trees, lie the remains of the great Shaykh Abd al-Malik. A little beyond this spot, rises suddenly from the plain a mass of castellated rock, the subject of many a wild superstition. Caravans always encamp beneath it, as whoso sleeps upon the summit loses his senses to evil spirits. At some future day Harar will be destroyed, and " Jannah Siri " will become a flourishing town. We ascended it, and found no life but hawks, coneys, an owl,[1] and a graceful species of black eagle[2]; there were many traces of buildings, walls, ruined houses, and wells, whilst the sides and summit were tufted with venerable sycamores. This act was an imprudence; the Badawin at once declared that we were " prospecting " for a fort, and the evil report preceded us to Harar.

After a mile's march from Jannah Siri, we crossed a ridge of rising ground, and suddenly, as though by magic, the scene shifted.

Before us lay a little Alp; the second step of the Ethiopian Highland. Around were high and jagged hills, their sides black with the Saj[3] and Somali pine,[4] and their upper brows veiled with a thin growth of cactus. Beneath was a deep valley, in the midst of which ran a serpentine of shining waters, the gladdest spectacle we had yet witnessed : further in front, masses of hill rose abruptly from shady valleys, encircled on the far horizon by a straight blue line of ground, resembling

---

1 The Somal call the owl " Shimbir libah "—the lion bird.

2 The plume was dark, chequered with white, but the bird was so wild that no specimen could be procured.

3 The Arabs apply this term to teak.

4 The Dayyib of the Somal, and the Sinaubar of the Arabs ; its line of growth is hereabouts an altitude of 5000 feet.

a distant sea.   Behind us glared the desert: we had now reached the outskirts of civilization, where man, abandoning his flocks and herds, settles, cultivates, and attends to the comforts of life.

The fields are either terraces upon the hill slopes or the sides of valleys, divided by flowery hedges with lanes between, not unlike those of rustic England; and on a nearer approach the daisy, the thistle, and the sweet briar pleasantly affected my European eyes.   The villages are no longer moveable: the Kraal and wigwam are replaced by the Gambisa or bell-shaped hut of Middle Africa,[1] circular cottages of holcus wattle, covered with coarse dab and surmounted by a stiff, conical, thatch roof, above which appears the central supporting post, crowned with a gourd or ostrich egg.[2]   A strong abattis of thorns protects these settlements, which stud the hills in all directions: near most of them are clumps of tall trees, to the southern sides of which are hung, like birdcages, long cylinders of matting, the hives of these regions.   Yellow crops of holcus rewarded the peasant's toil: in some places the long stems tied in bunches below the ears as piled muskets, stood ready for the reaper; in others, the barer ground showed that the task was done.   The boys sat perched upon reed platforms[3] in the trees, and with loud shouts drove away thieving birds, whilst their fathers cut the crop with diminutive sickles, or thrashed heaps of straw with rude

---

1 Travellers in Central Africa describe exactly similar buildings, bell-shaped huts, the materials of which are stakes, clay and reed, conical at the top, and looking like well-thatched corn-stacks.

2 Amongst the Fellatahs of Western Africa, only the royal huts are surmounted by the ostrich's egg.

3 These platforms are found even amongst the races inhabiting the regions watered by the Niger.

flails,[1] or winnowed grain by tossing it with a flat wooden shovel against the wind. The women husked the pineapple-formed heads in mortars composed of a hollowed trunk,[2] smeared the threshing floor with cow-dung and water to defend it from insects, piled the holcus heads into neat yellow heaps, spanned and crossed by streaks of various colours, brick-red and brownish-purple,[3] and stacked the Karbi or straw, which was surrounded like the grain with thorn, as a defence against the wild hog. All seemed to consider it a labour of love : the harvest-home song sounded pleasantly to our ears, and, contrasting with the silent desert, the hum of man's habitation was a music.

Descending the steep slope, we reposed, after a seven miles' march, on the banks of a bright rivulet, which bisects the Kobbo or valley : it runs according to my guides, from the north towards Ogadayn, and the direction is significant—about Harar I found neither hill nor stream trending from east to west. The people of the Kutti[4] flocked out to gaze upon us : they were unarmed, and did not, like the Badawin, receive us with cries of " Bori." During the halt, we bathed in the waters, upon whose banks were a multitude of huge Mantidæ, pink and tender green. Returning to the

---

1 Charred sticks about six feet long and curved at the handle.

2 Equally simple are the other implements. The plough, which in Eastern Africa has passed the limits of Egypt, is still the crooked tree of all primitive people, drawn by oxen ; and the hoe is a wooden blade inserted into a knobbed handle.

3 It is afterwards stored in deep dry holes, which are carefully covered to keep out rats and insects ; thus the grain is preserved undamaged for three or four years. Like the Matamores, or underground caves of Berbers, and the grain stores of Leghorn; cachettes or siloes of Algerines. When opened the grain must be eaten quickly.

4 This word is applied to the cultivated districts, the granaries of Somali land.

camels, I shot a kind of crow, afterwards frequently seen.[1] It is about three times the size of our English bird, of a bluish-black with a snow-white poll, and a beak of unnatural proportions : the quantity of lead which it carried off surprised me. A number of Widads assembled to greet us, and some Habr Awal, who were returning with a caravan, gave us the salam, and called my people cousins. " Verily," remarked the Hammal, " amongst friends we cut one another's throats; amongst enemies we become sons of uncles ! "

At 3 P.M. we pursued our way over rising ground, dotted with granite blocks fantastically piled, and everywhere in sight of fields and villages and flowing water. A furious wind was blowing, and the End of Time quoted the Somali proverb, " heat hurts, but cold kills : " the camels were so fatigued, and the air became so raw,[2] that after an hour and a half's march we planted our wigwams near a village distant about seven miles from the Gurays Hills. Till late at night we were kept awake by the crazy Widads : Ao Samattar had proposed the casuistical question, " Is it lawful to pray upon a mountain when a plain is at hand ? " Some took the *pro*, others the *contra*, and the wordy battle raged with uncommon fury.

On Wednesday morning at half past seven we started down hill towards " Wilensi," a small table-mountain, at the foot of which we expected to find the Jirad Adan awaiting us in one of his many houses, crossed a fertile valley, and ascended another steep slope by a bad and stony road. Passing the home of Shirwa,

---

1 " The huge raven with gibbous or inflated beak and white nape," writes Mr. Blyth, " is the corvus crassirostris of Ruppell, and, together with a nearly similar Cape species, is referred to the genus Corvultur of Lesson."

2 In these hills it is said sometimes to freeze ; I never saw ice.

who vainly offered hospitality, we toiled onwards, and after a mile and a half's march, which occupied at least two hours, our wayworn beasts arrived at the Jirad's village. On inquiry, it proved that the chief, who was engaged in selecting two horses and two hundred cows, the price of blood claimed by the Amir of Harar, for the murder of a citizen, had that day removed to Sagharrah, another settlement.

As we entered the long straggling village of Wilensi, our party was divided by the Jirad's two wives. The Hammal, the Kalandar, Shahrazad, and Dunyazad, remained with Beuh and his sister in her Gurgi, whilst Long Gulad, the End of Time, and I were conducted to the cottage of the Jirad's prettiest wife, Sudiyah. She was a tall woman, with a light complexion, handsomely dressed in a large Harar Tobe, with silver earrings, and the kind of necklace called Jilbah or Kardas.[1] The Jiradah (princess) at once ordered our hides to be spread in a comfortable part of the hut, and then supplied us with food—boiled beef, pumpkin, and Jowari cakes. During the short time spent in that Gambisa, I had an opportunity, dear L., of seeing the manners and customs of the settled Somal.

The interior of the cottage is simple. Entering the door, a single plank with pins for hinges fitted into sockets above and below the lintel—in fact, as artless a contrivance as ever seen in Spain or Corsica—you find a space, divided by dwarf walls of wattle and dab into three compartments, for the men, women, and cattle. The horses and cows, tethered at night on the left of the door, fill the cottage with the wherewithal to pass many a *nuit blanche:* the wives lie on the right, near a large fireplace of stones and raised clay, and the males occupy the most com-

---

1 It is a string of little silver bells and other ornaments made by the Arabs at Berberah.

fortable part, opposite to and farthest from the entrance. The thatched ceiling shines jetty with smoke, which when intolerable is allowed to escape by a diminutive window: this seldom happens, for smoke, like grease and dirt, keeping man warm, is enjoyed by savages. Equally simply is the furniture: the stem of a tree, with branches hacked into pegs, supports the shields, the assegais are planted against the wall, and divers bits of wood, projecting from the sides and the central roof-tree of the cottage, are hung with clothes and other articles that attract white ants. Gourds smoked inside, and coffee cups of coarse black Harar pottery, with deep wooden platters, and prettily carved spoons of the same material, compose the household supellex. The inmates are the Jiradah and her baby, Siddik a Galla serf, the slave girls and sundry Somal: thus we hear at all times three languages[1] spoken within the walls.

Long before dawn the goodwife rises, wakens her handmaidens, lights the fire, and prepares for the Afur or morning meal. The quern is here unknown.[2] A flat, smooth, oval slab, weighing about fifteen pounds, and a stone roller six inches in diameter, worked with both hands, and the weight of the body kneeling ungracefully upon it on "all fours," are used to triturate the holcus grain. At times water must be sprinkled over the meal, until a finely powdered paste is ready for the oven : thus several hours' labour is required to prepare a few pounds of bread. About 6 A.M. there appears a substantial breakfast of roast beef and mutton, with scones of Jowari grain, the whole drenched in broth. Of the men few

---

1 Harari, Somali and Galla, besides Arabic, and other more civilized dialects.

2 The Negroes of Senegal and the Hottentots use wooden mortars. At Natal and amongst the Amazulu Kafirs, the work is done with slabs and rollers like those described above.

perform any ablutions, but all use the tooth stick before
sitting down to eat. After the meal some squat in the
sun, others transact business, and drive their cattle to the
bush till 11 A.M., the dinner hour. There is no variety in
the repasts, which are always flesh and holcus: these
people despise fowls, and consider vegetables food for
cattle. During the day there is no privacy; men, women,
and children enter in crowds, and will not be driven away
by the Jiradah, who inquires screamingly if they come
to stare at a baboon. My kettle especially excites their
surprise; some opine that it is an ostrich, others, a
serpent: Sudiyah, however, soon discovered its use, and
begged irresistibly for the unique article. Throughout
the day her slave girls are busied in grinding, cooking,
and quarrelling with dissonant voices: the men have
little occupation beyond chewing tobacco, chatting, and
having their wigs frizzled by a professional coiffeur. In
the evening the horses and cattle return home to be
milked and stabled: this operation concluded, all apply
themselves to supper with a will. They sleep but little,
and sit deep into the night trimming the fire, and con-
versing merrily over their cups of Farshu or millet beer.[1]
I tried this mixture several times, and found it detestable:
the taste is sour, and it flies directly to the head, in consequence of being mixed with some poisonous bark. It
is served up in gourd bottles upon a basket of holcus
heads, and strained through a pledget of cotton fixed
across the narrow mouth, into cups of the same primitive
material: the drinkers sit around their liquor, and their
hilarity argues its intoxicating properties. In the morning they arise with headaches and heavy eyes; but these

---

1 In the Eastern World this well-known fermentation is
generally called " Buzah," whence the old German word " büsen "
and our "booze." The addition of a dose of garlic converts it into
an emetic.

symptoms, which we, an industrious race, deprecate, are not disliked by the Somal—they promote sleep and give something to occupy the vacant mind. I usually slumber through the noise except when Ambar, a half caste Somali, returning from a trip to Harar, astounds us with his *contes bleus*, or wild Abtidon howls forth some lay like this : —

I.

" 'Tis joyesse all in Ísa's home !
The fatted oxen bleed,
And slave girls range the pails of milk,
And strain the golden mead.

II.

" 'Tis joyesse all in Ísa's home !
This day the Chieftain's pride
Shall join the song, the dance, the feast,
And bear away a bride.

III.

" ' He cometh not ! ' the father cried,
Smiting with spear the wall ;
' And yet he sent the ghostly man,
Yestre'en before the fall ! '

IV.

" ' He cometh not ! ' the mother said,
A tear stood in her eye ;
' He cometh not, I dread, I dread,
And yet I know not why.'

V.

" ' He cometh not ! ' the maiden thought,
Yet in her glance was light,
Soft as the flash in summer's eve
Where sky and earth unite.

VI.

" The virgins, deck'd with tress and flower,
Danced in the purple shade,
And not a soul, perchance, but wished
Herself the chosen maid.

VII.

" The guests in groups sat gathering
    Where sunbeams warmed the air,
  Some laughed the feasters' laugh, and some
    Wore the bent brow of care.

VIII.

" ' 'Tis he !—'tis he ! '—all anxious peer,
    Towards the distant lea ;
  A courser feebly nears the throng—
    Ah ! 'tis his steed they see.

IX.

" The grief cry bursts from every lip,
    Fear sits on every brow,
  There's blood upon the courser's flank !—
    Blood on the saddle bow !

X.

" ' 'Tis he !—'tis he ! '—all arm and run
    Towards the Marar Plain,
  Where a dark horseman rides the waste
    With dust-cloud for a train.

XI.

" The horseman reins his foam-fleckt steed,
    Leans on his broken spear,
  Wipes his damp brow, and faint begins
    To tell a tale of fear.

XII.

" ' Where is my son ? '—' Go seek him there,
    Far on the Marar Plain,
  Where vultures and hyænas hold
    Their orgies o'er the slain.

XIII.

" ' We took our arms, we saddled horse,
    We rode the East countrie,
  And drove the flocks, and harried herds
    Betwixt the hills and sea.

XIV.

" ' We drove the flock across the hill,
    The herd across the wold—

The poorest spearboy had returned
That day, a man of gold.

xv.

" ' But Awal's children mann'd the vale
Where sweet the Arman flowers,
Their archers from each bush and tree
Rained shafts in venomed showers.

xvi.

" ' Full fifty warriors bold and true
Fell as becomes the brave ;
And whom the arrow spared, the spear
Reaped for the ravening grave.

xvii.

" ' Friend of my youth ! shall I remain
When ye are gone before ? '
He drew the wood from out his side,
And loosed the crimson gore.

xviii.

" Falling, he raised his broken spear,
Thrice wav'd it o'er his head,
Thrice raised the warrior's cry ' revenge ! '—
His soul was with the dead.

xix.

" Now, one by one, the wounded braves
Homeward were seen to wend,
Each holding on his saddle bow
A dead or dying friend.

xx.

" Two galliards bore the Ísa's son,
The corpse was stark and bare—
Low moaned the maid, the mother smote
Her breast in mute despair.

xxi.

" The father bent him o'er the dead,
The wounds were all before ;
Again his brow, in sorrow clad,
The garb of gladness wore.

XXII.

" ' Ho! sit ye down nor mourn for me,
　　Unto the guests he cried ;
' My son a warrior's life hath lived,
　　A warrior's death hath died.

XXIII.

" ' His wedding and his funeral feast
　　Are one, so Fate hath said ;
Death bore him from the brides of earth
　　The brides of Heaven to wed.'

XXIV.

" They drew their knives, they sat them down,
　　And fed as warriors feed ;
The flesh of sheep and beeves they ate,
　　And quaffed the golden mead.

XXV.

" And Ísa sat between the prayers
　　Until the fall of day,
When rose the guests and grasped their spears,
　　And each man went his way.

XXVI.

" But in the morn arose the cry,
　　For mortal spirit flown ;
The father's mighty heart had burst
　　With woe he might not own.

XXVII.

" On the high crest of yonder hill,
　　They buried sire and son,
Grant, Allah! grant them Paradise—
　　Gentles, my task is done ! "

·　　·　　·　　·　　·　　·　　·

Immediately after our arrival at Wilensi we sent
Yusuf Dira, the Jirad's second son to summon his
father. I had to compose many disputes between the
Hammal and the End of Time : the latter was swelling

with importance ; he was now accredited ambassador from the Hajj to the Girhi chief, consequently he aimed at commanding the Caravan. We then made preparations for departure, in case of the Jirad being unable to escort us. Shahrazad and Dunyazad, hearing that the small-pox raged at Harar, and fearing for their charms, begged hard to be left behind : the Kalandar was directed, despite his manly objections, to remain in charge of these dainty dames. The valiant Beuh was dressed in the grand Tobe promised to him ; as no consideration would induce him towards the city, he was dismissed with small presents, and an old Girhi Badawi, generally known as Sa'id Wal, or Mad Sa'id, was chosen as our escort. Camels being unable to travel over these rough mountain paths, our weary brutes were placed for rest and pasture under the surveillance of Shirwa : and not wishing the trouble and delay of hiring asses, the only transport in this country, certain moreover that our goods were safer here than nearer Harar, we selected the most necessary objects, and packed them in a pair of small leathern saddlebags which could be carried by a single mule.

All these dispositions duly made, at 10 A.M. on the 29th December we mounted our animals, and, guided by Mad Sa'id, trotted round the northern side of the Wilensi table-mountain down a lane fenced with fragrant dog roses. Then began the descent of a steep rocky hill, the wall of a woody chasm, through whose gloomy depths the shrunken stream of a large Fiumara wound like a thread of silver. The path would be safe to nought less surefooted than a mule : we rode slowly over rolling stones, steps of micaceous grit, and through thorny bush for about half an hour. In the plain below appeared a village of the Jirad's Midgans, who came out to see us pass, and followed the strangers to some distance. One happening to say, " Of what use is his gun ?—

before he could fetch fire, I should put this arrow through him!" I discharged a barrel over their heads, and derided the convulsions of terror caused by the unexpected sound.

Passing onwards we entered a continuation of the Wady Harirah. It is a long valley choked with dense vegetation, through which meandered a line of water brightly gilt by the sun's rays: my Somal remarked that were the elephants now infesting it destroyed, rice, the favourite luxury, might be grown upon its banks in abundance. Our road lay under clumps of shady trees, over rocky watercourses, through avenues of tall cactus, and down *tranchées* worn by man eight and ten feet below stiff banks of rich red clay. On every side appeared deep clefts, ravines, and earth cracks, all, at this season, dry. The unarmed cultivators thronged from the frequent settlements to stare, and my Somal, being no longer in their own country, laid aside for guns their ridiculous spears. On the way passing Ao Samattar's village, the worthy fellow made us halt whilst he went to fetch a large bowl of sour milk. About noon the fresh western breeze obscured the fierce sun with clouds, and we watered our mules in a mountain stream which crossed our path thrice within as many hundred yards. After six miles' ride reaching the valley's head, we began the descent of a rugged pass by a rough and rocky path. The scenery around us was remarkable. The hill sides were well wooded, and black with pine: their summits were bared of earth by the heavy monsun which spreads the valleys with rich soil; in many places the beds of waterfalls shone like sheets of metal upon the black rock; villages surrounded by fields and fences studded the country, and the distance was a mass of purple peak and blue table in long vanishing succession. Ascending the valley's opposite wall, we found the remains of primæval forests—little glades which had escaped the axe—they

resounded with the cries of pintados and cynocephali.[1]
Had the yellow crops of Holcus been wheat, I might
have fancied myself once more riding in the pleasant
neighbourhood of Tuscan Sienna.

At 4 P.M., after accomplishing fifteen miles on rough
ground, we sighted Sagharrah, a snug high-fenced village
of eight or nine huts nestling against a hill side with trees
above, and below a fertile grain-valley. Presently Mad
Sa'id pointed out to us the Jirad Adan, who, attended
by a little party, was returning homewards : we fired our
guns as a salute, he however hurried on to receive us
with due ceremony in his cottage. Dismounting at the
door we shook hands with him, were led through the idle
mob into a smoky closet contrived against the inside
wall, and were regaled with wheaten bread steeped in
honey and rancid butter. The host left us to eat, and
soon afterwards returned :—I looked with attention at a
man upon whom so much then depended.

Adan bin Kaushan was in appearance a strong wiry
Badawi—before obtaining from me a turband he wore
his bushy hair dyed dun—about forty-five years old, at
least six feet high, with decided features, a tricky smile,
and an uncertain eye. In character he proved to be one
of those cunning idiots so peculiarly difficult to deal with.
Ambitious and wild with greed of gain, he was withal so
fickle that his head appeared ever changing its contents ;
he could not sit quiet for half an hour, and this physical
restlessness was an outward sign of the uneasy inner
man. Though reputed brave, his treachery has won
him a permanent ill fame. Some years ago he betrothed
a daughter to the eldest son of Jirad Hirsi of the Berteri
tribe, and then, contrary to the Somali laws of honour,

---

1 The Somal will not kill these plundering brutes, like the
Western Africans believing them to be enchanted men.

married her to Mohammed Wa'iz of the Jibril Abokr. This led to a feud, in which the disappointed suitor was slain. Adan was celebrated for polygamy even in Eastern Africa: by means of his five sons and dozen daughters, he has succeeded in making extensive connections,[1] and his sister, the Gisti[2] Fátimah, was married to Abu Bakr, father of the present Amir. Yet the Jirad would walk into a crocodile's mouth as willingly as within the walls of Harar. His main reason for receiving us politely was an ephemeral fancy for building a fort, to control the country's trade, and rival or over-awe the city. Still he did not neglect the main chance: whatever he saw he asked for; and after receiving a sword, a Koran, a turband, an Arab waistcoat of gaudy satin, about seventy Tobes, and a similar proportion of indigo-dyed stuff, he privily complained to me that the Hammal had given him but twelve cloths. A list of his wants will best explain the man. He begged me to bring him from Berberah a silver-hilted sword and some soap, 1000 dollars, two sets of silver bracelets, twenty guns with powder and shot, snuff, a scarlet cloth coat embroidered with gold, some poison that would not fail, and any other little article of luxury which might be supposed to suit him. In return he was to present us with horses, mules, slaves, ivory, and other valuables: he forgot, however, to do so before we departed.

The Jirad Adan was powerful, being the head of a tribe of cultivators, not split up, like the Badawin, into independent clans, and he thus exercises a direct influence

---

1 Some years ago Adan plundered one of Sharmarkay's caravans; repenting the action, he offered in marriage a daughter, who, however died before nuptials.

2 Gisti is a "princess" in Harari, equivalent to the Somali Jiradah.

upon the conterminous races.[1]   The Girhi or "Giraffes"
inhabiting these hills are, like most of the other settled
Somal, a derivation from Darud, and descended from
Kombo.   Despite the unmerciful persecutions of the
Gallas, they gradually migrated westwards from Makhar,
their original nest, now number 5000 shields, possess
about 180 villages, and are accounted the power para-
mount.   Though friendly with the Habr Awal, the Girhi
seldom descend, unless compelled by want of pasture, into
the plains.

The other inhabitants of these hills are the Gallas
and the Somali clans of Berteri, Bursuk, Shaykhash,
Hawiyah, Usbayhan, Marayhan, and Abaskul.

The Gallas[2] about Harar are divided into four
several clans, separating as usual into a multitude of
septs.   The Alo extend westwards from the city; the
Nole inhabit the land to the east and north-east, about
two days' journey between the Ísa Somal, and Harar:
on the south, are situated the Babuli and the Jarsa at
Wilensi, Sagharrah, and Kondura—places described in
these pages.

The Berteri, who occupy the Gurays Range, south
of, and limitrophe to the Gallas, and thence extend eastward to the Jigjiga hills, are estimated at 3000 shields.[3]

---

1 They are, however, divided into clans, of which the following
are the principal :—

   1. Bahawiyah, the race which supplies the Jirads.
   2. Abu Yunis (divided into ten septs).
   3. Rer Ibrahim (similarly divided).
   4. Jibril.   8. Rer Auro.
   5. Bakasiyya.   9. Rer Walembo.
   6. Rer Mahmud.   10. Rer Khalid.
   7. Musa Dar.

2 I do not describe these people, the task having already been
performed by many abler pens than mine.

3 They are divided into the Bah Ambaro (the chief's family) and
the Shaykhashed.

Of Darud origin, they own allegiance to the Jirad Hirsi, and were, when I visited the country, on bad terms with the Girhi. The chief's family has, for several generations, been connected with the Amirs of Harar, and the caravan's route to and from Berberah lying through his country, makes him a useful friend and a dangerous foe. About the Jirad Hirsi different reports were rife: some described him as cruel, violent and avaricious; others spoke of him as a godly and a prayerful person: all, however, agreed that he *had* sowed wild oats. In token of repentance, he was fond of feeding Widads, and the Shaykh Jami of Harar was a frequent guest at his kraal.

The Bursuk number about 5000 shields, own no chief, and in 1854 were at war with the Girhi, the Berteri, and especially the Gallas. In this country, the feuds differ from those of the plains: the hill men fight for three days, as the End of Time phrased it, and make peace for three days. The maritime clans are not so abrupt in their changes; moreover they claim blood-money, a thing here unknown. The Shaykhash, or " Reverend " as the term means, are the only Somal of the mountains not derived from Dir and Darud. Claiming descent from the Caliph Abu Bakr, they assert that ten generations ago, one Ao Khutab bin Fakih Umar crossed over from Al-Hijaz, and settled in Eastern Africa with his six sons, Umar the greater, Umar the less, two Abdillahs, Ahmad, and lastly Siddik. This priestly tribe is dispersed, like that of Levi, amongst its brethren, and has spread from Efat to Ogadayn. Its principal sub-families are, Ao Umar, the elder, and Bah Dumma, the junior, branch.

The Hawiyah has been noticed in a previous chapter. Of the Usbayhan I saw but few individuals: they informed me that their tribe numbered forty villages, and about 1000 shields; that they had no chief of their own race, but owned the rule of the Girhi and Berteri Jirads.

Their principal clans are the Rer Yusuf, Rer Sa'id, Rer Abokr, and Yusuf Liyo.

In the Eastern Horn of Africa, and at Ogadayn, the Marahayn is a powerful tribe, here it is unconsequential, and affiliated to the Girhi. The Abaskul also lies scattered over the Harar hills, and owns the Jirad Adan as its chief. This tribe numbers fourteen villages, and between 400 and 500 shields, and is divided into the Rer Yusuf, the Jibrailah, and the Warra Dig:—the latter clan is said to be of Galla extraction.

On the morning after my arrival at Sagharrah I felt too ill to rise, and was treated with unaffected kindness by all the establishment. The Jirad sent to Harar for millet beer, Ao Samattar went to the gardens in search of Kat, the sons Yusuf Dera and a Dwarf[1] insisted upon firing me with such ardour, that no refusal could avail: and Khayrah the wife, with her daughters, two tall dark, smiling, and well-favoured girls of thirteen and fifteen, sacrificed a sheep as my Fida, or Expiatory offering. Even the Galla Christians, who flocked to see the stranger, wept for the evil fate which had brought him so far from his fatherland, to die under a tree. Nothing indeed, would have been easier than such operation: all required was the turning face to the wall, for four or five days. But to expire of an ignoble colic !—the thing was not to be thought of, and a firm resolution to live on sometimes, methinks, effects its object.

On the 1st January, 1855, feeling stronger, I clothed myself in my Arab best, and asked a palaver with the Jirad. We retired to a safe place behind the village, where I read with pomposity the Hajj Sharmarkay's letter. The chief appeared much pleased by our having

---

1 The only specimen of stunted humanity seen by me in the Somali country. He was about eighteen years old, and looked ten.

preferred his country to that of the Ísa : he at once opened the subject of the new fort, and informed me that I was the builder, as his eldest daughter had just dreamed that the stranger wonld settle in the land. Having discussed the project to the Jirad's satisfaction, we brought out the guns and shot a few birds for the benefit of the vulgar. Whilst engaged in this occupation, appeared a party of five strangers, and three mules with ornamented Morocco saddles, bridles, bells, and brass neck ornaments, after the fashion of Harar. Two of these men, Haji Umar, and Nur Ambar, were citizens; the others, Ali Hasan, Husayn Araleh, and Haji Mohammed, were Somal of the Habr Awal tribe, high in the Amir's confidence. They had been sent to settle with Adan the weighty matter of Blood-money. After sitting with us almost half an hour, during which they exchanged grave salutations with my attendants, inspected our asses with portentous countenances, and asked me a few questions concerning my business in those parts, they went privily to the Jirad, told him that the Arab was not one who bought and sold, that he had no design but to spy out the wealth of the land, and that the whole party should be sent prisoners in their hands to Harar. The chief curtly replied that we were his friends, and bade them, " throw far those words." Disappointed in their designs, they started late in the afternoon, driving off their 200 cows, and falsely promising to present our salams to the Amir.

It became evident that some decided step must be taken. The Jirad confessed fear of his Harari kinsman, and owned that he had lost all his villages in the immediate neighbourhood of the city. I asked him point-blank to escort us : he as frankly replied that it was impossible. The request was lowered—we begged him to accompany us as far as the frontier : he professed inability to do so, but promised to send his eldest son, Shirwa.

Nothing then remained, dear L., but *payer d'audace*, and, throwing all forethought to the dogs, to rely upon what has made many a small man great, the good star. I addressed my companions in a set speech, advising a mount without delay. They suggested a letter to the Amir, requesting permission to enter his city: this device was rejected for two reasons. In the first place, had a refusal been returned, our journey was cut short, and our labours stultified. Secondly, the End of Time had whispered that my two companions were plotting to prevent the letter reaching its destination. He had charged his own sin upon their shoulders: the Hammal and Long Gulad were incapable of such treachery. But our hedge-priest was thoroughly terrified; "a coward body after a'," his face brightened when ordered to remain with the Jirad at Sagharrah, and though openly taunted with poltroonery, he had not the decency to object. My companions were then informed that hitherto our acts had been those of old women, not soldiers, and that something savouring of manliness must be done before we could return. They saw my determination to start alone, if necessary, and to do them justice, they at once arose. This was the more courageous in them, as alarmists had done their worst: but a day before, some travelling Somali had advised them, as they valued dear life, not to accompany that Turk to Harar. Once in the saddle, they shook off sad thoughts, declaring that if they were slain, I should pay their blood-money, and if they escaped, that their reward was in my hands. When in some danger, the Hammal especially behaved with a sturdiness which produced the most beneficial results. Yet they were true Easterns. Wearied by delay at Harar, I employed myself in meditating flight; they drily declared that after-wit serves no good purpose: whilst I considered the possibility of escape, they looked only at the prospect of being dragged back with pinioned arms by the Amir's guard. Such is generally the effect of the vulgar Moslem's blind fatalism.

I then wrote an English letter[1] from the Political Agent at Aden to the Amir of Harar, proposing to deliver it in person, and throw off my disguise. Two reasons influenced me in adopting this "neck or nothing" plan. All the races amongst whom my travels lay, hold him nidering who hides his origin in places of danger; and secondly, my white face had converted me into a Turk, a nation more hated and suspected than any Europeans, without our *prestige*. Before leaving Sagharrah, I entrusted to the End of Time a few lines addressed to Lieut. Herne at Berberah, directing him how to act in case of necessity. Our baggage was again decimated: the greater part was left with Adan, and an ass carried only what was absolutely necessary, —a change of clothes, a book or two, a few biscuits, ammunition, and a little tobacco. My Girhi escort consisted of Shirwa, the Badawi Abtidon, and Mad Sa'id mounted on the End of Time's mule.

At 10 A.M. on the 2nd January, all the villagers assembled, and recited the Fatihah, consoling us with the information that we were dead men. By the worst of footpaths, we ascended the rough and stony hill behind Sagharrah, through bush and burn and over ridges of rock. At the summit was a village, where Shirwa halted, declaring that he dared not advance: a swordsman, however, was sent on to guard us through the Galla Pass. After an hour's ride, we reached the foot of a tall Table-mountain called Kondura, where our

---

1 At first I thought of writing it in Arabic; but having no seal, a *sine quâ non* in an Eastern letter, and reflecting upon the consequences of detection or even suspicion, it appeared more politic to come boldly as a European.

road, a goat-path rough with rocks or fallen trees, and here and there arched over with giant creepers, was reduced to a narrow ledge, with a forest above and a forest below. I could not but admire the beauty of this Valombrosa, which reminded me of scenes whilome enjoyed in fair Touraine. High up on our left rose the perpendicular walls of the misty hill, fringed with tufted pine, and on the right the shrub-clad folds fell into a deep valley. The cool wind whistled and sunbeams like golden shafts darted through tall shady trees—

Bearded with moss, and in garments green—

the ground was clothed with dank grass, and around the trunks grew thistles, daisies, and blue flowers which, at a distance, might well pass for violets.

Presently we were summarily stopped by half a dozen Gallas attending upon one Rabah, the Chief who owns the Pass.[1] This is the African style of toll-taking: the "pike" appears in the form of a plump of spearmen, and the gate is a pair of lances thrown across the road. Not without trouble, for they feared to depart from the *mos majorum*, we persuaded them that the ass carried no merchandise. Then rounding Kondura's northern flank, we entered the Amir's territory: about thirty miles distant, and separated by a series of blue valleys, lay a dark speck upon a tawny sheet of stubble—Harar.

Having paused for a moment to savour success, we began the descent. The ground was a slippery black soil—mist ever settles upon Kondura—and frequent springs oozing from the rock formed beds of black mire. A few huge Birbisa trees, the remnant of a forest still thick around the mountain's neck, marked out the road:

---

1 It belongs, I was informed, to two clans of Gallas, who year by year in turn monopolize the profits.

they were branchy from stem to stern, and many had
a girth of from twenty to twenty-five feet.[1]

After an hour's ride amongst thistles, whose flowers
of a bright red-like worsted were not less than a child's
head, we watered our mules at a rill below the slope.
Then remounting, we urged over hill and dale, where
Galla peasants were threshing and storing their grain
with loud songs of joy: they were easily distinguished
by their African features, mere caricatures of the Somal,
whose type has been Arabized by repeated immigrations
from Al-Yaman and Hadramaut. Late in the afternoon,
having gained ten miles in a straight direction, we
passed through a hedge of plantains, defending the
windward side of Gafra, a village of Midgans who
collect the Jirad Adan's grain. They shouted delight
on recognising their old friend, Mad Sa'id, led us to an
empty Gambisa, swept and cleaned it, lighted a fire,
turned our mules into a field to graze, and went forth to
seek food. Their hospitable thoughts, however, were
marred by the two citizens of Harar, who privately
threatened them with the Amir's wrath, if they dared to
feed that Turk.

As evening drew on, came a message from our
enemies, the Habr Awal, who offered, if we would wait
till sunrise, to enter the city in our train. The Jirad
Adan had counselled me not to provoke these men; so,
contrary to the advice of my two companions, I returned
a polite answer, purporting that we would expect them
till eight o'clock the next morning.

At 7 A.M., on the 3rd January, we heard that the
treacherous Habr Awal had driven away their cows
shortly after midnight. Seeing their hostile intentions,
I left my journal, sketches, and other books in charge

---

1 Of this tree are made the substantial doors, the basins and the
porringers of Harar.

of an old Midgan, with directions that they should be forwarded to the Jirad Adan, and determined to carry nothing but our arms and a few presents for the Amir. We saddled our mules, mounted and rode hurriedly along the edge of a picturesque chasm of tender pink granite, here and there obscured by luxuriant vegetation. In the centre, fringed with bright banks a shallow rill, called Doghlah, now brawls in tiny cascades, then whirls through huge boulders towards the Erar River. Presently, descending by a ladder of rock scarcely safe even for mules, we followed the course of the burn, and emerging into the valley beneath, we pricked forward rapidly, for day was wearing on, and we did not wish the Habr Awal to precede us.

About noon we crossed the Erar River. The bed is about one hundred yards broad, and a thin sheet of clear, cool, and sweet water covered with crystal the greater part of the sand. According to my guides, its course, like that of the hills, is southerly towards the Webbe of Ogadayn[1]: none, however, could satisfy my curiosity concerning the course of the only perennial stream which exists between Harar and the coast.

In the lower valley, a mass of waving holcus, we met a multitude of Galla peasants coming from the city market with new potlids and the empty gourds which had contained their butter, ghi, and milk; all wondered aloud at the Turk, concerning whom they had heard many horrors. As we commenced another ascent, appeared a Harar Grandee mounted upon a handsomely caparisoned mule and attended by seven servants who carried gourds and skins of grain. He was a pale-faced senior with a white beard, dressed in a fine Tobe and a snowy turband, with scarlet edges : he carried no shield, but an Abyssinian broadsword was slung over his left

---

1 The Webbe Shebayli or Haines River.

shoulder. We exchanged courteous salutations, and as I was thirsty he ordered a footman to fill a cup with water. Half way up the hill appeared the 200 Girhi cows, but those traitors, the Habr Awal, had hurried onwards. Upon the summit was pointed out to me the village of Elaoda : in former times it was a wealthy place belonging to the Jirad Adan.

At 2 P.M. we fell into a narrow fenced lane, and halted for a few minutes near a spreading tree, under which sat women selling ghi and unspun cotton. About two miles distant on the crest of a hill, stood the city— the end of my present travel—a long sombre line, strikingly contrasting with the white-washed towns of the East. The spectacle, materially speaking, was a disappointment : nothing conspicuous appeared but two grey minarets of rude shape : many would have grudged exposing three lives to win so paltry a prize. But of all that have attempted, none ever succeeded in entering that pile of stones : the thorough-bred traveller, dear L., will understand my exultation, although my two companions exchanged glances of wonder.

Spurring our mules, we advanced at a long trot, when Mad Sa'id stopped us to recite a Fatihah in honour of Ao Umar Siyad and Ao Rahmah, two great saints who repose under a clump of trees near the road. The soil on both sides of the path is rich and red : masses of plantains, limes, and pomegranates denote the gardens, which are defended by a bleached cow's skull, stuck upon a short stick[1] and between them are plantations of coffee, bastard saffron, and the graceful Kat. About half a mile eastward of the town appears a burn called Jalah or the Coffee Water : the crowd crossing it did not

---

1 This scarecrow is probably a talisman. In the Saharah, according to Richardson, the skull of an ass averts the evil eye from gardens.

prevent my companions bathing, and whilst they donned clean Tobes I retired to the wayside, and sketched the town.

These operations over, we resumed our way up a rough *tranchée* ridged with stone and hedged with tall cactus. This ascends to an open plain. On the right lie the holcus fields, which reach to the town wall: the left is a heap of rude cemetery, and in front are the dark defences of Harar, with groups of citizens loitering about the large gateway, and sitting in chat near the ruined tomb of Ao Abdal. We arrived at 3 P.M., after riding about five hours, which were required to accomplish twenty direct miles.[1]

Advancing to the gate, Mad Sa'id accosted a warder, known by his long wand of office, and sent our salams to the Amir, saying that we came from Aden, and requested the honour of audience. Whilst he sped upon his errand, we sat at the foot of a round bastion, and were scrutinized, derided, and catechized by the curious of both sexes,

---

1 The following is a table of our stations, directions, and distances :—

				Miles.	
1. From Zayla to Gudingaras	-	S.E. 165°	19		
2. To Kuranyali	-	-	-	145°	8
3. To Adad	-	-	-	225°	25
4. To Damal	-	-	-	205°	11
5. To Al-Armo	-	-	-	190°	11
6. To Jiyaf	-	-	-	202°	10
7. To Halimalah (the Holy Tree, about half-way)	-	-	192°	7	
				— 91 miles.	
8. To Aububah	-	-	-	245°	21
9. To Koralay	-	-	-	165°	25
10. To Harar	-	-	-	260°	65
				—111 miles.	

Total statute miles 202

especially by that conventionally termed the fair. The three Habr Awal presently approached and scowlingly inquired why we had not apprised them of our intention to enter the city. It was now " war to the knife "—we did not deign a reply.

CHAPTER VIII.

TEN DAYS AT HARAR.

AFTER waiting half an hour at the gate, we were told
by the returned warder to pass the threshold, and remounting guided our mules along the main street, a
narrow up-hill lane, with rocks cropping out from a
surface more irregular than a Perote pavement. Long
Gulad had given his animal into the hands of our two
Badawin: they did not appear till after our audience,
when they informed us that the people at the entrance
had advised them to escape with the beasts, an evil fate
having been prepared for the proprietors.

Arrived within a hundred yards of the gate of holcus-
stalks, which opens into the courtyard of this African St.
James's, our guide, a blear-eyed, surly-faced, angry-voiced
fellow, made signs—none of us understanding his Harari
—to dismount. We did so. He then began to trot, and
roared out apparently that we must do the same.[1] We
looked at one another, the Hammal swore that he would
perish foully rather than obey, and—conceive, dear L.,
the idea of a petticoated pilgrim venerable as to beard
and turband breaking into a long "double!"—I expressed

---

[1] The Ashantis at Customs' time (rites done on the death of
men of rank) run across the royal threshold to escape being seized
and sacrificed to wet the grave with slaves' blood (2000 prisoners
are killed when the King "makes a custom" at ancestral tombs);
possibly the trace of a pagan rite is still preserved by Moslem Harar,
where it is now held a mark of respect and always exacted from the
citizens.

much the same sentiment. Leading our mules leisurely, in spite of the guide's wrath, we entered the gate, strode down the yard, and were placed under a tree in its left corner, close to a low building of rough stone, which the clanking of frequent fetters argued to be a state prison.

This part of the court was crowded with Gallas, some lounging about, others squatting in the shade under the palace walls. The chiefs were known by their zinc arm-lets, composed of thin spiral circlets, closely joined, and extending in mass from the wrist almost to the elbow: all appeared to enjoy peculiar privileges—they carried their long spears, wore their sandals, and walked leisurely about the royal precincts. A delay of half an hour, during which state affairs were being transacted within, gave me time to inspect a place of which so many and such different accounts are current. The palace itself is, as Clapperton describes the Fellatah Sultan's state hall, a mere shed, a long, single storied, windowless barn of rough stone and reddish clay, with no other insignia but a thin coat of whitewash over the door. This is the royal and wazirial distinction at Harar, where no lesser man may stucco the walls of his house. The courtyard was about eighty yards long by thirty in breath, irregularly shaped, and surrounded by low buildings: in the centre, opposite the outer entrance, was a circle of masonry against which were propped divers doors.[1]

Presently the blear-eyed guide with the angry voice returned from within, released us from the importunities of certain forward and inquisitive youths, and motioned

---

1 I afterwards learned that when a man neglects a summons his door is removed to the royal court-yard on the first day; on the second, it is confiscated. The door is a valuable and venerable article in this part of Africa. According to Bruce, Ptolemy Euergetes engraved it upon the Axum Obelisk for the benefit of his newly conquered Æthiopian subjects, to whom it had been unknown.

us to doff our slippers at a stone step, or rather line, about twelve feet distant from the palace wall. We grumbled that we were not entering a mosque, but in vain. Then ensued a long dispute, in tongues mutually unintelligible, about giving up our weapons: by dint of obstinacy we retained our daggers and my revolver. The guide raised a door curtain, suggested a bow, and I stood in the presence of the dreaded chief.

The Amir, or, as he styles himself, the Sultan Ahmad bin Sultan Abu Bakr, sat in a dark room with whitewashed walls, to which hung—significant decorations—rusty matchlocks and polished fetters. His appearance was that of a little Indian Rajah, an etiolated youth twenty-four or twenty-five years old, plain and thin-bearded, with a yellow complexion, wrinkled brows and protruding eyes. His dress was a flowing robe of crimson cloth, edged with snowy fur, and a narrow white turband tightly twisted round a tall conical cap of red velvet, like the old Turkish headgear of our painters. His throne was a common Indian Kursi, or raised cot, about five feet long, with back and sides supported by a dwarf railing : being an invalid he rested his elbow upon a pillow, under which appeared the hilt of a Cutch sabre. Ranged in double line, perpendicular to the Amir, stood the "court," his cousins and nearest relations with right arms bared after fashion of Abyssinia.

I entered the room with a loud " Peace be upon ye !" to which H. H. replying graciously, and extending a hand, bony and yellow as a kite's claw, snapped his thumb and middle finger. Two chamberlains stepping forward, held my forearms, and assisted me to bend low over the fingers, which however I did not kiss, being naturally averse to performing that operation upon any but a woman's hand. My two servants then took their turn : in this case, after the back was saluted, the palm

was presented for a repetition.[1] These preliminaries
concluded, we were led to and seated upon a mat in
front of the Amir, who directed towards us a frowning
brow and inquisitive eye.

Some inquiries were made about the chief's health :
he shook his head captiously, and inquired our errand.
I drew from my pocket my own letter : it was carried by
a chamberlain, with hands veiled in his Tobe, to the
Amir, who after a brief glance laid it upon the couch,
and demanded further explanation. I then represented
in Arabic that we had come from Aden, bearing the
compliments of our Daulah or governor, and that we had
entered Harar to see the light of H. H.'s countenance :
this information concluded with a little speech, describing
the changes of Political Agents in Arabia, and alluding
to the friendship formerly existing between the English
and the deceased chief Abu Bakr.

The Amir smiled graciously.

This smile I must own, dear L., was a relief. We
had been prepared for the worst, and the aspect of affairs
in the palace was by no means reassuring.

Whispering to his Treasurer, a little ugly man with
a badly shaven head, coarse features, pug nose, angry
eyes, and stubby beard, the Amir made a sign for us to
retire. The *baise main* was repeated, and we backed out
of the audience-shed in high favour. According to
grandiloquent Bruce, "the Court of London and that
of Abyssinia are, in their principles, one " : the loiterers
in the Harar palace yards who had before regarded us
with cut-throat looks, now smiled as though they loved
us. Marshalled by the guard, we issued from the precincts, and after walking a hundred yards entered the
Amir's second palace, which we were told to consider
our home. There we found the Badawin, who, scarcely

---

1 In Abyssinia, according to the Lord of Geesh, this is a mark
of royal familiarity and confidence.

believing that we had escaped alive, grinned in the joy of their hearts, and we were at once provided from the chief's kitchen with a dish of Shabta, holcus cakes soaked in sour milk, and thickly powdered with red pepper, the salt of this inland region.

When we had eaten, the treasurer reappeared, bearing the Amir's command, that we should call upon his Wazir, the Jirad Mohammed. Resuming our peregrinations, we entered an abode distinguished by its external streak of chunam, and in a small room on the ground floor, cleanly white-washed and adorned, like an old English kitchen, with varnished wooden porringers of various sizes, we found a venerable old man whose benevolent countenance belied the reports current about him in Somali-land.[1] Half rising, although his wrinkled brow showed suffering, he seated me by his side upon the

---

[1] About seven years ago the Hajj Sharmarkay of Zayla chose as his agent at Harar, one of the Amir's officers, a certain Hajj Janitay. When this man died Sharmarkay demanded an account from his sons ; at Berberah they promised to give it, but returning to Harar they were persuaded, it is believed, by the Jirad Mohammed, to forget their word. Upon this Sharmarkay's friends and relations, incited by one Husayn, a Somali who had lived many years at Harar in the Amir's favour, wrote an insulting letter to the Jirad, beginning with, "No peace be upon thee, and no blessings of Allah, thou butcher ! son of a butcher, &c., &c. ! " and concluding with a threat to pinion him in the market-place as a warning to men. Husayn carried the letter, which at first excited general terror ; when, however, the attack did not take place, the Amir Abu Bakr imprisoned the imprudent Somali till he died. Sharmarkay by way of reprisals, persuaded Alu, son of Sahlah Salaseh, king of Shoa, to seize about three hundred Harari citizens living in his dominions and to keep them two years in durance.

The Amir Abu Bakr is said on his deathbed to have warned his son against the Jirad. When Ahmad reported his father's decease to Zayla, the Hajj Sharmarkay ordered a grand Maulid or Mass in honour of the departed. Since that time, however, there has been little intercourse and no cordiality between them.

carpeted masonry-bench, where lay the implements of his craft, reeds, inkstands and whitewashed boards for paper, politely welcomed me, and gravely stroking his cotton-coloured beard, in good Arabic desired my object.

I replied almost in the words used to the Amir, adding however some details how in the old day one Madar Farih had been charged by the late Sultan Abu Bakr with a present to the governor of Aden, and that it was the wish of our people to re-establish friendly relations and commercial intercourse with Harar.

"Khayr Inshallah!—it is well if Allah please!" ejaculated the Jirad: I then bent over his hand, and took leave.

Returning, we inquired anxiously of the treasurer about my servants' arms which had not been returned, and were assured that they had been placed in the safest of store-houses, the palace. I then sent a common six-barrelled revolver as a present to the Amir, explaining its use to the bearer, and we prepared to make ourselves as comfortable as possible. The interior of our new house was a clean room, with plain walls, and a floor of tamped earth; opposite the entrance were two broad steps of masonry, raised about two feet, and a yard above the ground, and covered with hard matting. I contrived to make upon the higher ledge a bed with the cushions which my companions used as shabracques, and, after seeing the mules fed and tethered, lay down to rest worn out by fatigue and profoundly impressed with the *poésie* of our position. I was under the roof of a bigoted prince whose least word was death; amongst a people who detest foreigners; the only European that h..d ever passed over their inhospitable threshold, and the fated instrument of their future downfall.

END OF VOLUME I.

H.H. AHMED BIN ABIBAKR AMIR OF HARAR

FIRST FOOTSTEPS

IN

EAST AFRICA

OR,

AN EXPLORATION OF HARAR

BY

CAPTAIN SIR RICHARD F. BURTON,

K.C.M.G., F.R.G.S., &c., &c., &c.

EDITED BY HIS WIFE,

ISABEL BURTON

Memorial Edition.

———

IN TWO VOLUMES.
VOLUME II.

CONTENTS

OF

THE SECOND VOLUME.

LIST OF ILLUSTRATIONS

IN VOLUME II.

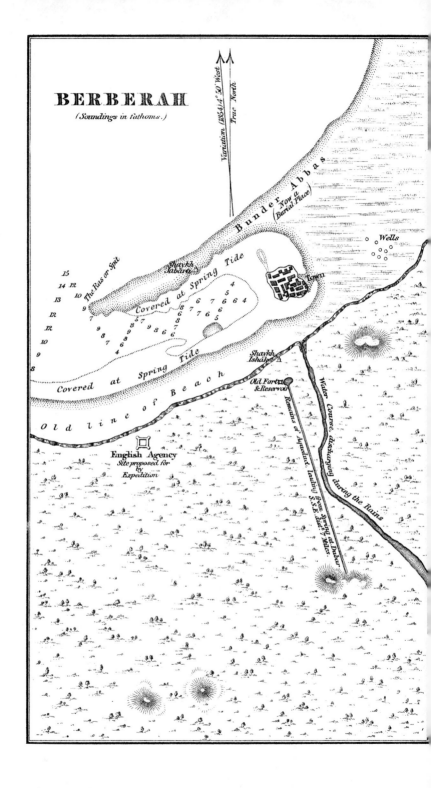

FIRST FOOTSTEPS

IN

EAST AFRICA.

CHAPTER VIII.—(*Continued.*)

TEN DAYS AT HARAR.

I now proceed to a description of unknown Harar.

The ancient capital of Hadiyah, called by the citizens " Harar Gay,[1]" by the Somal " Adari," by the Gallas "Adaray," and by the Arabs and ourselves " Harar,[2]" lies, according to my dead reckoning, 220° S.W. of, and 175 statute miles from, Zayla—257° W. of, and 219 miles distant from, Berberah. This would place it in 9° 20' N. lat., and 42° 7' E. long. The thermometer showed an altitude of about 5,500 feet above the level of the sea.[3] Its site is the slope of a

---

1 Thus M. Isenberg (Preface to Ambaric Grammar, p. iv.) calls the city Harrar or Arargê.

2 " Harar," is not an uncommon name in this part of Eastern Africa : according to some, the city is so called from a kind of tree, according to others, from the valley below it.

3 I say *about :* we were compelled to boil our thermometers at Wilensi, not venturing upon such operation within the city.

hill which falls gently from west to east. On the eastern side are cultivated fields ; westwards a terraced ridge is laid out in orchards; northwards is a detached eminence covered with tombs ; and to the south, the city declines into a low valley bisected by a mountain burn. This irregular position is well sheltered from high winds, especially on the northern side, by the range of which Kondura is the lofty apex ; hence, as the Persian poet sings of a heaven-favoured city—

"Its heat is not hot, nor its cold, cold."

During my short residence the air reminded me of Tuscany. On the afternoon of the 11th January there was thunder accompanied by rain : frequent showers fell on the 12th, and the morning of the 13th was clear ; but as we crossed the mountains, black clouds obscured the heavens. The monsún is heavy during one summer month ; before it begins the crops are planted, and they are reaped in December and January. At other seasons the air is dry, mild, and equable.

The province of Hadiyah[1] is mentioned by Makrizi as one of the seven members of the Zayla Empire,[2] founded by Arab invaders, who in the 7th century of our æra conquered and colonized the low tract between the Red Sea and the Highlands. Moslem Harar exercised a pernicious influence upon the fortunes of Christian Abyssinia.[3]

---

1 The province is eight days by nine in extent, with a large army, and money derived from the trade in eunuchs. I have chiefly borrowed from Taki al-Din Ahmad bin Ali al-Makrizi.

2 The other six were Ífat, Arabini, Duaro, Sharkah, Báli and Darah.

3 A circumstantial account of the Jihad or Moslem crusades is, I am told, given in the Fath al-Habashah, unfortunately a rare work, which was not procurable at Zanzibar. The Amir of Harar had but one volume, and the other is to be found at Mocha or Hudaydah.

The allegiance claimed by the Æthiopian Emperors from the Adel—the Dankali and ancient Somal—was evaded at a remote period, and the intractable Moslems were propitiated with rich presents, when they thought proper to visit the Christian court. The Abyssinians supplied the Adel with slaves, the latter returned the value in rock-salt, commercial intercourse united their interests, and from war resulted injury to both people. Nevertheless the fanatic lowlanders, propense to pillage and proselytizing, burned the Christian churches, massacred the infidels, and tortured the priests, until they provoked a blood feud of uncommon asperity.

In the 14th century (A.D. 1312—1342) Amda Sion, Emperor of Æthiopia, taunted by Amano, King of Hadiyah, as a monarch fit only to take care of women, overran and plundered the Lowlands from Tegulet to the Red Sea. The Amharas were commanded to spare nothing that drew the breath of life : to fulfil a prophecy which foretold the fall of Al-Islam, they perpetrated every kind of enormity.

Peace followed the death of Amda Sion. In the reign of Zara Yakub[1] (A.D. 1434—1468), the flame of war was again fanned in Hadiyah by a Zayla princess who was slighted by the Æthiopian monarch on account of the length of her foreteeth: the hostilities which ensued were not, however, of an important nature. Bœda Mariam, the next occupant of the throne, passed his life in a constant struggle for supremacy over the Adel : on his death-bed he caused himself to be so placed that his face looked towards those lowlands, upon whose subjugation the energies of ten years had been vainly expended.

At the close of the 15th century, Mahfuz, a bigoted Moslem, inflicted a deadly blow upon Abyssinia.

---

1 This prince built "Debra Berhan," the "Hill of Glory," a church dedicated to the Virgin Mary at Gondar.

Vowing that he would annually spend the forty days of Lent amongst his infidel neighbours, when, weakened by rigorous fasts, they were less capable of bearing arms, for thirty successive years he burned churches and monasteries, slew without mercy every male that fell in his way, and driving off the women and children, he sold some to strange slavers, and presented others to the Sharifs of Meccah. He bought over Za Salasah, commander in chief of the Emperor's body guard, and caused the assassination of Alexander (A.D. 1478—1495) at the ancient capital Tegulet. Naud, the successor, obtained some transient advantages over the Moslems. During the earlier reign of the next emperor, David III. son of Na'ud,[1] who being but eleven years old when called to the throne, was placed under the guardianship of his mother the Iteghe Helena, new combatants and new instruments of warfare appeared on both sides of the field.

After the conquest of Egypt and Arabia by Selim I. (A. D. 1516)[2] the caravans of Abyssinian pilgrims travelling to Jerusalem were attacked, the old were butchered and the young were swept into slavery. Many Arabian merchants fled from Turkish violence and injustice, to the opposite coast of Africa, whereupon the Ottomans took possession from Aden of Zayla, and not only laid the Indian trade under heavy contributions by means of their war-galleys, but threatened the total destruction of Abyssinia. They aided and encouraged Mahfuz to continue his depredations, whilst the Sharif of Meccah gave him command of Zayla, the key of the

---

1 A prince of many titles : he is generally called Wanag Suggud, " feared amongst the lions," because he spent the latter years of his life in the wild.

2 Al-Yaman submitted to Sulayman Pasha in A.D. 1538.

upper country, and presented him with the green banner of a Crusader.

On the other hand, the great Albuquerque at the same time (A. D. 1508—1515) was viceroy of India, and to him the Iteghe Helena applied for aid. Her ambassador arrived at Goa, " bearing a fragment of wood belonging to the true cross on which Christ died," which relic had been sent as a token of friendship to her brother Emanuel by the empress of Æthiopia. The overture was followed by the arrival at Masawwah of an embassy from the King of Portugal. Too proud, however, to await foreign aid, David at the age of sixteen took the field in person against the Moslems.

During the battle that ensued, Mahfuz, the Goliath of the Unbelievers, was slain in single combat by Gabriel Andreas, a soldier of tried valour, who had assumed the monastic life in consequence of having lost the tip of his tongue for treasonable freedom of speech : the green standard was captured, and 12,000 Moslems fell. David followed up his success by invading the lowlands, and, in defiance, struck his spear through the door of the king of Adel.

Harar was a mere mass of Badawi villages during the reign of Mohammed Gragne, the "left-handed" Attila of Adel.[1] Supplied with Arab mercenaries from Mocha, and by the Turks of Al-Yaman with a body of Janissaries and a train of artillery, he burst into Ífat and Fatigar. In A.D. 1528 he took possession of Shoa, overran Amhara, burned the churches and carried away an immense booty. The next campaign enabled him to winter at Begmeder : in the following year he hunted the Emperor David through Tigre to the borders of Sana'ar, gave battle to the Christians on the banks of

---

1 " Gragne," or in the Somali dialect " Guray," means a left-handed man ; Father Lobo errs in translating it " the Lame."

the Nile, and with his own hand killed the monk
Gabriel, then an old man. Reinforced by Gideon and
Judith, king and queen of the Saman Jews, and aided by
a violent famine which prostrated what had escaped the
spear, he perpetrated every manner of atrocity, captured
and burned Axum, destroyed the princes of the royal
blood on the mountain of Amba Gêshê,[1] and slew
in A.D. 1540, David, third of his name and last emperor
of Æthiopia who displayed the magnificence of " King
of Kings."

Claudius, the successor to the tottering throne, sent
as his ambassador to Europe, one John Bermudez, a
Portuguese who had been detained in Abyssinia, and
promised, it is said, submission to the Pontiff of Rome,
and the cession of a third of his dominions in return for
reinforcements. By order of John III., Don Stephen
and Don Christopher, sons of Don Vasco da Gama,
cruised up the Red Sea with a powerful flotilla, and the
younger brother, landing at Masawwah with 400 musqueteers, slew Nur the Governor, and sent his head to
Gondar, where the Iteghe Sabel Wenghel received it as
an omen of good fortune. Thence the Portuguese general
imprudently marched in the monsun season, and was
soon confronted upon the plain of Ballut by Mohammed
Gragne at the head of 10,000 spearmen and a host of
cavalry. On the other side stood a rabble rout of
Abyssinians, and a little band of 350 Portuguese heroes
headed by the most chivalrous soldier of a chivalrous age.

According to Father Jerome Lobo,[2] who heard the

---

1 This exploit has been erroneously attributed to Nur, the
successor of Mohammed.

2 This reverend Jesuit was commissioned in A.D. 1622, by the
Count de Vidigueira, Viceroy of the Indies, to discover where his
relative Don Christopher was buried, and to procure some of the
relics. Assisted by the son-in-law of the Abyssinian Emperor, Lobo
marched with an army through the Gallas, found the martyr's teeth

events from an eye-witness, a conference took place between the two captains. Mohammed encamped in a commanding position, sent a message to Don Christopher informing him that the treacherous Abyssinians had imposed upon the king of Portugal, and that in compassion of his opponent's youth, he would give him and his men free passage and supplies to their own country. The Christian presented the Moslem ambassador with a rich robe, and returned this gallant answer, "that he and his fellow-soldiers were come with an intention to drive Mohammed out of these countries which he had wrongfully usurped; that his present design was, instead of returning back the way he came, as Mohammed advised, to open himself a passage through the country of his enemies; that Mohammed should rather think of determining whether he would fight or yield up his ill-gotten territories than of prescribing measures to him; that he put his whole confidence in the omnipotence of God, and the justice of his cause; and that to show how full a sense he had of Mohammed's kindness, he took the liberty of presenting him with a looking-glass and a pair of pincers."

The answer and the present so provoked the Adel Monarch that he arose from table to attack the little

---

and lower jaw, his arms and a picture of the Holy Virgin which he always carried about with him. The precious remains were forwarded to Goa.

I love the style of this old father, so unjustly depreciated by our writers, and called ignorant peasant and liar by Bruce, because he claimed for his fellow countrymen the honour of having discovered the Coy Fountains. The Nemesis who never sleeps punished Bruce by the justest of retributions. His pompous and inflated style, his uncommon arrogance, and over-weening vanity, his affectation of pedantry, his many errors and misrepresentations, aroused against him a spirit which embittered the last years of his life. It is now the fashion to laud Bruce, and to pity his misfortunes. I cannot but think that he deserved them.

troop of Portuguese, posted upon the declivity of a hill near a wood. Above them stood the Abyssinians, who resolved to remain quiet spectators of the battle, and to declare themselves on the side favoured by victory.

Mohammed began the assault with only ten horse-men, against whom an equal number of Portuguese were detached : these fired with so much exactness that nine of the Moors fell and the king was wounded in the leg by Peter de Sa. In the mêlée which ensued, the Moslems, dismayed by their first failure, were soon broken by the Portuguese muskets and artillery. Mohammed preserved his life with difficulty, he however rallied his men, and entrenched himself at a strong place called Membret (Mamrat), intending to winter there and await succour.

The Portuguese more desirous of glory than wealth, pursued their enemies, hoping to cut them entirely off: finding, however, the camp impregnable, they entrenched themselves on a hill over against it. Their little host diminished day by day, their friends at Masawwah could not reinforce them, they knew not how to procure pro-visions, and could not depend on their Abyssinian allies. Yet memorious of their countrymen's great deeds, and depending upon divine protection, they made no doubt of surmounting all difficulties.

Mohammed on his part was not idle. He solicited the assistance of the Moslem princes, and by inflaming their religious zeal, obtained a reinforcement of 2000 musqueteers from the Arabs, and a train of artillery from the Turks of Al-Yaman. Animated by these succours, he marched out of his trenches to enter those of the Portuguese, who received him with the utmost bravery, destroyed many of his men, and made frequent sallies, not, however, without sustaining considerable losses.

Don Christopher had already one arm broken and a knee shattered by a musket shot. Valour was at length oppressed by superiority of numbers: the enemy entered the camp, and put the Christians to the spear. The Portuguese general escaped the slaughter with ten men, and retreated to a wood, where they were discovered by a detachment of the enemy.[1] Mohammed, overjoyed to see his most formidable enemy in his power, ordered Don Christopher to take care of a wounded uncle and nephew, telling him that he should answer for their lives, and upon their death, taxed him with having hastened it. The Portuguese roundly replied that he was come to destroy Moslems, not to save them. Enraged at this language, Mohammed placed a stone upon his captive's head, and exposed him to the insults of the soldiery, who inflicted upon him various tortures which he bore with the resolution of a martyr. At length, when offered a return to India as the price of apostacy, the hero's spirit took fire. He answered with the highest indignation, that nothing could make him forsake his Heavenly Master to follow an "imposter," and continued in the severest terms to vilify the "false Prophet," till Mohammed struck off his head.[2] The body was divided into quarters and sent to different places,[3] but the Catholics gathered their martyr's remains and interred them.

---

1 Bruce followed by most of our modern authors, relates a circumstantial and romantic story of the betrayal of Don Christopher by his mistress, a Turkish lady of uncommon beauty, who had been made prisoner.

The more truth-like pages of Father Lobo record no such silly scandal against the memory of the "brave and holy Portuguese." Those who are well read in the works of the earlier eastern travellers will remember their horror of "handling heathens after that fashion." And amongst those who fought for the faith an *affaire de cœur* with a pretty pagan was held to be a sin as deadly as heresy or magic.

2 Romantic writers relate that Mohammed decapitated the Christian with his left hand.

3 Others assert, in direct contradiction to Father Lobo, that the body was sent to different parts of Arabia, and the head to Constantinople

Every Moor who passed by threw a stone upon the grave, and raised in time such a heap that Father Lobo found difficulty in removing it to exhume the relics. He concludes with a pardonable superstition: " There is a tradition in the country, that in the place where Don Christopher's head fell, a fountain sprang up of wonderful virtue, which cured many diseases, otherwise past remedy."

Mohammed Gragne improved his victory by chasing the young Claudius over Abyssinia, where nothing opposed the progress of his arms. At last the few Portuguese survivors repaired to the Christian Emperor, who was persuaded to march an army against the King of Adel. Resolved to revenge their general, the harquebusiers demanded the post opposite Mohammed, and directed all their efforts against the part where the Moslem Attila stood. His fellow religionists still relate that when Gragne fell in action, his wife Talwambara,[1] the heroic daughter of Mahfuz, to prevent the destruction and dispersion of the host of Al-Islam, buried the corpse privately, and caused a slave to personate the prince until a retreat to safe lands enabled her to discover the stratagem to the nobles.[2]

Father Lobo tells a different tale. According to

---

1 Bruce followed by later authorities, writes this name Del Wumbarea.

2 Talwambara, according to the Christians, after her husband's death, and her army's defeat, threw herself into the wilds of Atbara, and recovered her son Ali Jirad by releasing Prince Menas, the brother of the Abyssinian emperor, who in David's reign had been carried prisoner to Adel.

The historian will admire these two widely different accounts of the left-handed hero's death. Upon the whole he will prefer the Moslem's tradition from the air of truth pervading it, and the various improbabilities which appear in the more detailed story of the Christians.

him, Peter Leon, a marksman of low stature, but passing valiant, who had been servant to Don Christopher, singled the Adel king out of the crowd, and shot him in the head as he was encouraging his men. Mohammed was followed by his enemy till he fell down dead: the Portuguese then alighting from his horse, cut off one of his ears and rejoined his fellow-countrymen. The Moslems were defeated with great slaughter, and an Abyssinian chief finding the Gragne's corpse upon the ground, presented the head to the Negush or Emperor, claiming the honour of having slain his country's deadliest foe. Having witnessed in silence this impudence, Peter asked whether the king had but one ear, and produced the other from his pocket to the confusion of the Abyssinian.

Thus perished, after fourteen years' uninterrupted fighting, the African hero, who dashed to pieces the structure of 2500 years. Like the " Kardillan " of the Holy Land, Mohammed Gragne is still the subject of many a wild and grisly legend. And to the present day the people of Shoa retain an inherited dread of the lowland Moslems.

Mohammed was succeeded on the throne of Adel by the Amir Nur, son of Majid, and, according to some, brother to the " Left-handed." He proposed marriage to Talwambara, who accepted him on condition that he should lay the head of the Emperor Claudius at her feet. In A.D. 1559, he sent a message of defiance to the Negush, who, having saved Abyssinia almost by a miracle, was rebuilding on Debra Work, the " Golden Mount," a celebrated shrine which had been burned by the Moslems. Claudius, despising the eclipses, evil prophecies, and portents which accompanied his enemy's progress, accepted the challenge. On the 22nd March 1559, the armies were upon the point of engaging, when the high priest of Debra Libanos, hastening into the presence of the Negush, declared that in a vision, Gabriel had ordered him to dissuade the Emperor of Æthiopia from needlessly risking life. The superstitious Abyssinians fled, leaving Claudius supported by a handful of Portuguese, who were soon slain around him, and he fell covered with wounds. The Amir Nur cut off his head, and laid it at the feet of Talwambara, who, in observance of her pledge, became his wife. This Amazon suspended the trophy by its hair to the branch of a tree opposite her abode, that her eyes might be gladdened by the sight: after hanging two years, it was purchased by an Armenian merchant, who interred it in the Sepulchre of St. Claudius at Antioch. The name of the Christian hero who won every action save that in which he perished, has been enrolled in the voluminous catalogue of Abyssinian saints, where it occupies a conspicuous place as the destroyer of Mohammed the Left-handed.

The Amir Nur has also been canonized by his countrymen, who have buried their favourite " Wali " under a little dome near the Jami Mosque at Harar. Shortly after his decisive victory over the Christians, he surrounded the city with its present wall—a circumstance now invested with the garb of Moslem fable. The warrior used to hold frequent conversations with Al-Khizr : on one occasion, when sitting upon a rock, still called Gay Humburti—Harar's Navel—he begged that some Sharif might be brought from Meccah, to aid him in building a permanent city. By the use of the " Great Name" the vagrant prophet instantly summoned from Arabia the Sharif Yunis, his son Fakr al-Din, and a descendant from the Ansar or Auxiliaries of the Prophet: they settled at Harar, which throve by the blessing of their presence. From this tradition we may gather that the city was restored, as it was first founded and colonized, by hungry Arabs.

The Sharifs continued to rule with some interruptions until but a few generations ago, when the present family rose to power. According to Bruce, they are Jabartis, who, having intermarried with Sayyid women, claim a noble origin. They derive themselves from the Caliph Abu Bakr, or from Akil, son of Abu Talib, and brother of Ali. The Olema, although lacking boldness to make the assertion, evidently believe them to be of Galla or pagan extraction.

The present city of Harar is about one mile long by half that breadth. An irregular wall, lately repaired,[1] but ignorant of cannon, is pierced with five large gates,[2] and supported by oval towers of artless construction. The material of the houses and defences is rough stones, the granites and sandstones of the hills, cemented. like the ancient Galla cities, with clay. The only large building is the Jami or Cathedral, a long barn of poverty-stricken appearance, with broken-down gates, and two white-washed minarets of truncated conoid shape. They

---

1 Formerly the Waraba, creeping through the holes in the wall, rendered the streets dangerous at night. They are now destroyed by opening the gates in the evening, enticing in the animals by slaughtering cattle, and closing the doors upon them, when they are safely speared.

2 The following are the names of the gates in Harari and Somali.

Eastward. Argob Bari (Bar in Amharic is a gate, *e.g.* Ankobar, the gate of Anko, a Galla Queen, and Argob is the name of a Galla clan living in this quarter), by the Somal called Erar.

North. Asum Bari (the gate of Axum), in Somali, Faldano or the Zayla entrance.

West. Asmadim Bari or Hamaraisa.

South. Badro Bari or Bab Bida.

South East. Sukutal Bari or Bisidimo.

At all times these gates are carefully guarded; in the evening the keys are taken to the Amir, after which no one can leave the city till dawn.

were built by Turkish architects from Mocha and
Hodaydah : one of them lately fell, and has been replaced by an inferior effort of Harari art. There are
a few trees in the city, but it contains none of those
gardens which give to Eastern settlements that pleasant
view of town and country combined. The streets are
narrow lanes, up hill and down dale, strewed with
gigantic rubbish heaps, upon which repose packs of
mangy or one-eyed dogs, and even the best are encum-
bered with rocks and stones. The habitations are
mostly long, flat-roofed sheds, double storied, with doors
composed of a single plank, and holes for windows
pierced high above the ground, and decorated with
miserable wood-work : the principal houses have separate apartments for the women, and stand at the
bottom of large court-yards closed by gates of Holcus
stalks. The poorest classes inhabit " Gambisa," the
thatched cottages of the hill-cultivators. The city
abounds in mosques, plain buildings without minarets,
and in graveyards stuffed with tombs—oblong troughs
formed by long slabs planted edgeways in the ground.
I need scarcely say that Harar is proud of her learning,
sanctity, and holy dead. The principal saint buried in
the city is Shaykh Umar Abadir al-Bakri, originally
from Jeddah, and now the patron of Harar : he lies
under a little dome in the southern quarter of the city,
near the Bisidimo Gate.

The ancient capital of Hadiyah shares with Zabid
in Al-Yaman, the reputation of being an Alma Mater,
and inundates the surrounding districts with poor
scholars and crazy " Widads." Where knowledge leads
to nothing, says philosophic Volney, nothing is done to
acquire it, and the mind remains in a state of barbarism. There are no establishments for learning, no
endowments, as generally in the East, and apparently
no encouragement to students : books also are rare and

costly. None but the religious sciences are cultivated. The chief Olema are the Kabir[1] Khalil, the Kabir Yunis, and the Shaykh Jami: the two former scarcely ever quit their houses, devoting all their time to study and tuition: the latter is a Somali who takes an active part in politics.

These professors teach Moslem literature through the medium of Harari, a peculiar dialect confined within the walls. Like the Somali and other tongues in this part of Eastern Africa, it appears to be partly Arabic in etymology and grammar: the Semitic scion being grafted upon an indigenous root: the frequent recurrence of the guttural *kh* renders it harsh and unpleasant, and it contains no literature except songs and tales, which are written in the modern Naskhi character. I would willingly have studied it deeply, but circumstances prevented: the explorer too frequently must rest satisfied with descrying from his Pisgah the Promised Land of Knowledge, which another more fortunate is destined to conquer. At Zayla, the Hajj sent to me an Abyssinian slave who was cunning in languages: but he, to use the popular phrase, "showed his right ear with his left hand." Inside Harar, we were so closely watched that it was found impossible to put pen to paper. Escaped, however, to Wilensi, I hastily collected the grammatical forms and a vocabulary, which will correct the popular assertion that "the language is Arabic: it has an affinity with the Amharic.[2]"

Harar has not only its own tongue, unintelligible to any save the citizens; even its little population of about

---

1 Kabir in Arabic means great, and is usually applied to the Almighty; here it is a title given to the principal professors of religious science.

2 This is equivalent to saying that the language of the Basque provinces is French with an affinity to English.

8000 souls is a distinct race. The Somal say of the city that it is a Paradise inhabited by asses: certainly the exterior of the people is highly unprepossessing. Amongst the men, I did not see a handsome face: their features are coarse and debauched; many of them squint, others have lost an eye by small-pox, and they are disfigured by scrofula and other diseases: the bad expression of their countenances justifies the proverb, "Hard as the heart of Harar." Generally the complexion is a yellowish brown, the beard short, stubby and untractable as the hair, and the hands and wrists, feet and ankles, are large and ill-made. The stature is moderate-sized, some of the elders show the "pudding sides" and the pulpy stomachs of Banyans, whilst others are lank and bony as Arabs or Jews. Their voices are loud and rude. The dress is a mixture of Arab and Abyssinian. They shave the head, and clip the mustachioes and imperial close, like the Shafe'i of Al-Yaman. Many are bareheaded, some wear a cap, generally the embroidered Indian work, or the common cotton Takiyah of Egypt: a few affect white turbands of the fine Harar work, loosely twisted over the ears. The body-garment is the Tobe, worn flowing as in the Somali country or girt with the dagger-strap round the waist: the richer classes bind under it a Futah or loin-cloth, and the dignitaries have wide Arab drawers of white calico. Coarse leathern sandals, a rosary and a tooth-stick rendered perpetually necessary by the habit of chewing tobacco, complete the costume: and arms being forbidden in the streets, the citizens carry wands five or six feet long.

The women, who, owing probably to the number of female slaves, are much the more numerous, appear beautiful by contrast with their lords. They have small heads, regular profiles, straight noses, large eyes, mouths approaching the Caucasian type, and light yellow complexions. Dress, however, here is a disguise to charms.

COSTUMES OF HARAR.

A long, wide, cotton shirt, with short arms as in the Arab's Aba, indigo-dyed or chocolate-coloured, and ornamented with a triangle of scarlet before and behind —the base on the shoulder and the apex at the waist— is girt round the middle with a sash of white cotton crimson-edged. Women of the upper class, when leaving the house, throw a blue sheet over the head, which, however, is rarely veiled. The front and back hair parted in the centre is gathered into two large bunches below the ears, and covered with dark blue muslin or network, whose ends meet under the chin. This coiffure is bound round the head at the junction of scalp and skin by a black satin ribbon which varies in breadth according to the wearer's means: some adorn the gear with large gilt pins, others twine in it a Taj or thin wreath of sweet-smelling creeper. The virgins collect their locks, which are generally wavy not wiry, and grow long as well as thick, into a knot tied *à la Diane* behind the head: a curtain of short close plaits escaping from the bunch, falls upon the shoulders, not ungracefully. Silver ornaments are worn only by persons of rank. The ear is decorated with Somali rings or red coral beads, the neck with necklaces of the same material, and the fore-arms with six or seven of the broad circles of buffalo and other dark horns prepared in Western India. Finally, stars are tattooed upon the bosom, the eyebrows are lengthened with dyes, the eyes fringed with Kohl, and the hands and feet stained with henna.

The female voice is harsh and screaming, especially when heard after the delicate organs of the Somal. The fair sex is occupied at home spinning cotton thread for weaving Tobes, sashes, and turbands; carrying their progeny perched upon their backs, they bring water from the wells in large gourds borne on the head; work in the gardens, and—the men considering, like the Abyssinians, such work a disgrace—sit and sell in the long street which here represents the Eastern bazar. Chewing tobacco enables them to pass much of their time, and the rich diligently anoint themselves with ghi, whilst the poorer classes use remnants of fat from the lamps. Their freedom of manners renders a public flogging occasionally indispensable. Before the operation begins, a few gourds full of cold water are poured over their heads and shoulders, after which a single-thonged whip is applied with vigour.[1]

Both sexes are celebrated for laxity of morals. High and low indulge freely in intoxicating drinks, beer, and mead. The Amir has established strict patrols, who unmercifully bastinado those caught in the streets after a certain hour. They are extremely bigoted, especially against Christians, the effect of their Abyssinian wars, and are fond of " Jihading " with the Gallas, over whom they boast many a victory. I have seen a letter addressed by the late Amir to the Hajj Sharmarkay, in which he boasts of having slain a thousand infidels, and, by way of bathos, begs for a few pounds of English gunpowder. The Harari hold foreigners in especial hate and contempt, and divide them into two orders, Arabs and Somal.[2] The latter,

---

1 When ladies are bastinadoed in more modest Persia, their hands are passed through a hole in the tent wall, and fastened for the infliction to a Falakah or pole outside.

2 The hate dates from old times. Abd al-Karim, uncle to the late Amir Abu Bakr, sent for sixty or seventy Arab mercenaries under Haydar Assal the Auliki, to save him against the Gallas. The matchlockmen failing in ammunition, lost twenty of their number in battle and retired to the town, where the Gallas, after capturing Abd al-Karim, and his brother Abd al-Rahman, seized the throne, and, aided by the citizens, attempted to massacre the strangers. These, however, defended themselves gallantly, and would have crowned the son of Abd al-Rahman, had he not in fear declined the dignity; they then drew their pay, and marched with all the honours of war to Zayla. Shortly before our arrival, the dozen of petty Arab pedlars at Harar, treacherous intriguers, like all

though nearly one third of the population, or 2500 souls, are, to use their own phrase, cheap as dust: their natural timidity is increased by the show of pomp and power, whilst the word " prison " gives them the horrors.

The other inhabitants are about 3000 Badawin, who " come and go." Up to the city gates the country is peopled by the Gallas. This unruly race requires to be propitiated by presents of cloth ; as many as 600 Tobes are annually distributed amongst them by the Amir. Lately, when the smallpox, spreading from the city, destroyed many of their number, the relations of the deceased demanded and received blood-money ; they might easily capture the place, but they preserve it for their own convenience. These Gallas are tolerably brave, avoid matchlock balls by throwing themselves upon the ground when they see the flash, ride well, use the spear skilfully, and although of proverbially bad breed, are favourably spoken of by the citizens. The Somal find no difficulty in travelling amongst them. I repeatedly heard at Zayla and at Harar that traders had visited the far West, traversing for seven months a country of pagans wearing golden bracelets,[1] till they reached the Salt Sea, upon which Franks sail in ships.[2]

---

their dangerous race, had been plotting against the Amir. One morning when they least expected it, their chief was thrown into a prison which proved his grave, and the rest were informed that any stranger found in the city should lose his head. After wandering some months among the neighbouring villages, they were allowed to return and live under surveillance. No one at Harar dared to speak of this event, and we were cautioned not to indulge our curiosity.

1 This agrees with the Hon. R. Curzon's belief in Central African " diggings." The traveller once saw an individual descending the Nile with a store of nuggets, bracelets, and gold rings similar to those used as money by the ancient Egyptians.

2 M. Krapf relates a tale current in Abyssinia; namely, that there is a remnant of the slave trade between Guineh (the Guinea coast) and Shoa. Connection between the east and west formerly

At Wilensi, one Mohammed, a Shaykhash, gave me his itinerary of fifteen stages to the sources of the Abbay or Blue Nile : he confirmed the vulgar Somali report that the Hawash and the Webbe Shebayli both take rise in the same range of well wooded mountains which gives birth to the river of Egypt.

The government of Harar is the Amir. These petty princes have a habit of killing and imprisoning all those who are suspected of aspiring to the throne.[2] Ahmad's greatgrandfather died in jail, and his father narrowly escaped the same fate. When the present Amir ascended the throne he was ordered, it is said, by the Makad or chief of the Nole Gallas, to release his prisoners, or to mount his horse and leave the city. Three of his cousins, however, were, when I visited Harar, in confinement : one of them since that time died, and has been buried in his fetters. The Somal declare that the state-dungeon of Harar is beneath the palace, and that he who once enters it, lives with unkempt beard and untrimmed nails until the day when death sets him free.

The Amir Ahmad's health is infirm. Some attribute his weakness to a fall from a horse, others declare him to have been poisoned by one of his wives.[1] I judged him consumptive. Shortly after my departure he was upon the point of death, and he afterwards sent for a physician to Aden. He has four wives. No. 1 is the daughter of

---

existed : in the time of John the Second, the Portuguese on the river Zaire in Congo learned the existence of the Abyssinian church. Travellers in Western Africa assert that Fakihs or priests, when performing the pilgrimage pass from the Fellatah country through Abyssinia to the coast of the Red Sea. And it has lately been proved that a caravan line is open from the Zanzibar coast to Benguela.

2 All male collaterals of the royal family, however, are not imprisoned by law, as was formerly the case at Shoa.

the Jirad Hirsi; No. 2, a Sayyid woman of Harar; No. 3,
an emancipated slave girl; and No. 4, a daughter of
Jirad Abd al-Majid, one of his nobles. He has two
sons, who will probably never ascend the throne; one is
an infant, the other is a boy now about five years old.

The Amir Ahmad succeeded his father about three
years ago. His rule is severe if not just, and it has
all the *prestige* of secrecy. As the Amharas say, the
"belly of the Master is not known[2]": even the Jirad
Mohammed, though summoned to council at all times,
in sickness as in health, dares not offer uncalled-for
advice, and the queen dowager, the Gisti Fatimah, was
threatened with fetters if she persisted in interference.
Ahmad's principal occupations are spying his many
stalwart cousins, indulging in vain fears of the English,
the Turks, and the Hajj Sharmarkay, and amassing
treasure by commerce and escheats. He judges civil
and religious causes in person, but he allows them with
little interference to be settled by the Kazi, Abd al-
Rahman bin Umar al-Harari: the latter, though a
highly respectable person, is seldom troubled; rapid
decision being the general predilection. The punishments, when money forms no part of them, are mostly
according to Koranic code. The murderer is placed in
the market street, blindfolded, and bound hand and foot;
the nearest of kin to the deceased then strikes his neck
with a sharp and heavy butcher's knife, and the corpse
is given over to the relations for Moslem burial. If the
blow prove ineffectual a pardon is generally granted.
When a citizen draws dagger upon another or commits
any petty offence, he is bastinadoed in a peculiar
manner: two men ply their horsewhips upon his back
and breast, and the prince, in whose presence the punish-

---

1 This is a mere superstition; none but the most credulous can
believe that a man ever lives after an Eastern dose.

2 "The King's heart is inscrutable."

ment is carried out, gives the order to stop. Theft is visited with amputation of the hand. The prison is the award of state offenders: it is terrible, because the captive is heavily ironed, lies in a filthy dungeon, and receives no food but what he can obtain from his own family—seldom liberal under such circumstances—or buy or beg from his guards. Fines and confiscations, as usual in the East, are favourite punishments with the ruler. I met at Wilensi an old Harari, whose gardens and property had all been escheated, because his son fled from justice, after slaying a man. The Amir is said to have large hoards of silver, coffee, and ivory: my attendant the Hammal was once admitted into the inner palace, where he saw huge boxes of ancient fashion supposed to contain dollars. The only specie current in Harar is a diminutive brass piece called Mahallak[1]— hand-worked and almost as artless a medium as a modern Italian coin. It bears on one side the words:

ضريبة الهر .

(Zaribet al-Harar, the coinage of Harar).

---

1 The name and coin are Abyssinian. According to Bruce,

20 Mahallaks are worth	-	-	1 Grush.
12 Grush	,,	,,	-	-	1 Miskal.
4 Miskal	,,	,,	-	-	1 Wakiyah (ounce).

At Harar twenty-two plantains (the only small change) = one Mahallak, twenty-two Mahallaks = one Ashrafi (now a nominal coin,) and three Ashrafi = one dollar.

Lieut. Cruttenden remarks, " The Ashrafi stamped at the Harar mint is a coin peculiar to the place. It is of silver and the twenty-second part of a dollar. The only specimen I have been able to procure bore the date of 910 of the Hagira, with the name of the Amir on one side, and, on its reverse, ' La Ilaha ill 'Allah.'" This traveller adds in a note, " the value of the Ashrafi changes with each successive ruler. In the reign of Emir Abd el Shukoor, some 200 years ago, it was of gold." At present the Ashrafi, as I have said above, is a fictitious medium used in accounts.

On the reverse is the date, A H. 1248. The Amir pitilessly punishes all those who pass in the city any other coin.

The Amir Ahmad is alive to the fact that some state should hedge in a prince. Neither weapons nor rosaries are allowed in his presence; a chamberlain's robe acts as spittoon; whenever anything is given to or taken from him, his hand must be kissed; even on horseback two attendants fan him with the hems of their garments. Except when engaged on the Haronic visits which he, like his father,[1] pays to the streets and byways at night, he is always surrounded by a strong body guard. He rides to mosque escorted by a dozen horsemen, and a score of footmen with guns and whips precede him: by his side walks an officer shading him with a huge and heavily fringed red satin umbrella—from India to Abyssinia the sign of princely dignity. Even at his prayers two or three chosen matchlockmen stand over him with lighted fusees. When he rides forth in public, he is escorted by a party of fifty men: the running footmen crack their whips and shout "Let! Let!" (Go! Go!) and the citizens avoid stripes by retreating into the nearest house, or running into another street.

The army of Harar is not imposing. There are between forty and fifty matchlockmen of Arab origin, long settled in the place, and commanded by a veteran Maghrabi. They receive for pay one dollar's worth of holcus per annum, a quantity sufficient to afford five or six loaves a day: the luxuries of life must be provided by

---

1 An old story is told of the Amir Abu Bakr, that during one of his nocturnal excursions, he heard three of his subjects talking treason, and coveting his food, his wife, and his throne. He sent for them next morning, filled the first with good things, and bastinadoed him for not eating more, flogged the second severely for being unable to describe the difference between his own wife and the princess, and put the third to death.

the exercise of some peaceful craft. Including slaves, the total of armed men may be two hundred : of these one carries a Somali or Galla spear, another a dagger, and a third a sword, which is generally the old German cavalry blade. Cannon of small calibre is supposed to be concealed in the palace, but none probably knows their use. The city may contain thirty horses, of which a dozen are royal property : they are miserable ponies, but well trained to the rocks and hills. The Galla Badawin would oppose an invader with a strong force of spearmen, the approaches to the city are difficult and dangerous, but it is commanded from the north and west, and the walls would crumble at the touch of a six-pounder. Three hundred Arabs and two gallopper guns would take Harar in an hour.

Harar is essentially a commercial town : its citizens live, like those of Zayla, by systematically defrauding the Galla Badawin, and the Amir has made it a penal offence to buy by weight and scale. He receives, as octroi, from eight to fifteen cubits of Cutch canvas for every donkey-load passing the gates, consequently the beast is so burdened that it must be supported by the drivers. Cultivators are taxed ten per cent., the general and easy rate of this part of Africa, but they pay in kind, which considerably increases the Government share. The greatest merchant may bring to Harar £50 worth of goods, and he who has £20 of capital is considered a wealthy man. The citizens seem to have a more than Asiatic apathy, even in pursuit of gain. When we entered, a caravan was to set out for Zayla on the morrow ; after ten days, hardly one half of its number had mustered. The four marches from the city eastward are rarely made under a fortnight, and the average rate of their Kafilahs is not so high even as that of the Somal.

The principal exports from Harar are slaves, ivory,

coffee, tobacco, Wars (safflower or bastard saffron), Tobes and woven cottons, mules, holcus, wheat, "Karanji," a kind of bread used by travellers, ghi, honey, gums (principally mastic and myrrh), and finally sheep's fat and tallows of all sorts. The imports are American sheeting, and other cottons, white and dyed, muslins, red shawls, silks, brass, sheet copper, cutlery (generally the cheap German), Birmingham trinkets, beads and coral, dates, rice, and loaf sugar, gunpowder, paper, and the various other wants of a city in the wild.

Harar is still, as of old,[1] the great "half way house" for slaves from Zangaro, Guragué, and the Galla tribes, Alo and others[2]: Abyssinians and Amharas, the most valued,[3] have become rare since the King of Shoa prohibited the exportation. Women vary in value from 100 to 400 Ashrafis, boys from 9 to 150: the worst are kept for domestic purposes, the best are driven and exported by the Western Arabs[4] or by the subjects of

---

1 Al Makrizi informs us that in his day Hadiyah supplied the East with black Eunuchs, although the infamous trade was expressly forbidden by the Emperor of Abyssinia.

2 The Arusi Gallas are generally driven direct from Ugadayn to Berberah.

3 "If you want a brother (in arms)," says the Eastern proverb, "buy a Nubian, if you would be rich, an Abyssinian, and if you require an ass, a Sawahili (negroid)." Formerly a small load of salt bought a boy in Southern Abyssinia; many of them however, died on their way to the coast.

4 The Firman lately issued by the Sultan and forwarded to the Pasha of Jeddah for the Kaimakan and the Kazi of Meccah, has lately caused a kind of revolution in Western Arabia. The Olema and the inhabitants denounced the rescript as opposed to the Koran, and forced the magistrate to take sanctuary. The Kaimakan came to his assistance with Turkish troops; the latter, however, were soon pressed back into their fort. At this time, the Sharif Abd al-Muttalib arrived at Meccah, from Taif, and almost simultaneously Rashid

H. H. the Imam of Maskat, in exchange for rice and dates. I need scarcely say that commerce would thrive on the decline of slavery : whilst the Felateas or man-razzias are allowed to continue, it is vain to expect industry in the land.

Ivory at Harar amongst the Kafirs is a royal monopoly, and the Amir carries on the one-sided system of trade, common to African monarchs. Elephants abound in Jarjar, the Erar forest, and in the Harirah and other valleys, where they resort during the hot season, in cold descending to the lower regions. The Gallas hunt the animals and receive for the spoil a little cloth : the Amir sends his ivory to Berberah, and sells it by means of a Wakil or agent. The smallest kind is called " Ruba Aj " (Quarter Ivory), the better descrip-tion " Nuss Aj " (Half Ivory), whilst " Aj," the best kind, fetches from thirty-two to forty dollars per Farasilah of 27 Arab pounds.[1]

The coffee of Harar is too well known in the markets of Europe to require description : it grows in the gardens about the town, in greater quantities amongst the Western Gallas, and in perfection at Jarjar, a district of about seven days' journey from Harar on the Ífat road. It is said that the Amir withholds this

---

Pasha came from Constantinople with orders to seize him, send him to the capital, and appoint the Sharif Nazír to act until the nomination of a successor, the state prisoner Mohammed bin Aun.

The tumult redoubled. The people attributing the rescript to the English and French Consuls of Jeddah, insisted upon pulling down their flags. The Pasha took them under his protection, and on the 14th January, 1856, the "Queen" steamer was despatched from Bombay, with orders to assist the government and to suppress the contest.

[1] This weight, as usual in the East, varies at every port. At Aden the Farasilah is 27 lbs., at Zayla, 20 lbs., and at Berberah, 35 lbs.

valuable article, fearing to glut the Berberah market: he has also forbidden the Harash, or coffee cultivators, to travel lest the art of tending the tree be lost. When I visited Harar, the price per parcel of twenty-seven pounds was a quarter of a dollar, and the hire of a camel carrying twelve parcels to Berberah was five dollars: the profit did not repay labour and risk.

The tobacco of Harar is of a light yellow colour, with good flavour, and might be advantageously mixed with Syrian and other growths. The Alo, or Western Gallas, the principal cultivators, plant it with the holcus, and reap it about five months afterwards. It is cocked for a fortnight, the woody part is removed, and the leaf is packed in sacks for transportation to Berberah. At Harar, men prefer it for chewing as well as smoking; women generally use Surat tobacco. It is bought, like all similar articles, by the eye, and about seventy pounds are to be had for a dollar.

The Wars or Safflower is cultivated in considerable quantities around the city: an abundance is grown in the lands of the Gallas. It is sown when the heavy rains have ceased, and is gathered about two months afterwards. This article, together with slaves, forms the staple commerce between Berberah and Maskat. In Arabia, men dye with it their cotton shirts, women and children use it to stain the skin a bright yellow; besides the purpose of a cosmetic, it also serves as a preservative against cold. When Wars is cheap at Harar, a pound may be bought for a quarter of a dollar.

The Tobes and sashes of Harar are considered equal to the celebrated cloths of Shoa: hand-woven, they as far surpass, in beauty and durability, the vapid produce of European manufactories, as the perfect hand of man excels the finest machinery. On the windward coast, one of these garments is considered a handsome present for a chief. The Harari Tobe consists of a double length of eleven cubits by two in breadth, with a border of bright scarlet, and the average value of a good article, even in the city, is eight dollars. They are made of the fine long-stapled cotton, which grows plentifully upon these hills, and are soft as silk, whilst their warmth admirably adapts them for winter wear. The thread is spun by women with two wooden pins; the loom is worked by both sexes.

Three caravans leave Harar every year for the Berberah market. The first starts early in January, laden with coffee, Tobes, Wars, ghi, gums, and other articles to be bartered for cottons, silks, shawls, and Surat tobacco. The second sets out in February. The principal caravan, conveying slaves, mules, and other valuable articles, enters Berberah a few days before the close of the season : it numbers about 3000 souls, and is commanded by one of the Amir's principal officers, who enjoys the title of Ebi or leader. Any or all of these kafilahs might be stopped by spending four or five hundred dollars amongst the Jibril Abokr tribe, or even by a sloop of war at the emporium. " He who commands at Berberah, holds the beard of Harar in his hand," is a saying which I heard even within the city walls.

The furniture of a house at Harar is simple—a few skins, and in rare cases a Persian rug, stools, coarse mats, and Somali pillows, wooden spoons, and porringers shaped with a hatchet, finished with a knife, stained red, and brightly polished. The gourd is a conspicuous article ; smoked inside and fitted with a cover of the same material, it serves as cup, bottle, pipe, and water-skin : a coarse and heavy kind of pottery, of black or brown clay, is used by some of the citizens.

The inhabitants of Harar live well. The best meat, as in Abyssinia, is beef : it rather resembled,

however, in the dry season when I ate it, the lean and
stringy sirloins of Old England in Hogarth's days. A hundred and twenty chickens, or sixty-six full-grown fowls,
may be purchased for a dollar, and the citizens do not,
like the Somal, consider them carrion. Goat's flesh is
good, and the black-faced Berberah sheep, after the
rains, is, here as elsewhere, delicious. The staff of life
is holcus. Fruit grows almost wild, but it is not prized
as an article of food: the plantains are coarse and
bad, grapes seldom come to maturity; although the
brab flourishes in every ravine, and the palm becomes
a lofty tree, it has not been taught to fructify, and the
citizens do not know how to dress, preserve or pickle
their limes and citrons. No vegetables but gourds are
known. From the cane, which thrives upon these hills,
a little sugar is made: the honey of which, as the
Abyssinians say, "the land stinks," is the general
sweetener. The condiment of East Africa is red pepper.

To resume, dear L., the thread of our adventures
at Harar.

Immediately after arrival, we were called upon by
the Arabs, a strange mixture. One, the Haji Mukhtar,
was a Maghrabi from Fez: an expatriation of forty
years had changed his hissing Arabic as little as his
"rocky face." This worthy had a coffee-garden as-
signed to him, as commander of the Amir's body-guard:
he introduced himself to us, however, as a merchant,
which led us to look upon him as a spy. Another, Haji
Hasan, was a thorough-bred Persian: he seemed to know
everybody, and was on terms of bosom friendship with
half the world from Cairo to Calcutta, Moslem, Christian
and Pagan. Amongst the rest was a boy from Meccah,
a Maskat man, a native of Suez, and a citizen of
Damascus: the others were Arabs from Al-Yaman. All

were most civil to us at first; but, afterwards, when our
interviews with the Amir ceased, they took alarm, and
prudently cut us.

The Arabs were succeeded by the Somal, amongst
whom the Hammal and Long Gulad found relatives,
friends, and acquaintances, who readily recognized them
as government servants at Aden. These visitors at first
came in fear and trembling with visions of the Harar
jail: they desired my men to return the visit by night,
and made frequent excuses for apparent want of hospitality. Their apprehensions, however, soon vanished:
presently they began to prepare entertainments, and, as
we were without money, they willingly supplied us with
certain comforts of life. Our three Habr Awal enemies,
seeing the tide of fortune settling in our favour, changed
their tactics: they threw the past upon their two Harari
companions, and proposed themselves as Abbans on our
return to Berberah. This offer was politely staved off;
in the first place we were already provided with protectors, and secondly these men belonged to the Ayyal
Shirdon, a clan most hostile to the Habr Girhajis.
They did not fail to do us all the harm in their power,
but again my good star triumphed.

After a day's repose, we were summoned by the
Treasurer, early in the forenoon, to wait upon the Jirad
Mohammed. Sword in hand, and followed by the
Hammal and Long Gulad, I walked to the " palace,"
and entering a little ground-floor room on the right of
and close to the audience-hall, found the minister sitting
upon a large dais covered with Persian carpets. He was
surrounded by six of his brother Jirads or councillors,
two of them in turbands, the rest with bare and shaven
heads: their Tobes, as is customary on such occasions
of ceremony, were allowed to fall beneath the waist.
The lower part of the hovel was covered with dependents,
amongst whom my Somal took their seats: it seemed to

be customs' time, for names were being registered, and
money changed hands. The Grandees were eating Kat,
or as it is here called " Ját.[1]" One of the party prepared
for the Prime Minister the tenderest twigs of the tree,
plucking off the points of even the softest leaves.
Another pounded the plant with a little water in a
wooden mortar : of this paste, called " Al-Madkuk,"
a bit was handed to each person, who, rolling it into
a ball, dropped it into his mouth. All at times, as is the
custom, drank cold water from a smoked gourd, and
seemed to dwell upon the sweet and pleasant draught.
I could not but remark the fine flavour of the plant after
the coarser quality grown in Al-Yaman. Europeans perceive but little effect from it—friend S. and I once tried
in vain a strong infusion—the Arabs, however, un-
accustomed to stimulants and narcotics, declare that,
like opium eaters, they cannot live without the excitement. It seems to produce in them a manner of dreamy
enjoyment, which, exaggerated by time and distance,
may have given rise to that splendid myth the Lotos,
and the Lotophagi. It is held by the Olema here as in
Arabia, " Akl al-Salikin," or the Food of the Pious, and
literati remark that it has the singular properties of en-
livening the imagination, clearing the ideas, cheering the
heart, diminishing sleep, and taking the place of food.
The people of Harar eat it every day from 9 A.M. till
near noon, when they dine and afterwards indulge in
something stronger—millet-beer and mead.

The Jirad, after polite inquiries, seated me by his
right hand upon the Dais, where I ate Kat and fingered
my rosary, whilst he transacted the business of the day.
Then one of the elders took from a little recess in the
wall a large book, and uncovering it, began to recite a

---

1 See Chap. iii. Al-Makrizi, describing the kingdom of Zayla,
uses the Harari, not the Arabic term ; he remarks that it is unknown
to Egypt and Syria, and compares its leaf to that of the orange.

long Dua or Blessing upon the Prophet: at the end of
each period all present intoned the response, " Allah
bless our Lord Mohammed with his Progeny and his
Companions, one and all ! " This exercise lasting half
an hour afforded me the opportunity—much desired—of
making an impression. The reader, misled by a mar-
ginal reference, happened to say, " Angels, Men, and
Jinnis : " the Jirad took the book and found written,
" Men, Angels, and Jinnis." Opinions were divided as
to the order of beings, when I explained that human
nature, which amongst Moslems is *not* a little lower than
the angelic, ranked highest, because of it were created
prophets, apostles, and saints, whereas the other is but
a " Wasitah " or connection between the Creator and his
creatures. My theology won general approbation and a
few kinder glances from the elders.

Prayer concluded, a chamberlain whispered the Jirad,
who arose, deposited his black coral rosary, took up an
inkstand, donned a white " Badan " or sleeveless Arab
cloak over his cotton shirt, shuffled off the Dais into his
slippers, and disappeared. Presently we were summoned to an interview with the Amir : this time I was
allowed to approach the outer door with covered feet.
Entering ceremoniously as before, I was motioned by
the Prince to sit near the Jirad, who occupied a Persian
rug on the ground to the right of the throne : my two
attendants squatted upon the humbler mats in front
and at a greater distance. After sundry inquiries about
the changes that had taken place at Aden, the letter was
suddenly produced by the Amir, who looked upon it
suspiciously and bade me explain its contents. I was
then asked by the Jirad whether it was my intention to
buy and sell at Harar : the reply was, " We are no
buyers nor sellers[1]; we have become your guests to pay

---

1 In conversational Arabic " we " is used without affectation
for " I."

our respects to the Amir—whom may Allah preserve!—
and that the friendship between the two powers may
endure." This appearing satisfactory, I added, in lively
remembrance of the proverbial delays of Africa, where
two or three months may elapse before a letter is
answered or a verbal message delivered, that perhaps
the Prince would be pleased to dismiss us soon, as the
air of Harar was too dry for me, and my attendants were
in danger of the small-pox, then raging in the town. The
Amir, who was chary of words, bent towards the Jirad,
who briefly ejaculated, " The reply will be vouchsafed:"
with this unsatisfactory answer the interview ended.

Shortly after arrival, I sent my Salam to one of the
Olema, Shaykh Jami of the Berteri Somal: he accepted
the excuse of ill health, and at once came to see me.
This personage appeared in the form of a little black
man aged about forty, deeply pitted by small-pox, with
a protruding brow, a tufty beard and rather delicate
features: his hands and feet were remarkably small.
Married to a descendant of the Sharif Yunis, he had
acquired great reputation as an Alim or Savan, a
peace-policy-man, and an ardent Moslem. Though an
imperfect Arabic scholar, he proved remarkably well
read in the religious sciences, and even the Meccans
had, it was said, paid him the respect of kissing his
hand during his pilgrimage. In his second character,
his success was not remarkable, the principal results
being a spear-thrust in the head, and being generally
told to read his books and leave men alone. Yet he is
always doing good "lillah," that is to say, gratis and
for Allah's sake : his pugnacity and bluntness—the prerogatives of the " peaceful"—gave him some authority
over the Amir, and he has often been employed on
political missions amongst the different chiefs. Nor
has his ardour for propagandism been thoroughly grati-
fied. He commenced his travels with an intention of

winning the crown of glory without delay, by murdering the British resident at Aden[1]: struck, however, with the order and justice of our rule, he changed his intentions and offered Al-Islam to the officer, who received it so urbanely, that the simple Eastern repenting having intended to cut the Kafir's throat, began to pray fervently for his conversion. Since that time he has made it a point of duty to attempt every infidel: I never heard, however, that he succeeded with a soul.

The Shaykh's first visit did not end well. He informed me that the old Osmanlis conquered Stambul in the days of Omar. I imprudently objected to the date, and he revenged himself for the injury done to his fame by the favourite ecclesiastical process of privily damning me for a heretic, and a worse than heathen. Moreover he had sent me a kind of ritual which I had perused in an hour and returned to him: this prepossessed the Shaykh strongly against me, lightly "skimming" books being a form of idleness as yet unknown to the ponderous East.

Our days at Harar were monotonous enough. In the morning we looked to the mules, drove out the cats—as great a nuisance here as at Aden—and ate for breakfast lumps of boiled beef with peppered holcus-scones. We were kindly looked upon by one Sultan, a sick and decrepid Eunuch, who having served five Amirs, was allowed to remain in the palace. To appearance he was mad: he wore upon his poll a motley scratch wig, half white and half black, like Day and Night in

---

1 The Shaykh himself gave me this information. As a rule it is most imprudent for Europeans holding high official positions in these barbarous regions, to live as they do, unarmed and unattended. The appearance of utter security may impose, where strong motives for assassination are wanting. At the same time the practice has occasioned many losses which singly, to use an Indian statesman's phrase, would have "dimmed a victory."

masquerades. But his conduct was sane. At dawn he sent us bad plantains, wheaten crusts, and cups of unpalatable coffee-tea,[1] and, assisted by a crone more decrepid than himself, prepared for me his water-pipe, a gourd fitted with two reeds and a tile of baked clay by way of bowl: now he "knagged" at the slave girls, who were slow to work, then burst into a fury because some visitor ate Kat without offering it to him, or crossed the royal threshold in sandal or slipper. The other inmates of the house were Galla slave-girls, a great nuisance, especially one Berille, an unlovely maid, whose shrill voice and shameless manners were a sad scandal to pilgrims and pious Moslems.

About 8 A.M. the Somal sent us gifts of citrons, plantains, sugar cane, limes, wheaten bread, and stewed fowls. At the same time the house became full of visitors, Harari and others, most of them pretexting inquiries after old Sultan's health. Noon was generally followed by a little solitude, the people retiring to dinner and siesta : we were then again provided with bread and beef from the Amir's kitchen. In the afternoon the house again filled, and the visitors dispersed only for supper. Before sunset we were careful to visit the mules tethered in the court-yard; being half starved they often attempted to desert.[2]

---

1 In the best coffee countries, Harar and Al-Yaman, the berry is reserved for exportation. The Southern Arabs use for economy and health—the bean being considered heating—the Kishr or follicle. This in Harar is a woman's drink. The men considering the berry too dry and heating for their arid atmosphere, toast the leaf on a girdle, pound it and prepare an infusion which they declare to be most wholesome, but which certainly suggests weak senna. The boiled coffee-leaf has been tried and approved of in England; we omit, however, to toast it.

2 In Harar a horse or a mule is never lost, whereas an ass straying from home is rarely seen again.

It was harvest home at Harar, a circumstance which worked us much annoy. In the mornings the Amir, attended by forty or fifty guards, rode to a hill north of the city, where he inspected his Galla reapers and threshers, and these men were feasted every evening at our quarters with flesh, beer, and mead.[1] The strong drinks caused many a wordy war, and we made a point of exhorting the pagans, with poor success I own, to purer lives.

We spent our *soirée* alternately bepreaching the Gallas, "chaffing" Mad Sa'id, who despite his seventy years was a hale old Badawi with a salt and sullen repartee, and quarrelling with the slave-girls. Berille the loud-lunged, or Aminah the pert, would insist upon extinguishing the fat-fed lamp long ere bed-time, or would enter the room singing, laughing, dancing, and clapping a measure with their palms, when, stoutly aided by old Sultan, who shrieked like a hyæna on these occasions, we ejected her in extreme indignation. All then was silence without: not so—alas!—within. Mad Sa'id snored fearfully, and Abtidon chatted half the night with some Badawi friend, who had dropped in to supper. On our hard couches we did not enjoy either the *noctes* or the *cœnæ deorum*.

The even tenour of such days was varied by a perpetual reference to the rosary, consulting sooth-sayers,

---

1 This is the Abyssinian "Tej," a word so strange to European organs, that some authors write it "Zatsh." At Harar it is made of honey dissolved in about fifteen parts of hot water, strained and fermented for seven days with the bark of a tree called Kudidah; when the operation is to be hurried, the vessel is placed near the fire. Ignorant Africa can ferment, not distil, yet it must be owned she is skilful in her rude art. Every traveller has praised the honey-wine of the Highlands, and some have not scrupled to prefer it to champagne. It exhilarates, excites and acts as an aphrodisiac; the consequence is, that at Harar all men, pagans and sages, priests and rulers, drink it.

and listening to reports and rumours brought to us by the Somal in such profusion that we all sighed for a discontinuance. The Jirad Mohammed, excited by the Habr Awal, was curious in his inquiries concerning me : the astute Senior had heard of our leaving the End of Time with the Jirad Adan, and his mind fell into the fancy that we were transacting some business for the Hajj Sharmarkay, the popular bugbear of Harar. Our fate was probably decided by the arrival of a youth of the Ayyal Gedid clan, who reported that three brothers had landed in the Somali country, that two of them were anxiously awaiting at Berberah the return of the third from Harar, and that, though dressed like Moslems, they were really Englishmen in government employ. Visions of cutting off caravans began to assume a hard and palpable form : the Habr Awal ceased intriguing, and the Jirad Mohammed resolved to adopt the *suaviter in modo* whilst dealing with his dangerous guest.

Some days after his first visit, the Shaykh Jami, sending for the Hammal, informed him of an intended trip from Harar : my follower suggested that we might well escort him. The good Shaykh at once offered to apply for leave from the Jirad Mohammed ; not, however, finding the minister at home, he asked us to meet him at the palace on the morrow, about the time of Kat-eating.

We had so often been disappointed in our hopes of a final " lay-public," that on this occasion much was not expected. However, about 6 A.M., we were all summoned and entering the Jirad's levee-room were, as usual, courteously received. I had distinguished his complaint—chronic bronchitis—and resolving to make a final impression, related to him all its symptoms, and promised, on reaching Aden, to send the different remedies employed by ourselves. He clung to the hope of escaping his sufferings, whilst the attendant courtiers looked on

approvingly, and begged me to lose no time. Presently
the Jirad was sent for by the Amir, and after a few
minutes I followed him, on this occasion alone. Ensued
a long conversation about the state of Aden, of Zayla, of
Berberah, and of Stambul. The chief put a variety of
questions about Arabia, and every object there: the
answer was that the necessity of commerce confined us
to the gloomy rock. He used some obliging expressions
about desiring our friendship, and having considerable
respect for a people who built, he understood, large ships.
I took the opportunity of praising Harar in cautious
phrase, and especially of regretting that its coffee was not
better known amongst the Franks. The small wizen-faced
man smiled, as Moslems say, the smile of Omar[1]: seeing
his brow relax for the first time, I told him that being now
restored to health, we requested his commands for Aden.
He signified consent with a nod, and the Jirad, with
many compliments, gave me a letter addressed to the
Political Resident, and requested me to take charge of a
mule as a present. I then arose, recited a short prayer,
the gist of which was that the Amir's days and reign
might be long in the land, and that the faces of his foes
might be blackened here and hereafter, bent over his
hand, and retired. Returning to the Jirad's levee-hut, I
saw by the countenances of my two attendants that they
were not a little anxious about the interview, and comforted them with the whispered word " Achha "—" all
right ! "

Presently appeared the Jirad, accompanied by two
men, who brought my servants' arms, and the revolver

1 The Caliph Omar is said to have smiled once and wept once.
The smile was caused by the recollection of his having eaten his
paste-gods in the days of ignorance. The tear was shed in remembrance of having buried alive, as was customary amongst the Pagan
Arabs, his infant daughter, who, whilst he placed her in the grave,
with her little hands beat the dust off his beard and garment.

which I had sent to the prince. This was a *contretemps*. It was clearly impossible to take back the present, besides which, I suspected some finesse to discover my feelings towards him : the other course would ensure delay. I told the Jirad that the weapon was intended especially to preserve the Amir's life, and for further effect, snapped caps in rapid succession to the infinite terror of the august company. The minister returned to his master, and soon brought back the information that after a day or two another mule should be given to me. With suitable acknowledgments we arose, blessed the Jirad, bade adieu to the assembly, and departed joyful, the Hammal in his glee speaking broken English, even in the Amir's courtyard.

Returning home, we found the good Shaykh Jami, to whom we communicated the news with many thanks for his friendly aid. I did my best to smooth his temper about Turkish history, and succeeded. Becoming communicative, he informed me that the original object of his visit was the offer of good offices, he having been informed that in the town was a man who brought down the birds from heaven, and the citizens having been thrown into great excitement by the probable intentions of such a personage. Whilst he sat with us, Kabir Khalil, one of the principal Olema, and one Haji Abdullah, a Shaykh of distinguished fame who had been dreaming dreams in our favour, sent their salams. This is one of the many occasions in which, during a long residence in the East, I have had reason to be grateful to the learned, whose influence over the people when unbiassed by bigotry is decidedly for good. That evening there was great joy amongst the Somal, who had been alarmed for the safety of my companions ; they brought them presents of Harari Tobes, and a feast of fowls, limes, and wheaten bread for the stranger.

On the 11th of January I was sent for by the Jirad

and received the second mule. At noon we were visited
by the Shaykh Jami, who, after a long discourse upon
the subject of Sufiism,[1] invited me to inspect his books.
When midday prayer was concluded we walked to his
house, which occupies the very centre of the city : in its
courtyard is "Gay Humburti," the historic rock upon
which Saint Nur held converse with the Prophet Khizr.
The Shaykh, after seating us in a room about ten feet
square, and lined with scholars and dusty tomes, began
reading out a treatise upon the genealogies of the Grand
Masters, and showed me in half a dozen tracts the tenets
of the different schools. The only valuable MS. in the
place was a fine old copy of the Koran ; the Kamus and
the Sihah were there,[2] but by no means remarkable for
beauty or correctness. Books at Harar are mostly
antiques, copyists being exceedingly rare, and the square
massive character is more like Cufic with diacritical
points, than the graceful modern Naskhi. I could not,
however, but admire the bindings : no Eastern country
save Persia surpasses them in strength and appearance.
After some desultory conversation the Shaykh ushered
us into an inner room, or rather a dark closet partitioned
off from the study, and ranged us around the usual dish
of boiled beef, holcus bread, and red pepper. After
returning to the study we sat for a few minutes—
Easterns rarely remain long after dinner—and took
leave, saying that we must call upon the Jirad
Mohammed.

Nothing worthy of mention occurred during our
final visit to the minister. He begged me not to forget
his remedies when we reached Aden : I told him that
without further loss of time we would start on the
morrow, Friday, after prayers, and he simply ejaculated,

---

1 The Eastern parent of Free-Masonry.
2 Two celebrated Arabic dictionaries.

" It is well, if Allah please ! " Scarcely had we returned
home, when the clouds, which had been gathering since
noon, began to discharge heavy showers, and a few loud
thunder-claps to reverberate amongst the hills. We
passed that evening surrounded by the Somal, who
charged us with letters and many messages to Berberah.
Our intention was to mount early on Friday morning.
When we awoke, however, a mule had strayed and was
not brought back for some hours. Before noon Shaykh
Jami called upon us, informed us that he would travel
on the most auspicious day—Monday—and exhorted us
to patience, deprecating departure upon Friday, the
Sabbath. Then he arose to take leave, blessed us at
some length, prayed that we might be borne upon the
wings of safety, again advised Monday, and promised at
all events to meet us at Wilensi.

I fear that the Shaykh's counsel was on this
occasion likely to be disregarded. We had been absent
from our goods and chattels a whole fortnight: the
people of Harar are famously fickle; we knew not what
the morrow might bring forth from the Amir's mind—in
fact, all these African cities are prisons on a large scale,
into which you enter by your own will, and, as the
significant proverb says, you leave by another's. However, when the mosque prayers ended, a heavy shower
and the stormy aspect of the sky preached patience more
effectually than did the divine : we carefully tethered
our mules, and unwillingly deferred our departure till
next morning.

CHAPTER IX.

A RIDE TO BERBERAH.

LONG before dawn on Saturday, 13th January, the mules were saddled, bridled, and charged with our scanty luggage. After a hasty breakfast we shook hands with old Sultan the Eunuch, mounted and pricked through the desert streets. Suddenly my weakness and sickness left me—so potent a drug is joy!—and, as we passed the gates loudly salaming to the warders, who were crouching over the fire inside, a weight of care and anxiety fell from me like a cloak of lead.

Yet, dear L., I had time, on the top of my mule for musing upon how melancholy a thing is success. Whilst failure inspirits a man, attainment reads the sad prosy lesson that all our glories

"Are shadows, not substantial things."

Truly said the sayer, "disappointment is the salt of life"—a salutary bitter which strengthens the mind for fresh exertion, and gives a double value to the prize.

This shade of melancholy soon passed away. The morning was beautiful. A cloudless sky, then untarnished by sun, tinged with reflected blue the mist-crowns of the distant peaks and the smoke wreaths hanging round the sleeping villages, and the air was a cordial after the rank atmosphere of the town. The dew hung in large diamonds from the coffee trees, the spur-fowl crew blithely in the bushes by the way-side :—briefly, never did the face of Nature appear to me so truly lovely.

We hurried forward, unwilling to lose time and fearing the sun of the Erar valley. With arms cocked, a precaution against the possibility of Galla spears in ambuscade, we crossed the river, entered the yawning chasm and ascended the steep path. My companions were in the highest spirits, nothing interfered with the general joy but the villain Abtidon, who loudly boasted in a road crowded with market people, that the mule which he was riding had been given to us by the Amir as a Jizyah or tribute. The Hammal, direfully wrath, threatened to shoot him upon the spot, and it was not without difficulty that I calmed the storm.

Passing Gafra we ascertained from the Midgans that the Jirad Adan had sent for my books and stored them in his own cottage. We made in a direct line for Kondura. At one P.M. we safely threaded the Galla's pass, and about an hour afterwards we exclaimed " Alhamdolillah " at the sight of Sagharrah and the distant Marah Prairie. Entering the village we discharged our fire-arms : the women received us with the Masharrad or joy-cry, and as I passed the enclosure the Jiradah Khayrah performed the " Fola " by throwing over me some handfuls of toasted grain.[1] The men gave cordial *poignées de mains*, some danced with joy to see us return alive; they had heard of our being imprisoned, bastinadoed, slaughtered ; they swore that the Jirad was raising an army to rescue or revenge us— in fact, had we been their kinsmen more excitement could not have been displayed. Lastly, in true humility, crept forward the End of Time, who, as he kissed my

---

1 It is an Arab as well as a Somali ceremony to throw a little Kaliyah or Salul (toasted grain) over the honoured traveller when he enters hut or tent.

hand, was upon the point of tears: he had been half-starved, despite his dignity as Sharmarkay's Mercury, and had spent his weary nights and days reciting the chapter Y.S. and fumbling the rosary for omens. The Jirad, he declared, would have given him a sheep and one of his daughters to wife, temporarily, but Shirwa had interfered, he had hindered the course of his sire's generosity: " Cursed be he," exclaimed the End of Time, " who with dirty feet defiles the pure water of the stream ! "

We entered the smoky cottage. The Jirad and his sons were at Wilensi settling the weighty matter of a caravan which had been plundered by the Usbayhan tribe—in their absence the good Khayrah and her daughters did the duties of hospitality by cooking rice and a couple of fowls. A pleasant evening was spent in recounting our perils as travellers will do, and complimenting one another upon the power of our star.

At eight the next morning we rode to Wilensi. As we approached it all the wayfarers and villagers inquired Hibernically if we were the party that had been put to death by the Amir of Harar. Loud congratulations and shouts of joy awaited our arrival. The Kalandar was in a paroxysm of delight: both Shahrazad and Dunyazad were affected with giggling and what might be blushing. We reviewed our property and found that the One-eyed had been a faithful steward, so faithful indeed, that he had well nigh starved the two women. Presently appeared the Jirad and his sons bringing with them my books ; the former was at once invested with a gaudy Abyssinian Tobe of many colours, in which he sallied forth from the cottage the admired of all admirers. The pretty wife Sudiyah and the good Khayrah were made happy by sundry gifts of huge Birmingham ear-rings, 'brooches and bracelets, scissors, needles, and thread. The evening as usual ended in a feast.

We halted a week at Wilensi to feed—in truth my companions had been faring lentenly at Harar—and to lay in stock and strength for the long desert march before us. A Somali was despatched to the city under orders to load an ass with onions, tobacco, spices, wooden platters, and Karanji,[1] which our penniless condition had prevented our purchasing. I spent the time collecting a vocabulary of the Harari tongue under the auspices of Mad Sa'id and Ali the poet, a Somali educated at the Alma Mater. He was a small black man, long-headed, and long-backed, with remarkably prominent eyes, a bulging brow, nose pertly turned up, and lean jaws almost unconscious of beard. He knew the Arabic, Somali, Galla, and Harari languages, and his acuteness was such, that I found no difficulty in what usually proves the hardest task—extracting the grammatical forms. " A poet, the son of a Poet," to use his own phrase, he evinced a Horatian respect for the beverage which bards love, and his discourse, whenever it strayed from the line of grammar, savoured of over reverence for the goddess whom Pagans associated with Bacchus and Ceres. He was also a patriot and a Tyrtæus. No clan ever attacked his Girhis without smarting under terrible sarcasms, and his sneers at the young warriors for want of ardour in resisting Gudabirsi encroachments were quoted as models of the " withering." Stimulated by the present of a Tobe, he composed a song in honour of the pilgrim : I will offer a literal translation of the exordium, though sentient of the fact that modesty shrinks from such quotations.

" Formerly, my sire and self held ourselves songsters :
Only to-day, however, I really begin to sing.
At the order of Abdullah, Allah sent, my tongue is loosed,

---

1 Bread made of holcus grain dried and broken into bits; it is thrown into broth or hot water, and thus readily supplies the traveller with a wholesome *panade.*

The son of the Kuraysh by a thousand generations,
He hath visited Audal, and Sahil and Adari [1];
A hundred of his ships float on the sea ;
His intellect," &c., &c., &c.

When not engaged with Ali the Poet I amused myself by consoling Mad Sa'id, who was deeply afflicted,
his son having received an ugly stab in the shoulder.
Thinking, perhaps, that the Senior anticipated some evil
results from the wound, I attempted to remove the
impression. "Alas, O Hajj!" groaned the old man, "it
is not that!—how can the boy be *my* boy, I who have
ever given instead of receiving stabs?" nor would he be
comforted, on account of the youth's progeniture. At
other times we summoned the heads of the clans and proceeded to write down their genealogies. This always led to
a scene beginning with piano, but rapidly rising to the
strepitoso. Each tribe and clan wished to rank first,
none would be even second—what was to be done?
When excitement was at its height, the paper and pencil
were torn out of my hand, stubbly beards were pitilessly
pulled, and daggers half started from their sheaths.
These quarrels were, however, easily composed, and
always passed off in storms of abuse, laughter, and
derision.

With the end of the week's repose came Shaykh
Jami, the Berteri, equipped as a traveller with sword,
praying-skin, and water-bottle. This bustling little
divine, whose hobby it was to make every man's
business his own, was accompanied by his brother, in
nowise so prayerful a person, and by four burly, black-
looking Widads, of whose birth, learning, piety, and
virtues he spoke in terms eloquent. I gave them a

---

1 The Somal invariably call Berberah the "Sahil," (meaning
in Arabic the sea-shore,) as Zayla with them is "Audal," and
Harar "Adari."

supper of rice, ghi, and dates in my hut, and with much difficulty excused myself on plea of ill health from a Samrah or night's entertainment—the chaunting some serious book from evening even to the small hours. The Shaykh informed me that his peaceful errand on that occasion was to determine a claim of blood-money amongst the neighbouring Badawin. The case was rich in Somali manners. One man gave medicine to another who happened to die about a month afterwards: the father of the deceased at once charged the mediciner with poisoning, and demanded the customary fine. Mad Sa'id grumbled certain disrespectful expressions about the propriety of divines confining themselves to prayers and Koran, whilst the Jirad Adan, after listening to the Shaykh's violent denunciation of the Somali doctrine, " Fire, but not shame![1] " conducted his head-scratcher, and with sly sarcasm declared that he had been Islamized afresh that day.

On Sunday, the 21st of January, our messenger returned from Harar, bringing with him supplies for the road: my vocabulary was finished, and as nothing delayed us at Wilensi, I determined to set out the next day. When the rumour went abroad every inhabitant of the village flocked to our hut, with the view of seeing what he could beg or borrow: we were soon obliged to close it, with peremptory orders that none be admitted but the Shaykh Jami. The divine appeared in the afternoon accompanied by all the incurables of the country side: after hearing the tale of the blood-money, I determined that talismans were the best and safest medicines in those mountains. The Shaykh at first doubted their efficacy. But when my diploma as a master Sufi was exhibited, a new light broke upon him and his attendant Widads.

---

1 " Al-Nár wa lá al-Ar," an Arabic maxim, somewhat more forcible than our "death rather than dishonour "=" Hell with Honour."

" Verily he hath declared himself this day!" whispered
each to his neighbour, still sorely mystified. Shaykh Jami
carefully inspected the document, raised it reverently to
his forehead, and muttered some prayers: he then in
humble phrase begged a copy, and required from me
" Ijazah " or permission to act as master. The former
request was granted without hesitation, about the latter I
preferred to temporize: he then owned himself my pupil,
and received, as a well-merited acknowledgment of his
services, a pencil and a silk turband.

The morning fixed for our departure came; no one,
however, seemed ready to move. The Hammal, who
but the night before had been full of ardour and activity,
now hung back; we had no coffee, no water-bags, and
Dunyazad had gone to buy gourds in some distant
village. This was truly African: twenty-six days had
not sufficed to do the work of a single watch! No
servants had been procured for us by the Jirad, although
he had promised a hundred whenever required. Long
Gulad had imprudently lent his dagger to the smooth-
tongued Yusuf Dira, who hearing of the departure,
naturally absconded. And, at the last moment, one
Abdi Aman, who had engaged himself at Harar as
guide to Berberah for the sum of ten dollars, asked
a score.

A display of energy was clearly necessary. I sent
the Jirad with directions to bring the camels at once,
and ordered the Hammal to pull down the huts. Abdi
Aman was told to go to Harar—or the other place—
Long Gulad was promised another dagger at Berberah;
a message was left directing Dunyazad to follow, and
the word was given to load.

By dint of shouting and rough language, the
caravan was ready at 9 A. M. The Jirad Adan and his
ragged tail leading, we skirted the eastern side of
Wilensi, and our heavily laden camels descended with

pain the rough and stony slope of the wide Kloof
dividing it from the Marar Prairie. At 1 P.M. the chief
summoned us to halt : we pushed on, however, without
regarding him. Presently, Long Gulad and the End of
Time were missing ; contrary to express orders they had
returned to seek the dagger. To ensure discipline, on
this occasion I must have blown out the long youth's
brains, which were, he declared, addled by the loss of
his weapon : the remedy appeared worse than the
disease.

Attended only by the Hammal, I entered with
pleasure the Marar Prairie. In vain the Jirad entreated
us not to venture upon a place swarming with lions ;
vainly he promised to kill sheep and oxen for a feast ;—
we took abrupt leave of him, and drove away the
camels.

Journeying slowly over the skirt of the plain, when
rejoined by the truants, we met a party of travellers,
who, as usual, stopped to inquire the news. Their chief,
mounted upon an old mule, proved to be Madar Farih,
a Somali well known at Aden. He consented to accompany us as far as the halting place, expressed
astonishment at our escaping Harar, and gave us intelligence which my companions judged grave. The Jirad
Hirsi of the Berteri, amongst whom Madar had been
living, was incensed with us for leaving the direct road.
Report informed him, moreover, that we had given 600
dollars and various valuables to the Jirad Adan—Why
then had he been neglected ? Madar sensibly advised
us to push forward that night, and to 'ware the bush,
whence Midgans might use their poisoned arrows.

We alighted at the village formerly beneath Gurays,
now shifted to a short distance from those hills. Presently appeared Dunyazad, hung round with gourds and
swelling with hurt feelings : she was accompanied by
Dahabo, sister of the valiant Beuh, who, having for

ever parted from her graceless husband, the Jirad, was returning under our escort to the Gurgi of her family. Then came Yusuf Dira with a smiling countenance and smooth manners, bringing the stolen dagger and many excuses for the mistake; he was accompanied by a knot of kinsmen deputed by the Jirad as usual for no good purpose. That worthy had been informed that his Berteri rival offered a hundred cows for our persons, dead or alive: he pathetically asked my attendants " Do you love your pilgrim? " and suggested that if they did so, they might as well send him a little more cloth, upon the receipt of which he would escort us with fifty horsemen.

My Somal lent a willing ear to a speech which smelt of falsehood a mile off: they sat down to debate; the subject was important, and for three mortal hours did that palaver endure. I proposed proceeding at once. They declared that the camels could not walk, and that the cold of the prairie was death to man. Pointing to a caravan of grain-carriers that awaited our escort, I then spoke of starting next morning. Still they hesitated. At length darkness came on, and knowing it to be a mere waste of time to debate over night about dangers to be faced next day, I ate my dates and drank my milk, and lay down to enjoy tranquil sleep in the deep silence of the desert.

The morning of the 23rd of January found my companions as usual in a state of faint-heartedness. The Hammal was deputed to obtain permission for fetching the Jirad and all the Jirad's men. This was positively refused. I could not, however, object to sending sundry Tobes to the cunning idiot, in order to back up a verbal request for the escort. Thereupon Yusuf Dira, Madar Farih, and the other worthies took leave, promising to despatch the troop before noon: I saw them depart with pleasure, feeling that we had bidden adieu to the Girhis.

The greatest danger we had run was from the Jirad Adan, a fact of which I was not aware till some time after my return to Berberah: he had always been plotting an *avanie* which, if attempted, would have cost him dear, but at the same time would certainly have proved fatal to us.

Noon arrived, but no cavalry. My companions had promised that if disappointed they would start before nightfall and march till morning. But when the camels were sent for, one, as usual if delay was judged advisable, had strayed: they went in search of him, so as to give time for preparation to the caravan. I then had a sharp explanation with my men, and told them in conclusion that it was my determination to cross the Prairie alone, if necessary, on the morrow.

That night heavy clouds rolled down from the Gurays Hills, and veiled the sky with a deeper gloom. Presently came a thin streak of blue lightning and a roar of thunder, which dispersed like flies the mob of gazers from around my Gurgi; then rain streamed through our hut as though we had been dwelling under a system of cullenders. Dunyazad declared herself too ill to move; Shahrazad swore that she would not work : briefly, that night was by no means pleasantly spent.

At dawn, on the 24th, we started across the Marar Prairie with a caravan of about twenty men and thirty women, driving camels, carrying grain, asses, and a few sheep. The long straggling line gave a " wide berth " to the doughty Hirsi and his Berteris, whose camp-fires were clearly visible in the morning grey. The air was raw ; piles of purple cloud settled upon the hills, whence cold and damp gusts swept the plain ; sometimes we had a shower, at others a Scotch mist, which did not fail to penetrate our thin raiment. My people trembled, and their teeth chattered as though they were walking upon ice. In our slow course we passed herds of quagga and gazelles, but the animals were wild, and both men and mules were unequal to the task of stalking them. About midday we closed up, for our path wound through the valley wooded with Acacia—fittest place for an ambuscade of archers. We dined in the saddle on huge lumps of sun-dried beef, and bits of gum gathered from the trees.

Having at length crossed the prairie without accident, the caravan people shook our hands, congratulated one another, and declared that they owed their lives to us. About an hour after sunset we arrived at Abtidon's home, a large kraal at the foot of the Konti cone : fear of lions drove my people into the enclosure, where we passed a night of scratching. I was now haunted by the dread of a certain complaint for which sulphur is said to be a specific. This is the pest of the inner parts of Somali-land ; the people declare it to arise from flies and fleas : the European would derive it from the deficiency, or rather the impossibility, of ablutions.

" Allah help the Goer, but the Return is Rolling : " this adage was ever upon the End of Time's tongue, yet my fate was apparently an exception to the general rule. On the 25th January, we were delayed by the weakness of the camels, which had been half starved in the Girhi mountains. And as we were about to enter the lands of the Habr Awal,[1] then at blood feud with my men, all

---

1 This is the second great division of the Somal people, the father of the tribe being Awal, the cadet of Ishak al-Hazrami.

The Habr Awal occupy the coast from Zayla and Siyaro to the lands bordering upon the Berteri tribe. They own the rule of a Jirad, who exercises merely a nominal authority. The late chief's name was " Bon," he died about four years ago, but his children have not yet received the turband. The royal race is the Ayyal Abdillah, a powerful clan extending from the Dabasanis Hills to near Jigjiga, skirting the Marar Prairie.

The Habr Awal are divided into a multitude of clans : of these I shall specify only the principal, the subject of the maritime Somal

Habr Girhajis, probably a week would elapse before we could provide ourselves with a fit and proper protector. Already I had been delayed ten days after the appointed time, my comrades at Berberah would be apprehensive of accidents, and although starting from Wilensi we had resolved to reach the coast within the fortnight, a month's march was in clear prospect.

Whilst thus chewing the cud of bitter thought where thought was of scant avail, suddenly appeared the valiant Beuh, sent to visit us by Dahabo his gay sister. He informed us that a guide was in the neighbourhood, and the news gave me an idea. I proposed that he should escort the women, camels, and baggage under the command of the Kalandar to Zayla, whilst we, mounting our mules and carrying only our arms and provisions for four days, might push through the lands of the Habr Awal. After some demur all consented.

It was not without apprehension that I pocketed all my remaining provisions, five biscuits, a few limes, and sundry lumps of sugar. Any delay or accident to our mules would starve us; in the first place, we were about to traverse a desert, and secondly where Habr Awal were, they would not sell meat or milk to Habr Girhajis. My attendants provided themselves with a small provision of sun-dried beef, grain, and sweetmeats: only one water-bottle, however was found amongst the whole party. We arose at dawn after a wet night on the 26th January, but we did not start till 7 A.M., the reason being that all the party, the Kalandar, Shahrazad and Dunyazad,

---

being already familiar to our countrymen. The Ísa Musa inhabit part of the mountains south of Berberah. The Mikahil tenant the lowlands on the coast from Berberah to Siyaro. Two large clans, the Ayyal Yunis and the Ayyal Ahmad, have established themselves in Berberah and at Bulhar. Besides these are the Ayyal Abdillah Sa'ad, the Ayyal Jira'ato, who live amongst the Ayyal Yunis—the Bahgobo and the Ayyal Hamid.

claimed and would have his or her several and distinct palaver.

Having taken leave of our friends and property,[1] we spurred our mules, and guided by Beuh, rode through cloud and mist towards Koralay the Saddle-back hill. After an hour's trot over rugged ground falling into the Harawwah valley, we came to a Gudabirsi village, where my companions halted to inquire the news, also to distend their stomachs with milk. Thence we advanced slowly, as the broken path required, through thickets of wild henna to the kraal occupied by Beuh's family. At a distance we were descried by an old acquaintance, Fahi, who straightways began to dance like a little Polyphemus, his shock-wig waving in the air: plentiful potations of milk again delayed my companions, who were now laying in a four days' stock.

Remounting, we resumed our journey over a mass of rock and thicket, watered our mules at holes in a Fiumara, and made our way to a village belonging to the Ugaz or chief of the Gudabirsi tribe. He was a middle-aged man of ordinary presence, and he did not neglect to hold out his hand for a gift which we could not but refuse. Halting for about an hour, we persuaded a guide, by the offer of five dollars and a pair of cloths, to accompany us. " Dubayr "—the Donkey—who belonged to the Bahgobo clan of the Habr Awal, was a " long Lankin," unable like all these Badawin, to endure fatigue. He could not ride,·the saddle cut him, and he found his mule restive ; lately married, he was incapacitated for walking, and he

---

1 My property arrived safe at Aden after about two months. The mule left under the Kalandar's charge never appeared, and the camels are, I believe, still grazing among the Ísa. The fair Shahrazad, having amassed a little fortune, lost no time in changing her condition, an example followed in due time by Dunyazad. And the Kalandar after a visit to Aden, returned to electrify his Zayla friends with long and terrible tales of travel.

sadly suffered from thirst. The Donkey little knew, when he promised to show Berberah on the third day what he had bound himself to perform: after the second march he was induced, only by the promise of a large present, and one continual talk of food, to proceed, and often he threw his lengthy form upon the ground, groaning that his supreme hour was at hand. In the land which we were to traverse every man's spear would be against us. By way of precaution, we ordered our protector to choose desert roads and carefully to avoid all kraals. At first, not understanding our reasons, and ever hankering after milk, he could not pass a thorn fence without eyeing it wistfully. On the next day, however, he became more tractable, and before reaching Berberah he showed him-self, in consequence of some old blood feud, more anxious even than ourselves to avoid villages.

Remounting, under the guidance of the Donkey, we resumed our eastward course. He was communicative even for a Somali, and began by pointing out, on the right of the road, the ruins of a stone-building, called, as customary in these countries, a fort. Beyond it we came to a kraal, whence all the inhabitants issued with shouts and cries for tobacco. Three o'clock P. M. brought us to a broad Fiumara choked with the thickest and most tangled vegetation: we were shown some curious old Galla wells, deep holes about twenty feet in diameter, excavated in the rock; some were dry, others overgrown with huge creepers, and one only supplied us with tolerable water. The Gudabirsi tribe received them from the Girhi in lieu of blood-money: beyond this watercourse, the ground belongs to the Rer Yunis Jibril, a powerful clan of the Habr Awal, and the hills are thickly studded with thorn-fence and kraal.

Without returning the salutations of the Badawin, who loudly summoned us to stop and give them the news, we trotted forwards in search of a deserted sheepfold. At sunset we passed, upon an eminence on our left, the ruins of an ancient settlement, called after its patron Saint, Ao Barhi : and both sides of the mountain road were flanked by tracts of prairie-land, beautifully purpling in the evening air. After a ride of thirty-five miles, we arrived at a large fold, where, by removing the inner thorn-fences, we found fresh grass for our starving beasts. The night was raw and windy, and thick mists deepened into a drizzle, which did not quench our thirst, but easily drenched the saddle cloths, our only bedding. In one sense, however, the foul weather was propitious to us. Our track might easily have been followed by some enterprising son of Yunis Jibril ; these tracts of thorny bush are favourite places for cattle lifting ; moreover the fire was kept blazing all night, yet our mules were not stolen.

We shook off our slumbers before dawn on the 27th. I remarked near our resting-place, one of those detached heaps of rock, common enough in the Somali country : at one extremity a huge block projects upwards, and suggests the idea of a gigantic canine tooth. The Donkey declared that the summit still bears traces of building, and related the legend connected with Moga Madir.[1] There, in times of old, dwelt a Galla maiden whose eye could distinguish a plundering party at a distance of five days' march. The enemies of her tribe, after sustaining heavy losses, hit upon the expedient of an attack, not *en chemise*, but with their heads muffled in bundles of hay. When Moga, the maiden, informed her sire and clan that a prairie was on its way towards the hill, they deemed her mad; the manœuvre succeeded, and the unhappy seer lost her life. The legend interested me by its wide diffusion. The history of Zarka, the blue-eyed witch of the Jadis tribe, who seized Yamamah by

---

1 " Moga's eye-tooth."

her gramarye, and our Scotch tale of Birnam wood's march, are Asiatic and European facsimiles of African " Moga's Tooth."

At 7 A.M. we started through the mist, and trotted eastwards in search of a well. The guide had deceived us : the day before he had promised water at every half mile ; he afterwards owned with groans that we should not drink before nightfall. These people seem to lie involuntarily : the habit of untruth with them becomes a second nature. They deceive without object for deceit, and the only way of obtaining from them correct information is to inquire, receive the answer, and determine it to be diametrically opposed to fact.

I will not trouble you, dear L., with descriptions of the uniform and uninteresting scenery through which we rode—horrid hills upon which withered aloes brandished their spears, plains apparently rained upon by a shower of stones, and rolling ground abounding only with thorns like the " wait-a-bits " of Kafir land, created to tear man's skin or clothes. Our toil was rendered doubly toilsome by the Eastern travellers' dread—the demon of Thirst rode like Care behind us. For twenty-four hours we did not taste water, the sun parched our brains, the mirage mocked us at every turn, and the effect was a species of monomania. As I jogged along with eyes closed against the fiery air, no image unconnected with the want suggested itself. Water ever lay before me— water lying deep in the shady well—water in streams bubbling icy from the rock—water in pellucid lakes inviting me to plunge and revel in their treasures. Now an Indian cloud was showering upon me fluid more precious than molten pearl, then an invisible hand offered a bowl for which the mortal part would gladly have bartered years of life. Then—drear contrast !—I opened my eyes to a heat-reeking plain, and a sky of that eternal metallic blue so lovely to painter and poet, so blank and death-like to us, whose χαλον was tempest, rain-storm, and the huge purple nimbus. I tried to talk—it was in vain, to sing in vain, vainly to think; every idea was bound up in one subject, water.[1]

As the sun sank into the East we descended the wide Gogaysa valley. With unspeakable delight we saw in the distance a patch of lively green: our animals scented the blessing from afar, they raised their drooping ears, and started with us at a canter, till, turning a corner, we suddenly sighted sundry little wells. To spring from the saddle, to race with our mules, who now feared not the crumbling sides of the pits, to throw ourselves into the muddy pools, to drink a long slow draught, and to dash the water over our burning faces, took less time to do than to recount. A calmer inspection showed a necessity for caution—the surface was alive with tadpoles and insects: prudence, however, had little power at that time, we drank, and drank, and then drank again. As our mules had fallen with avidity upon the grass, I proposed to pass a few hours near the well. My companions, however, pleading the old fear of lions, led the way to a deserted kraal upon a neighbouring hill. We had marched about thirty miles eastward, and had entered a safe country belonging to the Bahgoba, our guide's clan.

At sunrise on the 28th of January, the Donkey, whose limbs refused to work, was lifted into the saddle, declaring that the white man must have been sent from heaven, as a special curse upon the children of Ishak. We started, after filling the water-bottle, down the Gogaysa valley. Our mules were becoming foot-sore,

---

1 As a rule, twelve hours without water in the desert during hot weather, kill a man. I never suffered severely from thirst but on this occasion; probably it was in consequence of being at the time but in weak health.

and the saddles had already galled their backs; we were therefore compelled to the additional mortification of travelling at snail's pace over the dreary hills, and through the uninteresting bush.

About noon we entered Wady Danan, or "The Sour," a deep chasm in the rocks; the centre is a winding sandy watercourse, here and there grassy with tall rushes, and affording at every half mile a plentiful supply of sweet water. The walls of the ravine are steep and rugged, and the thorny jungle clustering at the sides gives a wild appearance to the scene. Traces of animals, quagga and gazelle, everywhere abounded: not being however, in "Dianic humour," and unwilling to apprise Badawin of our vicinity, I did not fire a shot. As we advanced, large trees freshly barked and more tender plants torn up by the roots, showed the late passage of a herd of elephants: my mule, though the bravest of our beasts, was in a state of terror all the way. The little grey honey-bird[1] tempted us to wander

---

[1] I have never shot this feathered friend of man, although frequent opportunities presented themselves. He appears to be the Cuculus Indicator (le Concou Indicateur) and the Om-Shlanvo of the Kafirs; the Somal call him Maris. Described by Father Lobo and Bruce, he is treated as a myth by Le Vaillant; M. Wiedman makes him cry "Shirt! Shirt! Shirt!" Dr. Sparrman "Tcherr! Tcherr!" Mr. Delegorgue "Chir! Chir! Chir!" His note suggested to me the shrill chirrup of a sparrow, and his appearance that of a greenfinch.

Buffon has repeated what a traveller had related, namely, that the honey-bird is a little traitor who conducts men into ambuscades prepared by wild beasts. The Lion-Slayer in S. Africa asserts it to be the belief of Hottentots and the interior tribes, that the bird often lures the unwary pursuer to danger, sometimes guiding him to the midday retreat of a grizzly lion, or bringing him suddenly upon the den of the crouching panther. M. Delegorgue observes that the feeble bird probably seeks aid in removing carrion for the purpose of picking up flies and worms; he acquits him of malice prepense, believing that where the prey is, there carnivorous beasts may be met. The Somal, however, carry their superstition still farther.

with all his art: now he sat upon the nearest tree chirping his invitation to a feast, then he preceded us with short jerking flights to point out the path. My people, however, despite the fondness for honey inherent in the Somali palate,[1] would not follow him, deciding that on this occasion his motives for inviting us were not of the purest.

Emerging from the valley, we urged on our animals over comparatively level ground, in the fallacious hope of seeing the sea that night. The trees became rarer as we advanced and the surface metallic. In spots the path led over ironstone that resembled slag. In other places the soil was ochre-coloured[2]: the cattle lick it, probably on account of the aluminous matter with which it is mixed. Everywhere the surface was burnt up by the sun, and withered from want of rain. Towards evening we entered a broad slope called by the Somal Dihh Murodi, or Murodilay, the Elephants' Valley. Crossing its breadth from west to east, we traversed two Fiumaras, the nearer " Hamar," the further " Las Dorhhay," or the Tamarisk water-holes. They were similar in appearance, the usual Wady about 100 yards wide, pearly sand lined with borders of leek green, pitted with dry wells around which lay heaps of withered thorns and a herd of gazelles tripping gracefully over the quartz carpet.

After spanning the valley we began to descend the

The honey-bird is never trusted by them; he leads, they say, either to the lion's den or the snakes' hiding-place, and often guides his victim into the jaws of the Kaum or plundering party.

1 The Somal have several kinds of honey. The Donyale or wasp-honey, is scanty and bad; it is found in trees and obtained by smoking and cutting the branch. The Malab Shinni or bee-honey, is either white, red or brown; the first is considered the most delicate in flavour.

2 The Somal call it Arrah As.

lower slopes of a high range, whose folds formed like a curtain the bold background of the view. This is the landward face of the Ghauts, over which we were to pass before sighting the sea. Masses of cold grey cloud rolled from the table-formed summit, we were presently shrouded in mist, and as we advanced, rain began to fall. The light of day vanishing, we again descended into a Fiumara with a tortuous and rocky bed, the main drain of the landward mountain side. My companions, now half-starved—they had lived through three days on a handful of dates and sweetmeats—devoured with avidity the wild Jujube berries that strewed the stones. The guide had preceded us : when we came up with him, he was found seated upon a grassy bank on the edge of the rugged torrent bed. We sprang in pleased astonishment from the saddle, dire had been the anticipations that our mules—one of them already required driving with the spear—would, after another night of starvation, leave us to carry their loads upon our own backs. The cause of the phenomenon soon revealed itself. In the rock was a hole about two feet wide, whence a crystal sheet welled over the Fiumara bank, forming a paradise for frog and tadpole. This " Ga'angal " is considered by the Somal a " fairies' well ": all, however, that the Donkey could inform me was, that when the Nomads settle in the valley, the water sinks deep below the earth—a knot which methinks might be unravelled without the inter-position of a god. The same authority declared it to be the work of the " old ancient " Arabs.

The mules fell hungrily upon the succulent grass, and we, with the most frugal of suppers prepared to pass the rainy night. Presently, however, the doves and Katas,[1] the only birds here requiring water, approached in flights, and fearing to drink, fluttered around us with

[1] The sand-grouse of Egypt and Arabia, the rock-pigeon of Sind and the surrounding countries.

shrill cries.   They suggested to my companions the
possibility of being visited in sleep by more formidable
beasts, and even man: after a short halt, an advance
was proposed ; and this was an offer which, on principle,
I never refused.   We remounted our mules, now refreshed
and in good spirits, and began to ascend the stony face
of the Eastern hill through a thick mist, deepening the
darkness.   As we reached the bleak summit, a heavy
shower gave my companions a pretext to stop: they
readily found a deserted thorn fence, in which we passed
a wet night.   That day we had travelled at fewest thirty-
five miles without seeing the face of man : the country
was parched to a cinder for want of water, and all the
Nomads had migrated to the plains.

The morning of the 29th January was unusually
fine : the last night's rain hung in masses of mist about
the hill-sides, and the rapid evaporation clothed the clear
background with deep blue.   We began the day by
ascending a steep goat-track : it led to a sandy Fiumara,
overgrown with Jujubes and other thorns, abounding in
water, and showing in the rocky sides, caverns fit for a
race of Troglodytes.   Pursuing the path over a stony
valley lying between parallel ranges of hill, we halted at
about 10 A.M. in a large patch of grass-land, the produce
of the rain, which for some days past had been fertilizing
the hill-tops.   Whilst our beasts grazed greedily, we sat
under a bush, and saw far beneath us the low country
which separates the Ghauts from the sea.   Through an
avenue in the rolling nimbus, we could trace the long
courses of Fiumaras, and below, where mist did not
obstruct the sight, the tawny plains, cut with watercourses glistening white, shone in their eternal summer.

Shortly after 10 A. M., we resumed our march, and
began the descent of the Ghauts by a ravine to which
the guide gave the name of " Kadar."   No sandy
watercourse, the " Pass " of this barbarous land, here

facilitates the travellers' advance : the rapid slope of the hill presents a succession of blocks and boulders piled one upon the other in rugged steps, apparently impossible to a laden camel. This ravine, the Splugen of Somaliland, led us, after an hour's ride, to the Wady Duntu, a gigantic mountain-cleft formed by the violent action of torrents. The chasm winds abruptly between lofty walls of syenite and pink granite, glittering with flaky mica, and streaked with dykes and veins of snowy quartz : the strata of the sandstones that here and there projected into the bed were wonderfully twisted around a central nucleus, as green boughs might be bent about a tree. Above, the hill-tops towered in the air, here denuded of vegetable soil by the heavy monsun, there clothed from base to brow with gum trees, whose verdure was delicious to behold. The channel was now sandy, then flagged with limestone in slippery sheets, or horrid with rough boulders : at times the path was clear and easy ; at others, a precipice of twenty or thirty feet, which must be a little cataract after rain, forced us to fight our way through the obstinate thorns that defended some spur of ragged hill. As the noontide heat, concentrated in this funnel, began to affect man and beast, we found a granite block, under whose shady brow clear water, oozing from the sand, formed a natural bath, and sat there for a while to enjoy the spectacle and the atmosphere, perfumed, as in part of Persia and Northern Arabia, by the aromatic shrubs of the desert.

After a short half-hour, we remounted and pursued our way down the Duntu chasm. As we advanced, the hills shrank in size, the bed became more level, and the walls of rock, gradually widening out, sank into the plain. Brisk and elastic above, the air, here soft, damp, and tepid, and the sun burning with a more malignant heat, convinced us that we stood once more below the Ghauts. For two hours we urged our mules in a south-

east direction down the broad and winding Fiumara,
taking care to inspect every well, but finding them all
full of dry sand. Then turning eastwards, we crossed a
plain called by the Donkey "Battaladayti Taranay"—
the Flats of Taranay—an exact representation of the
maritime regions about Zayla. Herds of camels and
flocks of milky sheep browsing amongst thorny Acacia
and the tufted Kulan, suggested pleasing visions to
starving travellers, and for the first time after three days
of hard riding, we saw the face of man. The shepherds,
Mikahil of the Habr Awal tribe, all fled as we approached : at last one was bold enough to stand and
deliver the news. My companions were refreshed by good
reports : there had been few murders, and the sea-board
was tolerably clear of our doughty enemies, the Ayyal
Ahmad. We pricked over the undulating growth of
parched grass, shaping our course for Jabal Almis, to
sailors the chief landmark of this coast, and for a certain
thin blue stripe on the far horizon, upon which we gazed
with gladdened eyes.

Our road lay between low brown hills of lime and
sandstone, the Sub-Ghauts forming a scattered line
between the maritime mountains and the sea. Presently
the path was choked by dense scrub of the Arman
Acacia : its yellow blossoms scented the air, but hardly
made amends for the injuries of a thorn nearly two
inches long, and tipped with a wooden point sharp as a
needle. Emerging, towards evening, from this bush, we
saw large herds of camels, and called their guardians to
come and meet us. For all reply they ran like ostriches
to the nearest rocks, uttering the cry of alarm, and when
we drew near, each man implored us to harry his
neighbour's cattle. Throughout our wanderings in
Somaliland this had never occurred : it impressed me
strongly with the disturbed state of the regions inhabited
by the Habr Awal. After some time we persuaded a

Badawi who, with frantic gestures, was screaming and flogging his camels, to listen: reassured by our oaths, he declared himself to be a Bahgoba, and promised to show us a village of the Ayyal Gadid. The Hammal, who had married a daughter of this clan, and had constituted his father-in-law my protector at Berberah, made sure of a hospitable reception : " To-night we shall sleep under cover and drink milk," quoth one hungry man to another, who straightways rejoined, "And we shall eat mutton ! "

After dark we arrived at a kraal, we unsaddled our mules and sat down near it, indulging in Epicurean anticipations. Opposite us, by the door of a hut, was a group of men who observed our arrival, but did not advance or salute us. Impatient, I fired a pistol, when a gruff voice asked why we disturbed the camels that were being milked. " We have fallen upon the Ayyal Shirdon "—our bitterest enemies—whispered the End of Time. The same voice then demanded in angrier accents, " Of what tribe be ye ? " We boldly answered, " Of the Habr Girhajis." Thereupon ensued a war of words. The Ayyal Shirdon inquired what we wanted, where we had been, and how we dared, seeing that peace had not been concluded between the tribes, to enter their lands. We replied civilly as our disappointment would permit, but apparently gained little by soft words. The inhospitable Badawin declared our arrival to be in the seventeenth house of Geomancy—an advent probable as the Greek Kalends—and rudely insisted upon knowing what had taken us to Harar. At last, a warrior, armed with two spears, came to meet us, and bending down recognized the End of Time : after a few short sentences he turned on his heel and retired. I then directed Long Gulad to approach the group, and say that a traveller was at their doors ready and willing to give tobacco in exchange for a draught of milk. They refused point-blank, and spoke of fighting: we at once made ready with our weapons, and showing the plain, bade them come on and receive a " belly full." During the lull which followed this obliging proposal we saddled our mules and rode off, in the grimmest of humours, loudly cursing the craven churls who knew not the value of a guest.

We visited successively three villages of the Ayyal Gadid: the Hammal failed to obtain even a drop of water from his connexions, and was taunted accordingly. He explained their inhospitality by the fact that all the warriors being at Berberah, the villages contained nothing but women, children, servants, and flocks. The Donkey when strictly questioned declared that no well nearer than Bulhar was to be found: as men and mules were faint with thirst, I determined to push forward to water that night. Many times the animals were stopped, a mute hint that they could go no further: I spurred onwards, and the rest, as on such occasions they had now learned to do, followed without a word. Our path lay across a plain called Banka Hadla, intersected in many places by deep watercourses, and thinly strewed with Kulan clumps. The moon arose, but cast a cloud-veiled and uncertain light: our path, moreover, was not clear, as the guide, worn out by fatigue, tottered on far in the rear.

About midnight we heard—delightful sound!—the murmur of the distant sea. Revived by the music, we pushed on more cheerily. At last the Donkey preceded us, and about 3 A.M. we found, in a Fiumara, some holes which supplied us with bitter water, truly delicious after fifteen hours of thirst. Repeated draughts of the element, which the late rains had rendered potable, relieved our pain, and hard by we found a place where coarse stubbly grass saved our mules from starvation. Then rain coming on, we coiled ourselves under the saddle cloths, and, reckless alike of Ayyal Ahmad and Ayyal Shirdon, slept like the dead.

At dawn on the 30th January, I arose and inspected the site of Bulhar. It was then deserted, a huge heap of bleached bones being the only object suggestive of a settlement. This, at different times, has been a thriving place, owing to its roadstead, and the feuds of Berberah: it was generally a village of Gurgis, with some stone-houses built by Arabs. The coast however is open and havenless, and the Shimal wind, feared even at the Great Port, here rages with resistless violence. Yet the place revives when plundering parties render the plain unsafe: the timid merchants here embark their goods and persons, whilst their camels are marched round the bay.

Mounting at 6 A.M. we started slowly along the sea coast, and frequently halted on the bushy Fiumara-cut plain. About noon we bathed in the sea, and sat on the sands for a while, my people praying for permission to pass the kraals of their enemies, the Ayyal Ahmad, by night. This, their last request, was graciously granted: to say sooth rapid travelling was now impossible; the spear failed to urge on one mule, and the Hammal was obliged to flog before him another wretched animal. We then traversed an alluvial plain, lately flooded, where slippery mud doubled the fatigue of our cattle; and, at 3 P.M., again halted on a patch of grass below the rocky spur of Dabasenis, a hill half way between Bulhar and Berberah. On the summit I was shown an object that makes travellers shudder, a thorn-tree, under which the Habr Girhajis[1] and their friends of the Ísa Musa sit, vulture-

---

1 The Habr Girhajis, or eldest branch of the sons of Ishak (generally including the children of " Arab "), inhabit the Ghauts behind Berberah, whence they extend for several days' march towards Ogadayn, the southern region. This tribe is divided into a multitude of clans. The Ismail Arrah supply the Sultan, a nominal chief like

like, on the look-out for plunder and murder. Advancing another mile, we came to some wells, where we were obliged to rest our animals. Having there finished our last mouthful of food, we remounted, and following the plain eastward, prepared for a long night-march.

As the light of day waned we passed on the right hand a table-formed hill, apparently a detached fragment of the sub-Ghauts or coast range. This spot is celebrated in local legends as " Auliya Kumbo," the Mount of Saints, where the forty-four Arab Santons sat in solemn conclave before dispersing over the Somali country to preach Al-Islam. It lies about six hours of hard walking from Berberah.

At midnight we skirted Bulho Faranji, the Franks' Watering-place,[1] a strip of ground thickly covered with trees. Abounding in grass and water, it has been the site of a village: when we passed it, however, all was desert. By the moon's light we descried, as we silently skirted the sea, the kraals and folds of our foe the Ayyal Ahmad, and at times we could distinguish the lowing

---

the Ísa Ugaz; they extend from Makhar to the south of Gulays number about 15,000 shields and are sub-divided into three septs. The Musa Arrah hold the land between Gulays and the seats of the Mijjarthayn and Warsingali tribes on the windward coast. The Ishak Arrah count 5,000 or 6,000 shields, and inhabit the Gulays Range. The other sons of Arrah (the fourth in descent from Ishak), namely, Mikahil, Gambah, Daudan, and others, also became founders of small clans. The Ayyal Da'ud, facetiously called " Idagallah " or earth-burrowers, and sprung from the second son of Girhajis, claim the country south of the Habr Awal, reckon about 4,000 shields, and are divided into 11 or 12 septs.

As has been noticed, the Habr Girhajis have a perpetual blood feud with the Habr Awal, and, even at Aden, they have fought out their quarrels with clubs and stones. Yet as cousins they willingly unite against a common enemy, the Ísa for instance, and become the best of friends

So called from the Mary Anne brig, here plundered in 1825.

of their cattle : my companions chuckled hugely at the success of their manœuvre, and perhaps not without reason. At Berberah we were afterwards informed that a shepherd in the bush had witnessed and reported our having passed, when the Ayyal Ahmad cursed the star that had enabled us to slip unhurt through their hands.

Our mules could scarcely walk : after every bow-shot they rolled upon the ground and were raised only by the whip. A last halt was called when arrived within four miles of Berberah : the End of Time and Long Gulad, completely worn out, fell fast asleep upon the stones. Of all the party the Hammal alone retained strength and spirits : the sturdy fellow talked, sang, and shouted, and, whilst the others could scarcely sit their mules, he danced his war-dance and brandished his spear. I was delighted with his " pluck."

Now a long dark line appears upon the sandy horizon—it grows more distinct in the shades of night—the silhouettes of shipping appear against sea and sky. A cry of joy bursts from every mouth : cheer, boys, cheer, our toils here touch their end !

The End of Time first listened to the small still voice of Caution. He whispered anxiously to make no noise lest enemies might arise, that my other attendants had protectors at Berberah, but that he, the hated and feared, as the *locum tenens* of Sharmarkay—the great *bête noire*—depended wholly upon my defence. The Donkey led us slowly and cautiously round the southern quarter of the sleeping town, through bone heaps and jackals tearing their unsavoury prey : at last he marched straight into the quarter appropriated to the Ayyal Gadid our protectors. Anxiously I inquired if my comrades had left Berberah, and heard with delight that they awaited me there.

It was then 2 A.M. and we had marched at least

forty miles. The Somal, when in fear of forays, drive laden camels over this distance in about ten hours.

I dismounted at the huts where my comrades were living. A glad welcome, a dish of rice, and a glass of strong waters—pardon, dear L., these details—made amends for past privations and fatigue. The servants and the wretched mules were duly provided for, and I fell asleep, conscious of having performed a feat which, like a certain ride to York, will live in local annals for many and many a year.

CHAPTER X.

BERBERAH AND ITS ENVIRONS.

It is interesting to compare the earliest with the latest account of the great emporium of Eastern Africa.[1]

Bartema, writing in the sixteenth century "of Barbara and the Island of Ethiope," offers the following brief description:—"After that the tempests were appeased, we gave wind to our sails, and in short time arrived at an island named Barbara, the prince whereof is a Mahometan.[2] The island is not great but fruitful and well peopled: it hath abundance of flesh. The inhabitants are of colour inclining to black. All their riches is in herds of cattle."

Lieut. Cruttenden of the I.N., writing in 1848, thus describes the place:—"The annual fair is one of the most interesting sights on the coast, if only from the fact of many different and distant tribes being drawn together for a short time, to be again scattered in all directions. Before the towers of Berbera were built,[3]

---

1 In 1567 (the year after Zayla's fall) Lopez Suarez took without resistance—the inhabitants having fled—and burned the City "Barbora near to Zayla, a place not unlike to it, but much less."

2 I cannot guess why Bartema decided "Barbara" to be an island, except that he used "insula" in the sense of "peninsula." The town is at very high tides flooded round, but the old traveller manifestly speaks of the country.

3 These are the four martello towers erected, upon the spot where the town of huts generally stands, by the Hajj Sharmarkay,

the place from April to the early part of October was utterly deserted, not even a fisherman being found there; but no sooner did the season change, than the inland tribes commenced moving down towards the coast, and preparing their huts for their expected visitors. Small craft from the ports of Yemen, anxious to have an opportunity of purchasing before vessels from the gulf could arrive, hastened across, followed about a fortnight to three weeks later by their larger brethren from Muscat, Soor, and Ras el Khyma, and the valuably freighted Bagalas[1] from Bahrein, Bussorah, and Graen. Lastly, the fat and wealthy Banian traders from Pore-bunder, Mandavie, and Bombay, rolled across in their clumsy Kotias,[1] and with a formidable row of empty ghee jars slung over the quarters of their vessels, elbowed themselves into a permanent position in the front tier of craft in the harbour, and by their superior capital, cunning, and influence, soon distanced all competitors."

" During the height of the fair, Berbera is a perfect Babel, in confusion as in languages: no chief is acknow-ledged, and the customs of bygone days are the laws of the place. Disputes between the inland tribes daily arise, and are settled by the spear and dagger, the com-batants retiring to the beach at a short distance from the town, in order that they may not disturb the trade. Long strings of camels are arriving and departing day and night, escorted generally by women alone, until at a distance from the town ; and an occasional group of dusky and travel-worn children marks the arrival of the slave Cafila from Hurrur and Efat."

" At Berbera, the Gurague and Hurrur slave mer-

---

who garrisoned them with thirty Arab and Negro matchlockmen. They are now in ruins, having been dismantled by orders from Aden.

1 The former is an Arab craft, the latter belongs to the Northern Coasts of Western India.

chant meets his correspondent from Bussorah, Bagdad, or Bunder Abbas: and the savage Gidrbeersi (Guda-birsi), with his head tastefully ornamented with a scarlet sheepskin in lieu of a wig, is seen peacefully bartering his ostrich feathers and gums with the smooth-spoken Banian from Porebunder, who prudently living on board his ark, and locking up his puggree,[1] which would infallibly be knocked off the instant he was seen wearing it, exhibits but a small portion of his wares at a time, under a miserable mat spread on the beach."

" By the end of March the fair is nearly at a close, and craft of all kinds, deeply laden, and sailing generally in parties of three and four, commence their homeward journey. The Soori boats are generally the last to leave, and by the first week in April, Berbera is again deserted, nothing being left to mark the site of a town lately containing 20,000 inhabitants, beyond bones of slaughtered camels and sheep, and the framework of a few huts, which is carefully piled on the beach in readiness for the ensuing year. Beasts of prey now take the opportunity to approach the sea: lions are commonly seen at the town well during the hot weather; and in April last year, but a week after the fair had ended, I observed three ostriches quietly walking on the beach.[2]"

Of the origin of Berberah little is known. Al-Firuzabadi derives it, with great probability, from two Himyar chiefs of Southern Arabia.[3] About A.D. 522 the troops of Anushirwan expelled the Abyssinians from Al-Yaman, and re-established there a Himyari prince under vassalage of the Persian Monarch. Tradition

---

1 A turband.

2 The wild animals have now almost entirely disappeared. As will afterwards be shown, the fair since 1848 has diminished to one third its former dimensions.

3 This subject has been fully discussed in Chap. IV.

asserts the port to have been occupied in turns by the Furs,[1] the Arabs, the Turks, the Gallas, and the Somal. And its future fortunes are likely to be as varied as the past.

The present decadence of Berberah is caused by petty internal feuds. Girhajis the eldest son of Ishak al-Hazrami, seized the mountain ranges of Gulays and Wagar lying about forty miles behind the coast, whilst Awal, the cadet, established himself and his descendants upon the lowlands from Berberah to Zayla. Both these powerful tribes assert a claim to the customs and profits of the port on the grounds that they jointly conquered it from the Gallas.[2] The Habr Awal, however, being in possession, would monopolize the right : a blood feud rages, and the commerce of the place suffers from the dissensions of the owners.

Moreover the Habr Awal tribe is not without internal feuds. Two kindred septs, the Ayyal Yunis Nuh and the Ayyal Ahmad Nuh,[3] established themselves originally at Berberah. The former, though the more numerous, admitted the latter for some years to a participation of profits, but when Aden, occupied by the British, rendered the trade valuable, they drove out the weaker sept, and declared themselves sole " Abbans " to strangers during the fair. A war ensued. The sons of

---

1 The old Persians.

2 Especially the sea-board Habr Girhajis clans—the Musa Arrah, the Ali Sa'id, and the Sa'ad Yunis—are interested in asserting their claims.

3 Yunis and Ahmad were brothers, children of Nuh, the ninth in descent from Ishak al-Hazrami. The former had four sons, Hosh Yunis, Gadid Yunis, Mahmud Yunis, and Shirdon Yunis; their descendants are all known as the Ayyal or progeny of Yunis. The Ayyal Ahmad Nuh hold the land immediately behind the town, and towards the Ghauts, blend with the Ísa Musa. The Mikahil claim the Eastern country from Siyaro to Illanti, a wooded valley affording good water and bad anchorage to wind-bound vessels.

Yunis obtained aid of the Mijjarthayn tribe. The sons of Ahmad called in the Habr Girhajis, especially the Musa Arrah clan, to which the Hajj Sharmarkay belongs, and, with his assistance, defeated and drove out the Ayyal Yunis. These, flying from Berberah, settled at the haven of Bulhar, and by their old connection with the Indian and other foreign traders, succeeded in drawing off a considerable amount of traffic. But the roadstead was insecure: many vessels were lost, and in 1847 the Ísa Somal slaughtered the women and children of the new-comers, compelling them to sue the Ayyal Ahmad for peace. Though the feud thus ended, the fact of its having had existence ensures bad blood: amongst these savages treaties are of no avail, and the slightest provocation on either side becomes a signal for renewed hostilities.

. . . . . .

After this dry disquisition we will return, dear L., to my doings at Berberah.

Great fatigue is seldom followed by long sleep. Soon after sunrise I awoke, hearing loud voices proceeding from a mass of black face and tawny wig, that blocked up the doorway, pressing forward to see their new stranger. The Berberah people had been informed by the Donkey of our having ridden from the Girhi hills in five days: they swore that not only the thing was impossible, but moreover that we had never sighted Harar. Having undergone the usual catechizing with credit, I left the thatched hut in which my comrades were living, and proceeded to inspect my attendants and cattle. The former smiled blandly: they had acquitted themselves of their trust, they had outwitted the Ayyal Ahmad, who would be furious thereat, they had filled themselves with dates, rice, and sugared tea—another potent element of moral satisfaction—and they trusted that a few days would show them their wives and families. The End of Time's brow, however, betrayed an *arrière pensée;* once more his cowardice crept forth, and he anxiously whispered that his existence depended upon my protection. The poor mules were by no means so easily restored. Their backs, cut to the bone by the saddles, stood up like those of angry cats, their heads drooped sadly, and their hams showed red marks of the spear-point. Directing them to be washed in the sea, dressed with cold-water bandages, and copiously fed, I proceeded to inspect the Berberah Plain.

The " Mother of the Poor," as the Arabs call the place, in position resembles Zayla. The town—if such name can be given to what is now a wretched clump of dirty mat-huts — is situated on the northern edge of alluvial ground, sloping almost imperceptibly from the base of the Southern hills. The rapacity of these short-sighted savages has contracted its dimensions to about one-sixth of its former extent : for nearly a mile around, the now desert land is strewed with bits of glass and broken pottery. Their ignorance has chosen the worst position : *Mos Majorum* is the Somali code, where father built there son builds, and there shall grandson build. To the S. and E. lies a saline sand-flat, partially over-flowed by high tides : here are the wells of bitter water, and the filth and garbage make the spot truly offensive. Northwards the sea-strand has become a huge cemetery, crowded with graves whose dimensions explain the Somali legend that once there were giants in the land : tradition assigns to it the name of Bunder Abbas. Westward, close up to. the town, runs the creek, which forms the wealth of Berberah. A long strip of sand and limestone—the general formation of the coast—defends its length from the northern gales, the breadth is about three quarters of a mile, and the depth varies from six to fifteen fathoms near the Ras or Spit at which ships anchor before putting out to sea.

Behind the town, and distant about seven miles, lie the Sub-Ghauts, a bold background of lime and sand-stone. Through a broad gap called Duss Malablay[1] appear in fine weather the granite walls of Wagar and Gulays, whose altitude by aneroid was found to be 5700 feet above the level of the sea.[2] On the eastward the Berberah plain is bounded by the hills of Siyaro, and westwards the heights of Dabasenis limit the prospect.[3]

It was with astonishment that I reflected upon the impolicy of having preferred Aden to this place.

The Emporium of Eastern Africa has a salubrious

---

1 In the centre of the gap is a detached rock called Daga Malablay.

2 It was measured by Lt. Herne, who remarks of this range that "cold in winter, as the presence of the pine-tree proves, and cooled in summer by the Monsoon, abounding in game from a spur fowl to an elephant; this hill would make an admirable Sanitarium." Unfortunately Gulays is tenanted by the Habr Girhajis, and Wagar by the Ísa Musa, treacherous races.

3 This part of Somali land is a sandy plain, thinly covered with thorns and bounded by two ranges, the Ghauts and Sub-Ghauts. The latter or maritime mountains begin at Tajurrah, and extend to Karam (long. 46° E.), where they break into detached groups; the distance from the coast varies from 6 to 15 miles, the height from 2000 to 3000 feet, and the surface is barren, the rock being denuded of soil by rain. The Ghauts lie from 8 to 40 miles from the sea, they average from 4000 to 6000 feet, are thickly covered with gum-arabic and frankincense trees, the wild fig and the Somali pine, and form the seaward wall of the great table-land of the interior. The Northern or maritime face is precipitous, the summit is tabular and slopes gently southwards. The general direction is E. by N. and W. by S., there are, however, some spurs at the three hills termed "Ourat," which project towards the north. Each portion of the plain between these ranges has some local name, such as the "Shimberali Valley" extending westwards from the detached hill Dimoli, to Geuli, Dinanjir and Gularkar. Intersected with Fiumaras which roll torrents dur i n the monsun, they are covered with a scrub of thorns, wild fig, aloe, and different kinds of Cactus.

climate,[1] abundance of sweet water—a luxury to be
"fully appreciated only after a residence at Aden"[2]—a
mild monsun, a fine open country, an excellent harbour,
and a soil highly productive. It is the meeting-place of
commerce, has few rivals, and with half the sums
lavished in Arabia upon engineer follies of stone and
lime, the environs might at this time have been covered
with houses, gardens, and trees.

The Eye of Al-Yaman, to quote Carlyle, is a
"mountain of misery towering sheer up like a bleak
Pisgah, with outlooks only into desolation, sand, salt water
and despair." The camp is in a " Devil's Punchbowl,"
stiflingly hot during nine months of the year, and subject
to alternations of sandstorm and Samun, "without either
seed, water, or trees," as Ibn Batutah described it 500
years ago, unproductive for want of rain—not a sparrow
can exist there, nor will a crow thrive[3]—and essentially

---

1 The climate of Berberah is cool during the winter, and though
the sun is at all times burning, the atmosphere, as in Somali land
generally, is healthy. In the dry season the plain is subject to great
heats, but lying open to the north, the sea-breeze is strong and regular.
In the monsun the air is cloudy, light showers frequently fall, and
occasionally heavy storms come up from the southern hills.

2 I quote Lieut. Cruttenden. The Berberah water has acquired
a bad name because the people confine themselves to digging holes
three or four feet deep in the sand, about half-a-mile from high-water
mark. They are reconciled to it by its beneficial effects, especially
after and before a journey. Good water, however, can be procured
in any of the Fiumaras intersecting the plain ; when the Hajj Sharmarkay's towers commanded the town wells, the people sank pits in
low ground a few hundred yards distant, and procured a purer
beverage. The Banyans, who are particular about their potations,
drink the sweet produce of Siyaro, a roadstead about nineteen miles
eastward of Berberah.

3 The experiment was tried by an officer who brought from
Bombay a batch of sparrows and crows. The former died, scorbutic
I presume ; the latter lingered through an unhappy life, and to judge
from the absence of young, refused to entail their miseries upon
posterity.

unhealthy.[1] Our loss in operatives is only equalled by our waste of rupees; and the general wish of Western India is, that the extinct sea of fire would, Vesuvius-like, once more convert this dismal cape into a living crater.

After a day's rest—physical not spiritual, for the Somal were as usual disputing violently about the Abbanship[2]—I went with my comrades to visit an

---

1 The climate of Aden, it may be observed, has a reputation for salubrity which it does not deserve. The returns of deaths prove it to be healthy for the European soldier as London, and there are many who have built their belief upon the sandy soil of statistics. But it is the practice of every sensible medical man to hurry his patients out of Aden; they die elsewhere—some I believe recover— and thus the deaths caused by the crater are attributed statistically to Bombay or the Red Sea.

Aden is for Asiatics a hot bed of scurvy and ulcer. Of the former disease my own corps, I am informed, had in hospital at one time 200 cases above the usual amount of sickness; this arises from the brackish water, the want of vegetables, and lastly the cachexy induced by an utter absence of change, diversion, and excitement. The ulcer is a disease endemic in Southern Arabia; it is frequently fatal, especially to the poorer classes of operatives, when worn out by privation, hardship, and fatigue.

2 The Abban is now the pest of Berberah. Before vessels have cast anchor, or indeed have rounded the Spit, a crowd of Somal, eager as hotel-touters, may be seen running along the strand. They swim off, and the first who arrives on board inquires the name of the Abban; if there be none he touches the captain or one of the crew and constitutes himself protector. For merchandize sent forward, the man who conveys it becomes answerable.

The system of dues has become complicated, Formerly, the standard of value at Berberah was two cubits of the blue cotton-stuff called Sauda; this is now converted into four pice of specie. Dollars form the principal currency; rupees are taken at a discount. Traders pay according to degree, the lowest being one per cent., taken from Maskat and Suri merchants. The shopkeeper provides food for his Abban, and presents him at the close of the season with a Tobe, a pair of sandals, and half-a-dozen dollars. Wealthy Banyans and Mehmans give food and raiment, and before departure from 50 to 200 dollars. This class, however, derive large profits:

interesting ruin near the town. On the way we were
shown pits of coarse sulphur and alum mixed with sand;
in the low lands senna and colocynth were growing wild.
After walking a mile south-south-east, from present
Berberah to a rise in the plain, we found the remains of
a small building about eight yards square divided into
two compartments. It is apparently a Mosque: one
portion, the sole of which is raised, shows traces of the
prayer niche; the other might have contained the tomb
of some saint now obsolete, or might have been a fort to
protect a neighbouring tank. The walls are of rubble
masonry and mud, revetted with a coating of cement
hard as stone, and mixed with small round pebbles.[1]
Near it is a shallow reservoir of stone and lime, about
five yards by ten, proved by the aqueduct, part of which
still remains, to be a tank of supply. Removing the
upper slabs, we found the interior lined with a deposit of
sulphate of lime and choked with fine drift sand; the

---

they will lend a few dollars to the Badawi at the end of the Fair,
on condition of receiving cent. per cent., at the opening of the next
season. Travellers not transacting business must feed the protector,
but cannot properly be forced to pay him. Of course the Somal
take every advantage of Europeans. Mr. Angelo, a merchant from
Zanzibar, resided two months at Bulhar; his broker of the Ayyal
Gadid tribe, and an Arab who accompanied him, extracted, it is
said, 3000 dollars. As a rule the Abban claims one per cent. on
sales and purchases, and two dollars per head of slaves. For each
bale of cloth, half-a-dollar in coin is taken; on gums and coffee the
duty is one pound in twenty-seven. Cowhides pay half-a-dollar
each, sheep and goat's skins four pice, and ghi about one per cent.

Lieut. Herne calculates that the total money dues during the
Fair-season amount to 2000 dollars, and that, in the present reduced
state of Berberah, not more than 10,000*l.* worth of merchandize is
sold. This estimate the natives of the place declare to be considerably under the mark.

1 The similarity between the Persian "Gach" and this cement,
which is found in many ruins about Berberah, has been remarked
by other travellers.

breadth is about fifteen inches and the depth nine.
After following it fifty yards toward the hills, we lost the
trace; the loose stones had probably been removed for
graves, and the soil may have buried the firmer portion.

Mounting our mules we then rode in a south-south-
east direction towards the Dubar Hills. The surface of
the ground, apparently level, rises about 100 feet per
mile. In most parts a soft sand overlying hard loam,
like work *en pisé*, limestone and coralline; it shows
evidences of inundation: water-worn stones of a lime
almost as compact as marble, pieces of quartz, selenite,
basalt, granite, and syenite in nodules are everywhere
sprinkled over the surface.[1] Here and there torrents
from the hills had cut channels five or six feet below the
level, and a thicker vegetation denoted the lines of bed.
The growth of wild plants, scanty near the coast, became

---

[1] The following note by Dr. Carter of Bombay will be interesting to Indian geologists.

" Of the collection of geological specimens and fossils from Berberah above mentioned, Lieut. Burton states that the latter are
found on the plain of Berberah, and the former in the following
order between the sea and the summits of mountains (600 feet high),
above it—that is, the ridge immediate behind Berberah.

" 1. Country along the coast consists of a coralline limestone,
(tertiary formation,) with drifts of sand, &c. 2. Sub-Ghauts and
lower ranges (say 2000 feet high), of sandstone capped with limestone, the former preponderating. 3. Above the Ghauts a plateau
of primitive rocks mixed with sandstone, granite, syenite, mica
schiste, quartz rock, micaceous grit, &c.

" The fawn-coloured fossils from his coralline limestone are
evidently the same as those of the tertiary formation along the
south-east coast of Arabia, and therefore, the same as those of
Cutch ; and it is exceedingly interesting to find that among the blue-
coloured fossils which are accompanied by specimens of the blue
shale, composing the beds from which they have been weathered
out, are species of Terebratula Belemnites, identical with those
figured in Grant's Geology of Cutch; thus enabling us to extend
those beds of the Jurassic formation which exist in Cutch, and along
the south-eastern coast of Arabia, across to Africa."

more luxuriant as we approached the hills ; the Arman Acacia flourished, the Kulan tree grew in clumps, and the Tamarisk formed here and there a dense thicket. Except a few shy antelopes,[1] we saw no game.

A ride of seven or eight miles led us to the dry bed of a watercourse overgrown with bright green rushes, and known to the people as Dubar Wena, or Great Dubar. The strip of ground, about half a mile long, collects the drainage of the hills above it : numerous Las or Pits, in the centre of the bed, four or five feet deep, abundantly supply the flocks and herds. Although the surface of the ground, where dry, was white with impure nitre, the water tasted tolerably sweet. Advancing half a mile over the southern shoulder of a coarse and shelly mass of limestone, we found the other rushy swamp, called Dubar Yir or Little Dubar. A spring of warm and bitter water flowed from the hill over the surface to a distance of 400 or 500 yards, where it was absorbed by the soil. The temperature of the sources immediately under the hill was 106° Fahr., the thermometer standing at 80° in the air, and the aneroid gave an altitude of 728 feet above the sea.

The rocks behind these springs were covered with ruins of mosques and houses. We visited a little tower commanding the source : it was built in steps, the hill being cut away to form the two lower rooms, and the second story showed three compartments. The material was rubble and the form resembled Galla buildings ; we found, however, fine mortar mixed with coarse gravel, bits of glass bottles and blue glazed pottery, articles now unknown to this part of Africa. On the summit of the highest peak our guides pointed out remains of another fort similar to the old Turkish watch-towers at Aden.

---

1 These animals are tolerably tame in the morning, as day advances their apprehension of man increases.

About three quarters of a mile from the Little Dubar, we found the head of the Berberah Aqueduct. Thrown across a watercourse apparently of low level, it is here more substantially built than near the beach, and probably served as a force pipe until the water found a fall. We traced the line to a distance of ten yards, where it disappeared beneath the soil, and saw nothing resembling a supply-tank except an irregularly shaped natural pool.[1]

A few days afterwards, accompanied by Lieut. Herne, I rode out to inspect the Biyu Gora or Night-running Water. After advancing about ten miles in a south-east direction from Berberah, we entered rough and broken ground, and suddenly came upon a Fiumara, about 250 yards broad. The banks were fringed with Brab and Tamarisk, the Daum palm and green rushes: a clear sparkling and shallow stream bisected the sandy

---

1 Lieut. Cruttenden in considering what nation could have constructed, and at what period the commerce of Berberah warranted, so costly an undertaking, is disposed to attribute it to the Persian conquerors of Aden in the days of Anushirwan. He remarks that the trade carried on in the Red Sea was then great, the ancient emporia of Hisn Ghorab and Aden prosperous and wealthy, and Berberah doubtless exported, as it does now, ivory, gums, and ostrich feathers. But though all the maritime Somali country abounds in traditions of the Furs or ancient Persians, none of the buildings near Berberah justifies our assigning to them, in a country of monsun rain and high winds, an antiquity of 1300 years ago.

The Somal assert that ten generations ago their ancestors drove out the Gallas from Berberah, and attribute these works to the ancient Pagans. That nation of savages, however, was never capable of constructing a scientific aqueduct. I therefore prefer attributing these remains at Berberah to the Ottomans, who, after the conquest of Aden by Sulayman Pasha in A.D. 1538, held Al-Yaman for about 100 years, and as auxiliaries of the King of Adel, penetrated as far as Abyssinia. Traces of their architecture are found at Zayla and Harar, and according to tradition, they possessed at Berberah a settlement called, after its founder, Bunder Abbas.

bed, and smaller branches wandered over the surface. This river, the main drain of the Ghauts and Sub-Ghauts, derives its name from the increased volume of the waters during night: evaporation by day causes the absorption of about a hundred yards. We found its temperature 73° Fahr. (in the air 78°), and our people dug holes in the sand instead of drinking from the stream, a proof that they feared leeches.[1] The taste of the water was bitter and nauseous.[2]

Following the course of the Biyu Gora through two low parallel ranges of conglomerate, we entered a narrow gorge, in which lime and sandstone abound. The dip of the strata is about 45° west, the strike north and south. Water springs from under every stone, drops copiously from the shelves of rock, oozes out of the sand, and bubbles up from the mould. The temperature is exceedingly variable: in some places the water is icy cold, in others, the thermometer shows 68° Fahr., in others, 101°—the maximum, when we visited it, being 126°. The colours are equally diverse. Here, the polished surface of the sandstone is covered with a hoar of salt and nitre.[3] There, where the stream does not flow, are pools dyed greenish-black or rust-red by iron sediment. The gorge's sides are a vivid red: a peculiar creeper

---

1 Here, as elsewhere in Somali land, the leech is of the horse-variety. It might be worth while to attempt breeding a more useful species after the manner recommended by Capt. R. Johnston, the Sub-Assistant Commissary General in Sind (10th April, 1845). In these streams leeches must always be suspected; inadvertently swallowed, they fix upon the inner coat of the stomach, and in Northern Africa have caused, it is said, some deaths among the French soldiers.

2 Yet we observed frogs and a small species of fish.

3 Either this or the sulphate of magnesia, formed by the decomposition of limestone, may account for the bitterness of the water.

hangs from the rocks, and water trickles down its metallic leaves. The upper cliffs are crowned with tufts of the dragon's-blood tree.

Leaving our mules with an attendant, we began to climb the rough and rocky gorge, which, as the breadth diminishes, becomes exceedingly picturesque. In one part, the side of a limestone hill hundreds of feet in height, has slipped into the chasm, half filling it with gigantic boulders: through these the noisy stream whirls, now falling in small cascades, then gliding over slabs of sheet rock: here it cuts grooved channels and deep basins clean and sharp as artificial baths in the sandstone, there it flows quietly down a bed of pure sparkling sand. The high hills above are of a tawny yellow: the huge boulders, grisly white, bear upon their summits the drift wood of the last year's inundation. During the monsun, when a furious torrent sweeps down from the Wagar Hills, this chasm must afford a curiously wild spectacle.

Returning from a toilsome climb, we found some of the Ayyal Ahmad building near the spot where Biyu Gora is absorbed, the usual small stone tower. The fact had excited attention at Berberah; the erection was intended to store grain, but the suspicious savages, the Ísa Musa, and Mikahil, who hold the land, saw in it an attempt to threaten their liberties. On our way home we passed through some extensive cemeteries: the tombs were in good preservation; there was nothing peculiar in their construction, yet the Somal were positive that they belonged to a race preceding their own. Near them were some ruins of kilns—comparatively modern, for bits of charcoal were mixed with broken pieces of pottery— and the oblong tracery of a dwelling-house divided into several compartments: its material was the sun-dried brick of Central Asia, here a rarity.

After visiting these ruins there was little to detain

me at Berberah.　The town had become intolerable, the heat under a mat hut was extreme, the wind and dust were almost as bad as Aden, and the dirt perhaps even worse.　As usual we had not a moment's privacy, Arabs as well as the Somal assuming the right of walking in, sitting down, looking hard, chatting with one another, and departing.　Before the voyage, however, I was called upon to compose a difficulty upon the subject of Abbanship.　The Hammal had naturally constituted his father-in-law, one Burhali Nuh, of the Ayyal Gadid, protector to Lieut. Herne and myself.　Burhali had proved himself a rascal: he had been insolent as well as dishonest, and had thrown frequent obstacles in his employer's way; yet custom does not permit the Abban to be put away like a wife, and the Hammal's services entitled him to the fullest consideration.　On the other hand Jami Hasan, a chief and a doughty man of the Ayyal Ahmad, had met me at Aden early in 1854, and had received from me a ring in token of Abbanship. During my absence at Harar, he had taken charge of Lieut. Stroyan.　On the very morning of my arrival he came to the hut, sat down spear in hand, produced the ring and claimed my promise.　In vain I objected that the token had been given when a previous trip was intended, and that the Hammal must not be disappointed: Jami replied that once an Abban always an Abban, that he hated the Hammal and all his tribe, and that he would enter into no partnership with Burhali Nuh:—to complicate matters, Lieut. Stroyan spoke highly of his courage and conduct.　Presently he insisted rudely upon removing his *protégé* to another part of the town: this passed the limits of our patience, and decided the case against him.

　　For some days discord raged between the rivals. At last it was settled that I should choose my own Abban in presence of a general council of the Elders.

The chiefs took their places upon the shore, each with his followers forming a distinct semicircle, and all squatting with shield and spear planted upright in the ground. When sent for, I entered the circle sword in hand, and sat down awaiting their pleasure. After much murmuring had subsided, Jami asked in a loud voice, " Who is thy protector ? " The reply was, " Burhali Nuh! " Knowing, however, how little laconism is prized by an East-African audience, I did not fail to follow up this answer with an Arabic speech of the dimensions of an average sermon, and then shouldering my blade left the circle abruptly. The effect was success. Our wild friends sat from afternoon till sunset: as we finished supper one of them came in with the glad tidings of a " peace conference." Jami had asked Burhali to swear that he intended no personal offence in taking away a *protégé* pledged to himself : Burhali had sworn, and once more the olive waved over the braves of Berberah.

On the 5th February 1855, taking leave of my comrades, I went on board Al-Kasab or the Reed—such was the ill-omened name of our cranky craft—to the undisguised satisfaction of the Hammal, Long Gulad, and the End of Time, who could scarcely believe in their departure from Berberah with sound skins.[1] Coast in with a light breeze, early after noon on the next day we arrived at Siyaro, a noted watering-place for shipping, about nineteen miles east of the emporium. The roadstead is open to the north, but a bluff buttress of limestone rock defends it from the north-east gales. Upon a barren strip of sand lies the material of the town; two houses of

---

1 They had been in some danger : a treacherous murder perpetrated a few days before our arrival had caused all the Habr Girhajis to fly from the town and assemble 5,000 men at Bulhar for battle and murder. This proceeding irritated the Habr Awal, and certainly, but for our presence, the strangers would have been scurvily treated by their "cousins."

stone and mud, one yet unfinished, the other completed
about thirty years ago by Farih Binni, a Mikahil chief.

Some dozen Badawi spearmen, Mikahil of a neighbouring kraal, squatted like a line of crows upon the
shore to receive us as we waded from the vessel. They
demanded money in too authoritative a tone before
allowing us to visit the wells, which form their principal
wealth. Resolved not to risk a quarrel so near Berberah,
I was returning to moralize upon the fate of Burckhardt
—after a successful pilgrimage refused admittance to
Aaron's tomb at Sinai—when a Badawi ran to tell us
that we might wander where we pleased. He excused
himself and his companions by pleading necessity, and
his leanness lent conviction to the plea.

The larger well lies close to the eastern wall of the
dwelling-house: it is about eighteen feet deep, one third
sunk through ground, the other two thirds through limestone, and at the bottom is a small supply of sweet clear
water. Near it I observed some ruined tanks, built
with fine mortar like that of the Berberah ruins. The
other well lies about half a mile to the westward of the
former: it is also dug in the limestone rock. A few yards
to the north-east of the building is the Furzah or custom-
house, whose pristine simplicity tempts me to describe
it :—a square of ground surrounded by a dwarf rubble
enclosure, and provided wlth a proportional mosque, a
tabular block of coralline niched in the direction of
Meccah. On a little eminence of rock to the westward,
rise ruined walls, said by my companions to have been
built by a Frank, who bought land from the Mikahil
and settled on this dismal strand.

Taking leave of the Badawin, whose hearts were
gladdened by a few small presents, we resumed our
voyage eastwards along the coast. Next morning, we
passed two broken pyramids of dark rock called Dubada
Gumbar Madu—the Two Black Hills. After a tedious

day's sail, twenty miles in twenty-four hours, the Captain of Al-Kasab landed us in a creek west of Aynterad. A few sheep boats lay at anchor in this " back-bay," as usual when the sea is heavy at the roadstead, and the crews informed us that a body of Badawin was marching to attack the village. Abdi Mohammed Diban, pro- prietor of the Aynterad Fort, having constituted me his protector, and remained at Berberah, I armed my men, and ordering the captain of the " Reed " to bring his vessel round at early dawn, walked hurriedly over the three miles that separated us from the place. Arrived at the fort, we found that Abdi's slaves knew nothing of the reported attack. They received me, however, hospitably, and brought a supper of their only provision, vile dates and dried meat. Unwilling to diminish the scanty store, the Hammal and I but dipped our hands in the dish : Long Gulad and the End of Time, however, soon cleared the platters, while abusing roundly the unpalatable food. After supper, a dispute arose between the Hammal and one of the Habr Tul Jailah, the tribe to whom the land belongs. The Badawi, not liking my looks, pro- posed to put a spear into me. The Hammal objected that if the measure were carried out, he would return the compliment in kind. Ensued a long dispute, and the listeners laughed heartily at the utter indifference with which I gave ear. When it concluded, amicably as may be expected, the slaves spread a carpet upon a coarse Berberah couch, and having again vented their hilarity in a roar of laughter, left me to sleep.

We had eaten at least one sheep per diem, and mutton baked in the ship's oven is delicious to the Somali mouth. Remained on board another dinner, a circumstance which possibly influenced the weak mind of the Captain of the " Reed." Awaking at dawn, I went out, expecting to find the vessel within stone's throw : it was nowhere visible. About 8 A.M., it appeared in sight, a mere speck upon the sea-horizon, and whilst it approached, I inspected the settlement.

Aynterad, an inconsiderable place lying east-north-east of, and about forty miles from, Berberah, is a favourite roadstead principally on account of its water, which rivals that of Siyaro. The anchorage is bad: the Shimal or north wind sweeps long lines of heavy wave into the open bay, and the bottom is a mass of rock and sand-reef. The fifty sunburnt and windsoiled huts which compose the settlement, are built upon a bank of sand overlying the normal limestone: at the time when I visited it, the male population had emigrated *en masse* to Berberah. It is principally supported by the slave trade, the Arabs preferring to ship their purchases at some distance from the chief emporium.[1] Lieut. Herne, when he visited it, found a considerable amount of "black bullion" in the market.

The fort of Aynterad, erected thirty years ago by Mohammed Diban, is a stone and mud house square and flat-roofed, with high windows, an attempt at crenelles, and, for some reason intelligible only to its own Vitruvius, but a single bastion at the northern angle. There is no well, and the mass of huts cluster close to the walls. The five guns here deposited by Sharmarkay when expelled from Berberah, stand on the ground outside the fort, which is scarcely calculated to bear heavy carronades: they are unprovided with balls, but

---

1 Of all the slave-dealers on this coast, the Arabs are the most unscrupulous. In 1855, one Mohammed of Maskat, a ship-owner, who, moreover, constantly visits Aden, bought within sight of our flag a free-born Arab girl of the Yafa'i tribe, from the Akarib of Bir Hamid, and sold her at Berberah to a compatriot. Such a crime merits severe punishment; even the Abyssinians visit with hanging the Christian convicted of selling a fellow religionist. The Arab slaver generally marries his property as a ruse, and arrived at Maskat or Bushiri, divorces and sells them. Free Somali women have not unfrequently met with this fate.

that is a trifle where pebbles abound. Moreover, Abdi's slaves are well armed with matchlock and pistol, and the Badawi Tul Jailah[1] find the spear ineffectual against stone walls. The garrison has frequently been blockaded by its troublesome neighbours, whose prowess, however, never extended beyond preliminaries.

To allay my impatience, that morning I was invited into several huts for the purpose of drinking sour milk. A malicious joy filled my soul, as about noon, the Machiavellian Captain of the " Reed " managed to cast anchor, after driving his crazy craft through a sea which the violent Shimal was flinging in hollow curves foam-fringed upon the strand. I stood on the shore making signs for a canoe. My desires were disregarded, as long as decency admitted. At last, about 1 P.M., I found myself upon the quarter-deck.

" Dawwir al-farman,"—shift the yard !—I shouted with a voice of thunder.

---

1 The Habr Tul Jailah (mother of the tribe of Jailah) descendants of Ishak al-Hazrami by a slave girl, inhabit the land eastward of Berberah. Their principal settlements after Aynterad are the three small ports of Karam, Unkor, and Hays. The former, according to Lieut. Cruttenden, is " the most important from its possessing a tolerable harbour, and from its being the nearest point from Aden, the course to which place is N. N. W.,—consequently the wind is fair, and the boats laden with sheep for the Aden market pass but one night at sea, whilst those from Berberah are generally three. What greatly enhances the value of Kurrum (Karam), however, is its proximity to the country of the Dulbahanteh, who approach within four days of Kurrum, and who therefore naturally have their chief trade through that port. The Ahl Yusuf, a branch of the Habertel Jahleh, at present hold possession of Kurrum, and between them and the tribes to windward there exists a most bitter and irreconcileable feud, the consequence of sundry murders perpetrated about five years since at Kurrum, and which hitherto have not been avenged. The small ports of Enterad, Unkor, Heis, and Rukudah are not worthy of mention, with the exception of the first-named place, which has a trade with Aden in sheep."

The answer was a general hubbub. "He surely will not sail in a sea like this?" asked the trembling Captain of my companions.

"He will!" sententiously quoth the Hammal, with a Burleigh nod.

"It blows wind—" remonstrated the Rais.

"And if it blew fire?" asked the Hammal with the air *goguenard*, meaning that from the calamity of Frankish obstinacy there was no refuge.

A kind of death-wail arose, during which, to hide untimely laughter, I retreated to a large drawer, in the stern of the vessel, called a cabin. There my ears could distinguish the loud entreaties of the crew vainly urging my attendants to propose a day's delay. Then one of the garrison, accompanied by the Captain who shook as with fever, resolved to act forlorn hope, and bring a *feu d'enfer* of phrases to bear upon the Frank's hard brain. Scarcely, however, had the head of the sentence been delivered, before he was playfully upraised by his bushy hair and a handle somewhat more substantial, carried out of the cabin, and thrown, like a bag of biscuit, on the deck.

The case was hopeless. All strangers plunged into the sea—the popular way of landing in East Africa—the anchor was weighed, the ton of sail shaken out, and the "Reed" began to dip and rise in the yeasty sea laboriously as an alderman dancing a polka.

For the first time in my life I had the satisfaction of seeing the Somal unable to eat—unable to eat mutton. In sea-sickness and needless terror, the captain, crew, and passengers abandoned to us all the baked sheep, which we three, not being believers in the Evil Eye, ate from head to trotters with especial pleasure. That night the waves broke over us. The End of Time occupied himself in roaring certain orisons, which are reputed to calm stormy seas: he desisted only when Long Gulad pointed out that a wilder gust seemed to follow as in derision each more emphatic period. The Captain, a noted reprobate, renowned on shore for his knowledge of erotic verse and admiration of the fair sex, prayed with fervour: he was joined by several of the crew, who apparently found the charm of novelty in the edifying exercise. About midnight a Sultan al-Bahr or Sea-king —a species of whale—appeared close to our counter; and as these animals are infamous for upsetting vessels in waggishness, the sight elicited a yell of terror and a chorus of religious exclamations.

On the morning of Friday, the 9th February 1855, we hove in sight of Jabal Shamsan, the loftiest peak of the Aden Crater. And ere evening fell, I had the pleasure of seeing the faces of friends and comrades once more.

POSTSCRIPT.

On Saturday, the 7th April 1855, the H. E. I. Company's Schooner " Mahi," Lieut. King, I. N., commanding, entered the harbour of Berberah, where her guns roared forth a parting salute to the " Somali Expedition."

The Emporium of East Africa was at the time of my landing, in a state of confusion. But a day before, the great Harar caravan, numbering 3000 souls, and as many cattle, had entered for the purpose of laying in the usual eight months' supplies, and purchase, barter, and exchange were transacted in most hurried and un-business-like manner. All day, and during the greater part of night, the town rang with the voices of buyer and seller: to specify no other articles of traffic, 500 slaves of both sexes were in the market.[1] Long lines of

---

[1] The Fair-season of 1854-55 began on the 15th November, and may be said to have broken up on the 15th April.

The principal caravans which visit Berberah are from Harar the Western, and Ogadayn, the Southern region: they collect the produce of the numerous intermediate tribes of the Somal. The former has been described in the preceding pages. The following remarks upon the subject of the Ogadayn caravan are the result of Lieuts. Stroyan and Herne's observations at Berberah.

"Large caravans from Ogadayn descend to the coast at the beginning and the end of the Fair-season. They bring slaves from the Arusa country, cattle in great quantities, gums of sorts, clarified

laden and unladen camels were to be seen pacing the glaring yellow shore; rumours of plundering parties at times brought swarms of spear-men, bounding and yelling like wild beasts, from the town: already small parties of travellers had broken ground for their return journey; and the foul heap of mat hovels, to which this celebrated mart had been reduced, was steadily shrinking in dimensions.

Our little party consisted of forty-two souls. At Aden I had applied officially for some well-trained Somali policemen, but as an increase of that establishment had been urged upon the home authorities, my request was refused. We were fain to content ourselves with a dozen recruits of various races, Egyptian, Nubian, Arab and Negro, whom we armed with sabres and flint muskets. The other members of the expedition were our private servants, and about a score of Somal under our rival protectors Jami Hasan and Burhali Nuh. The Ras or Captain of the Kafilah was one Mahmud of the

---

butter, ivory, ostrich feathers, and rhinoceros horns to be made into handles for weapons. These are bartered for coarse cotton cloth of three kinds, for English and American sheeting in pieces of seventy-five, sixty-six, sixty-two, and forty-eight yards, black and indigo-dyed calicos in lengths of sixteen yards, nets or fillets worn by the married women, iron and steel in small bars, lead and zinc, beads of various kinds, especially white porcelain and speckled glass, dates and rice."

The Ayyal Ahmad and Ayyal Yunis classes of the Habr Awal Somal have constituted themselves Abbans or brokers to the Ogadayn Caravans, and the rapacity of the patron has produced a due development of roguery in the client. The principal trader of this coast is the Banyan from Aden and Cutch, facetiously termed by the Somal their "Milch-cows." The African cheats by mis-measuring the bad cotton cloth, and the Indian by falsely weighing the coffee, ivory, ostrich feathers and other valuable articles which he receives in return. Dollars and even rupees are now preferred to the double breadth of eight cubits which constitutes the well known "Tobe."

Mijjarthayn, better known at Aden as Al-Balyuz or the Envoy : he had the reputation of being a shrewd manager, thoroughly acquainted with the habits and customs, as well as the geography, of Somaliland.

Our camp was pitched near the site of the proposed Agency, upon a rocky ridge within musket-shot of the southern extremity of the creek, and about three quarters of a mile distant from the town. This position had been selected for the benefit of the " Mahi's " guns. Political exigencies required the " Mahi " to relieve the " Elphinstone," then blockading the seaboard of our old Arab foe, the Fazli chief ; she was unable to remain upon the coast, and superintend our departure, a measure which I had strongly urged. Our tents were pitched in one line : Lieut. Stroyan's was on the extreme right, about a dozen paces distant was the " Rowtie[1]" occupied by Lieut. Herne and myself, and at a similar distance on the left of the camp was that in which Lieut. Speke slept. The baggage was placed between the two latter, the camels were tethered in front upon a sandy bed beneath the ridge our camping-ground, and in rear stood the horses and mules. During day-time all were on the alert : at night two sentries were posted, regularly relieved, and visited at times by the Ras and ourselves.

I had little reason to complain of my reception at Berberah. The chiefs appeared dissatisfied with the confinement of one Mohammed Sammattar, the Abban who accompanied Lieut. Speke to the Eastern country : they listened, however, with respectful attention to a letter in which the Political Resident at Aden enjoined them to treat us with consideration and hospitality.

There had been petty disputes with Burhali Nuh, and the elders of the Ísa Musa tribe, touching the hire

---

1 A Sepoy's tent, pent-house shaped, supported by a single transverse and two upright poles and open at one of the long ends

of horse-keepers and camel-drivers : such events, however, are not worthy to excite attention in Africa. My
friend at Harar, the Shaykh Jami, had repeatedly called
upon us, eaten bread and salt, recommended us to his
fellow countrymen, and used my intervention in persuading avaricious ship-owners to transport, gratis,
pauper pilgrims to Arabia. The people, after seeing
the deaths of a few elephants, gradually lowered their
loud boasts and brawling claims : they assisted us in
digging a well, offered their services as guides and camel-
drivers, and in some cases insisted upon encamping near
us for protection. Briefly, we saw no grounds of apprehension. During thirty years, not an Englishman of the
many that had visited it had been molested at Berberah,
and apparently there was as little to fear in it as within
the fortifications of Aden.[1]

Under these favourable circumstances we might
have set out at once towards the interior. Our camels,
fifty-six in number, had been purchased,[2] and the

---

1 Since returning I have been informed, however, by the
celebrated Abyssinian traveller M. Antoine d'Abbadie, that in no
part of the wild countries which he visited was his life so much
perilled as at Berberah.

2 Lieut. Speke had landed at Karam harbour on the 24th of
March, in company with the Ras, in order to purchase camels. For
the Ayyun or best description he paid seven dollars and a half; the
Gal Ad (white camels) cost on an average four. In five days he had
collected twenty-six, the number required, and he then marched
overland from Karam to Berberah.

I had taken the precaution of detaching Lieut. Speke to Karam
in lively remembrance of my detention for want of carriage at
Zayla, and in consequence of a report raised by the Somal of Aden
that a sufficient number of camels was not procurable at Berberah.
This proved false. Lieuts. Stroyan and Herne found no difficulty
whatever in purchasing animals at the moderate price of five dollars
and three quarters a head : for the same sum they could have
bought any reasonable number. Future travellers, however, would

Ogadayn Caravan was desirous of our escort. But we wished to witness the close of the Berberah fair, and we expected instruments and other necessaries by the mid-April mail from Europe.[1]

About 3 P.M., on the 9th April, a shower, accompanied by thunder and lightning, came up from the southern hills, where rain had been falling for some days, and gave notice that the Gugi or Somali monsun had begun. This was the signal for the Badawin to migrate to the plateau above the hills.[2] Throughout the town the mats were stripped from the frameworks of stick and pole,[3] the camels were laden, and thousands of travellers lined the roads. The next day Berberah was almost deserted except by the pilgrims who intended to take ship, and by merchants, who, fearful of plundering parties, awaited the first favourable hour for setting sail. Our protectors, Jami and Burhali, receiving permission to accompany their families and flocks, left us in charge of their sons and relations. On the 15th April the last vessel sailed out of the creek, and our little party remained in undisputed possession of the place.

Three days afterwards, about noon, an Aynterad craft *en route* from Aden entered the solitary harbour freighted with about a dozen Somal desirous of accompanying us towards Ogadayn, the southern region. She

---

do well not to rely solely upon Berberah for a supply of this necessary, especially at seasons when the place is not crowded with caravans.

1 The Elders of the Habr Awal, I have since been informed, falsely asserted that they repeatedly urged us, with warnings of danger, to leave Berberah at the end of the fair, but that we positively refused compliance, for other reasons. The facts of the case are those stated in the text.

2 They prefer travelling during the monsun, on account of the abundance of water.

3 The framework is allowed to remain for use next Fair-season.

would have sailed that evening ; fortunately, however I had ordered our people to feast her commander and crew with rice and the irresistible dates.

At sunset on the same day we were startled by a discharge of musketry behind the tents: the cause proved to be three horsemen, over whose heads our guide had fired in case they might be a foraging party. I reprimanded our people sharply for this act of folly, ordering them in future to reserve their fire, and when necessary to shoot into, not above, a crowd. After this we proceeded to catechize the strangers, suspecting them to be scouts, the usual forerunners of a Somali raid: the reply was so plausible that even the Balyuz, with all his acuteness, was deceived. The Badawin had forged a report that their ancient enemy the Hajj Sharmarkay was awaiting with four ships at the neighbouring port, Siyaro, the opportunity of seizing Berberah whilst deserted, and re-erecting his forts there for the third time. Our visitors swore by the divorce-oath—the most solemn which the religious know—that a vessel entering the creek at such unusual season, they had been sent to ascertain whether it had been freighted with materials for building, and concluded by laughingly asking if we feared danger from the tribe of our own protectors. Believing them, we posted as usual two sentries for the night, and retired to rest in our wonted security.

Between 2 and 3 A.M. of the 19th April I was suddenly aroused by the Balyuz, who cried aloud that the enemy was upon us.[1] Hearing a rush of men like a stormy wind, I sprang up, called for my sabre, and sent Lieut. Herne to ascertain the force of the foray. Armed with a " Colt," he went to the rear and left of

---

1 The attacking party, it appears, was 350 strong; 12 of the Mikahil, 15 of the Habr Girhajis, and the rest Ísa Musa. One Ao Ali wore, it is said, the ostrich feather for the murder of Lieut. Stroyan.

the camp, the direction of danger, collected some of the guard—others having already disappeared—and fired two shots into the assailants. Then finding himself alone, he turned hastily towards the tent; in so doing he was tripped up by the ropes, and as he arose, a Somali appeared in the act of striking at him with a club. Lieut. Herne fired, floored the man, and rejoining me, declared that the enemy was in great force and the guard nowhere. Meanwhile, I had aroused Lieuts. Stroyan and Speke, who were sleeping in the extreme right and left tents. The former, it is presumed, arose to defend himself, but, as the sequel shows, we never saw him alive.[1] Lieut. Speke, awakened by the report of fire-arms, but supposing it the normal false alarm— a warning to plunderers—he remained where he was: presently hearing clubs rattling upon his tent, and feet shuffling around, he ran to my Rowtie, which we prepared to defend as long as possible.

The enemy swarmed like hornets with shouts and screams intending to terrify, and proving that overwhelming odds were against us: it was by no means easy to avoid in the shades of night the jobbing of javelins, and the long heavy daggers thrown at our legs from under and through the opening of the tent. We three remained together: Lieut. Herne knelt by my right, on my left was Lieut. Speke guarding the entrance, I stood in the centre, having nothing but a sabre. The revolvers were used by my companions with deadly effect: unfortunately there was but one pair. When the fire was exhausted, Lieut. Herne went to search for his powder-horn, and that failing, to find some spears

---

[1] Mohammed, his Indian servant, stated that rising at my summons he had rushed to his tent, armed himself with a revolver, and fired six times upon his assassins. Unhappily, however, Mohammed did not see his master fall, and as he was foremost amongst the fugitives, scant importance attaches to his evidence.

usually tied to the tent-pole. Whilst thus engaged, he saw a man breaking into the rear of our Rowtie, and came back to inform me of the circumstance.

At this time, about five minutes after the beginning of the affray, the tent had been almost beaten down, an Arab custom with which we were all familiar, and had we been entangled in its folds we should have been speared with unpleasant facility. I gave the word for escape, and sallied out, closely followed by Lieut. Herne, with Lieut. Speke in the rear. The prospect was not agreeable. About twenty men were kneeling and crouching at the tent entrance, whilst many dusk figures stood further off, or ran about shouting the war-cry, or with shouts and blows drove away our camels. Among the enemy were many of our friends and attendants: the coast being open to them, they naturally ran away, firing a few useless shots and receiving a modicum of flesh wounds.

After breaking through the mob at the tent entrance, imagining that I saw the form of Lieut. Stroyan lying upon the sand, I cut my way towards it amongst a dozen Somal, whose war-clubs worked without mercy, whilst the Balyuz, who was violently pushing me out of the fray, rendered the strokes of my sabre uncertain. This individual was cool and collected: though incapacitated by a sore right-thumb from using the spear, he did not shun danger, and passed unhurt through the midst of the enemy: his efforts, however, only illustrated the venerable adage, " defend me from my friends." I turned to cut him down: he cried out in alarm; the well-known voice caused an instant's hesitation: at that moment a spearman stepped forward, left his javelin in my mouth, and retired before he could be punished. Escaping as by a miracle, I sought some support: many of our Somal and servants lurking in the darkness offered to advance, but " tailed off " to a man as we approached the foe. Presently the Balyuz reappeared, and led me towards the place where he believed my three comrades had taken refuge. I followed him, sending the only man that showed presence of mind, one Golab of the Yusuf tribe, to bring back the Aynterad craft from the Spit into the centre of the harbour.[1]

Again losing the Balyuz in the darkness, I spent the interval before dawn wandering in search of my comrades, and lying down when overpowered with faintness and pain: as the day broke, with my remaining strength I reached the head of the creek, was carried into the vessel, and persuaded the crew to arm themselves and visit the scene of our disasters.

Meanwhile, Lieut. Herne, who had closely followed me, fell back, using the butt-end of his discharged six-shooter upon the hard heads around him: in so doing he came upon a dozen men, who though they loudly vociferated, " Kill the Franks who are killing the Somal! " allowed him to pass uninjured.

He then sought his comrades in the empty huts of the town, and at early dawn was joined by the Balyuz, who was similarly employed. When day broke he sent a Negro to stop the native craft, which was apparently sailing out of the harbour, and in due time came on board. With the exception of sundry stiff blows with the war-club, Lieut. Herne had the fortune to escape unhurt.

On the other hand, Lieut. Speke's escape was in every way wonderful. Sallying from the tent he levelled his " Dean and Adams " close to his assailant's breast. The pistol refused to revolve. A sharp blow of a war-

---

1 At this season native craft quitting Berberah make for the Spit late in the evening, cast anchor there, and set sail with the land breeze before dawn. Our lives hung upon a thread. Had the vessel departed, as she intended, the night before the attack, nothing could have saved us from destruction.

club upon the chest felled our comrade, who was in the rear and unseen. When he fell, two or three men sprang upon him, pinioned his hands behind, felt him for concealed weapons—an operation to which he submitted in some alarm—and led him towards the rear, as he supposed to be slaughtered. There, Lieut. Speke, who could scarcely breathe from the pain of the blow, asked a captor to tie his hands before, instead of behind, and begged a drop of water to relieve his excruciating thirst. The savage defended him against a number of the Somal who came up threatening and brandishing their spears, he brought a cloth for the wounded man to lie upon, and lost no time in procuring a draught of water.

Lieut. Speke remained upon the ground till dawn. During the interval he witnessed the war-dance of the savages—a scene striking in the extreme. The tallest and largest warriors marched in a ring round the tents and booty, singing, with the deepest and most solemn tones, the song of thanksgiving. At a little distance the grey uncertain light disclosed four or five men, lying desperately hurt, whilst their kinsmen kneaded their limbs, poured water upon their wounds, and placed lumps of dates in their stiffening hands.[1] As day broke, the division of plunder caused angry passions to rise. The dead and dying were abandoned. One party made a rush upon the cattle, and with shouts and yells drove them off towards the wild, some loaded themselves with goods, others fought over pieces of cloth, which they tore with hand and dagger, whilst the disappointed, vociferating with rage, struck at one another and brandished their spears. More than once during these scenes, a panic seized them; they moved off in a body

---

[1] The Somal place dates in the hands of the fallen to ascertain the extent of injury: he who cannot eat that delicacy is justly decided to be *in articulo*.

to some distance; and there is little doubt that had our guard struck one blow, we might still have won the day.

Lieut. Speke's captor went to seek his own portion of the spoil, when a Somali came up and asked in Hindustani, what business the Frank had in their country, and added that he would kill him if a Christian, but spare the life of a brother Moslem. The wounded man replied that he was going to Zanzibar, that he was still a Nazarene, and therefore that the work had better be done at once :—the savage laughed and passed on. He was succeeded by a second, who, equally compassionate, whirled a sword round his head, twice pretended to strike, but returned to the plunder without doing damage. Presently came another manner of assailant. Lieut. Speke, who had extricated his hands, caught the spear levelled at his breast, but received at the same moment a blow from a club which, paralyzing his arm, caused him to lose his hold. In defending his heart from a succession of thrusts, he received severe wounds on the back of his hand, his right shoulder, and his left thigh. Pausing a little, the wretch crossed to the other side, and suddenly passed his spear clean through the right leg of the wounded man : the latter " smelling death," then leapt up, and taking advantage of his assailant's terror, rushed headlong towards the sea. Looking behind, he avoided the javelin hurled at his back, and had the good fortune to run, without further accident, the gauntlet of a score of missiles. When pursuit was discontinued, he sat down faint from loss of blood upon a sandhill. Recovering strength by a few minutes' rest, he staggered on to the town, where some old women directed him to us. Then, pursuing his way, he fell in with the party sent to seek him, and by their aid reached the craft, having walked and run at least three miles, after receiving eleven wounds, two of which had pierced his thighs. A touching lesson how difficult it is to kill a man in sound health![1]

When the three survivors had reached the craft, Yusuf, the captain, armed his men with muskets and spears, landed them near the camp, and ascertained that the enemy expecting a fresh attack, had fled, carrying away our cloth, tobacco, swords, and other weapons.[2] The corpse of Lieut. Stroyan was then brought on board. Our lamented comrade was already stark and cold. A spear had traversed his heart, another had pierced his abdomen, and a frightful gash, apparently of a sword, had opened the upper part of his forehead: the body had been bruised with war-clubs, and the thighs showed marks of violence after death. This was the severest affliction that befell us. We had lived together like brothers: Lieut. Stroyan was a universal favourite, and his sterling qualities of manly courage, physical endurance, and steady perseverance had augured for him a bright career, thus prematurely cut off. Truly melancholy to us was the contrast between the evening when he sat with us full of life and spirits, and the morning when we saw amongst us a livid corpse.

We had hoped to preserve the remains of our friend for interment at Aden. But so rapid were the effects of

---

1 In less than a month after receiving such injuries, Lieut. Speke was on his way to England: he has never felt the least inconvenience from the wounds, which closed up like cuts in Indian-rubber.

2 They had despised the heavy sacks of grain, the books, broken boxes, injured instruments, and a variety of articles which they did not understand. We spent that day at Berberah, bringing off our property, and firing guns to recall six servants who were missing. They did not appear, having lost no time in starting for Karam and Aynterad, whence they made their way in safety to Aden. On the evening of the 19th of April, unable to remove the heavier effects, and anxious to return with the least possible delay, I ordered them to be set on fire.

exposure, that we were compelled most reluctantly, on the morning of the 20th April, to commit them to the deep, Lieut. Herne reading the funeral service.

Then with heavy hearts we set sail for the near Arabian shore, and, after a tedious two days, carried to our friends the news of unexpected disaster.

APPENDIX I.

DIARY AND OBSERVATIONS

MADE BY LIEUTENANT SPEKE, WHEN ATTEMPTING
TO REACH THE WADY NOGAL.

DIARY.

On the 28th October, 1854, Lieutenant Speke arrived at Kurayat, a small village near Las Kuray (Goree Bunder), in the country called by the Somal " Makhar," or the eastern maritime region. During the period of three months and a half he was enabled to make a short excursion above the coast-mountains, visiting the Warsingali, the Dulbahanta, and the Habr Girhajis tribes, and penetrating into a region unknown to Europeans. The bad conduct of his Abban, and the warlike state of the country, prevented his reaching the " Wady Nogal," which, under more favourable circumstances and with more ample leisure than our plans allowed him, he conceives to be a work of little difficulty and no danger. He has brought back with him ample notices of the region visited, and has been enabled to make a valuable collection of the Fauna, which have been forwarded to the Curator of the Royal As. Society's Museum, Calcutta. On the 15th February, 1855, Lieutenant Speke revisited Kurayat, and there embarked for Aden.

Before proceeding to Lieutenant Speke's Journal, it may be useful to give a brief and general account of the region explored.

The portion of the Somali country visited by Lieutenant Speke may be divided into a Maritime Plain, a Range of Mountains, and an elevated Plateau.

The Maritime Plain, at the points visited by Lieutenant Speke, is a sandy tract overlying limestone, level to the foot of the hills, and varying from half a mile to two miles in breadth. Water is not everywhere procurable. At the village of Las Kuray, there is an old and well built well, about twelve feet deep, producing an abundant and excellent supply. It appears that the people have no implements, and are too barbarous to be capable of so simple an engineering operation as digging. The vegetation presents the usual appearance of salsolaceous plants thinly scattered over the surface, with here and there a stunted growth of Arman or Acacia. The watershed is of course from south to north, and the rain from the hills is carried off by a number of Fiumaras or freshets, with broad shallow beds, denoting that much of the monsun rain falling in the mountains is there absorbed, and that little finds its way to the sea. At this season (the dry weather) the plain is thinly inhabited ; there are no villages except on the sea-shore, and even these were found by the traveller almost entirely deserted, mostly women occupying the houses, whilst the men were absent, trading and tending cattle in the hills. The harbours are, generally speaking, open and shallow roadsteads, where ships find no protection; there is, however, one place (Las Galwayta), where, it is said, deep water extends to the shore.

Meteorological observations show a moderate temperature, clear air, and a regular north-easterly wind. It is probable that, unlike the Berberah Plain, the monsun rain here falls in considerable quantities. This land belongs in part to the Warsingali. Westwards of Las Galwayta, which is the frontier, the Habr Girhajis lay claim to the coast. The two tribes, as usual in that unhappy land, are on terms of " Dam " or blood-feud ; yet they intermarry.

The animals observed were, the Waraba, a dark-coloured cynhyena, with a tail partly white, a grey jackal, and three different kinds of antelopes. Besides gulls, butcher birds, and a description of sparrow, no birds were found on the Maritime Plain.

The Range of Mountains is that long line which fringes the Somali coast from Tajurrah to Ras Jerd Hafun (Cape Guardafui). In the portion visited by Lieutenant Speke it is composed principally of lime-stones, some white, others brownish, and full of fossil shells. The seaward face is a gradual slope, yet as usual more abrupt than the landward side, especially in the upper regions. Steep irregular ravines divide the several masses of hill. The range was thinly covered with Acacia scrub in the lower folds. The upper portion was thickly clad with acacia and other thorns, and upon the summit, the Somali pine tree observed by me near Harar, and by Lieutenant Herne at Gulays, first appeared. Rain had freshly fallen.

The animal creation was represented by the leopard, hyena, rhinoceros, Waraba, four kinds of antelopes, hares and rats, tailless and long-tailed. It is poor in sea birds (specimens of those collected have been forwarded to the As. Society's Museum), and but one description of snake was observed. These hills belong partly to the Warsingali, and partly to the Habr Girhajis. The frontier is in some places denoted by piles of rough stones. As usual, violations of territorial right form the rule, not the exception, and trespass is sure to be followed by a "war." The meteorology of these hills is peculiar. The temperature appears to be but little lower than the plain : the wind was north-easterly; and both monsuns bring heavy rains.

At Yafir, on the summit of the hill, Lieutenant Speke's thermometer showed an altitude of about 7,500 feet. The people of the country do not know what ice means. Water is very scarce in these hills, except

during the monsun : it is found in springs which are far
apart ; and in the lower slopes collected rain water is
the sole resource. This scarcity renders the habits of
the people peculiarly filthy.

After descending about 2,000 feet from the crest of
the mountains to the southern fall, Lieutenant Speke
entered upon the platform which forms the country of
the Eastern Somal. He is persuaded that the watershed
of this extensive tract is from N.W. to S.E., contrary
to the opinion of Lieutenant Cruttenden, who, from
information derived from the Somal, determined the
slope to be due south. " Nogal " appears, according
to Lieutenant Speke, to be the name of a tract of land
occupied by the Warsingali, the Mijjarthayn, and the
northern clan of the Dulbahantas, as Bohodlay in Haud
is inhabited by the southern. Nogal is a sterile table-
land, here and there thinly grown with thorns, perfectly
useless for agriculture, and, unless it possess some
mineral wealth, valueless. The soil is white and stony,
whereas Haud or Ogadayn is a deep red, and is
described as having some extensive jungles. Between
the two lies a large watercourse, called " Tuk Der," or
the Long River. It is dry during the cold season, but
during the rains forms a flood, tending towards the
Eastern Ocean. This probably is the line which in our
maps is put down as " Wady Nogal, a very fertile and
beautiful valley."

The surface of the plateau is about 4100 feet above
the level of the sea : it is a space of rolling ground, stony
and white with broken limestone. Water is found in
pools, and in widely scattered springs : it is very scarce,
and owing to the total absence of this necessary further
south than the hills Lieutenant Speke was stopped by its
want. The climate appeared to our traveller delightful.
In some places the glass fell at 6 A.M. to 25°, yet at noon
on the same day the mercury rose to 76°. The wind was

always N.E., sometimes gentle, and occasionally blowing strongly but without dust. The rainy monsun must break here with violence, and the heat be fearful in the hot season. The principal vegetation of this plateau was Acacia, scarce and stunted ; in some places under the hills and in the watercourses these trees are numerous and well grown. On the other hand, extensive tracts towards the south are almost barren. The natives speak of Malmal (myrrh) and the Luban (incense) trees. The wild animals are principally antelopes ; there are also ostriches, onagers, Waraba, lions (reported to exist), jackals, and vermin. The bustard and florikan appear here. The Nomads possess large flocks of sheep, the camels, cows, and goats being chiefly found at this season on the seaward side of the hills, where forage is procurable. The horses were stunted tattoos, tolerably well-bred, but soft for want of proper food. It is said that the country abounds in horses, but Lieutenant Speke " doubts the fact." The eastern portion of the plateau visited by our traveller belongs to the Warsingali, the western to the Dulbahantas : the former tribe extends to the S.E., whilst the latter possesses the lands lying about the Tuk Der, the Nogal, and Haud. These two tribes are at present on bad terms, owing to a murder which led to a battle : the quarrel has been allowed to rest till lately, when it was revived at a fitting opportunity. But there is no hostility between the Southern Dulbahantas and the Warsingali, on the old principle that " an enemy's enemy is a friend."

On the 21st October, 1854, Lieutenant Speke, from the effects of a stiff easterly wind and a heavy sea, made by mistake the harbour of Rakúdah. This place has been occupied by the Rer Dud, descendants of Sambur, son of Ishak. It is said to consist of a small fort, and two or three huts of matting, lately re-erected. About two years ago the settlement was laid waste by the rightful owners of the soil, the Musa Abokr, a sub-family of the Habr Tal Jailah.

22nd October.—Without landing, Lieutenant Speke coasted along to Bunder Hais, where he went on shore. Hais is a harbour belonging to the Musa Abokr. It contains a " fort," a single-storied, flat-roofed, stone and mud house, about 20 feet square, one of those artless constructions to which only Somal could attach importance. There are neither muskets nor cannon among the braves of Hais. The " town " consists of half a dozen mud huts, mostly skeletons. The anchoring ground is shallow, but partly protected by a spur of hill, and the sea abounds in fish. Four Buggaloes (native craft) were anchored here, waiting for a cargo of Dumbah sheep and clarified butter, the staple produce of the place. Hais exports to Aden, Mocha, and other parts of Arabia ; it also manufactures mats, with the leaves of the Daum palm and other trees. Lieutenant Speke was well received by one Ali, the Agil, or petty chief of the place : he presented two sheep to the traveller. On the way from Bunder Jadid to Las Kuray, Lieutenant Speke remarks that Las Galwayta would be a favourable site for a Somali settlement. The water is deep even close to the shore, and there is an easy ascent from it to the summit of the mountains. The consequence is that it is coveted by the Warsingali, who are opposed by the present proprietors, the Habr Girhajis. The Sultan of the former family resists any settlement for fear of dividing and weakening their force ; it is too far from their pastures, and they have not men enough for both purposes.

28th October.—Lieutenant Speke landed at Kurayat, near Las Kuray, and sent a messenger to summon the chief, Mohammed Ali, Jirad or Prince of the Warsingali tribe.

During a halt of twenty-one days, the traveller had

an opportunity of being initiated into the mysteries of Somali medicine and money hiding. The people have but two cures for disease, one the actual cautery, the other a purgative, by means of melted sheep's-tail, followed by such a draught of camel's milk that the stomach, having escaped the danger of bursting, is suddenly and completely relieved. It is here the custom of the wealthy to bury their hoards, and to reveal the secret only when at the point of death. Lieutenant Speke went to a place where it is said a rich man had deposited a considerable sum, and described his "cache" as being "on a path in a direct line between two trees as far as the arms can reach with a stick." The hoarder died between forty and fifty years ago, and his children have been prevented by the rocky nature of the ground, and their forgetting to ask which was the right side of the tree, from succeeding in anything beyond turning up the stones.

Las Kuray is an open roadstead for native craft. The town is considered one of the principal strongholds of the coast. There are three large and six small "forts," similar in construction to those of Hais ; all are occupied by merchants, and are said to belong to the Sultan. The mass of huts may be between twenty and thirty in number. They are matted buildings, long and flat-roofed ; half a dozen families inhabit the same house, which is portioned off for such accommodation. Public buildings there is none, and no wall protects the place. It is in the territory of the Warsingali, and owns the rule of the Jirad or Prince, who sometimes lives here, and at other times inhabits the Jungle. Las Kuray exports gums, Dumbah sheep, and guano, the latter considered valuable, and sent to Makalla in Arabia, to manure the date plantations.

Four miles westward of Las Kuray is Kurayat, also called Little Kuray. It resembles the other settlement, and is not worth description. Lieutenant Speke here occupied a fort or stone house belonging to his Abban; finding the people very suspicious, he did not enter Las Kuray for prudential motives. There the Sultan has no habitation; when he visited the place he lodged in the house of a Nacoda or ship-captain.

Lieutenant Speke was delayed at Kurayat by the pretext of want of cattle; in reality to be plundered. The Sultan who inhabits the Jungle, did not make his appearance till repeatedly summoned. About the tenth day the old man arrived on foot, attended by a dozen followers; he was carefully placed in the centre of a double line bristling with spears, and marched past to his own fort. Lieutenant Speke posted his servants with orders to fire a salute of small firearms. The consequence was that the evening was spent in prayers.

During Lieutenant Speke's first visit to the Sultan, who received him squatting on the ground outside the house in which he lodged, with his guards about him, the dignitary showed great trepidation, but returned salams with politeness. He is described as a fine-looking man, between forty-eight and fifty years of age; he was dressed in an old and dirty Tobe, had no turband, and appeared unarmed. He had consulted the claims of "dignity" by keeping the traveller waiting ten days whilst he journeyed twenty miles. Before showing himself he had privily held a Durbar at Las Kuray; it was attended by the Agils of the tribe, by Mohammed Samattar (Lieutenant Speke's Abban), and the people generally. Here the question was debated whether the traveller was to be permitted to see the country. The voice of the multitude was as usual *contra*, fearing to admit a wolf into the fold. It was silenced however by the Sultan, who thought fit to favour the English, and by the Abban, who settled the question, saying that he, as the Sultan's subject, was answerable for all that might

happen, and that the chief might believe him or not ;—
"how could such Jungle-folk know anything ? "

On the morning of the 8th November the Sultan
returned Lieutenant Speke's visit. The traveller took
the occasion of "opening his desire to visit the Warsingali
country and the lands on the road to Berberah, keeping
inland about 200 miles, more or less according to circumstances, and passing through the Dulbahantas." To
this the Sultan replied, that "as far as his dominions
extended the traveller was perfectly at liberty to go
where he liked; but as for visiting the Dulbahantas, he
could not hear of or countenance it." Mahmud Ali, Jirad
or Prince of the southern Dulbahantas, was too far away
for communication, and Mohammed Ali Jirad, the nearest
chief, had only ruled seven or eight years; his power
therefore was not great. Moreover, these two were at
war: the former having captured, it is said, 2000 horses,
400 camels, and a great number of goats and sheep,
besides wounding a man. During the visit, which lasted
from 8 A.M. to 2 P.M., the Sultan refused nothing but permission to cross the frontier, fearing, he said, lest an
accident should embroil him with our Government.
Lieutenant Speke gave them to understand that he
visited their country, not as a servant of the Company,
but merely as a traveller wishing to see sport. This of
course raised a laugh; it was completely beyond their
comprehension. They assured him, however, that he
had nothing to apprehend in the Warsingali country,
where the Sultan's order was like that of the English.
The Abban then dismissed the Sultan to Las Kuray,
fearing the appetites of his followers ; and the guard, on
departure, demanded a cloth each by way of honorarium.
This was duly refused, and they departed in discontent.
The people frequently alluded to two grand grievances.
In the first place they complained of an interference on
the part of our Government, in consequence of a quarrel

which took place seven years ago at Aden, between them and the Habr Tal Jailah tribe of Karam. The Political Resident, it is said, seized three vessels belonging to the Warsingali, who had captured one of the ships belonging to their enemies; the former had command of the sea, but since that event they have been reduced to a secondary rank. This grievance appears to be based on solid grounds. Secondly, they complained of the corruption of their brethren by intercourse with a civilized people, especially by visiting Aden: the remedy for this evil lies in their own hands, but desire of gain would doubtless defeat any moral sanitary measure which their Elders could devise. They instanced the state of depravity into which the Somal about Berberah had fallen, and prided themselves highly upon their respect for the rights of *meum* and *tuum*, so completely disregarded by the Western States. But this virtue may arise from the severity of their chastisements: mutilation of the hand being the usual award to theft.

Moreover Lieutenant Speke's Journal does not impress the reader highly with their honesty. And lastly, I have found the Habr Awal at Berberah, on the whole, a more respectable race than the Warsingali.

Lieutenant Speke's delay at Kurayat was caused by want of carriage. He justly remarks that "every one in this country appeals to precedent"; the traveller, therefore, should carefully ascertain the price of everything, and adhere to it, as those who follow him twenty years afterwards will be charged the same. One of the principal obstacles to Lieutenant Speke's progress was the large sum given to the natives by an officer who visited this coast some years ago. Future travellers should send before them a trusty Warsingali to the Sultan, with a letter specifying the necessary arrangements, a measure which would save trouble and annoyance to both parties.

On the 10th of November the Sultan came early to Lieutenant Speke's house. He received a present of cloth worth about forty rupees. After comparing his forearm with every other man's and ascertaining the mean, he measured and re-measured each piece, an operation which lasted several hours. A flint gun was presented to him, evidently the first he had ever handled; he could scarcely bring it up to his shoulder, and persisted in shutting the wrong eye. Then he began as usual to beg for more cloth, powder, and lead. By his assistance Lieutenant Speke bought eight camels, inferior animals, at rather a high price, from 10 to $16\frac{1}{2}$ cloths (equivalent to dollars) per head. It is the custom for the Sultan, or in his absence, for an Agil to receive a tithe of the price; and it is his part to see that the traveller is not overcharged. He appears to have discharged his duty very inefficiently, a dollar a day being charged for the hire of a single donkey. Lieutenant Speke regrets that he did not bring dollars or rupees, cloth on the coast being now at a discount.

After the usual troubles and vexations of a first move in Africa, on the 16th of November, 1854, Lieutenant Speke marched about three miles along the coast, and pitched at a well close to Las Kuray. He was obliged to leave about a quarter of his baggage behind, finding it impossible with his means to hire donkeys, the best conveyance across the mountains, where camels must be very lightly laden. The Sultan could not change, he said, the route settled by a former Sahib. He appears, though famed for honesty and justice, to have taken a partial view of Lieutenant Speke's property. When the traveller complained of his Abban, the reply was, " This is the custom of the country, I can see no fault; all you bring is the Abban's, and he can do what he likes with it."

The next day was passed unpleasantly enough in

the open air, to force a march, and the Sultan and his party stuck to the date-bag, demanding to be fed as servants till rations were served out to them.

18*th November.*—About 2 A.M. the camels (eleven in number) were lightly loaded, portions of the luggage being sent back to Kurayat till more carriage could be procured. The caravan crossed the plain southwards, and after about two miles' march entered a deep stony watercourse winding through the barren hills. After five miles' progress over rough ground, Lieutenant Speke unloaded under a tree early in the afternoon near some pools of sweet rain water collected in natural basins of limestone dotting the watercourse. The place is called Iskodubuk; the name of the watercourse is Duktura. The Sultan and the Abban were both left behind to escort the baggage from Las Kuray to Kurayat. They promised to rejoin Lieutenant Speke before nightfall; the former appeared after five, the latter after ten, days. The Sultan sent his son Abdallah, a youth of about fifteen years old, who proved so troublesome that Lieutenant Speke was forced repeatedly to dismiss him : still the lad would not leave the caravan till it reached the Dulbahanta frontier. And the Abban delayed a Negro servant, Lieutenant Speke's gun-bearer, trying by many offers and promises to seduce him from service.

19*th November.*—At dawn the camels were brought in ; they had been feeding at large all night, which proves the safety of the country. After three hours' work at loading, the caravan started up the watercourse. The road was rugged; at times the watercourse was blocked up with boulders, which compelled the travellers temporarily to leave it. With a little cutting away of projecting rocks which are of soft stone, the road might be made tolerably easy. Scattered and stunted Acacias, fringed with fresh green foliage, relieved the eye: all else was barren rock. After marching about two miles, the traveller was obliged to halt by the Sultan; a messenger arrived with the order. The halting-place is called Damalay. It is in the bed of the watercourse, stagnating rain, foul-looking but sweet, lying close by. As in all other parts of this Fiumara, the bed was dotted with a bright green tree, sometimes four feet high, resembling a willow. Lieutenant Speke spread his mat in the shade, and spent the rest of the day at his diary, and in conversation with the natives.

The next day was also spent at Damalay. The interpreter, Mohammed Ahmad, a Somali of the Warsingali tribe, and all the people, refused positively to advance. Lieutenant Speke started on foot to Las Kuray in search of the Abban: he was followed at some distance by the Somal, and the whole party returned on hearing a report that the chief and the Abban were on the way. The traveller seems on this occasion to have formed a very low estimate of the people. He stopped their food until they promised to start the next day.

21st November.—The caravan marched at gun-fire, and, after a mile, left the watercourse, and ascended by a rough camel-path a buttress of hill leading to the ridge of the mountains. The ascent was not steep, but the camels were so bad that they could scarcely be induced to advance. The country was of a more pleasant aspect, a shower of rain having lately fallen. At this height the trees grow thicker and finer, the stones are hidden by grass and heather, and the air becomes somewhat cooler. After a six miles' march Lieutenant Speke encamped at a place called Adhai. Sweet water was found within a mile's walk;—the first spring from which our traveller drank. Here he pitched a tent.

At Adhai Lieutenant Speke was detained nine days by the non-appearance of his " Protector" and the refusal of his followers to march without him. The camels were sent back with the greatest difficulty to fetch the portion of the baggage left behind. On the 24th Lieutenant Speke sent his Hindustani servant to Las Kuray, with orders to bring up the baggage. "Imam" started alone and on foot, not being permitted to ride a pony hired by the traveller: he reported that there is a much better road for laden camels from the coast to the crest of the hills. Though unprotected, he met with no difficulty, and returned two days afterwards, having seen the baggage *en route*. During Lieutenant Speke's detention, the Somal battened on his provisions, seeing that his two servants were absent, and that no one guarded the bags. Half the rice had been changed at Las Kuray for an inferior description. The camel drivers refused their rations because all their friends (thirty in number) were not fed. The Sultan's son taught them to win the day by emptying and hiding the water skins, by threatening to kill the servants if they fetched water, and by refusing to do work. During the discussion, which appears to have been lively, the eldest of the Sultan's four sons, Mohammed Aul, appeared from Las Kuray. He seems to have taken a friendly part, stopped the discussion, and sent away the young prince as a nuisance. Unfortunately, however, the latter reappeared immediately that the date bags were opened, and Mohammed Aul stayed only two days in Lieutenant Speke's neighbourhood. On the 28th November the Abban appeared. The Sultan then forced upon Lieutenant Speke his brother Hasan as a second Abban, although this proceeding is contrary to the custom of the country. The new burden, however, after vain attempts at extortion, soon disappeared, carrying away with him a gun.

For tanning water-skins the Somal here always use, when they can procure it, a rugged bark with a smooth epidermis of a reddish tinge, a pleasant aromatic odour, and a strong astringent flavour. They call it Mohur: powdered and sprinkled dry on a wound, it acts as a styptic. Here was observed an aloe-formed plant, with a strong and woody thorn on the top.   It is called Haskul or Hig ; the fibres are beaten out with sticks or stones, rotted in water, and then made into cord.   In other parts the young bark of the acacia is used ; it is first charred on one side, then reduced to fibre by mastication, and lastly twisted into the semblance of a rope.

From a little manuscript belonging to the Abban, Lieutenant Speke learned that about 440 years ago (A.D. 1413), one Darud bin Ismail, unable to live with his elder brother at Meccah, fled with a few followers to these shores.   In those days the land was ruled, they say, by a Christian chief called Kín, whose Wazir, Wharrah, was the terror of all men.   Darud collected around him, probably by proselytizing, a strong party: he gradually increased his power, and ended by expelling the owners of the country, who fled to the N.W. as far as Abyssinia.   Darud, by an Asyri damsel, had a son called Kabl Ullah, whose son Harti had, as progeny, Warsingali, Dulbahanta, and Mijjarthayn.   These three divided the country into as many portions, which, though great territorial changes have taken place, to this day bear their respective owners' names.

Of this I have to observe, that universal tradition represents the Somal to be a people of half-caste origin, African and Arabian ; moreover, that they expelled the Gallas from the coast, until the latter took refuge in the hills of Harar.   The Gallas are a people partly Moslem, partly Christian, and partly Pagan ; this may account for the tradition above recorded.   Most Somal, however, declare " Darud " to be a man of ignoble origin, and do not derive him from the Holy City.   Some declare he was driven from Arabia for theft.   Of course each tribe exaggerates its own nobility with as reckless a defiance of truth as its neighbours depreciate it.   But I have made a rule always to doubt what semi-barbarians write. Writing is the great source of historical confusion, because falsehoods accumulate in books, persons are confounded, and fictions assume, as in the mythologic genealogies of India, Persia, Greece, and Rome, a regular and systematic form. On the other hand, oral tradition is more trustworthy; witness the annals and genealogies preserved in verse by the Bhats of Cutch, the Arab Nassab, and the Bards of Baluchistan.

30th November.—The Sultan took leave of Lieutenant Speke, and the latter prepared to march in company with the Abban, the interpreter, the Sultan's two sons, and a large party. By throwing the tent down and sitting in the sun he managed to effect a move. In the evening the camels started from Adhai up a gradual ascent along a strong path. The way was covered with bush, jungle, and trees. The frankincense, it is said, abounded; gum trees of various kinds were found; and the traveller remarked a single stunted sycamore growing out of a rock. I found the tree in all the upper regions of the Somali country, and abundant in the Harar Hills. After two miles' march the caravan halted at Habál Ishawálay, on the northern side of the mountains, within three miles of the crest. The halting-ground was tolerably level, and not distant from the waters of Adhai, the only spring in the vicinity. The travellers slept in a deserted Kraal, surrounded by a stout fence of Acacia thorns heaped up to keep out the leopards and hyenas. During the heat Lieutenant Speke sat under a tree. Here he remained three days; the first in order to bring up part of his baggage which had been left behind: the second to send on a portion to the next halting-place; and the third in consequence of the Abban's resolution to procure Ghi or clarified butter. The Sultan could not resist the opportunity of extorting something by a final visit—for a goat, killed and eaten by the camel-drivers contrary to Lieutenant Speke's orders, a dollar was demanded.

4th December, 1854.—About dawn the caravan was loaded, and then proceeded along a tolerably level pathway through a thick growth of thorn trees towards a bluff hill. The steep was reached about 9 A.M., and the camels toiled up the ascent by a stony way, dropping their loads for want of ropes, and stumbling on their road. The summit, about 500 yards distant, was reached in an hour. At Yafir, on the crest of the mountains, the caravan halted two hours for refreshment. Lieutenant Speke describes the spot in the enthusiastic language of all travellers who have visited the Seaward Range of the Somali Hills. It appears, however, that it is destitute of water. About noon the camels were again loaded, and the caravan proceeded across the mountains by a winding road over level ground for four miles. This point commanded an extensive view of the Southern Plateau. In that direction the mountains drop in steps or terraces, and are almost bare; as in other parts rough and flat topped piles of stones, reminding the traveller of the Tartar Cairns, were observed. I remarked the same in the Northern Somali country; and in both places the people gave a similar account of them, namely, that they are the work of an earlier race, probably the Gallas. Some of them are certainly tombs, for human bones are turned up: in others empty chambers are discovered; and in a few are found earthern and large copper pots. Lieutenant Speke on one occasion saw an excavated mound propped up inside by pieces of timber, and apparently built without inlet. It was opened about six years ago by a Warsingali, in order to bury his wife, when a bar of metal (afterwards proved by an Arab to be gold) and a gold ring, similar to what is worn by women in the nose, were discovered. In other places the natives find, it is said, women's bracelets, beads, and similar articles still used by the Gallas.

After nightfall the caravan arrived at Mukur, a halting-place in the southern declivity of the hills. Here Lieutenant Speke remarked that the large watercourse in which he halted becomes a torrent during the rains, carrying off the drainage towards the eastern coast. He had marched that day seventeen miles, when the party made a Kraal with a few bushes. Water was found within a mile in a rocky basin ; it was fetid and full of animalculæ. Here appeared an old woman driving sheep and goats into Las Kuray, a circumstance which shows that the country is by no means dangerous.

After one day's halt at Mukur to refresh the camels, on the 6th December Lieutenant Speke started at about 10 A.M. across the last spur of the hills, and presently entered a depression dividing the hills from the Plateau. Here the country was stony and white-coloured, with watercourses full of rounded stones. The Jujube and Acacias were here observed to be on a large scale, especially in the lowest ground. After five miles the traveller halted at a shallow watercourse, and at about half a mile distant found sweet but dirty water in a deep hole in the rock. The name of this station was Karrah.

8th December.—Early in the morning the caravan moved on to Rhat, a distance of eight miles : it arrived at about noon. The road lay through the depression at the foot of the hills. In the patches of heather Florikan was found. The Jujube-tree was very large. In the rains this country is a grassy belt, running from west to east, along a deep and narrow watercourse, called Rhat Tug, or the Fiumara of Rhat, which flows eastward towards the ocean. At this season, having been " eaten up," the land was almost entirely deserted ; the Kraals lay desolate, the herdsmen had driven off their cows to the hills, and the horses had been sent towards the Mijjarthayn country. A few camels and donkeys were seen : considering that their breeding is left to chance, the blood is not contemptible. The sheep and goats are small, and their coats, as usual in these hot countries, remain short. Lieutenant Speke was informed that, owing to want of rain, and it being the breeding season, the inland and Nomad Warsingali live entirely on flesh, one meal serving for three days. This was a sad change of affairs from what took place six weeks before the traveller's arrival, when there had been a fall of rain, and the people spent their time revelling on milk, and sleeping all day under the shade of the trees—the Somali idea of perfect happiness.

On the 9th December Lieutenant Speke, halting at Rhat, visited one of " Kin's " cities, now ruined by time, and changed by the Somal having converted it into a cemetery. The remains were of stone and mud, as usual in this part of the world. The houses are built in an economical manner ; one straight wall, nearly 30 feet long, runs down the centre, and is supported by a number of lateral chambers facing opposite ways, *e.g.*

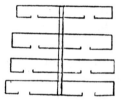

This appears to compose the village, and suggests a

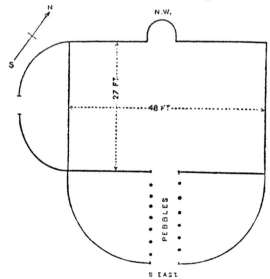

convent or a monastery. To the west, and about fifty
yards distant, are ruins of stone and good white mortar,
probably procured by burning the limestone rock. The
annexed ground plan will give an idea of these interesting remains, which are said to be those of a Christian
house of worship. In some parts the walls are still
10 feet high, and they show an extent of civilization now
completely beyond the Warsingali. It may be remarked
of them that the direction of the niche, as well as the
disposition of the building, would denote a Moslem
mosque. At the same time it must be remembered that
the churches of the Eastern Christians are almost always
made to front Jerusalem, and the Gallas being a Moslem
and Christian race, the sects would borrow their architecture from each other. The people assert these ruins
to be those of Nazarenes. Yet in the Jid Ali valley of
the Dulbahantas Lieutenant Speke found similar remains,
which the natives declared to be one of their forefathers'
mosques ; the plan and the direction were the same as
those now described. Nothing, however, is easier than
to convert St. Sophia into the Aya Sufiyyah mosque.
Moreover, at Jid Ali, the traveller found it still the
custom of the people to erect a Mala, or cross of stone or
wood covered with plaster, at the head and foot of
every tomb.

The Dulbahantas, when asked about these crosses,
said it was their custom, derived from sire and grandsire.
This again would argue that a Christian people once
inhabited these now benighted lands.

North of the building now described is a cemetery,
in which the Somal still bury their dead. Here Lieu-

tenant Speke also observed crosses, but he was prevented by the superstition of the people from examining them.

On an eminence S.W. of, and about seventy yards from the main building, are the isolated remains of another erection, said by the people to be a fort. The foundation is level with the ground, and shows two compartments opening into each other.

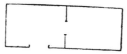

Rhat was the most southerly point reached by Lieutenant Speke. He places it about thirty miles distant from the coast, and at the entrance of the great Plateau. Here he was obliged to turn westward, because at that season of the year the country to the southward is desolate for want of rain—a warning to future visitors. During the monsun this part of the land is preferred by the people : grass grows, and there would be no obstacle to travellers.

Before quitting Rhat, the Abban and the interpreter went to the length of ordering Lieutenant Speke not to fire a gun. This detained him a whole day.

11*th December.*—Early in the morning, Lieutenant Speke started in a westerly direction, still within sight of the mountains, where not obstructed by the inequalities of the ground. The line taken was over an elevated flat, in places covered with the roots of parched up grass; here it was barren, and there appeared a few Acacias. The view to the south was shortened by rolling ground : hollow basins, sometimes fifteen miles broad, succeed each other; each sends forth from its centre a watercourse to drain off the water eastward. The face of the country, however, is very irregular, and consequently description is imperfect. This day ostriches and antelopes were observed in considerable numbers. After marching ten miles the caravan halted at Barham, where they found a spring of clear and brackish water from the limestone rock, and flowing about 600 yards down a deep rocky channel, in parts lined with fine Acacias. A Kraal was found here, and the traveller passed a comfortable night.

12th December.—About 9 A.M. the caravan started, and threaded a valley, which, if blessed with a fair supply of water, would be very fertile. Whilst every-thing else is burned up by the sun on the high ground, a nutritious weed, called Buskallay, fattens the sheep and goats. Wherever, therefore, a spring is found, men flock to the place and fence themselves in a Kraal. About half-way the travellers reached Darud bin Ismail's tomb, a parallelogram of loose stones about one foot high, of a battered and ignoble appearance; at one extremity stood a large sloping stone, with a little mortar still clinging to it. No outer fence surrounded the tomb, which might easily be passed by unnoticed: no honours were paid to the memory of the first founder of the tribe, and the Somal did not even recite a Fatihah over his dust. After marching about twelve miles, the caravan encamped at Labbahdilay, in the bed of a little watercourse which runs into the Yubbay Tug. Here they found a small pool of bad rain water. They made a rude fence to keep out the wild beasts, and in it passed the night.

13th December.—The Somal showed superior activity in marching three successive days; the reason appears to be that the Abban was progressing towards his home. At sunrise the camels were loaded, and at 8 A.M. the caravan started up a valley along the left bank of a watercourse called the Yubbay Tug. This was out of the line, but the depth of the perpendicular sides pre-vented any attempt at crossing it. The people of the country have made a peculiar use of this feature of ground. During the last war, ten or eleven years ago, between the Warsingali and the Dulbahantas, the latter sent a large foraging party over the frontier. The Warsingali stationed a strong force at the head of the watercourse to prevent its being turned, and exposed their flocks and herds on the eastern bank to tantalize the hungry enemy. The Dulbahantas, unable to cross the chasm, and unwilling, like all Somali heroes even in their wrath, to come to blows with the foe, retired in huge disgust. After marching five miles, the caravan halted, the Abban declaring that he and the Sultan's younger son must go forward to feel the way; in other words, to visit his home. His pretext was a good one. In countries where postal arrangements do not exist, intelligence flies quicker than on the wings of paper. Many evil rumours had preceded Lieutenant Speke, and the inland tribe professed, it was reported, to despise a people who can only threaten the coast. The Dulbahantas had been quarrelling amongst themselves for the last thirteen years, and were now determined to settle the dispute by a battle. Formerly they were all under one head; but one Ali Harram, an Akil or minor chief, determined to make his son, Mohammed Ali, Jirad or Prince of the clans inhabiting the northern provinces. After five years' intrigue the son was proclaimed, and carried on the wars caused by his father, declaring an intention to fight to the last. He has, however, been successfully opposed by Mahmud Ali, the rightful chief of the Dulbahanta family, the southern clans of Haud and beyond the Nogal being more numerous and more powerful than the northern divisions. No merchant, Arab or other, thinks of penetrating into this country, principally on account of the expense. Lieutenant Speke is of opinion that his cloth and rice would easily have stopped the war for a time: the Dulbahantas threatened and blustered, but allowed themselves easily to be pacified.

It is illustrative of the customs of this people that, when the Dulbahantas had their hands engaged, and left their rear unprotected, under the impression that no enemies were behind, the Warsingali instantly remembered that one of their number had been murdered by the other race many years ago. The blood-money had been paid, and peace had been concluded, but the opportunity was too tempting to be resisted.

The Yubbay Tug watercourse begins abruptly, being as broad and deep at the head as it is in the trunk. When Lieutenant Speke visited it, it was dry; there was but a thin growth of trees in it, showing that water does not long remain there. Immediately north of it lies a woody belt, running up to the foot of the mountains, and there bifurcating along the base. Southwards, the Yubbay is said to extend to a considerable distance, but Somali ideas of distance are peculiar, and absorption is a powerful agent in these latitudes.

Till the 21st December Lieutenant Speke was delayed at the Yubbay Tug. His ropes had been stolen by discharged camel-men, and he was unable to replace them.

On the 15th December one of the Midgan or Serviles was tried for stealing venison from one of his fellows. The Sultan, before his departure, had commissioned three of Lieutenant Speke's attendants to act as judges in case of such emergency: on this occasion the interpreter was on the Woolsack, and he sensibly fined the criminal two sheep to be eaten on the road. From inquiries, I have no doubt that these Midgan are actually reduced by famine at times to live on a food which human nature abhors. In the northern part of the Somali country I never heard of cannibalism, although the Servile tribes will eat birds and other articles of food disdained by Somal of gentle blood. Lieutenant Speke complains of the scarcity and the quality of the water, " which resembles the mixture commonly known as black draught." Yet it appears not to injure health ; and the only disease found endemic is an ophthalmia, said to return periodically every three years. The animals have learned to use sparingly what elsewhere is a daily necessary ; camels are watered twice a month, sheep thrice, and horses every two or three days. No wild beasts or birds, except the rock pigeon and duck, ever drink except when rain falls.

The pickaxe and spade belonging to the traveller were greatly desired : in one place water was found, but more generally the people preferred digging for honey in the rocks. Of the inhabitants we find it recorded that, like all Nomads, they are idle to the last degree, contenting themselves with tanned skins for dress and miserable huts for lodging. Changing ground for the flocks and herds is a work of little trouble ; one camel and a donkey carry all the goods and chattels, including water, wife, and baby. Milk in all stages (but never polluted by fire), wild honey, and flesh, are their only diet ; some old men have never tasted grain. Armed with spear and shield, they are in perpetual dread of an attack. It is not strange that under such circumstances the population should be thin and scattered ; they talk of thousands going to war, but the wary traveller suspects gross exaggeration. They preserve the abominable Galla practice of murdering pregnant women in hopes of mutilating a male fœtus.

On the 20th December Lieutenant Speke was informed by the Sultan's son that the Dulbahantas would not permit him to enter their country. As a favour, however, they would allow him to pass towards the home of the Abban, who, having married a Dulbahanta girl was naturalized amongst them.

21st December.—Early in the morning Lieutenant Speke, accompanied by the interpreter, the Sultan's son, one servant, and two or three men to lead a pair of camels, started eastward. The rest of the animals (nine in number) were left behind in charge of Imam, a Hindustani boy, and six or seven men under him. The reason for this step was that Husayn Haji, and Agil of the Dulbahantas and a connection of the Abban, demanded, as sole condition for permitting Lieutenant Speke to visit " Jid Ali," that the traveller should give up all his property. Before leaving the valley, he observed a hillock glistening white: it appears from its salt, bitter taste, to have been some kind of nitrate efflorescing from the ground. The caravan marched about a mile across the deep valley of Yubbay Tug, and ascended its right side by a beaten track: they then emerged from a thin jungle in the lower grounds to the stony hills which compose the country. Here the line pursued was apparently parallel to the mountains bordering upon the sea : between the two ridges was a depression, in which lay a small watercourse. The road ran along bleak undulating ground, with belts of Acacia in the hollows : here and there appeared a sycamore tree. On the road two springs were observed, both of bitter water, one deep below the surface, the other close to the ground; patches of green grass grew around them. Having entered the Dulbahanta frontier, the caravan unloaded in the evening, after a march of thirteen miles, at a depression called Ali. No water was found there.

22nd December.—Early in the morning the traveller started westward, from Ali, wishing that night to make Jid Ali, about eighteen miles distant. After marching thirteen miles over the same monotonous country as before, Lieutenant Speke was stopped by Husayn Haji, the Agil, who declared that Gulad Ali, another Agil, was opposed to his progress. After a long conversation, Lieutenant Speke reasoned him into compliance ; but that night they were obliged to halt at Birhamir, within five miles of Jid Ali. The traveller was offered as many horses as he wanted, and a free passage to Berberah, if he would take part in the battle preparing between the two rival clans of Dulbahantas: he refused, on plea of having other engagements. But whenever the question of penetrating the country was started, there came the same dry answer: " No beggar had even attempted to visit them—what, then, did the Englishman want?" The Abban's mother came out from her hut, which was by the wayside, and with many terrors endeavoured to stop the traveller.

23rd December.—Next morning the Abban appeared, and, by his sorrowful surprise at seeing Lieutenant Speke across the frontier, showed that he only had made the difficulty. The caravan started early, and, travelling five miles over stony ground, reached the Jid Ali valley. This is a long belt of fertile soil, running perpendicular to the seaward range; it begins opposite Bunder Jadid, at a gap in the mountains through which the sea is, they say, visible. In breadth, at the part first visited by Lieutenant Speke, it is about two miles: it runs southward, and during rain probably extends to about twenty miles inland. Near the head of the valley is a spring of bitter water, absorbed by the soil after a quarter of a mile's course: in the monsun, however, a considerable torrent must flow down this depression. Ducks and snipe are found here. The valley shows, even at this season, extensive patches of grass, large acacia trees, bushes, and many different kinds of thorns: it is the most wooded lowland seen by Lieutenant Speke. Already the Nomads are here changing their habits; two small enclosures have been cultivated by an old Dulbahanta, who had studied agriculture during a pilgrimage to Meccah. The Jowari grows luxuriantly, with stalks 8 and 9 feet high, and in this first effort had well rewarded the enterpriser. Lieutenant Speke lent the slave Farhan, to show the art of digging; for this he received the present of a goat. I may here remark that everywhere in the Somali country the people are prepared to cultivate grain, and only want someone to take the initiative. As yet they have nothing but their hands to dig with. A few scattered huts were observed near Jid Ali, the grass not being yet sufficiently abundant to support collected herds.

Lieutenant Speke was delayed nineteen days at Jid Ali by various pretexts. The roads were reported closed. The cloth and provisions were exhausted. Five horses must be bought from the Abban for thirty dollars a head (they were worth one fourth that sum), as presents. The first European that visited the Western Country had stopped rain for six months, and the Somal feared for the next monsun. All the people would flock in, demanding at least what the Warsingali had received; otherwise they threatened the traveller's life. On the 26th of December Lieutenant Speke moved three miles up the valley to some distance from water, the crowd being troublesome, and preventing his servants eating. On the 31st of December all the baggage was brought up from near Abi: one of the camels, being upon the point of death, was killed and devoured. It was impossible to keep the Abban from his home, which was distant about four miles: numerous messages were sent in vain, but Lieutenant Speke drew him from his hut by " sitting in Dhurna," or dunning him into compliance. At last arose a violent altercation. All the Warsingali and Dulbahanta servants were taken away, water was stopped, the cattle were cast loose, and the traveller was told to arm and defend himself and his two men :— they would all be slain that night and the Abban would abandon them to the consequences of their obstinacy. They were not killed, however, and about an hour afterwards the Somal reappeared, declaring that they had no intention of deserting.

11th January, 1855.—About 10 A. M. the caravan started without the Abban across the head of the Jid Ali valley. The land was flat, abounding in Acacia, and showing signs of sun-parched grass cropped close by the cattle. After a five miles' march the travellers came to a place called Biyu Hablay; they unloaded under a tree and made a Kraal. Water was distant. Around were some courses, ending abruptly in the soft absorbing ground. Here the traveller was met by two Dulbahantas, who demanded his right to enter their lands, and insinuated that a force was gathering to oppose him. They went away, however, after a short time, threatening with smiles to come again. Lieutenant Speke was also informed that the Southern Dulbahanta tribes had been defeated with loss by the northern clans, and that his journey would be interrupted by them. Here the traveller remarked how willing are the Somal to study: as usual in this country, any man who reads the Koran and can write out a verset upon a board is an object of envy. The people are fanatic. They rebuked the interpreter for not praying regularly, for eating from a Christian's cooking pot, and for cutting deer's throats low down (to serve as specimens); they also did not approve of the traveller's throwing date stones into the fire. As usual, they are fearful boasters. Their ancestors turned Christians out of the country. They despise guns. They consider the Frank formidable only behind walls: they are ready to fight it out in the plain, and they would gallop around cannon so that not a shot would tell. Vain words to conceal the hearts of hares! Lieutenant Speke justly remarks that, on account of the rough way in which they are brought up, the Somal would become excellent policemen; they should, however, be separated from their own people, and doubtless the second generation might be trained into courage.

At Biyu Hablay Lieutenant Speke, finding time as

well as means deficient, dropped all idea of marching to Berberah. He wished to attempt a north-western route to Hais, but the Rer Hamaturwa (a clan of the Habr Girhajis who occupy the mountain) positively refused passage. Permission was accorded by that clan to march due north upon Bunder Jadid, where, however, the traveller feared that no vessel might be found. As a last resource he determined to turn to the north-east, and, by a new road through the Habr Girhajis, to make Las Kuray.

18*th January.*—The Abban again returned from his home, and accompanied Lieutenant Speke on his first march to the north-east. Early in the morning the caravan started over the ground before described : on this occasion, however, it traversed the belt of jungle at the foot of the mountains. After a march of six miles they halted at " Mirhiddo," under a tree on elevated ground, in a mere desert, no water being nearer than the spring of Jid Ali. The Abban took the opportunity of Lieutenant Speke going out specimen-hunting to return home, contrary to orders, and he did not reappear till the traveller walked back and induced him to march. Here a second camel, being " in articulo," was cut up and greedily devoured.

21*st January.*—The Abban appeared in the morning, and the caravan started about noon, over the stony ground at the foot of the hills. After a mile's march, the " Protector " again disappeared, in open defiance of orders. That day's work was about ten miles. The caravan halted, late at night, in the bed of a watercourse, called Hanfallal. Lieutenant Speke visited the spring, which is of extraordinary sweetness for the Warsingali country : it flows from a cleft in the rock broad enough to admit a man's body, and about 60 feet deep.

23*rd January.*—Lieutenant Speke was about to set out under the guidance of Awado, the Abban's mother, when her graceless son reappeared.   At noon the caravan travelled along a rough road, over the lower spurs of the mountains : they went five miles, and it was evening when they unloaded in a watercourse a little distance up the hills, at a place called Dallmálay.   The bed was about 150 yards broad, full of jungle, and showed signs of a strong deep stream during the monsun. The travellers made up a Kraal, but found no water there.

24th January.—Early in the morning the caravan started, and ascended by a path over the hills.   The way was bare of verdure, but easy : here a camel unable to walk, though unloaded, was left behind.   One of Lieutenant Speke's discharged camel-men, a Warsingali, being refused passage by the Habr Girhajis, on account of some previous quarrel, found a stray camel, and carried it off to his home amongst the Dulbahantas. He afterwards appeared at Las Kuray, having taken the road by which the travellers entered the country.   Having marched eleven miles, the caravan arrived in the evening at Gobamiray, a flat on the crest of the mountains.   Here again thick jungle appeared, and the traveller stood over more on the seaward side.   Water was distant.

On arriving, the camels were seized by the Urus Sugay, a clan of the Habr Girhajis.   The poor wretches pretended to show fight, and asked if they were considered a nation of women, that their country was to be entered without permission.   Next morning they volunteered to act as escort.

25th January.—Loading was forbidden by the valiant sons of Habr Girhajis ; but as they were few in number, and the Warsingali clan was near, it went on without interruption.   This day, like the latter, was cloudy ; heavy showers fell for some hours, and the grass was springing up.   Rain had lasted for some time, and had not improved the road.   This fall is called by the people " Dairti " : it is confined to the hills, whereas the Gugi or monsun is general over the plateau.

About noon the caravan marched, late, because the Abban's two horses had strayed. These animals belonged to a relation of the " Protector," who called them his own, and wished as a civility to sell the garrons at the highest possible price to his client. The caravan marched down a tortuous and difficult road, descending about four miles. It unloaded as evening drew near, and the travellers found at Gambagahh a good dormitory, a cave which kept out the rain. Water was standing close by in a pool. The whole way was a thick jungle of bush and thorn.

26th January.—The Somal insisted upon halting to eat, and the caravan did not start before noon. The road was tolerable and the descent oblique. The jungle was thick and the clouds thicker ; rain fell heavily as usual in the afternoon. Five cloths were given to the Habr Girhajis as a bribe for passage. After a march of six miles the caravan halted at a place called Minan. Here they again found a cave which protected them from the rain. Water was abundant in the hollows of the rock.

27th January.—Early in the morning the caravan set out, and descended the hill obliquely by a tolerable road. They passed a number of thorn trees bearing a gum called Falafala or Luban Meyti, a kind of frankincense : it is thrown upon the fire, and the women are in the habit of standing over it. After travelling six miles the travellers unloaded at Hundurgal, on the bank of a watercourse leading to Las Galwayta : some pools of rain-water were observed in the rocky hollows of the bed.

28th January.—At about 9 A.M. the caravan crossed one of the lower ridges of the mountains by a tolerable road. Lieutenant Speke had preceded his camels, and was sitting down to rest, when he was startled by hearing the rapid discharge of a revolver. His valiant Abban, either in real or in pretended terror of the Habr Girhajis, had fired the pistol as a warning. It had the effect of collecting a number of Badawin to stare at the travellers, and cogitate on what they could obtain : they offered, however, no opposition.

At midday the caravan reached a broad and deep Fiumara, which contained a spring of good sweet water flowing towards the sea. Here they halted for refreshment. Again advancing, they traversed another ridge, and, after a march of twelve miles, arrived in the evening at another little watercourse on the Maritime Plain. That day was clear and warm, the rain being confined to the upper ranges. The name of the halting-place was Farjeh.

29th January.—The caravan marched over the plain into Kurayat, or Little Las Kuray, where Lieutenant Speke, after a detention of upwards of a fortnight, took boat, and after five days' sail arrived at Aden, where I was expecting him. He was charged forty dollars—five times the proper sum—for a place in a loaded Buggalow : from Aden to Bombay thirty-five dollars is the hire of the whole cabin. This was the last act of the Abban, who is now by the just orders of the acting Political Resident, Aden, expiating his divers offences in the Station Jail.

CONCLUSION.

Lieutenant Speke has passed through three large tribes, the Warsingali, the Dulbahanta, and the Habr Girhajis.

The Warsingali have a Sultan or Chief, whose orders are obeyed after a fashion by all the clans save one, the Bihidur. He cannot demand the attendance of a subject even to protect the country, and has no power to raise

recruits ; consequently increase of territory is never con-
templated in this part of the Somali country.   In case
of murder, theft, or dispute between different tribes, the
aggrieved consult the Sultan, who, assembling the elders,
deputes them to feel the inclinations of the " public."
The people prefer revenging themselves by violence, as
every man thereby hopes to gain something.   The war
ends when the enemy has more spears than cattle left—
most frequently, however, by mutual consent, when both
are tired of riding the country.   Expeditions seldom
meet one another, this retiring as that advances, and he
is deemed a brave who can lift a few head of cattle and
return home in safety.   The commissariat department is
rudely organized : at the trysting-place, generally some
water, the people assemble on a day fixed by the Sultan,
and slaughter sheep : each person provides himself by
hanging some dried meat upon his pony.   It is said that
on many occasions men have passed upwards of a week
with no other sustenance than water.   This extensive
branch of the Somal is divided into eighteen principal
clans, viz. :

1. Rer Jirad (the royal family).	10. Nuh Umar.
2. Rer Fatih.	11. Adan Sa'id.
3. Rer Abdullah.	12. Rer Haji.
4. Rer Bihidur.	13. Dubbays.
5. Bohogay Salabay.	14. Warlabah.
6. Adan Yakub.	15. Bayabarhay.
7. Jirad Umar.	16. Rer Yasif.
8. Jirad Yusuf.	17. Hindudub.
9. Jirad Liban.	18. Rer Garwayna.

The Northern Dulbahantas are suffering greatly
from intestine war.   They are even less tractable than
the Warsingali.   Their Sultan is a ruler only in name ;
no one respects his person or consults him in matters of

importance : their Jirad was in the vicinity of the traveller ; but evasive answers were returned (probably in consequence of the Abban's machinations) to every inquiry. The elders and men of substance settle local matters, and all have a voice in everything that concerns the general weal : such, for instance, as the transit of a traveller. Lieutenant Speke saw two tribes, the Mahmud Jirad and Rer Ali Nalay. The latter is subdivided into six septs.

The Habr Girhajis, here scattered and cut up, have little power. Their royal family resides near Berberah, but no one as yet wears the turband ; and even when investiture takes place, a ruler's authority will not extend to Makhur. Three clans of this tribe inhabit this part of the Somali country, viz. : Bah Gummaron, Rer Hamturwa, and Urus Sugay.

I venture to submit a few remarks upon the subject of the preceding diary.

It is evident from the perusal of these pages that though the traveller suffered from the system of black-mail to which the inhospitable Somal of Makhar subject all strangers, though he was delayed, persecuted by his " protector," and threatened with war, danger, and destruction, his life was never in real peril. Some allowance must also be made for the people of the country. Lieutenant Speke was of course recognized as a servant of Government ; and savages cannot believe that a man wastes his rice and cloth to collect dead beasts and to ascertain the direction of streams. He was known to be a Christian ; he is ignorant of the Moslem faith ; and, most fatal to his enterprise, he was limited in time. Not knowing either the Arabic or the Somali tongue, he was forced to communicate with the people through the medium of his dishonest interpreter and Abban.

I have permitted myself to comment upon the

system of interference pursued by the former authorities of Aden towards the inhabitants of the Somali coast. A partial intermeddling with the quarrels of these people is unwise. We have the whole line completely in our power. An armed cruiser, by a complete blockade, would compel the inhabitants to comply with any requisitions. But either our intervention should be complete—either we should constitute ourselves sole judges of all disputes, or we should sedulously turn a deaf ear to their complaints. The former I not only understand to be deprecated by our rulers, but I also hold it to be imprudent. Nothing is more dangerous than to influence in any way the savage balance of power between these tribes : by throwing our weight on one side we may do them incalculable mischief. The Somal, like the Arab Badawin, live in a highly artificial though an apparently artless state of political relations ; and the imperfect attempt of strangers to interfere would be turned to the worst account by the designing adventurer and the turbulent spirit who expect to rise by means of anarchy and confusion. Hitherto our partial intervention between the Habr Awal of Berberah and the Habr Girhajis of Zayla has been fraught with evils to them, and consequently to us.

But it is a rapidly prevailing custom for merchants and travellers to engage an Abban or Protector, not on the African coast, as was formerly the case, but at Aden. It is clearly advantageous to encourage this practice, since it gives us a right in case of fraud or violence to punish the Abban as he deserves.

Lastly, we cannot expect great things without some establishment at Berberah. Were a British agent settled there, he could easily select the most influential and respectable men, to be provided with a certificate entitling them to the honour and emolument of protecting strangers. Nothing would tend more surely than this measure to open up the new country to commerce and civilization. And it must not be inferred, from a perusal of the foregoing pages, that the land is valueless. Lieutenant Speke saw but a small portion of it, and that, too, during the dead season. Its exports speak for themselves: guano, valuable gums, hides, peltries, mats, clarified butter, honey, and Dumbah sheep. From the ruins and the traditions of the country, it is clear that a more civilized race once held these now savage shores, and the disposition of the people does not discourage the hope entertained by every Englishman—that of raising his fellow man in the scale of civilization.

Camp, Aden, March, 1855.

METEOROLOGICAL OBSERVATIONS

Made by Lieutenant Speke, during his Experimental Tour in Eastern Africa, portions of Warsingali, Dulbahanta, &c.

Date.	6 A.M.	Noon.	3 P.M.	Meteorological Notices.
1854.				
Oct. 29.	70°	87°	[1]112°	Wind from N. E. strong. [1]Ex-
,, 30.	70	87	85	Ditto. [posed to sun.
,, 31.	68	88	85	Ditto.
Nov. 1.	67	88	82	Ditto. (These observations
,, 2.	62	86	85	Ditto. from the 29th Oct.
,, 3.	59	86	,,	to the 7th Nov.,
,, 4.	65	86	84	Ditto. were taken in the
,, 5.	65	88	-	Ditto. tent.)
,, 6.	63	88	86	Ditto.
,, 7.	74	90	88	Cloudy in the morning.
,, 8.	66	83	88	Wind strong from the N. E. (In
,, 9.	64	84	82	Ditto. open air, but not ex-
,, 10.	69	84	82	Ditto. posed to the sun.)
,, 11.	70	84	82	Ditto.
,, 12.	68	83	82	
,, 13.	64	85	82	
,, 14.	77	82	82	
,, 15.	70	83	83	
,, 16.	72	83	82	
,, 17.	62	110	104	In open air exposed to sun.
,, 18.	62	95	96	
,, 19.	62	102	95	All these observations were taken
,, 20.	-	98	103	during the N. E. monsun, when
,, 21.	,,	,,	,,	the wind comes from that quar-
,, 22.	59	74	77	ter. It generally makes its
,, 23.	56	81	75	appearance about half-past 9
,, 24.	59	78	82	A.M.
,, 25.	58	78	79	
,, 26.	60	74	75	
,, 27.	59	82	77	
,, 28.	59	82	72	
,, 29.	59	-	80	
,, 30.	61	82	80	
Dec. 1.	52	78	86	
,, 2.	50	86	89	
,, 3.	,,	,,	,,	
,, 4.	-	69	,,	
,, 5.	54	84	84	
,, 6.	-	97	98	
,, 7.	52	-	89	
,, 8.	52	95	100	
,, 9.	38	90	94	
,, 10.	42	92	91	

Date.	6 A.M.	Noon.	3 P.M.	Meteorological Notices.
1854.				
Dec. 11.	42°	,,	,,	
,, 12.	45	73	,,	
,, 13.	40	81	82	
,, 14.	25	76	82	
,, 15.	33	80	82	
,, 16.	47	91	89	
,, 17.	36	84	90	
,, 18.	34	82	84	
,, 19.	54	78	84	
,, 20.	52	77	83	
,, 31.	-	89	88	
1855.				
Jan. 1.	40	98	98	In open air exposed to the sun.
,, 2.	43	84	86	All these observations were taken
,, 3.	34	84	86	during the N.E. monsun, when
,, 4.	32	86	84	the wind comes from that quar-
,, 5.	28	96	87	ter ; generally making its ap-
,, 6.	34	92	94	pearance about half-past 9 A.M.
,, 7.	39	91	80	
,, 8.	39	95	,,	
,, 9.	40	81	,,	
,, 10.	55	-	72	
,, 11.	50	91	90	
,, 12.	53	87	90	
,, 13.	51	94	94	
,, 14.	39	84	95	
,, 16.	40	81	87	
,, 17.	46	78	81	
,, 18.	42	86	88	
,, 19.	44	82	83	
,, 20.	40	,,	,,	
,, 21.	38	87	93	
,, 22.	50	91	84	
,, 23.	52	86	98	
,, 24.	52	-	62	On the north or sea face of the
,, 25.	51	79	66	Warsingali Hills, during 24th,
,, 26.	58	65	63	25th, and 26th, had rain and
,, 27.	58	,,	,,	heavy clouds during the day :
,, 30.	72	82	82	blowing off towards the evening.
,, 31.	71	88	93	From the 27th to the 7th the ob-
Feb. 1.	67	96	80	servations were taken at the sea.
,, 2.	74	89	80	
,, 3.	68	87	88	
,, 4.	68	89	,,	
,, 5.	68	84	83	
,, 6.	72	88	,,	On the 7th observations were taken
,, 7.	68	83	,,	in tent.

		Govern. Therm. boiled.	Therm.	Feet.
1854.				
Nov. 1st.	At Las Guray - - -	212°	88°	0000
22nd.	At Adhai - - - -	204·25	81	4577
30th.	At Habl Ishawalay - -	203·	58	5052
Dec. 4th.	At Yafir, top of range - -	200·25	69	6704
5th.	At Mukur, on plateau - -	205·5	67	3660
7th.	At Rhat Tug, on plateau -	206·5	62	3077
15th.	At Yubbay Tug, on plateau -	204·	62	4498
	Government boiling therm. broke here. Common. therm. out of bazar boiled at sea level - 209° Thermometer - 76			
1855.		Com. ther.		
Jan. 1st.	At Jid Ali, on plateau - -	202°	62	3884
12th.	At Biyu Hablay - - -	201·	62	4449

APPENDIX II.

GRAMMATICAL OUTLINE AND VOCABULARY

OF THE

HARARI LANGUAGE.

GRAMMATICAL OUTLINE.

PRELIMINARY REMARKS.

THE caution necessary for the stranger who would avoid exciting the suspicions of an African despot and Moslem bigots prevented my making any progress, during my short residence at the capital, in the Harari language. But once more safe among the Girhi Mountains, circumspection was no longer necessary. The literati who assisted in my studies were a banished citizen of Harar; Sa'id Wal, an old Badawi; and Ali Sha'ir, "the Poet," a Girhi Somal celebrated for his wit, his poetry, and his eloquence. I found the last most useful, and his linguistic sagacity enabled me to perform a feat of no ordinary difficulty, that of drawing out a grammatical sketch of the language. But time pressed, and few days remained for work. Our hours were spent in unremitting toil: we began at sunrise, the hut was ever crowded with Badawi critics, and it was late at night before the manuscript was laid by. On the evening of the third day, my three literati started upon their feet, and shook my hand, declaring that I knew as much as they themselves did.

Returning to Aden, I was fortunate enough to find there a friend, Lieutenant Dansey, 1st Bombay European regiment, who, seeing me embarrassed by preparations for an expedition, kindly volunteered to write out, and, with the assistance of one Farih Dibani, a Somali of the Habr Jul Jailah clan, to revise my notes. He spent much time and more trouble over his self-imposed task, and the attention which he bestowed upon each word may be considered a guarantee of accuracy.[1]

"Whether the scholars of the Hebrew, Ethiopic, and Arabic," I may remark in the words of M. Krapf ("Outline of the Kisuaheli Language," p. 6), "will derive any important aid from the knowledge of this tongue, is a question which I must answer in the negative; though it cannot be uninteresting to the Arabic scholar to observe the manner in which the Arabic has been amalgamated with the African language."

———

1. THE people of Harar ignore the origin of their language. It probably dates from our mediæval times, when the Hadiyah Empire flourished upon the ruins of the Christian states. In the present day it is absolutely confined within the walls of the city, which is surrounded on all sides by Gallas. Through the medium of Harari the Arabic language and the religious sciences are explained to the inhabitants : almost all the women and not a few of the citizens can speak no other tongue. The numerous Somal who visit and temporarily settle at Harar usually learn some sentences. But few penetrate deep into the language : at this moment, in Aden,

---

1 Afterwards at Berberah I met the Harar caravan ; and here my difficulty of procuring an instructor was truly characteristic. The timid merchants feared to lose their heads, and I should have failed but for the presence of a Sayyid, Aydrus bin Mohammed al-Barr al-Madani, who, with the real Sharif spirit, aided me, in the hope that one day   might revenge his wrongs upon the Amir of Harar.

amongst about 2000, one only is found capable of revising the vocabulary.

2. The Harari appears, like the Galla, the Dankali, and the Somali, its sisters, to be a Semitic graft inserted into an indigenous stock.[1] The pronouns, for instance, and many of the numerals are clearly Arabic, whilst the forms of the verb are African, and not unlike the vulgar tongues of modern India. Again, many of the popular expressions, without which conversation could not be carried on (*e. g. Labbay,* " here I am," in answer to a call), are pure Arabic. We are justified then in determining this dialect to be, like the Galla, the Dankali, and the Somali, a semi-Semite.[2]

---

1 " In the Abyssinian language, especially in the Ethiopic (or Ghiz), and in the Tigre and Gurague, its dialects, we find the Semitic element is still predominant; the Amharic manifests already a strong inclination of breaking through this barrier. The Somali and Galla languages have still more thrown off the Semitic fetter, whilst the Kisuaheli and its cognate idioms have entirely kept the Semitic aloof."—*Krapf, Preface.*

2 Lieutenant (now Captain) Rigby, 16th Regiment Bom. N. I., in an excellent paper published by the Bombay Asiatic Society, under the modest title of an " Outline of the Somauli Language, with Vocabulary," asserts that the dialect of which he is writing " has not the slightest similarity to Arabic in construction." A comparison of the singular persons of the pronouns will, I believe, lead to a different conclusion.

ARABIC.		SOMALI.
1. Ana, *I*	- -	Ana or Anega.
2. Anta, *thou*	- -	Adega.
3. Huwa, *he*	- -	Husagga.

The affixed article again suggests an Arabic derivation, which at first sight might escape the eye. Mindí, is *a* knife; Mindí-dá, *the* knife. The vulgar corruption of Ha' za' (هذا), *this,* affixed to the noun, as in Egypt and in many parts of Arabia (*e. g.* Al-Rajul dá, الرجل اد, *this* man), may have given rise to this and to the other forms of the Somali article ká, kí, gá, and gí. The interrogative pronoun

3. The Harari is not a written language, and the Arabic character imperfectly expresses its sound. It excites our wonder to see tongues so elaborate, with rules of eloquence and a poetry cultivated after the canons of rhythm and rhyme, destitute of an alphabet.[1] In Sind and India, on the contrary, every local variety of dialect has its own syllabarium modified from the Arabic or the Sanscrit. To account for the phenomenon, we must take refuge in some psychical cause hitherto unexplained. The Harari, when writing their songs and translations, use the Koranic character.

4. The pronunciation of the Harari dialect,[2] unlike

Ayw (*who ?*) is clearly a corruption of the Arabic Ay (ﺍﻱ), and Mahá (*what ?*) of Má (ﻣﺎ). Similarly the reciprocal Naf (*I myself*) is a contraction of the noun Nafs (ﻧﻔﺲ) used in this sense throughout Arabia. In many Somali words there is a direct derivation from the Arabic, which cannot be detected without a knowledge of the people's inability to articulate certain sounds. *Khubz* (ﺧﺒﺰ) in Arabic is *bread*. The Somali, avoiding the harsh khá (ﺥ), and generally converting zá (ﺯ) into sin (ﺱ) have changed the vocable into *kibis*. They have preserved intact the Arabic form of the Ism al-nisbah (ﺍﺳﻢ ﺍﻟﻨﺴﺒﻪ), adjective: for instance, Adáríyah means *belonging to Adári* (Harar); Aushíyah, *belonging to the Aushi* (Abyssinians). Of the Somali numerals, two only present any resemblance to the Arabic: Sadah, three, to Salásah (ﺛﻼﺛﺔ); and Afar, four, to Arba (ﺍﺭﺑﻊ). Both are derived through the Galla " Shadi " and "Afur."

1 Whether the Galla tongue possesses a distinct syllabarium is still a disputed point.

2 The pronunciation of the Somali tongue is partly Semitic, partly Indo-Germanic.

Of the Semitic we find two characteristic sounds :—

　　1. *Gh.* The Arabic Ghayn (ﻍ) occurs but rarely; as in the word Agh*al, a house.*

　　2. *H.* The Arabic Há (ﺡ) is common ; as in Ri*h* (ﺭﺡ), *a goat ;* Di*h* (ﺩﺡ), *a valley.*

The Sanscrit sounds are :—

　　1. *D* cerebral (ड); as in the words *Deg* (ﺩﺞ), *drowned ;* Ga*d* (ﮔﺪ), *a beard.*

the soft Galla and Somali, is harsh and guttural; a fact which causes astonishment, as it is spoken in a warm climate and within walls, where men generally soften sound. The Arabic letter khá (خ) is its characteristic.

The LETTERS which require comment in this sketch are—

1. The Arabic *hamzah* or broken *a'* (ء); *e.g.* ma'altu, day, bá'u, a merchant.[1]

2. A peculiar sound resembling *chya* (च) in Sanscrit; *e.g. koch* (قوچ) a eunuch. In pronunciation it is sometimes confounded with *sh; e.g.* abosh or abo*ch*, a man.

3. The Arabic *há* (ح); as in gi*h* (ﻎ), a live coal; zike*h*, gold.

4. The Arabic *káf* (ﺀﺎﻧ); as in *k*aytal (ﻗﻴﺘﻞ), a ship: this sound is also common in Somali.

5. The Sanscrit *l* (ळ); as in hi*ll*u (وحﻻ), truly.

6. The Sanscrit nasal *n* (ण); as in the pronoun I*n*yash (اﻧﺎﺵ), we.

7. The Cerebral *t* (ट); as in the word á*t* (آﺖ), a bone.

----

2. *L.* (ळ); as in Go*l* (ﮔﻮﻝ), *a barren woman.*

3. *N.* nasal (ण); as in the prohibitive, Há thigi*n* (ﻫﺎﺛﮕﻦ), *go not.*

4. *R.* cerebral (ड); as in the word Ga*r* (ﮔﺮ), *governments, an order.*

And, finally, the Somal, finding a difficulty in articulating the sounds Ch, P, and Z, change them into J, B, and S: *e.g.,*

> Ajjá, *for* Achha (in Hindustani, *good*).
> Bahár, *for* Pahár (in Hindustani *a hill*).
> Jasirah, *for* Jazírah (in Arabic, *an island*).

[1] The Semitic Ayn (ع) in Harari as in Hindustani, is converted into a simple *a*.

Like the Somali, the Harari tongue is remarkable for the hardness and the distinctness with which the consonants, those great discriminators of language, are articulated. To investigate this phenomenon, which has the peculiarity of varying according to the position of the letter, would lead me into a digression for which I have neither time nor space. Whenever a consonant is to be emphasized, it is denoted in the following pages by reduplication.

The system of orthography is the modified form of Sir W. Jones's alphabet : accents, however, have been used to denote the long vowels.

    1. *a* is pronounced as in the English "hat."

    2. *á*, as in "father."

    3. *ay*, as in "hay."

    4. *áy*, as in the Spanish "ay."

    5. *i*, as in the English "if."

    6. *í*, as ee in the English "sheer.[1]"

OF THE ARTICLE.

    5. THE definite is like the indefinite article, inherent in the noun.

    e.g. A horse and an ass; faras wá wajayrá.

        The son of the king; nagárshí lijjay.

The following examples will show the peculiarity of this part of speech:—

    A plate and the knife; Sehan wá masháh.

    The town of Aden; Aden bád.

    He went to the king; Nagárshí de hárá.

    The child and the father; Lijjay wá au-zo (literally, his father).

---

1 The other long and short vowels are omitted from this list, their pronunciation being according to the Italianized system now in vogue.

OF THE NOUN.

6. THE noun has two *genders*, Masculine and Feminine.

Masculine nouns may be converted into feminines by three processes. The first changes the terminal vowel into -*it*, or adds -*it* to the terminal consonant.

e.g. rágá, an old man ;   rágít, an old woman.
  bushshí, a dog ; bushshít, a bitch.
  wasíf, a slave boy ; wasífít, a slave girl.

Animals of different sexes have different names, and this forms the second process.

  e.g bárá, an ox ; lám, a cow.

The third and the most common way of expressing sex is by means of *abosh* (ابوش), "male or man," and *inistí* (corrupted from the Arabic unsa انثى), woman, "female." They correspond with our " he-" and " she-."

e.g. faras, a stallion ; inisti faras, a mare.
  abosh baghl, a he mule; inisti baghl, a she mule.

7. The noun has two *numbers*, Singular and Plural. The affix -*ásh* changes singulars into plurals.

e.g. abosh, a man ; aboshásh, men.
  wandag, a servant ; wandagásh, servants.
  gár, a house ; gárásh, houses.

Nouns ending in the long *á* become plural without reduplicating this letter.

e.g. gáfá, a slave ; gáfásh (for gáfáásh), slaves.
  gubná, a harlot ; gubnásh, harlots.

When the singular terminates in the sound -*ay*, so common in the Somali and Harari dialects, the plural is formed by affixing -*ásh* to the consonant preceding that diphthong.

e.g. lijjay, a son ;   lijjásh (for lijjiásh), sons.

The same is the case with nouns terminating in *í*.

e.g. kabri, a grave ;   kabrásh (for kabriásh), graves.

When the singular ends in the soft sibilant, it is usually changed into *z*.

e.g. faras, a horse ;   farazásh, horses.
       irás, a cloth ;   irázásh, cloths.

8. The noun in Harari, as in the Somali language, has no *cases :* the following is the way in which casal relations are expressed :—

Nom. and Acc., amír, *a chief.*
Dative,   amír lay, *to a chief.*
Vocative,   amir-o ! *O chief.*[1]
Ablative,   amír bay, *or* be, *from a chief.*

The Genitive case, as in the Somali, is expressed by simply prefixing the name of the person to the thing possessed.

e.g. The Amir's son, Amír lijjay (literally, Amir-son).
       The Sultan's house, Sultán gár.
       The gardens of Harar, Gay Harshásh.

To obviate the unintelligibility often arising from this formation, or rather absence of formation, the word *zo* or *so* (his) is sometimes added to the name of the thing possessed.

e.g. Ahmad's turban, Ahmad imamah-zo (literally,
           Ahmad his turban).
       The Kazi's brother, Kází íh-zo.

---

1 This *o* is generally added, as in the Somali tongue, to titles and proper names: *e.g.* Amir-o ! Arab-o ! Ahmad-o ! Sometimes the purely Arabic yá (ِ) is used, and when the address is unceremonious, Akhákh yá, *O thou !*

OF THE ADJECTIVE.

9. THE adjective, like the noun, has no cases properly so called. In some instances they precede their nouns.

> *e.g.* Táy barti, a black staff.
> Gidor abbá, a tall man.

At other times they follow their substantives.

> *e.g.* Shundud zike*h*, a golden necklace.
> Majlis gidir, a large assembly.

Adjectives, like nouns, alter their terminations in the *feminine* form.

> *e.g.* Uzn zalayla, a deaf man ; in the feminine, Uzn zalaylít.
> Kibrí zálá, a proud man ; in the feminine, Kibrí zálí.

As in the Somali tongue, degrees of *comparison* are expressed by phrases, not by any change of the adjective.

e.g.

Comparative. { This is greater than that.
Yá be yí igadrí hal (lit. that than this great is).

Superlative. { This is the greatest.
Yí jammí be igadrí hal (lit. this all than great is).

OF NUMERALS.

10. THE following are the *cardinal* numbers :—

1. Ahad (احد).
2. Kot.
3. Shíshtí.
4. Harad (هرد).
5. Hamistí (همستی).
6. Saddistí.
7. Sátí.
8. Sot or Sút.

9. Sehtan (Zehtayn).
10. Assir.
11. Ahad assir.
12. Kot wá assir.
20. Koyah.
30. Sáseh.
40. Arbaín (?).
50. Hamistí assir.

60. Siddistí assir.
70. Sát assir.
80. Sút assir.
90. Zehtaná or Sehtaná.
100. Baklá or Boghol (بوغل, the Somali word).
1000. Kum (Somali) or Alfí (Arabic).

11. The *ordinals* are formed by affixing *-khá* to the numerals.

e.g. Ahad-khá, first. Harad-khá, fourth.
Kot-khá, second. Hamistí-khá, fifth.
Shíshtí-khá, third.

12. The fractional numbers are :

¼ Rubá (Arab. ربع).   ¾ Shíshtíruba.

½ Nus (Ar. نصف) or Keni.   ⅓ Shíshtísam.

OF PRONOUNS.

13. THE system of pronouns in Harari, as in the Somali language, is artful and somewhat complicated. Like the Arabic it may be divided into separate and affixed. The *separate* or *personal* pronouns which have neither gender nor case are :—

Singular.	Plural.
1st Pers. Án (آن).	Innásh or Inyásh.
2nd ,, Akhákh (اخاخ).	Akhákhásh (اخاخاش)
3rd ,, Huwa (هه).[1]	Hiyyásh.

14. The *affixed* pronouns or possessives attached to nouns are :—

---

[1] Itta, *she* (near).   Yata, *she* (far).

Singular.

1st Pers. - e, *my* or *mine.*   *e.g.* Gár-e, my house.
2nd ,, - khá, *thy* or *thine.*   Gár-khá, thy house.
3rd ,, - zo, *or* - so, *his.*   Gár-zo, his house.[1]

Plural.

1st Pers.- zinya *or* sinya, *our.* *e.g.* Gár-zinya, our house.
2nd ,, - kho, *your.*   Gár-kho, your house.
3rd ,, - zinyo *or* sinyo, *their.*   Gár-zinyo, their house.

In the same way attached pronouns are affixed to verbs :—

> *e.g.* Sit-ayn, give (thou to) me.
> Sit-ana, give (thou to) us.

15. The *demonstrative* pronouns are :—

> Sing. Yí, *this.*
> Yá, *that.*
> Plur. Yíash, *or* yí'a*ch, these.*
> Yá'ash, *or* yá'ách, *those.*

16. The *interrogative* pronouns are the following :—

> Mántá (ماننا), *who ?*
> Mintá (منتا), *what ?*

17. The *reciprocal* pronoun is expressed in Harari, as in Somali, by *naf.* Another common word is *atte,*

> *e.g.* Án atte hárkho, I myself went,
> Akhákh attekh hárkhí, thou thyself wentest,
> Huwa attezo hára, he himself went.

The Arabic word Ruh (روح, life or soul) is also used for "self" in such phrases as this :—

> Mahatkho ruh-e, I smote myself.

---

1 These words are also pronounced zú, sú and khú. Of the former pronouns there are also singular and plural separate forms,
> *e.g.* Azo *or* Azu, *his.*
> Azyásh *or* Ayách, *their.*

OF VERBS.

18. THE Harari verb, like the Somali, has only two tenses, a Past and a Present. The Future of the Indicative, as well as the Conditional and the Optative tenses, is formed by adding significant particles and the use of the substantive verb. The root is the 2nd person of the Imperative, and a Prohibitive is obtained by prefixing *at* (اتِ), or by affixing *mekh*. In the negative forms, the Harari is more artfully constructed than the Somali verb.

19. The following are the two *auxiliary* verbs.

PAST TENSE.
(Affirmative Form.)

Singular.	1.	*I was,*	Án narkho (نارخُو).
	2.	*Thou wast,*	Akhákh nárkhí.
	3.	*He was,*	Huwa nárá.
Plural.	1.	*We were,*	Inyásh nárná.
	2.	*Ye were,*	Akhákhásh narkhú (نارخُو).
	3.	*They were,*	Hiyyásh nárú.

(Negative Form.)

Sing.	1.	*I was not,*	Án alnárkhúm (النارخوم).
	2.	*Thou wast not,*	Akhákh alnárkhím.
	3.	*He was not,*	Huwa alnárum.
Plur.	1.	*We were not,*	Inyásh alnárnám.
	2.	*Ye were not,*	Akhákhásh alnárkhúm.
	3.	*They were not,*	Hiyyásh alnárúm.

PRESENT TENSE.
(Affirmative Form.)

Singular.		*Plural.*	
1. *I am,*	Án halko.	1. *We are,*	Inyásh halna (هَلْنَ).
2. *Thou art.*	Akhákh halkhí.	2. *Ye* ,,	Akhákhásh halkhú.
3. *He is,*	Huwa hal (هل).	3. *They* ,,	Hiyyásh halú.

(Negative Form.)

1. *I am not,* Án elkhúm. 1. Inyásh elnám.
2. *Thou art not,* Akhákh elkhím. 2. Akhákhásh elkhúm.
3. *He is not,* Huwa elúm. 3. Hiyyásh elúm.

IMPERATIVE.

Singular. *Plural.*

2. *Be thou,* Hal (هل). 2. *Be ye,* Halkhú (هلخو).

The second auxiliary has the sense of *to become,* and corresponds with "jirrah" of the Somal, who express "I am" by wá jogá, literally, "I stand."

PAST TENSE.

Sing. 1. *I became,* Án ikaní (اقانى) nárkho.
2. *Thou becamest,* Akhákh tikání nárkhí.
3. *He became,* Huwa ikání nárá.
Plur. 1. *We became,* Inyásh nikání nárná.
2. *Ye became,* Akhákhásh tikání nárkhú.
3. *They became,* Hiyyásh ikání nárú.

PRESENT TENSE.

Sing. 1. *I become,* Án ikánákh (اقاناخ).
2. *Thou becomest,* Akhákh tikánákh.
3. *He becomes,* Huwa ikánál.
Plur. 1. *We become,* Inyásh nikánáná (نقانانا).
2. *Ye become,* Akhákhásh tikánákhu.
3. *They become,* Hiyyásh ikánálú.

IMPERATIVE.

Singular. *Plural.*

2. *Become thou,* Kánní (قانى). 2. *Become ye,* Kánnú (قانو).

PROHIBITIVE.

Sing. 2. *Become not,* ikánnimekh (اقانّيمِج).

Plur. 2. *Become not ye,* ikánnumekh (اقانّيمِج).

23. The following is a specimen of a verb regularly conjugated.

Past Tense.

(Affirmative Form.)

Sing. 1. *I went,*   Án letkho.
     2. *Thou wentest,* Akhákh letkhí.
     3. *He went,*   Huwa leta (ليت).
Plur. 1. *We went,*   Inyásh letna (ليتن).
     2. *Ye went,*   Akhákhásh letkhú.
     3. *They went,*   Hiyyásh letú.

(Negative Form.)

Sing. 1. *I went not,*   Án alletkhúm.
     2. *Thou wentest not,* Akhákh alletkhím.
     3. *He went not,*   Huwa alletám.
Plur. 1. *We went not,*   Inyásh alletnám.
     2. *Ye went not,*   Akhákásh alletkhúm.
     3. *They went not,*   Hiyyásh alletúm.

Present Tense.

(Affirmative Form.)

Singular.	Plural.
1. *I go,* Án iletákh (اليتاخ).	1. Inyásh niletáná.
2. *Thou goest,* Akhákh tiletínakh.	2. Akhákhásh tiletákhú.
3. *He goes,* Huwa yiletál.	3. Hiyyásh yiletálú.

(Negative Form.)

Sing. 1. *I go not,*   Án iletumekh.
     2. *Thou goest not,* Akhákh tiletumekh.
     3. *He goes not,*   Huwa iletumel.
Plur. 1. *We go not,*   Inyásh niletumena.
     2. *Ye go not,*   Akhákhásh tiletumekhú.
     3. *They go not,*   Hiyyásh iletumelú.

As in the Somali tongue and in the Semitic dialects generally, the Present serves for a Future tense: " I go," for " I shall or will go." A definite future is formed

in Harari by adding the substantive verb to a participial
form of the verb required to express futurity; *e. g.*

Sing.	1.	*I will go,*	Án iletle halkho.
	2.	*Thou wilt go,*	Akháhk tiletle halkhí.
	3.	*They will go,*	Huwa iletle hal.
Plur.	1.	*We will go,*	Inyásh niletle halna.
	2.	*Ye will go,*	Akhákhásh tiletle halkhú.
	3.	*They will go,*	Hiyyásh niletle halna.

IMPERATIVE.

Singular.	*Plural.*
2. *Go thou,* Let.	2. *Go ye,* Letú.

PROHIBITIVE.

2. *Go not thou,* At let.	2. *Go not ye,* At letú.

PARTICIPLES.

Going, Yiletál (بليتال)   *Not going,* Iletumel.

Gone, Itletle.

DIALOGUES AND SENTENCES.

Art thou well? Amánta khí?
Are ye well? Amánta khú?
Madam (to elderly female). Abbáy.
Sir. Abbá. Yá Sayyidí.
Are you well this morning? Amán hadarkhú?
Are you well this evening? Amán wa'alkhú?
Good morning. Amán be kero.
Good night. Amán be hedero.
I am well. Amán íntaná.
I am unwell. Nattú halbaná.
What is the matter with you? Min aganyekh?
Is your family well? Gár hawázum amánta khú?
I am better. Orintáy.
What news to-day? Hújí min war hal?
Good news to-day. Amán intá hújí.
It is cooler to-day than yesterday. Tájíná be hújí
    baradtá.
The air is cold. Dúf bárid intá.
Come in and sit down. Ná tageb.
What is thy name? Sumkhá mintá?
Come here (to woman). Lakambay.
Dost thou drink coffee? Bun tiseshákhi?
I want milk. Háy ikháshákh.
Is water to be had here? Mí halí ye atáybe?
Where goest thou? Ayde tahurákh?
I go to Harar. Gay uhurákh.
Send away the people. Walamosh yí uso'o.
I love you. An wadad khúsh.
What is thine age? Karníkhá aygay sintá?
Don't laugh. Asehak.
Raise your legs. Igir hafúshí.
Don't go there. At har yadde.

This man is good.   Yí abbá korám intá.

He is a great rascal.   Huwa gidir harámintá.

I don't want you (woman).   Ikháshá shúmekh.

Go from this.   Let yibí,—Jehannam har.

Leave my house.   Gár-e be witá.

Farewell!   Allahu le amánat!   (literally, "In Allah's charge.")

Allah pardon thee!   Aufi ashkhúkh!

What is the price of this coffee?   Yí bun min betasímakh?

Five ashrafi[1] a bale.   Ahad firasilah hamisti ashrafí.

This is dear.   Yí gál intá.

This is very cheap.   Yí kanná rakhís intá.

Give me bread.   Sitain úkhát.

I will beat thee.   Án imet akhákh.

I will not give.   Án istámekh.

I am hungry.   Ráhábenya.

I am thirsty.   Tararenya.   *

I am tired.   Dálágenya.

Where is thy house?   Aydenta gárkhá?

I have much to do to-day.   Húji bajíh habí halbayn.

We are about to travel.   Safar nahuráná.

How large is Harar?   Gay aygay sintá?

How far from this to Harar?   Yí atáy wá Gay aygay sintá?

How many people at Harar?   Gay uso'o aygay sintá?

Dost thou know him?   Akhákh tokakhí?

Dost thou know Arabic?   Arab sinán tokákhí?

I don't know it.   An úkumekh.

Hold my horse.   Faras lahadlayn.

The price of this horse is a hundred dollars.   Yí faras baklá kirshi[2] yakúchál.

---

2 The Ashrafi is a nominal coin used in accounts: three of these compose a dollar.

1 The Arabic *kirsh* (girsh, karsh, or garsh), probably derived from "groschen," is used as well as *riyal* in the Somali country, and at Harar.

There is.   Hal.
What delayed you ?   Min lahadekh ?
Is this knife thine ?   Yí masháh dínatkhánta ?
How many horses hast thou ?   Misti farazásh halakh ?
He killed him with a knife.   Nifti bayn gadalú.
Open the door.   Argabgí fitah.
Shut the door.   Argabgí igad.
Fill my pipe.   Gáyá milálay*n*.
Where is the book ?   Belá kitáb ?
It is in the box.   Sandúk bayn hal.
What o'clock is it ?   Min sá' anta ?
It is one P.M.   Zohr be ahad sá' ate hará.
It is new moon.   Warhe bakalá.
The sun is eclipsed.   Khusúf khána irr.

SPECIMEN OF A SONG IN HARARI.

BUKÁHÁ, bukáhá wá tazkirat bukáhá :
Nabi ba*k*ale surúre fánkazebay.
Alif lám kutub zál be diú wá ímánin tutúr.
Sabrí wá salátin tutúr.
Hamistáyn zobe nabbí azíowin tutúr.
Nabbi gárkho be, gár kho zarára be
Jannat shíra be, nabbí afosha be
Allah ! iláhíyo, hurtay maláhiyo !

TRANSLATION.

I weep, I weep, and I weep with (fond) remembrance,
(Thinking of) the Prophet's mule (he sitting) beautiful
    upon her back.
Alif-lám was written, faith and religion carrying,
Patience and prayer carrying,
(For the) fifth time the Prophet carrying,
The Prophet from his house, from the enclosure of his
    house,
To the midst of Paradise, the Prophet near—
Allah ! O my Allah ! near him place us !

THE names of the months are:—
1. Ashúrá (meharram).
2. Safarwarhe.
3. Harar maulúd { including the two Rabia and the two Jamádí.
7. Rajab.
7. Sha'abán.
9. Ramazán.
10. Shawwál.
11. Zulka'adah.
12. Zulhijjah.

———

Corn, holcus, and other grains are sold by this measure:

9 Handfuls = 1 Sugud (سَكد).
5 Sugud = 1 Tít tárad (تارد).
6 Tít tárad = 1 Tárad.

The usual measures of length are:

Zumzurti (زمزرتی), the span.
Kúrú (کورو), the cubit.

The common weights are:

Nuss Ratli, the half pound.
Ratli, the pound.
Nuss farásilah, ten pounds.
Farásilah, the maund, twenty pounds.

VOCABULARY.

N.B.—In the following pages, A. denotes that the word is pure Arabic;
A.c. corrupt Arabic; Amh. Amharic; S. Somali. The mark (?)
shows that the word is uncertain.

A.

Abandon, *v.*	- -	Giffarr (كفر).
Abdomen	- -	Karsí (A. c.).
Abide	- -	Tageb.
Abode	- -	Gár.
Above	- -	Lá'ay (لاءى).
Absence -	-	Zalaylkho (?).
Abuse	- -	Masdab.
Accumulate	-	Sámtí.
Adulterer	-	Fásik (A.), *fem.* Fásikít.
Afraid	- -	Fírat.
After	- -	Ehirr.
Afternoon	-	Asrí. Asr (A.).
Age	- -	Umrí (A.).
Air -	- -	Dúf.
Alive (well)	-	Or (اؤر).
All -	- -	Jammí.
Also (thus)	-	Azzokút.
Always -	-	Dáime (A.).
Amir's wife	-	Gístí.
Ancient -	-	Rágá, *fem.* Rágít.
Angel	- -	Maláikah (A.).
Anger, *s.* -	-	Ghazab (A.).
Angry	- -	Ghazbán (A.).
Another -	-	Alái (الاءى).

Answer -	-	Jawáb (A.).
Ant (black)	-	Chúch.
„ (white)	-	Kaynhúr.
Arise, *v.* -	-	Halfbal.
Arm	-	Íji (ايجى).
Arm-pit -	-	Kilkílát.
Army	-	Mákhedá (ماخيدا) Askar (A.), Amír Askar, the Amir's army.
Arrow -	-	Láwá.
Artificer -	-	Sáigh (A. esp. " goldsmith ").
Ash (ashes)	-	Hamad, *pl.* Hamadásh.
Ask	-	Athebrí (?).
Asleep -	-	Manyít.
Ass	-	Wajayrá.
Ate (*pret.*)	-	Balá.
At once -	-	Ahad sá'ah (A.).
Aunt (maternal)	-	Ikhistá.
„ (paternal)	-	Anná (انّا).
Avaricious	-	Bakhíl.
Awake -	-	Hafbal.
Away! (begone!)	-	Let !
Axe	-	Kalká, *pl.* Kalkásh.

B.

Back	-	Háchí.
Bad	-	Yegassí.
Bag	-	Kís (A.).
Baggage	-	Mahawá.
Baker	-	Ukhát- Zálí (*fem.* as only women sell bread).
Ball (bullet)	-	Rasás (A.).
Band	-	Nází (the black satin ribbon worn by women round the head to fasten the fillet which contains the hair).

Band	- - -	Nagárat (the Amir's kettle-drums, beaten at the hour of night prayers, as tocsin in times of danger, at the two festivals, and whenever the Prince leaves the palace).
Barren (women)	-	Zat wilat, Goblan.
Barter	- - -	Manáwat.
Base	- - -	Yegassí.
Basket	- - -	Mudáí.
Bath, *s.*	- - -	Sagará (prop. a privy).
Bathe	- - -	Háteb.
Battle	- - -	Gádal.
Bazaar	- - -	Magálah.
Beard	- - -	Daban.
Beat (kill)	- - -	Mahat.
Beautiful	- - -	*K*orám. *K*or-zálah, *fem.* *K*orzálí.
Bed	- - -	Firásh (A.).
Bedstead	- - -	Dúfán.
Bee	- - -	Nijját, Akús (?).
Beef	- - -	Lám Basar.
Beer (boozah)	-	Gohay. (Dakhbí is beer mixed with mead.)
Before	- - -	Ay*k*ad (ايقد). " In early part of," Nadí (ندی).
Beggar	- - -	Sakadad-báy (A. c. صدقه).
Behind	- - -	Ehirr.
Behold, *v.*	-	Hayj.
Belly	- - -	Kars (A. c.).
Below (beneath)	-	Taháy (تهای).
Bet -	- - -	Shart (A.).
Beyond (outside)	-	Káchí.
Bile	- - -	Safrá (A.).
Bird	- - -	Úf, *plur.* Úfásh.
Bitch	- - -	Bushít (Bushshít).
Bitter	- - -	Marrí (A. c. مّر).

Black	- - -	Táy.
Blacksmith	- -	Tumtú.
Blind, *adj.*	- -	Ín-zalaylá, *fem.* Ín-zalaylít.
Blood	- - -	Dam (A.).
Blood-money	- -	Diyah (A.).
Blunt, *adj.*	- -	Dumdum, bárid (A.).
Boat	- - -	Za'ímah (A.).
Body	- - -	Kám (A. c. فامة).
Bone	- - -	At (آت).
Book	- - -	Kitáb.
Bottle	- - -	Kirárat (A. c.).
Bow	- - -	Digáu.
Box	- - -	Sátán (?).
Boy (son)	- -	Lijjay.
Bracelet (ivory)	-	Áj (A.).
,, (man's)	-	Mál dáyá (the pewter armlet of a Galla chief).
,, (woman's)	-	Shánkháyt.
Brain	- - -	Hangullá.
Bran (chaff)	- -	Hanshar.
Brave	- - -	Gisí (S.), ishullo (?).
Bread	- - -	'Ukhát.
Break	- - -	Síbarr.
Breast (girl's)	-	Kunná.
Breeches	- -	Gannáfí, Kannáfí (?).
Bride	- - -	Arúzít (A. c.).
Bridegroom	- -	Arúz (A. c.).
Bring	- - -	Adej.
Broadcloth	- -	Júh (جوح ; Ar. جُوْخ Jokh).
Broken	- - -	Dallál (A.).
Brothers	- - -	Ih (اح, A. c.).
Bug	- - -	Tukhán (A. c.).
Bull	- - -	Bárá.
Burn, *v. imp.*	- -	Mágdí.
Burnt	- - -	Mágad.
But	- - -	Lákin (A.).

Butcher - - - Suwíyyá (A.).
Buttocks - - Fuddí (S.).
Buy - - - Khab (خب).
Buying and selling - Mokhab.
By all means - - Lá budd (A.).
By fair means - - Amán be.
By foul means - Yegassí be.

C.

Calf, *m.* - - - Rahas.
Carpenter - - Najjár (A.).
Carpet - - - Firásh (A.). Prayer-carpet, Sijjájah
(A. c.).
Camel - - - Gamaylah (A. c.), *fem.* Gamaylít.
Cannon - - - Madfá (A.).
Cat - - - - Adúrrú, Adan (?).
Cathedral - - Jámi (A.).
Cattle - - - Dínat.
Certainly - - Dirkhí (S.).
Chain - - - Silsilah (A.).
Change (barter) - Manáwat.
Charcoal - - Kasal.
Charm (talisman) - Kirtás (A.).
Cheap - - - Rakhís (A.).
Child - - - Waldí (A. c.), *pl.* Wildásh.
Cinnamon - - Korfá (A. c.).
Circumcision - - Absum.
Citron - - - Turungá (A. c.).
City - - - Magálah.
Clarified butter - Nazíf (A.).
Clay - - - *Ch*ebá.
Clean - - - Muk ishísh.
Climb, *v.* - - Isal.
Cloth (man's "tobe") Irás, *pl.* irázásh.
,, (woman's) - Gúlúbáy (worn out of doors over
the head). "Láy morad" is that
thrown over the shoulders.

Cloth (man's shirt) - Gidir kamís.
Clouds - - - Dánah.
Clove - - - Korunful (A.).
Club - - - Gidir bartí.
Coal (live) - - Gi*h*.
Coffee - - - Bun (A.). "*K*utti" is the decoction
of the leaf drunk by the Hararis.
Cold (catarrh) - - Hargab.
„ *adj.* - - - Birdí (A. c.).
Colour - - - Jinsí (A. c.).
Comb - - - Filá (S. firin).
Come! - - - Ná!
Containing (doing) - — Zála.
Cook (man) - - Dirig-zálá, Lelí (?).
„ (woman) - - Dirig-zálí, Kibábah-zálí.
Cooked - - - Khánah.
Cooking-pot (earthen) Makáto.
Copper - - - Nihás (A.).
Coral - - - Murjain (A. c.).
Corpse - - - Janáis (A. c.).
Corn - - - Ays (A. c. ?).
„ Indian - - Arab ikhí, *lit.* Arab holcus.
Corn (Indian roasted) Arab ikhí únká.
Cotton - - - *T*út (توت).
Cough - - - Ú*h* (اوح).
Court-yard - - Katam barí.
Cousin (female) - Zer kahat.
„ (male) - - Zer waldí, *pl.* Zer waldásh.
Cow - - - Lám
„ (milch) - - Háy-zálí.
Coward - - - Wahaylo, *fem.* Wahaylít.
Creeper - - - Táj (so called when worn by men
upon their turbands and women
upon their fillets).
Crepitus - - - Fas (A.).
Crooked - - - Wandállá.

Crow - - - Kurrá.
Cubit - - - Kúrú.
Cultivation - - Zará (A.).
Cultivator - - Argatá (opposed to " Gallá," a Nomad).
Cummin seed - - Kamún (A.).
Cup - - - Geb.
Cupping-horn - - Mahgút (Mahgút-ináí is the operator).
Cut - - - *Koch.*
Cuts (in cheek) - Makdad (beauty-marks).

D.

Dagger - - - Shotal.
Daily - - - Jammí yámúm.
Dance - - - Fakarr.
Danger (fright) - Firít.
Darkness - Jilmah (A. c.).
Date (the fruit) - Timir (A. c.). " Barni " is the Maskat date; "Sehárí"the small black date; " Farad " the large and juicy red variety.
Daughter - - Kahat.
Day - - - Ma'altú.
To-day - - - Hújí.
Yesterday - Tájená.
Third day ago - - Sestiná.
Fourth day ago - Rátiná.
Day after to-morrow Sestá.
Third day hence - Ra'atá.
Fourth day hence - Zirabe'itá (?).
Fifth day hence - Zikurkustá (?).
Dead (man) - - Janáis (A. c.); Mayyit (A.).
Deaf (man) - - Uzn-zalaylá.
 „ (woman)- - Uzn-zalaylít.
Deaf and dumb - Dúdah, fem. Dúdít; it also means idiotic.

Dear, *adj.*	-	Ghálí (A.); Kímah tabig.
Death	-	Maut (A.).
Debt	-	Mugot.
Deer	-	Waydalí.
Delay	-	Kaláh (قلاح).
Denial	-	Nakír (A.); Háshá (A.).
Deponent (witness)	-	Rágá.
Deposit	-	Amánat (A.).
Descend, *v.*	-	Wirad (?).
Descent	-	Maurad.
Desert, *s.*	-	Udmá bád.
Desert, *adj.*	-	Udmá (generally applied to land without trees).
Deserving	-	Wájib (A.).
Desire (want)	-	Fáj.
Devil (Satan)	-	Iblís (A.); Shaytán (A.).
Devil (sand-storm)	-	Dúf.
Die (dice)	-	Lafo (S.).
Difficult	-	Tabíg.
Dig	-	Hifarr. (A. c.); Khirr (?).
Dirt	-	Wasakh (A.).
Discharge (release)	-	Gifarr.
Disease	-	Mattú.
„ (venereal)	-	Jabtú (S. Jabtí).
Dish	-	Sehní (A. c.).
Dish-cover	-	Mot; mo'ot (generally made of plaited straw).
Distant	-	Ru*h*uk (رحق).
Ditch (pit)	-	Chayr.
Doer (*masc. or fem.*)	-	Ináí (?).
Dog	-	Bushshí.
Dollar	-	*K*arshí (Ar. *K*irsh).
Door	-	Gebtí.
Doubt	-	Shakk (A.).
Doubtful	-	Shaka*n*yá (A. c.).
Dream	-	Birzáz.

Dress	- - -	Libáshá (A. c.); Irázásh.
Dried	- - -	Daraká.
Drink, *v.*	- -	Sích.
Drinkables	- -	Mashjá.
Drug	- - -	Dawá (A.).
Drum	- - -	Karabú.
Drummer	- -	Karabú-zálá.
Drunk (intoxicated)		Sakhrá (A. c.).
Dry, *v.*	- - -	Darak; Darag.
Dumb, *masc.*	- -	Jabaká; arrát-zalaylá.
„ *fem.*	- -	Jabakít; arrat-zalaylít.
Dust	- - -	Sísá (Sesá S.).
Dwarf, *masc.*	- -	Hajayr.
„ *fem.*	- -	Hajayrít.

E.

Each	- - -	Ahad (A. c.).
Ear	- - -	Uzn. Uzun (A. c.).
Ear-ring	- -	Faror.
Earth	- - -	Dashí (Tashshí ?).
East	- - -	Írrtúj.
Easy	- - -	Yasír (A.).
Eat ! *v.*	- - -	Bilá.
Eatables	- -	Mablá. " Eatables and drink-ables," mablá wá mashjá.
Egg	- - -	Ukoh (أُقُوح).
Eight	- - -	Sot.
Eighth	- - -	Sotkhá.
Eighty	- - -	Sot assir.
Elder, eldest	- -	Gidirr.
Elephant	- -	Dukhun.
Eleven	- - -	Assir ahad.
Eloquent	- -	Tihayn.
Employment	- -	Habí.
Empty	- - -	Kof.

End ! (finish !)	-	*T*abosh.
Ended	- -	*T*abayyá.
Enemy	- -	Díná.
Enough	- -	Hidak. Yokál.
Envy	- -	Husúd (A.).
Envious	- -	Hasíd (A.c.)
Escape	- -	Sik.
Eunuch	- -	*K*oc*h*. Towásh (A.).
Evening	- -	Mashá (A.).
Every	- -	Jammí (A. c.).
Everything	- -	Jammí Shiyún (A. c.).
Evidence	- -	Rágá.
Exchange	- -	Manáwat.
Expense	- -	Farzí.
Eye	- -	Ín (A. c.).
Eyelash	- -	In chigar.

F.

Face	- -	Fít.
Fæces	- -	Gaf : Kaf (S.).
Faith (religion)	-	Dín (A.).
Fall, *v.*	- -	Wida*k*.
False	- -	Kizbá*n*yá.
Fame	- -	Námús (A.).
Fan (fly-flapper)	-	Zimbi Marwahah (A.).
Far	- -	Ruhug.
Farewell !	-	Amán ! (A.).
Farmer	- -	Harrásh.
Fast, *adv.*	-	Fitan.
Fast, *s.*	- -	Soman (A. c.).
Fat (strong)	-	Jabábir (A. c.); *K*assá (S.) Wadal.
Fate	- -	Ayyám (A.).
Father	- -	Áwa.
Fault	- -	Ghalat (A.).
Fear ! *v.*	- -	Fir.
Fearful	- -	Fírat.

Feather	- - -	Bállí (S. Bál).
Feet	- - -	Ingirásh. Pl. of Ingir.
Female	- - -	Inistí (A. c. ?).
Fetch	- - -	Adej.
Fetters	- - -	Ingir birat.
Fever	- - -	Wiyí nattú.
Few	- - -	Tinne'o.
Fillet (for woman's hair)	- - -	Gúftá.
Finger	- - -	Aťabinyá. Pl. Aťábinyásh.
Fire	- - -	Isád.
Fire-wood	- -	Mamágad.
First	- - -	Ahadkhá.
Fish	- - -	Túlam.
Fist	- - -	Dubuj.
Five	- - -	Hamistí.
Fifth	- - -	Hamistikhá.
Fifty	- - -	Hamistí assir.
Flag	- - -	Álan (A. c. and S.).
Flea	- - -	Kunáj; Takfí (?); injir bodo (S.).
Flesh	- - -	Basar.
Fly	- - -	Zimbí (A. c.).
Fodder	- - -	Sa'ar.
Food	- - -	Mablá.
Fool	- - -	Jinám (A. c.).
Foot (leg)	- -	Ingir.
Footstep	-	Hardá
Force	- - -	Tákh (A. c.).
By force	- - -	Yegassí be.
Forehead	- -	Fi'it.
Fort	- - -	Kalaí gár; darbí-gár.
Forty	- - -	Arbaín (A.).
Foul (impure)	- -	Najis (A.).
Four	- - -	Harad; harat.
Fourth	- - -	Haratkhá.
Fowl	- - -	Atáwág, *fem.* atáwágít.

Friend - - - Rafík (A.); marren (?).
Frog - - - Ankuráratí.
From - - - Be; bay.
Full - - - Mullu (?).

G.

Gall (bile) - - Safrá (A.).
Game - - - Dabál (esp. the La'ab al-Khayl).
Gambler - - Kammár (A.).
Garden - - - Harshí.
Gardener - - Harshi-wandag.
Garlic - - - Tummá (A. c.); ton (S.).
Gate - - - Bárí (A.).
Gate-keeper - Bárí-goitá.
Gather, *v.* - - Sámtí.
Gazelle - - - Sagáro (S.)
Generous - - Sakhí (A.).
Generosity - - Sakháwat (A.).
Get up ! *v.* - - Hafbal.
Gift - - - Hadiyah (A.); mastá (?).
Ginger - - - Zanjabílí.
Giraffe - - - Girhí (S.).
Girl (marriageable)- Wahashí. Pl. Wahashi'ách.
„ (aged) - - Gidir Wahashí.
Puella suta - - Duffun Wahashí (sicut est mos
    Somalorum et nationis Gallæ).

„ aperta - - Kufut Wahashí.
Girl (slave) - - Wasifít ; Amharet.
Girl - - - Kahat.
Give, *v.* - - - Sit (S.).
Glad - - - Tass ; tasstass.
Glass (cup) - - Kás (A.).
„ (looking) - Murá'it (A. c.).
„ (bootle, black) Kirárat *T*áy.
„ (red) - - *K*ay*h* (قيح).
Glory - - - Námús (A.).

Glue (gum)	- -	Mukát.
Go! *v.*	- - -	Let (to a woman, Lechí).
Gone (*pret.*)	- -	Letá.
Let go!	- - -	Hidak; Gifarr.
Goat (he)	- -	Kurmá.
„ (she)	- -	Dau.
God	- - -	Goitá. N.B.—The Argobbas call the Supreme Being "Gaeto," the Gallas "Goite" or "Wák," and the Somal "Aybah" (ایبه).
Gold	- - -	Zikeh (A. c.).
Goods	- - -	Maháwá.
Good	- - -	Korám.
Good news	- -	War amán.
Governor	- -	Nagáshí.
Grandfather	- -	Bábá.
Grandmother	- -	Ummá.
Grape	- - -	Anab (A.).
Grass	- - -	Sa'ar.
Grass-cutter (sickle)		Záhabí.
Gratis	- -	Bilásh (A.).
Grave	- - -	Kabrí (A.) ; Plur. Kabrásh.
Grave (saint's)	-	Awásh Kabrí.
Gravel	- - -	Ún.
Great, *adj.*	-	Gidír.
Greatest	- -	Jammí be Gadrí.
Green	- - -	Dámá : *fem.* Dámít. Akhzar (A.)
Groom	- - -	Záhabí.
Ground	- -	Tashshí. (?).
Ground (sloping)	-	Gobaná.
Guest	- - -	Nugda.
Guide	- - -	Úga yúkzalinta (?).
Guinea Fowl	-	Zikrá.
Gum	- - -	Mukát.
Gun	- - -	Nifti.
Gunpowder	- -	Bárúd (A. c.).

H.

Habitation	Gár.
Hail, *s.*	Ún Zináb.
Hail, *v.*	Amán bidíchkhú.
Hair	Chigar.
Hair (pecten)	Foc*h* chigar.
Hair-pin (woman's)	Filá.
Half	Nuss (A. c.) : Kení.
Hammer	Madoshá ; Buruj (?).
Hand	Ijí.
Handful	Mahfass ; Antobo (?).
Handwriting	Kitab.
Hang (tie, *v.*)	Igad ; Bal*n*aya (S.).
Harbour	Marsá (A.).
Hare	Askokí ; Bakhayla (S.).
Harlot	Gubná.
Haste !	Fitan.
Hatchet	Kalká.
Hay	Sa'ar.
Head	Urus (A. c.).
Health	Áfet (A. c.).
Hear	Simá (A. c.)
Heart	Wazanah.
Heavy	Razín (A.).
He	Huwa.
Heel	Kúb (A. c.).
Heir	Yurs Zálintá. (The Arabic word "Mirás" is used for a legacy.)
Hell	Azáb (A.) ; Jahanam (A.).
Here	Idday. "Here I am," Labbay (A.).
High (tall, long)	Gidorr.
Hill, *s.*	Sarí.
His	Zo or So.
Ho !	Yáhú (S.) ; Akhákh yá.
Hog	Hariyyá.
Holcus Sorghum	Ikhí.

Hole	- - -	Gadú.
Holloa!	- - -	Akhákh yá.
Honey	- - -	Dús.
Hoof	- - -	Ingir.
Horn (beast's)	-	*Karr* (A. c.).
„ (cupping)	-	Mahgút.
Horse	- - -	Faras (in Ar. a mare; in Som. a horse).
Hot	- - -	Wiyí.
House	- - -	Gár.
„ (thatched)	-	Sa'ar gár; Gambisa.
„ (stone) -	-	Darbí gár.
How much?	- -	Mistí?
Humble -	-	Miskín (A.).
Hundred	-	Baklá.
Hunger -	-	Abár.
Hungry -	-	Rahab.
Husband	-	Abosh.
Hut	- - -	Wantaf gár (the Badawi's mat tents, called by the Somal, Gurgí).

I.

I, *pers. pron.*	- -	Án.
Ice -	- - -	Mí darak.
Idle (useless) -	-	Mablúl.
If -	- - -	Girr (?).
Ignorant	-	Jáhil (A.); Wíj (the latter generally means " young ").
Immense	-	Bajíh.
Immerse, *v.*	-	Esbí.
Immediately -	-	Fitan.
In -	- - -	Bayn (A. ?).
In that place -	-	Yadday.
Infirm	- -	Gofáí.
Inform, *v.*	-	Warosh.

Information	- -	War (Amh.).
Injury	- - -	Khasárá (A.).
Ink	- - -	Maddí (A. c. from مداد ?).
Inkstand	- -	Dibet (A. c.).
Inquire, *v.*	- -	Athebrí (?).
Inside	- - -	Ustú.
Instead	- - -	Manáwat; Tanáwat.
Intelligent	- -	A'kil (A.).
Inter, *v.*	- - -	*K*ibarr.
Interest (usury)	-	Ribáh (A.).
Intestines (lower)	-	Mara*ch*í.
„ (higher)	-	Kars (A. c.).
Intoxication	- -	Kayf (A.).
Intoxicating articles		Khamrí (A.).
Iron	- - -	Birat (S. bir.).
Itch, *s.*	- - -	Wi'ir.
Ivory	- - -	Áj; dukhun-sin.

J.

Jackal	- - -	Aizagadú (S. ídagalá, "burrowing below ground").
Jail-	- - -	Hasbí (A. c.).
Javelin	- - -	Waram (S.).
Jewel	- - -	Jauhar (A.).
Joke	- - -	*Ch*arrá*k*ah (جرافه).
Joker	- - -	Fúhá*ch*.
Journey	- - -	Safar (A.).
„ (by day)	-	Hújí Safar.
„ (by night)	-	Mishayt Safar.
Jowari (holcus)	-	Ikhí.
„ (straw)	-	*K*arah.
Joy	- - -	Farhah (A.); Tast.
Judge	- - -	Fikíh (A.); Kází (A.).
Jump, *v.*	- -	Shafbal.
Just	- - -	A'dil.
Juvenile	- - -	Darmá.

K.

Kat-plant (القات)	-	Ját.
Kettle	- -	Disdí (A. c.); Ma*k*atú.
Key	- -	Miftah (A.); Mifcháh (A. c.).
Kick, *v.*	- -	Rigat.
Kidney	- -	Kuláy (A. c.).
Kill	- -	Gidal.
Kiss, *v.*	- -	Ma*h* (as among the Somal it is disliked.)
Kitchen	-	Aweládá.
Kite (bird)	-	*T*illí.
Knee	- -	Gilib.
Knife	- -	Mashá*h*.
Knot	- -	*K*uturr.
Know	- -	Ú*k*.
Knowledge	-	Ilm (A.).
Koosoo	- -	Sútí (the well-known vermifuge, called Hedo by the Somal).

L.

Labour	- -	Ta'ab (A.).
Lake (colour)	-	*K*ay*h* (قيم).
Lame	- -	Ingir zalaylá.
Lamp	- -	Makhtút.
Landlord	-	Gár-zálá.
Lane	- -	Kachín úga.
Language	- -	Sinán.
Large	- -	Gidir.
Lass	- -	Kahat.
Laughter	-	Sa*h*a*k* (سحق A. c.); Mashak (?).
Law	- -	Sharíah (A.).
Lazy	- -	Mablúl.
Lead	- -	Risás.
Leaf	- -	Wara*k* (A.); Kuttí.
Leak (hole)	-	Nudúl.

Lean	- - -	Gofáy.
Learning, *s.*	- -	Ilm (A.).
Learned (man)	-	Kabír (A.) ; Shaykh (A.).
Least	- -	Jammí be angál.
Leather (hide)	-	Gogá.
Leech	- -	Ayktí ulá'úl (S.).
Left	- -	Gurá (Gragnay Amh. Guray S. " left-handed ").
Left hand	-	Gurá igí.
Leg	- -	Ingir.
Lend, *v.*	-	Likc*h*.
Leopard	-	Gargorá.
Less	- -	Ansál.
Liar	- -	Kizba*n*yá.
Lie	- -	Kiz (A. c.).
Light, *adj.*	-	Khafíf (A.) ; Kafíf (A. c.).
Lightning	-	Biri*k* (A. c.) ; Birig.
Like	- -	Kut (yí kut, "like this." Azzokut, " like unto him").
Lime (fruit)	-	Zarbissí.
Lime (cement)	-	Núrat (A.).
Lion	- -	Wanág.
Lips	- -	Laflaf.
Listen, *v.*	-	Simá.
Little	- -	*Tít* (تِّيت).
Liver	- -	Kút.
Living	- -	Húí (حوی A. c.).
Lo !	- -	Haych.
Load	- -	Tá'an.
Locust	- -	Kafjor.
Look, *v.* -	-	Haych.
Loose (open), *v.*	-	Fitah; Matmas.
Loss	- -	Khasárá (A.); Kobul.
Lose (the way, &c.)	(Úga) *K*abad.
Love	- -	Ishkí (A.).
In love (man) -	-	Abosh áshaká.

In love (woman) - Indosh áshaktí.
Louse - - - Kúmáy (A. c. ?).
Low, *adj*. - - Háchír.

M.

Mad - - - Jinám.
Mad-dog - - Jinám bushí.
Madam - - - Abbáy.
Magic - - - Falá (S.).
Magician - - Falá-zálá.
Maid servant - - Gáfít.
Main mast - - Gidir dagal.
Make, *v*. - - - Úsh.
Malady - - - Nattú.
Male - - - Abosh.
Malice - - - Dínah.
Man - - - Abosh.
Many - - - Bají*h*.
Many times - - Bají*h* gir.
March, *s*. - - Malayt.
Mare - - - Inistí faras.
Mariner - - - Bahrí (A.).
Mark, *s*. - - - Astá.
Market place - - Magálah.
Marriage - - Mansá.
Marriage-portion - Mehr (A.).
Married (man) - Mishtí-hálá.
  „ (woman) - Abosh-hálí.
Master - - - Marí*n*.
Mat - - - Saylan.
Match (gun's) - Niftí fatílat.
Mead - - - *T*aj.
Meal (ground corn) Ays fíchah.
Measure - - - Sifar.
Meat - - - Basar.
Merchant - - Bá'u: tájir.

Message -	- -	Lo'okh.
Middle -	- -	Guttí; ustú (?): in the middle, guttí bayn.
Milk	- -	Háy.
Milk-pot -	-	Kadádah.
Milk-pot cover	-	Offá.
Minaret -	-	Khutbá.
Mine (it is)	-	Án zád intá.
Misery -	-	Masíbah (A. c.).
Model -	-	Áyinah (A.).
Money -	-	Mahallak (a brass coin current at Harar).
Monkey -	-	Zágarú.
Month -	-	Warhay.
Moon -	-	Charaká.
In the morning	-	Subhí (A.).
Mortar -	-	Mokaj (the pestle is called " Kaballá ").
Mortgage	-	Rahan (A.); Luhut.
Mosquito	-	Bimbí.
Mother -	-	A'e.
Mould (earth) -	-	Afar.
Mountain	-	Sarí.
Mouse -	-	Fúr (A. c.).
Mouth -	-	Afe (Amh. S.).
Mud -	-	Chebá.
Mule -	-	Baghl.
Murder -	-	Motá.
Murderer	-	Igadlí-zál; Gadáy (?).
Murdered	-	Gidalú.
Musjid (mosque)	-	Masgít.
Musk -	-	Misk (A). Zabád (A. civet, generally confounded by Orientals with musk).
Mustachio	-	Shárib (A.).
My -	- -	—e.
Myrrh -	-	Karabí.

N.

Nail	-	-	-	Mismár (A.).
Nail (hand)	-	-	Tifir (A. c.).
Naked	-	-	Kofh.
Name	-	-	Sum (A. c.).
Narrow	-	-	Chinkí.
Nasty	-	-	Yegassí.
Navel	-	-	Hamburtí.
Near	-	-	Kurrá.
Necessary (it is)	-	Yakhúnál.
Necessity	-	-	Hájah (A.).
Neck	-	-	Angat.
Necklace	-	-	Shandúd.
Needle	-	-	Morfí.
Needy	-	-	Fukrá.
Negro	-	-	Gáfá.
Neighbour	-	-	Afoshá.
Nest	-	-	Úf gár.
Never	-	-	Abadan (A.).
Never mind	-	-	Ahadúm aylá.
New	-	-	Hajís.
News	-	-	War (S.).
Night	-	-	Artú.
By night	-	-	Mushayt.
Nine	-	-	Sehtan ; Zehtáyn.
Ninth	-	-	Sehtan khá.
Ninety	-	-	Sehtaná.
Nipple (man's)	-	Tút (توت).
„ (woman's)	-	Kunná.
No !	-	-	May !
Nobody (there is)	-	Uso'o aylúm.
Nonsense	-	-	Kishná.
North	-	-	Jáh (A.); Kiblah (A.).
Nose	-	-	Úf.
Nostril	-	-	Úf nudúl.

There is nothing	-	Aylúm.
Now	- -	Akhkhá.
Number -	-	Helkí.

O.

Oath	- -	Tirayt.
Ocean	- -	Bahr (A.).
Oil -	- -	Salayt (A.).
Old	- -	Rágá, *fem.* Rágít.
Omen	- -	Fál (A.).
On (upon)	-	Lá'ay.
Once	-	Ahad muttí; Ahad gír.
At once -	-	Fitan.
One	- -	Ahad.
One third	-	Shíshtí-sám (A. ست).
One-armed	-	Ahad íjí zalaylá.
One-eyed	-	Ahad ín zalaylá.
One-legged	-	Ahad ingir zalaylá.
Onion	- -	Shunkortá.
Open, *v.* -	-	Fitah.
Opened -	-	Futoh.
Oppressor	-	Zálim (A.).
Oppression	-	Zulmí (A. c.).
Or -	- -	Walau (?). Ammá (A.).
Order	-	Amr (A.).
Orphan -	-	Yetím (A.) ; "á'e zalaylá," motherless ; "áwa zalaylá," fatherless.
Ostrich -	-	Guráyyá (S.).
Our	- -	Zinya.
Outside -	-	Mantá.
Owner	-	Zálá, *fem.* Zálí
Ox -	- -	Bárá.

P.

Pace - - -	Malaytá.
Pair - - -	Kut; Ko'ot.
Palace - - -	Nagáshí gár.
Palm (hand's) - -	Kaff'í (A. c.).
Paper - - -	Talhayyá.
Paramour (*fem.*) -	Gazan.
Partner - - -	Sharík (A.).
Pass, *v.* - - -	Let.
Path - - -	Kachín úga.
Pauper - - -	Zaygá.
Pawn - - -	Rahan (A.).
Peace - - -	Amán (A.).
Pearl - - -	Lúl (A.).
Pen - - -	Kalam (A.).
Penis - - -	Gantir.
People - - -	Uso 'o.
Pepper (black) -	Arab barbarí.
„ (red) -	Barbarí.
Perform, *v.* - -	Osh.
Perspiration - -	Wizí.
Pestle - - -	Kaballá.
Piece - - -	Koch (?).
Pig - - -	Hariyyá; Karkarrú.
Pigeon - - -	Hamímí (A. c.).
Pillow - - -	Makhaddá (A.).
Pimple - - -	Kím.
Pin - - -	Filá.
Pinch, *v.* - -	Kontá.
Pipe (smoking) -	Gáyá (the Indian " Gurgurí ").
„ tube -	Búk.
Pistol - - -	Tinneo Naftí.
Pit (cesspool) - -	Gadú.
Pity - - -	Rahmah (A.).
Place - - -	Attáí.
Plain - - -	Dídá.

Plantain - - - Mauz (A.).
Plate(forbakingbread) Kibábah (A. c.) ; Tábah (?).
Platter (wooden) - Gabatá.
Plough - - - Willítá ; Mahras (A.).
Plunder - - - Mahmat.
Pocket - - - Kís (A.).
Poetry - - - Fakarr.
Poison - - - Summí (A.).
Poisoned - - Summi-zálá.
Pomegranate - - Rummán (A.).
Ponderous - - Razín (A.).
Possible (it is) - Yakhúnál.
Pot (earthen) - Makatú.
Pot-bellied - - Kasá-zálá.
Pound (weight) - Ratlí.
Pox - - - Kitin.
Pretence - - Haylah (A.).
Pregnant - - Karsí ; Zálí.
Price - - - Báy.
Pride - - - Kibrí (A.).
Priest - - - Fakíh (A.).
Prison - - - Hasbí (A.).
Prisoner - - - Úgud.
Privy - - - Sagara.
Procurable - - Yaganyo.
Prodigious - - Ajab (A.).
Profit - - - Nafí (A. c.).
Proof - - - Ragá.
Proud (man) - - Kibrí-zálá ; Kibranyá.
„ (woman) - Kibrí-zálí ; Kibríyyít.
Provisions - - Mablá.
Pud. γυναικεîα - - Dúr.
Pumpkin - - Arab dubbá (S.).
Purse - - - Kís (A.).

Q.

Quadruped	- -	Dínat.
Quantity	-	Mistí.
Quarter -	-	Rubá (A.).
Quarter (of town)	-	Afochá.
Queen	- -	Gístí.
Question	-	Mathebar.
Quickly -	-	Fitan.
Quill	- -	Bállí (S.).
Quiver -	- -	Hinnách.

R.

Rage	- -	Za'al (A.); herár.
Raid	- -	Dína.
Raiment -	-	Irázásh.
Rain	- -	Zináb.
Raise, *v.* -	-	Hafush.
Raisin	- -	Zabíb (A.).
Ram	- -	Táy.
Ran, *v. pret.*	-	Saká.
Rapid	- -	Fitan.
Rascal -	-	Mablúl.
Rat	- -	Fúr (A.).
Raven	- -	Kurrá.
Raw	- -	Terí.
Razor	- -	Sháldá (?).
Read	- -	*K*ira (A. c.).
Real (dollar) -	-	*K*arshí.
Rebel	- -	Ásí (A.).
Rebellion	-	Balwá (A.).
Receive -	-	Nisá.
Red	- -	*K*ay*h* : *fem.* Kayhít.
Region	- -	Bád.
Regret	- -	Hammá (A. c.); Ghammá (A. c.).

Rein (bridle) - -	Hakamá (S.).
Relations - -	Ahl (A.).
Remain - - -	*K*irr (A. c.).
Remainder - -	*K*arrá.
Remedy - - -	Dawá.
Remote - - -	Ruhuk, ruhug.
Remove - - -	Ústí.
Repletion - -	Tufá (?).
Reply - - -	War. (Bring a reply: "War adej." Take my reply: "Ware ustí.")
Reptile - - -	Hubáb.
Residence - -	Gár.
Rest, *s.* - - -	Rá*h*ah (A.).
Return (*i.e.* give me back) - - -	Argabgilay*n*.
Revenge, *s.* - -	*K*isás (A.).
Take revenge - -	*K*isás ushú.
Reverse, *v.* - -	Gargab.
Reward - - -	Sakah ; dínat (?).
Rib - - -	Maytak.
Rich - - -	Ghaní (A.).
Rice - - -	Ruz (A.).
Ride, *v.* - - -	Isal.
Right (proper) -	*K*orám.
Right hand -	Kai*n*yít.
Right and left - -	Gurá wá Kai*n*yít.
Ring - - -	Makhtar.
Riot - - -	Matmáhat.
Rise up - - -	Hafbal.
Rising (ground) -	Karát.
Risk - - -	Fir.
River - - -	Zar ; Masrí (?).
Road - - -	Úga.
Roast, *v.* - -	Absil. (Roast the meat. "Basar absil.")

Rob, *v.* - - -	Rojh. (He robbed me. " Rojhá-bay*n*.")
Robber - - -	Rojhí.
Robbery - - -	Márojha.
Robe (woman's) -	Indosh írás.
,, (blue) - -	*T*áy írás.
,, (white) - -	Nají*h* írás.
Rock - - -	Sarí.
Rogue - - -	Mablúl.
Roof - - -	Darbenjí.
Room - - -	Kitrat.
Root - - -	Sirr ; Hedid (S.).
Rosary - - -	Tasbi*h* (A.).
Rose-water - -	Má-ward (A.).
Rope - - -	Fatít.
Ruin - - -	Kh'ráb (A.).
Ruler - - -	Nagáshí.
Run, *v.* - - -	Taráwat.
Run away ! - -	Rot ! Sik !

S.

Sack (ox-skin) -	Dawullá (large bags used on journeys).
,, (sheep-skin) -	Jíráb (A. c. small saddle-bags ; the bags for asses are called " Matan ").
Saddle - - -	Ko*r* (S. Ko*r*e) ; Hánká (?).
Saffron - - -	Waras (A.).
Saint - - -	Walí.
Salt - - -	Assú.
Sand - - -	Afar.
Sandals - - -	Ashín.
Sash (girdle) - -	Hankot.
Say, *v.* - - -	Asaynní.
Scales - - -	Mízá*n* (A.).
A single scale - -	Kaffí.

Scent	- - -	Súchná.
Scissors -	- -	Makrajah.
Scout	- - -	Ilálah (S.).
Scum	- - -	Wasakh (A.).
Sea	- - -	Bahr (A.).
Sea-coast	- -	Bahr aff.
By sea and by land		Bahrí wá barri (A.).
Seal	- - -	Tábá (A. c.).
Seal-ring	- -	Makhtar.
Search	- - -	Mafách.
Second (*ordinal n.*)	-	Kotkhá.
Secret	- - -	Sirrí (A.).
Secretly -	- -	Shemakna.
See, *v.*	- - -	Haych.
Self	- - -	Rúh (A.); Naf (A. c.).
Sell, *v.*	- - -	Assím.
Sepulchre	- -	Kabrí.
Serpent -	- -	Hifin; Hubáb.
Servant -	- -	Wandag.
Servile caste -	-	Bon (Dankalí word).
Seven	- - -	Sátí.
Seventh -	- -	Sátí khá.
Seventy -	- -	Sát assir.
Sew, *v.* -	- -	Sif. (" Sew the cloth," irás Sif.)
Shade (shadow)	-	*Ch*áyá (Sanscrit ?).
Shallow water	-	Tinneo mí.
Shame -	- -	Hayá (A.).
Shank -	- -	*K*ultum.
Sharp, *adj.*	-	Balah (ﻝ).
Shave, *v.*	-	Mashaylad.
She	- - -	Ittá.
Sheath (swords)	-	Síf gár (dagger's sheath, " shotal gár ").
Sheep	- - -	Táy.
Sheet	- - -	Láy morad ; irás.
Shepherd	- -	Agabarí.

Shirt	- - -	Kamís (A.).
Shield	- - -	Agrí.
Shop	- - -	Dukkán (A. There are no regular shops at Harar).
Short	- - -	Hájír.
Shot, s.	- - -	Risás (A.).
Shut, v.	- - -	Galab.
Sick	- - -	Nattú.
Sickle	- - -	Manja.
Silence, v.	- -	Ús.
Silver	- - -	Me'et.
Sin -	- - -	Abbá.
Sister	- - -	Ihít (A. c.).
Sit ! v.	- - -	Tageb.
Six -	- - -	Siddistí.
Sixth	- - -	Siddistíkhá.
Sixty	- - -	Siddistí assir.
Skin	- - -	Gogá.
„ (for water)	-	Kárbat (A. c.).
Skullcap -	- -	Kalotá (la Calotte).
Sky	- - -	Samí.
Slave (*mas.*)	-	Gáfá ; Wasíf ; Amhara.
„ (*fem.*)	-	Gafít ; Wasífít ; Amharít.
Sleep, v. -	- -	Manyít (Pass the night. "Heder"); Niyen (?).
Slippers -	- -	Ashín.
Small	- - -	Tinnéo ; Ted (?).
Small-pox	- -	Gifrí (in S. Fantú).
Smell (perfume)	-	Súchná.
Smoke, s.	- -	Tan.
„ v.	- -	Sich.
Snot	- - -	Infít.
Snuff (tobacco)	-	Jamalí (Give me a pinch of snuff, " Jamalí Makonat ").
Sole (of foot) -	-	Hardá.
Somali	- - -	Tumurr (a slighting name).

Son	-	-	- Lijgay.
Song	-	-	- Fa*k*arr.
Sore	-	-	- *Túlú.*
South	-	-	- Ke'ebá.
Span	-	-	- Zumzurtí.
Spear	-	-	- Waram.
Spider	-	-	- Asháráráhtí.
Spider's web	-		- Asháráráhtí gár.
Spittle	-	-	- Mirá*k* (A.).
Spoon	-	-	- Fanălah (S. Fandál).
Staff, *s.*	-	-	- Bartí.
Star	-	-	- *Túí* (توى).
Stench	-	-	- Chikná.
Stick	-	-	- Bartí.
Stone	-	-	- Ún.
Stop (hush)	-		- Sambal.
Street	-	-	- Magálah úga.
Strong	- '	-	- Tákh-zálá.
Stupravi matrem tuam (vulgar abuse)			A'e khá lagatkho.
Stuprari patrem tuum			Aukhá ligat.
It suffices	-		- Yokál.
Sugar	-	-	- Sukkar (A.).
Sugar-cane	-		- Âla Shankorr (S.).
Sun	-	-	- Írr.
Sweat	-	-	- Wizí.
Sweet	-	-	- Yatímál.
Switch	-	-	- Tinne'o bartí.
Sword	-	-	- Síf (A.).

T.

Take, *v.*	-	-	- Yakh (to woman " Yash ").
Take hold of	-		- La*h*at.
Take care		-	- Takayráh bá.

Tall	-	-	-	Gidorr.
Talisman	-	-	Kartás (A.).
Tax (on merchan- dise)	Ashúr (A. c.).
Tax (on land)	-	Zakáh (A.).
Tear	-	-	-	Ibí.
Ten	-	-	-	Assir (A. c.).
Tenth	-	-	Assirkhá.
That (*pr.*)	-	-	Yá.
Thatched hut	-	-	Gambisá.
Their	-	-	Ziꞥyo.
Then	-	-	Yí sá'ah.
Thence	-	-	Yí attay.
There	-	-	Yadday.
Here and there	-	Idday wá yadday.
Therefore	-	Yí le báytí.
These	-	-	Yí 'ach.
Thief	-	-	Rojhí (*fem.* Rojhít).
Thick	-	-	Wadal.
Thigh	-	-	Badú (?); Gonjí.
Thin	-	-	Gofáy.
Thine (thy)	-	-	-khá.
Thing	-	-	Sha'í (A. c.).
Third	-	-	Shíshtí khá.
Thirty	-	-	Saseh.
Thirst	-	-	*T*irrá.
Thirsty	-	-	*T*irrár.
This	-	-	Yí.
Thorn	-	-	Usukh.
Thorn fence	-	Hutur (Chuguf ?).
Thread	-	-	Fatlí (A. c.).
Three	-	-	Shíshtí.
Three quarters	-	Shíshtí rubá.
Thrice	-	-	Shíshtí muttí.
Throat	-	-	Hangúr ; marmar.
Throne	-	-	Tifán (?).

Throw, *v.*	- -	Ghínbá (?); ginyă.
Thumb -	- -	Gidir A*t*abi*n*yá.
Thunder -	- -	Birák (?); birág (A. c.).
Tie, *v.*	- - -	Ígad. (Tie the camel with a cord. "Gamaylah fatít be ígad.")
Tie (knot)	- -	Kátre (Knot with your cloth. " Irás be Kátre."); akoflí (?).
Time	- -	Sá'ah.
At what time?	-	Ay Sá'ah?
At all times	-	Kullu gírum.
Tired	- -	Dalágay.
Tobacco -	- -	Tunbákhú.
To -	- - -	Lay; le.
To-day -	- -	Hújí.
Toe	- -	Ingir a*t*abi*n*yá.
Together (with)	-	Báh. (I will go with you. "Án akhákh báh ilitákh.")
Tomb	- -	Kabrí.
To-morrow	- -	Gísh.
Tongue -	- -	Arrát.
Tooth	- -	Sin (A.).
Town	- -	Magálah.
Town-wall	- -	Jugal.
Travel, *v.*	- -	Sifar (A. c.).
Tree	- -	Lafú.
Tripe	- -	An*k*ar.
True	- -	*Hil*lú; *h*ullú.
Truly	- -	do. do.
Turband -	- -	imámat (A.).
Turband (Amir's)	-	Ká'úk (Turk.).
Turmeric	-	Húrdí injí.
Twenty -	- -	Koyah.
Tweezers	' - -	Ne*ch*; *K*arabah (?).
Twice	- -	Kot muttí.
Two	- - -	Kot.

U.

Ugly	- - -	Yagassál.
Ulcer	- - -	*Túlu*, *pl. Túlú'ash.*
Unarmed	- -	Agra waram zaltá (*lit.* shieldless and spearless).
Uncle (paternal)	-	Zer.
„ (maternal)	-	Káka.
Under	- - -	Taháy.
Understand	- -	Tukákh.
Unfortunate	- -	Ayyámúm aylá, *fem.* Ayyámúm aylí.
Unjust	- - -	Zálim (A.).
Unkind	- - -	Rahmatúm aylá, *fem.* rahmatúm aylí.
Unsafe	- - -	Amánúm altá, *fem.* amánúm altí.
Untie	- - -	Fitá*h* (A. c.).
Untrue	- - -	Kiz (A. c.).
Up -	- - -	Lá'ay.
Up and down	- -	Lá'ay wá taháy.
Go up !	- - -	Isal.
Bring up !	-	Lá'ay hafúsh.
Upon (it)	-	Usú lá'ay.
Urine	- - -	Shahad.
Us -	- - -	—ena.

V.

Value	- - -	Báy (What is the price of this ? " Báy zo mintá ? ")
Veil	- - -	Gulub (blue muslin fillet on women's hair).
Vein	- - -	Watar (A.).
Vengeance	- -	Kisás (A.).
Venom	- - -	Summí (A.).
Venomous	- -	Summí-zálá.
Venereal (disease)	-	Chob*t*ú ; Kitin.

Very	- - -	Bají*h*.
Very good	- -	Baji*h* korám.
Vile	- - -	Yegassí.
Village	- - -	Gandá; Tinne'o geh; tinne'o bád.
Viper	- - -	Hubáb summi-zálá.
Virgin	- - -	Wahashí.
Void (naked)	- -	Kofh.
Voice	- - -	*T*abă.
Vomit	- - -	Nataka.
Vow	- - -	Ballamá. (He vowed a mare. " Ballamá zi*n*ya inistí faras.")
Vulture	- - -	Áumar̈.

W.

Waist	- - -	Hankot.
Wall (house)	-	Digadag.
„ (town)	- -	Úgal.
Want, *s.*	- -	Hájah (A.).
„ *v.*	-	" Ahad ifájakh :" I want something. "Wandag akháshákh :" I want a servant.
War	- - -	Matmáhat.
Warm	- - -	Wiyí.
Was	- - -	Nár; fem. nártí.
Wash, *v. imp.* -	-	Mayeh.
Washing	- -	Wessá (the ablution called " Wuzú ").
Wätch	- - -	Zola*n*yá (night patrols through the city).
Water	- - -	Mí.
Water-pot	- -	Hán (S.).
Watered (garden, field, &c.)	- -	Masnú.
Wax	- - -	Shama (A.).
Way (road)	- -	Uga.
We	- - -	I*n*ya; i*n*yásh.

Weak	- - -	Tákhúm aylá.
Wealth	- - -	Bajíh dínat.
Weaver	- - -	Hayyák (A.).
Weigh	- - -	Amezní.
Weight	- - -	Mízán (A.).
Well (water)	- -	Zar (?).
Well (being)	- -	Amán (A.).
West	- - -	Írr kitbo (?); Kilmash (?).
Wet	- - -	Ruttá.
What ?	- - -	Mintá ?
Of what sort ?	-	Min Sinya (?).
Wheat	- - -	Ays (A. c.?).
Whence?	- -	Áyde ? (Whence comest thou ? " Áyde be díchkhi ? ").
Where?	- -	Baylá ? belá ?
Whetstone	- -	Moláh.
Whip	- - -	Kaytal (A. S.).
Whisper *v.*	- -	Íshayt be assayní.
Whistle	- - -	Afíj.
White	- - -	Najíh.
Who ?	- - -	Min ? (Who art thou ? " Min Sinyintakh ?").
Whore?	- - -	Gubnít.
Why?	- - -	Millay ? (Why dost thou beat me ? " Millay gadalkháyn ?").
Wick	- - -	Fatílat (A.).
Widow	- - -	Armalah (A.).
Widower	- -	Indosh motbá.
Wife	- - -	Indosh ; mishtí.
Wig (sheep-skin-dyed red)		Gurud; arabjí karr; timá bayt (S.).
Wind	- - -	Dúf.
Window	- - -	Taket (A. c.).
Wine	- - -	Gohay.
Wipe, *v.*	- -	Másh.
Within	- - -	Usto.

Without (outside) - Ká*ch*ay.
Without - - Aylám; aylúm (?).
Without reason - Sabab biláy.
Without hope - Haylad biláy.
Wolf - - - Warábá (S.).
Woman - - - Indosh; mishtí.
  ,, (barren) - Tuldúmayt.
  ,, (pregnant) - Karsí-zálí.
Wonder - - - Dink.
Wonderful - - Ajab (A.).
Wood - - - Inchí.
Word - - - Sinán.
Wound - - - Mahjá.
Write - - - Kitab.
Writing-board - Lo*h* (A.).

Y.

Yard (court) - . Katam-barí.
Year - - - Amad.
Last year - - Amná.
Every year - - Jammí ammatúm.
Yellow - - - Hurdí, *fem.* Hurdít.
Yes! - - - Í; áy.
Yet - - - Wílí.
You - - - Akhákhásh.
Young - - - Darmá.
Youth - - - Darmásh (?).

Z.

Zebra - - - Farrú (S.).
Zinc - - - *K*ay*h* birat.

APPENDIX III.

METEOROLOGICAL OBSERVATIONS IN THE COLD SEASON OF 1854—5

BY

Lieutenants HERNE, STROYAN, AND BURTON.

METEOROLOGICAL OBSERVATIONS by LIEUT. HERNE, at and near BERBERAH,

During the months of November and December, 1854.

Date.	Mountain Barometer 9 A.M. Barom.	Therm.	3 P.M. Barom.	Therm.	Aneroid Barometer 9 A.M. Barom.	Therm.	3 P.M. Barom.	Therm.	
1854. Nov. 17	-	-	-	-	30·065	78°	30·000	85°	At Aynterad.
„ 22	30·190	89°	-	-	30·200	89	-	-	At Berberah.
„ 23	30·190	88	30·150	87°	30·200	88	30·087	87	Ditto.
„ 24	-	-	30·150	87	-	-	30·100	87	Ditto.
„ 28	-	-	-	-	-	-	-	-	At the foot of the second range [of hills.
Dec. 2	-	-	-	-	27·025	73	-	-	At Garbadir.
„ 4	-	-	-	-	27·175	72	27·150	81	At half-past 1 P.M., barom. 24·600, therm. 68°, top of
„ 5	-	-	-	-	26·600	71	-	-	At the foot of Gulays. [Gulays.
„ 6	-	-	30·190	81	26·600	73	26·625	80	Ditto.
„ 15	-	-	-	-	26·625	73	-	-	At Berberah.
„ 16	30·300	88	-	-					
„ 21	30·250	80	30·130	81					
„ 22	30·200	80	-	-					
„ 24	30·190	79	30·050	83					
„ 25	30·150	88	30·050	83					
„ 26	30·182	86	-	-					
„ 27	30·190	70	30·050	82					
„ 28	30·150	86	30·050	82					
„ 29	30·200	88	30·080	84					
„ 30	30·190	87	30·080	84					
„ 31	30·200	85	-	-					

Corrections for Mountain Barometer.

Capacities. 1/50. Neutral point, 29·762. Capillary action, +·050. Temperature, 60°. Reading higher than Observatory Standard, 0·030.

METEOROLOGICAL OBSERVATIONS by LIEUT. HERNE, at and near BERBERAH, In January, 1855.

Date.	Mountain Barometer 9 A.M. Barom.	Therm.	Mountain Barometer 3 P.M. Barom.	Therm.	Aneroid Barometer 9 A.M. Barom.	Therm.	Aneroid Barometer 3 P.M. Barom.	Therm.	
1855.									These were taken at Berberah during what is termed the N.E. Monsun, the wind invariably coming from that quarter. The wind used to set in about half-past 9 A.M. and died away about 10 P.M.
Jan. 2	30·200	88°	30·100	87°					A gentle land wind always set in towards the morning.
„ 3	30·180	83	30·080	84					
„ 4	30·150	84	30·080	82					
„ 5	-	-	30·033	83					
„ 6	30·136	84	30·040	85	30·030	84°	29·975	84°	
„ 7	30·128	84	-	-	30·075	81	30·025	84	
„ 8	30·150	81	30·044	84	30·050	82	30·025	84	
„ 10	30·170	78	30·100	83	30·100	81	-	-	
„ 11	30·200	80	30·090	83	30·125	83	30·050	83	
„ 12	30·228	82	-	-	30·125	83	30·100	82	
„ 13	30·240	81	30·120	83	30·150	84	30·090	82	
„ 15	30·025	78	30·150	82	30·150	85	-	-	
„ 16	30·280	80	30·150	81	30·175	85	30·025	82	
„ 17	30·290	80	-	-	30·130	81	30·025	83	
„ 18	30·230	80	30·116	81	30·075	80	29·950	82	
„ 19	30·132	77	30·100	82	30·050	83	29·950	82	
„ 20	30·150	77	30·032	81	30·025	80	-	-	
„ 21	30·150	78	30·028	81	30·025	83	29·950	82	
„ 22	-	-	-	-	-	-	-	-	
„ 23	30·190	78	30·072	82	30·075	80	30·000	83	
„ 24	30·226	80	30·124	81	30·125	82	30·025	82	
„ 25	30·246	79	-	-	30·150	82	-	-	
„ 26	30·250	80	30·192	82	30·175	82	30·100	83	
„ 27	30·250	80	30·150	82	30·175	83	30·075	83	
„ 28	30·250	80	30·100	82	30·150	81	30·025	83	
„ 29	30·160	79	-	-	30·075	82	-	-	
„ 30	30·150	79	30·050	83	30·075	82	29·975	84	

Corrections for Mountain Barometer.

Capacities $\frac{1}{80}$. Neutral point, 29·762. Capillary action, +·050. Temperature, 60°. Reading higher than Observatory Standard, 0·030.

Date (1855)		Half-past 6 A.M. Barom.	Therm.	Half-past 9 A.M. Barom.	Therm.	Noon Barom.	Therm.	Half-past 3 P.M. Barom.	Therm.	Remarks
Feb. 8	Aner.	30·238	76°	30·286	79°	30·210	82°	30·150	81°	A little rain this morning.
		30·125	76	30·200	78	30·125	80	30·050	80	
„ 9	Aner.	30·160	74	–	–	–	–	–	–	Cloudy, and having the appearance of rain.
„ 10	Aner.	30·060	74	30·210	83	30·140	84	30·091	82	The last two at half-past 4.
		30·150	76	30·130	83	30·050	82	30·000	80	
„ 11	Aner.	30·050	76	30·180	81	30·118	82	30·056	82	
		30·140	77	30·100	81	30·100	80	30·000	80	
„ 12	Aner.	30·030	76	30·114	80	30·025	83	30·042	82	
		30·110	76	30·075	79	29·960	82	29·960	80	
„ 13	Aner.	30·010	76	30·114	79	30·092	80	30·038	81	Raining among the hills close to Berberah.
		30·116	77	30·070	78	30·025	78·5	29·975	79	
„ 14	Aner.	30·030	77	30·118	78	30·116	77	30·040	75	Had rain more or less up to 3 P.M.
		30·086	77	30·090	77	30·050	76	29·950	74	
„ 15	Aner.	30·015	76	–	–	30·110	76	29·950	75	Rain more or less the whole day.
		30·100	74	–	–	30·025	74	29·950	74	
„ 16	Aner.	30·000	73	–	–	30·026	79·5	29·982	77·5	Ditto.
„ 17	Aner.	–	–	30·100	77	29·912	78	29·900	76	Rain in the morning; remainder of day fine.
		–	–	30·000	76	30·046	80	30·000	79	
„ 18	Aner.	–	–	30·100	79	29·950	79	29·915	78	Rain in the morning.
*„ 19	Aner.	–	–	30·012	78	30·068	78	30·016	78	Rain in the afternoon.
„ 20	Aner.	29·925	73	–	–	29·960	76	29·925	77	Rain the whole day.
„ 21	„	29·950	73	30·000	79	29·975	86	29·915	76	Mountain barom. packed up.
„ 22	„	30·000	75	30·025	77	29·960	83	29·925	83	
„ 23	„	–	–	30·075	81	30·000	84	29·950	82	
„ 24	Moun.	30·025	77	30·060	84	30·050	84	30·000	85	
„ 25	Aner.	30·142	74	30·075	83	30·060	88			
„ 26	Moun.	30·012	73	30·125	83	30·200	88	30·000	84	Mountain barometer.
	Aner.			30·304	82	30·110	86	–	–	
„ 27	Aner.	–	–	30·175	83	30·246	87	30·200	84	
„ 28	Aner.	30·200	70	30·284	81	30·218	86	30·075	83	
Mar. 1	Aner.	30·060	68	30·264	82	30·112	85	30·148	83	
	Aner.	30·184	72	30·160	83	30·228	86	30·050	85	
„ 2		30·050	72	–	82	30·125	85	30·120	85	
„ 5	Aner.	–	–	–	–	30·172	86	30·050	84	
„ 6	Aner.	Dubar Aner.	72	30·050	82	29·500	85	30·134	84·5	
„ 7	Aner.	29·460	80	29·500	84	29·460	86	30·050	83	
						29·500	83	29·425	82	
						29·460	82	29·400	82	

N.B.—The Aneroid for February, 1855, was ·027 higher than Mountain barometer corrected for temperature.

* Moved into a tent from temporary house.

Mountain Barometer—Capacities, $\frac{1}{60}$. Neutral point, 29·762. Capillary action, +·050. Temperature, 60°. Reading higher than Observatory Standard, ·090.

THERMOMETRIC OBSERVATIONS by Lieut. BURTON,
During the month of November, 1854.

Date.	Temperature.			Remarks.
	6 A.M.	Noon	4 P.M.	
Nov. 4	78°	83°	83°	At Zayla. Thermometer placed in a room opening to the S. and W. Day cloudy, cirri; nights cool, heavy dew. Sea breeze from N.E.
5	81	82	-	Cirro-cumuli.
6	77	82	82	On the terrace at dawn 71°; in the sun at noon 118°. Sky clear; heavy dew at night.
7	78	81	-	Misty morning; dark horizon.
8	77	81	83	Air oppressive.
9	76	82	82	Zayla is open to both the land breeze (al-barri) and the sea breeze (al-bahri).
10	76	82	78	The sea breeze usually set in at 10 A.M., and continued as at Aden until sunset. Wind from W. and S.W.
11	77	82	-	The land breeze endured from nightfall till 8 A.M., when there was generally a a calm. Wind from N.E.
12	78	83	83	Nimbus in morning from E. and N.E. Cloudy day. Horizon dark at nightfall.
13	77	83	-	Hazy day; cold clear night.
14	75	81	83	Cold night; clear day.
15	79	83	83	Rain clouds gathering. Rain expected by people about this time.
16	79	83	84	Cloudy morning. In afternoon rain fell upon southern hills. Atmosphere close in plain.
17	82	83	84	Thunder in morning; close and cloudy at noon. At night rain fell on hills.
18	80	83	84	Cloudy morning.
19	81	83	83	Cloudy forenoon.
20	82	82	82	Rained heavily at Zayla from 9 A.M. to 2 P.M. Rain from N.E.
21	81	82	-	Fine clear day. Lightning at night.
22	82	83	-	Black clouds in morning from S.E. Windy night. Lightning from N.
23	82	83	83	Cloudy morning. Clear day.
24	76	82	82	Cool morning. Hot cloudy day.
25	78	82	-	Ditto. Ditto.
26	77	82	82	Fresh morning. Cloudless day. Fine evening. All signs of rain have vanished.
27	76	82	-	Cloudless day. Cool night.
28	-	88	88	Left Zayla at 3 P.M. on 27th Nov. In hut at Gudingaras on Zayla Plain. Sea breeze at 10 A.M.
29	73	-	88	At same place. Rain expected.
30	-	88	86	Cloudy morning. Cool day.

THERMOMETRIC OBSERVATIONS by Lieut. BURTON,
During the months of December 1854 and Jan. 1855.

Date.	Temperature.			Remarks.
	6 A.M.	Noon	4 P.M.	
1854.				
Dec. 1	72°	86°	84°	In hut. Light clouds at dawn. Hot day.
3	-	82	80	In hut below hills. Nimbus in morning. Hot sun.
4	70	80	-	Rain at 8 A.M. Cloudy day. Heavy dew at night.
5	-	80	-	In open air under tree. Hot sun. Cold night breeze.
6	-	79	80	In hut at foot of ascent. Wind gusty. Day cool and cloudy.
7	63	-	71	Under tree. Clear cold day. Hot sun at noon 107°.
8	52	73	-	Under tree. Cloudy morning. Cold day.
10	51	74	72	In hut below hills. Clear day; cold in shade; hot in sun.
11	56	72	-	Fine clear day. Atmosphere resembling that of Pisa, in Tuscany.
12	52	-	-	In hut. Hot sun. Cold wind.
13	61	78	80	In hut at Harawwah valley. No rain; season sickly; drought and dysentery.
14	54	-	-	Sun very hot, 120° at noon.
17	52	79	-	In hut at Agjogsi. At dawn 41°.
18	50	76	-	At Agjogsi, under the hill Koralay. Fine clear weather. Nomads lament want of rain.
19	41	71	-	
20	40	72	-	
21	42	74	-	
22	41	82	-	In hut under Konti hill. Close day.
23	51	-	-	Observations taken in open air.
24	-	73	72	In hut under Gurays hills. Sun powerful.
25	42	72	71	At the same place. Cool day.
26	51	-	-	Ditto. Till end of December cold winds and hot suns.
1855.				
Jan. 3	68	-	-	In hut below Kondura.
15	61	71	68	High wind. Cumuli. Furious wind at night.
16	58	69	69	Fine clear day.
17	56	72	6	Clouds on hill tops. Cold night and high wind. In hut, at Wilensi.
18	-	70	70	Hot day. No wind or clouds.
19	56	77	73	Hot day. Cloudless warm night.
20	56	78	-	Day hot and cloudless.
21	57	77	-	Fine warm day.
22	56	-	-	Left Wilensi. Hot day. Nimbi at 2 P.M. No rain. Warm night.
23	66	73	77	In the Marar Prairie. Warm cloudy day.

THERMOMETER BOILED.

Place.	Degrees.	Temperature.	Corrected Altitude.
Zayla (sea level) - - - -	210°	83°	
Halimalah (hill-top) - - -	204	64	3,347
Agjogsi (foot of Harar hills) -	201	79	5,133
Wilensi (near Harar) - - -	200	70	5,656
			Harar about 5,500
Berberah (level of sea) - -	210	86	

APPENDIX IV.

APPENDIX IV.

The Publishers of the First Edition of this Book found it "necessary to omit this Appendix," as to which see p. xxvii, vol. i, *ante*.

APPENDIX V.

APPENDIX V.

CONDENSED ACCOUNT

OF

AN ATTEMPT TO REACH HARAR FROM ANKOBAR.

The author Lieutenant, now Commander, WILLIAM BARKER of the Indian Navy, was one of the travellers who accompanied Sir William Cornwallis, then Captain, Harris on his mission to the court of Shoa. His services being required by the Bombay Government, he was directed by Captain Harris, on October 14th, 1841, to repair to the coast *viâ* Harar, by a road "hitherto untrodden by Europeans." These pages will reward perusal as a narrative of adventure, especially as they admirably show what obstacles the suspicious characters and the vain terrors of the Badawin have thrown in the way of energy and enterprise.

A CONDENSED ACCOUNT, &c.

———————

"*Aden, February* 28, 1842.

"SHORTLY after I had closed my last communication to Captain Harris of the Bombay Engineers on special duty at the Court of Shoa (14. Jan. 1842), a report arrived at Allio Amba that Demetrius, an Albanian who had been for ten years resident in the Kingdom of Shoa, and who had left it for Tajoorah, accompanied by "Johannes," another Albanian, by three Arabs, formerly servants of the Embassy, and by several slaves, had been murdered by the Bedoos (Badawin) near Murroo. This caused a panic among my servants. I allayed it with difficulty, but my interpreter declared his final intention of deserting me, as the Hurruri caravan had threatened to kill him if he persisted in accompanying me. Before proceeding farther it may be as well to mention that I had with me four servants, one a mere lad, six mules and nine asses to carry my luggage and provisions.

"I had now made every arrangement, having as the Wallasena Mahomed Abugas suggested, purchased a fine horse and a Tobe for my protector and guide, Datah Mahomed of the clan Seedy Habroo, a subtribe of the Debenah. It was too late to recede: accordingly at an early hour on Saturday, the 15th January, 1842, I commenced packing, and at about 8 A.M. took my departure from the village of Allio Amba. I had spent there a weary three months, and left it with that mixture of pleasure and regret felt only by those who traverse unknown and inhospitable regions. I had made many friends, who accompanied me for some distance on the road, and took leave of me with a deep feeling which assured me of their sympathy. Many endeavoured to dissuade me from the journey, but my lot was cast.

" About five miles from Allio, I met the nephew of the Wallasena, who accompanied me to Farri, furnished me with a house there, and ordered my mules and asses to be taken care of. Shortly after my arrival the guide, an old man, made his appearance and seemed much pleased by my punctuality.

" At noon on Sunday the 16th, the Wallasena arrived, and sent over his compliments, with a present of five loaves of bread. I called upon him in the evening, and reminded him of the letter he had promised me; he ordered it to be prepared, taking for copy the letter which the king (Sahala Salassah of Shoa) had given to me.

" My guide having again promised to forward me in safety, the Wallasena presented him with a spear, a shield, and a Tobe, together with the horse and the cloth which I had purchased for him. About noon on Monday the 17th, we quitted Farri with a slave-caravan bound for Tajoorah. I was acquainted with many of these people, the Wallasena also recommended me strongly to the care of Mahomed ibn Buraitoo and Dorranu ibn Kamil. We proceeded to Datharal, the Wallasena and his nephew having escorted me as far as Denehmelli, where they took leave. I found the Caffilah to consist of fifteen Tajoorians, and about fifty camels laden with provisions for the road, fifty male and about twenty female slaves, mostly children from eight to ten years of age. My guide had with him five camels laden with grain, two men and two women.

"The Ras el Caffilah (chief of the caravan) was one Ibrahim ibn Boorantoo, who it appears had been chief of the embassy caravan, although Essakh (Ishak) gave out that *he* was. It is certain that this man always gave orders for pitching the camp and for loading; but we being unaware of the fact that he was Ras el Caffilah, he had not received presents on the arrival of the Embassy at Shoa. Whilst unloading the camels, the following conversation took place. 'Yá Kabtán!' (O Captain) said he addressing me with a sneer, 'where are you going to?—do you think the Bedoos will let you pass through their country? We shall see! Now I will tell you!—you Feringis have treated me very ill!—you loaded Essakh and others with presents, but never gave me anything. I have as it were a knife in my stomach which is continually cutting me—this knife you have placed there! But, inshallah! it is now my turn! I will be equal with you!—you think of going to Hurrur—we shall see!' I replied, 'You know me not! It is true I was ignorant that you were Ras el Caffilah on our way to Shoa. You say you have a knive cutting your inside—I can remove that knife! Those who treat me well, now that I am returning to my country, shall be rewarded; for, the Lord be praised! there I have the means of repaying my friends, but in Shoa I am a beggar. Those that treat me ill shall also receive their reward.'

"My mules, being frightened at the sight of the camels, were exceedingly restive: one of them strayed and was brought back by Deeni ibn Hamed, a young man who was indebted to me for some medicines and a trifling present which he had received from the embassy. Ibrahim, the Ras el Caffilah, seeing him lead it back, called out, 'So you also have become servant to the Kafir (infidel)!' At the same time Datah Mahomed, the guide, addressed to me some remark which he asked Ibrahim to explain ; the latter replied in a sarcastic manner in Arabic, a language with which I am unacquainted.[1] This determined hostility on the part of the Ras el Caffilah was particularly distressing to me, as I feared he would do me much mischief. I therefore determined to gain him over to my interests, and accordingly, taking Deeni on one side, I promised him a handsome present if he would take an opportunity of explaining to Ibrahim that he should be well rewarded if he behaved properly, and at the same time that if he acted badly, that a line or two sent to Aden would do him harm. I also begged him to act as my interpreter as long as we were together, and he cheerfully agreed to do so.

" We were on the point of resuming our journey on Tuesday the 18th, when it was found that the mule of the Ras el Caffilah had strayed. After his conduct on the preceding evening, he was ashamed to come to me, but he deputed one of the caravan people to request the loan of one of my mules to go in quest of his. I gave him one readily. We were detained that day as the missing animal was not brought back till late. Notwithstanding my civility, I observed him in close conversation with Datah Mahomed, about the rich presents which the Feringis had given to Essakh and others, and I frequently observed him pointing to my luggage in an expressive manner. Towards evening the guide came to me and said, ' My son! I am an old man, my teeth are bad, I cannot eat this parched grain—I see you eat bread. Now we are friends, you must give me some of it ! ' I replied that several times after preparing for the journey, I had been disappointed and at last started on a short notice—that I was but scantily supplied with provisions, and had a long journey before me : notwith-

---

[1] Thus in the original. It may be a mistake, for Captain Barker is, I am informed, a proficient in conversational Arabic.

standing which I was perfectly willing that he should share with me what I had as long as it lasted, and that as he was a great chief, I expected that he would furnish me with a fresh supply on arriving at his country. He then said, 'it is well! but why did you not buy me a mule instead of a horse?' My reply was that I had supposed that the latter would be more acceptable to him. I divided the night into three watches: my servants kept the first and middle, and myself the morning.

" We quitted Dattenab, the frontier station, at about 7 o'clock A.M., on Wednesday the 19th. The country at this season presented a more lively appearance than when we travelled over it before, grass being abundant: on the trees by the roadside was much gum Acacia, which the Caffilah people collected as they passed. I was pleased to remark that Ibrahim was the only person ill-disposed towards me, the rest of the travellers were civil and respectful. At noon we halted under some trees by the wayside. Presently we were accosted by six Bedoos of the Woëmah tribe who were travelling from Keelulho to Shoa : they informed us that Demetrius had been plundered and stripped by the Takyle tribe, that one Arab and three male slaves had been slain, and that another Arab had fled on horseback to the Etoh (Ittu) Gallas, whence nothing more had been heard of him : the rest of the party were living under the protection of Shaykh Omar Buttoo of the Takyle. The Bedoos added that plunderers were lying in wait on the banks of the River Howash for the white people that were about to leave Shoa. The Ras el Caffilah communicated to me this intelligence, and concluded by saying: ' Now, if you wish to return, I will take you back, but if you say forward, let us proceed! ' I answered, ' let us proceed! ' I must own that the intelligence pleased me not: two of my servants were for returning, but they were persuaded to go on to the next station, where we would be guided by circumstances. About 2 o'clock P. M. we again proceeded, after a long "Cullam" or talk, which ended in Datah Mahomed, sending for assistance to a neighbouring tribe. During a conversation with the Ras el Caffilah, I found out that the Bedoos were lying in wait, not for the white people, but for our caravan. It came out these Bedouins had had the worst of a quarrel with the last Caffilah from Tajoorah : they then threatened to attack it in force on its return. The Ras el Caffilah was assured that as long as we journeyed together, I should consider his enemies my enemies, and that being well supplied with firearms, I would assist him on all occasions. This offer pleased him, and we became more friendly. We passed several deserted villages of the Bedoos, who had retired for want of water towards the Wadys, and about 7 o'clock P. M. halted at the lake Leadoo.

"On the morning of Thursday the 20th, Datah Mahomed came to me and delivered himself through Deeni as follows : 'My son ! our father the Wallasena entrusted you to my care, we feasted together in Gouchoo —you are to me as the son of my house ! Yesterday I heard that the Bedoos were waiting to kill, but fear not, for I have sent to the Seedy Habroo for some soldiers, who will be here soon. Now these soldiers are sent for on your account ; they will want much cloth, but you are a sensible person, and will of course pay them well. They will accompany us beyond the Howash !' I replied, 'It is true, the Wallasena entrusted me to your care. He also told me that you were a great chief, and could forward me on my journey. I therefore did not prepare a large supply of cloth—a long journey is before me—what can be spared shall be freely given, but you must tell the soldiers that I have but little. You are now my father !'

" Scarcely had I ceased when the soldiers, fine stout-looking savages, armed with spear, shield, and crease, mustering about twenty-five, made their appearance. It was then 10 A.M. The word was given to load the camels, and we soon moved forward. I found my worthy protector exceedingly good-natured and civil, dragging on my asses and leading my mules. Near the Howash we passed several villages, in which I could not but remark the great proportion of children. At about 3 P.M. we forded the river, which was waist-deep, and on the banks of which were at least 3,000 head of horned cattle. Seeing no signs of the expected enemy, we journeyed on till 5 P.M., when we halted at the south-eastern extremity of the Howash Plain, about one mile to the eastward of a small pool of water.

" At daylight on Friday the 21st it was discovered that Datah Mahomed's horse had disappeared. This was entirely his fault ; my servants had brought it back when it strayed during the night, but he said, ' Let it feed, it will not run away ! ' When I condoled with him on the loss of so noble an animal, he replied, ' I know very well who has taken it : one of my cousins asked me for it yesterday, and because I refused to give it he has stolen it ; never mind, Inshallah ! I will steal some of his camels.' After a ' Cullam ' about what was to be given to our worthy protectors, it was settled that I should contribute three cloths and the Caffilah ten ; receiving these, they departed much satisfied. Having filled our water-skins, we resumed our march a little before noon. Several herds of antelope and wild asses appeared on the way. At 7 P.M. we halted near Hano. Prevented from lighting a fire for fear of the Galla, I was obliged to content myself with some parched grain, of which I had prepared a large supply.

" At sunrise on the 22nd we resumed our journey, the weather becoming warm and the grass scanty. At noon we halted near Shaykh Othman. I was glad to find that Deeni had succeeded in converting the Ras el Caffilah from an avowed enemy to a staunch friend, at least outwardly so; he has now become as civil and obliging as he was before the contrary. There being no water at this station, I desired my servant Adam not to make any bread, contenting myself with the same fare as that of the preceding evening. This displeasing Datah Mahomed, some misunderstanding arose, which, from their ignorance of each other's language, might, but for the interference of the Ras el Caffilah and Deeni, have led to serious results. An explanation ensued, which ended in Datah Mahomed seizing me by the beard, hugging and embracing me in a manner truly unpleasant. I then desired Adam to make him some bread and coffee, and harmony was once more restored. This little disturbance convinced me that if once left among these savages without any interpreter, that I should be placed in a very dangerous situation. The Ras el Caffilah also told me that unless he saw that the road was clear for me to Hurrur, and that there was no danger to be apprehended, that he could not think of leaving me, but should take me with him to Tajoorah. He continued, 'You know not the Emir of Hurrur: when he hears of your approach he will cause you to be waylaid by the Galla. Why not come with me to Tajoorah? If you fear being in want of provisions we have plenty, and you shall share all we have!' I was much surprised at this change of conduct on the part of the Ras el Caffilah, and by way of encouraging him to continue friendly, spared not to flatter him, saying it was true I did not know him before, but now I saw he was a man of excellent disposition. At 3 P.M. we again moved forward. Grass became more abundant; in some places it was luxuriant and yet green. We halted at 8 P.M. The night was cold with a heavy dew, and there being no fuel, I again contented myself with parched grain.

" At daylight on the 23rd we resumed our march. Datah Mahomed asked for two mules, that he and his friend might ride forward to prepare for my reception at his village. I lent him the animals, but after a few minutes he returned to say that I had given him the two worst, and he would not go till I dismounted and gave him the mule which I was riding. About noon we arrived at the lake Toor Erain Murroo, where the Bedouins were in great numbers watering their flocks and herds, at least 3,000 head of horned cattle and sheep innumerable. Datah Mahomed, on my arrival, invited me to be seated under the shade of a spreading tree, and having introduced me to his people as his guest and the friend of the Wallasena, immediately ordered some milk, which was brought in a huge bowl fresh and warm from the cow ; my servants were similarly provided. During the night Adam shot a fox, which greatly astonished the Bedouins, and gave them even more dread of our fire-arms. Hearing that Demetrius and his party, who had been plundered of everything, were living at a village not far distant, I offered to pay the Ras el Caffilah any expense he might be put to if he would permit them to accompany our caravan to Tajoorah. He said that he had no objection to their joining the Caffilah, but that he had been informed their wish was to return to Shoa. I had a long conversation with the Ras, who begged of me not to go to Hurrur ; 'for,' he said, ' it is well known that the Hurruri caravan remained behind solely on your account. You will therefore enter the town, should you by good fortune arrive there at all, under unfavourable circumstances. I am sure that the Emir,[1] who may receive you kindly, will eventually do you much mischief, besides which these Bedouins will plunder you of all your property.' The other people of the caravan, who are all

---

1 This chief was the Emir Abubakr, father of Ahmed : the latter was ruling when I entered Harar in 1855.

my friends, also spoke in the same strain. This being noted as a bad halting place, all kept watch with us during the night.

"The mules and camels having had their morning feed, we set out at about 10 A.M. on Monday the 24th for the village of Datah Mahomed, he having invited the Caffilah's people and ourselves to partake of his hospitality and be present at his marriage festivities. The place is situated about half a mile to the E. N. E. of the lake; it consists of about sixty huts, surrounded by a thorn fence with separate enclosures for the cattle. The huts are formed of curved sticks, with their ends fastened in the ground, covered with mats, in shape approaching to oval, about five feet high, fifteen feet long, and eight broad. Arrived at the village, we found the elders seated under the shade of a venerable Acacia feasting; six bullocks were immediately slaughtered for the Caffilah and ourselves. At sunset a camel was brought out in front of the building and killed—the Bedoos are extremely fond of this meat. In the evening I had a long conversation with Datah Mahomed, who said, 'My son! you have as yet given me nothing. The Wallasena gave me everything. My horse has been stolen—I want a mule and much cloth.' Deeni replied for me that the mules were presents from the king (Sahala Salassah) to the Governor of Aden: this the old man would not believe. I told him that I had given him the horse and Tobe, but he exclaimed, 'No, no! my son; the Wallasena is our father; he told me that he had given them to me, and also that you would give me great things when you arrived at my village. My son! the Wallasena would not lie.' Datah was then called away.

"Early on the morning of Tuesday the 25th, Datah Mahomed invited me and the elders of the Caffilah to his hut, where he supplied us liberally with milk; clarified butter was then handed round, and the Tajoorians anointed their bodies. After we had left his hut, he came to me, and in presence of the Ras el Caffilah and Deeni said, ' You see I have treated you with great honour, you must give me a mule and plenty of cloth, as all my people want cloth. You have given me nothing as yet !' Seeing that I became rather angry, and declared solemnly that I had given him the horse and Tobe, he smiled and said, ' I know that, but I want a mule, my horse has been stolen.' I replied that I would see about it. He then asked for all my blue cloth and my Arab 'Camblee' (blanket). My portmanteau being rather the worse for wear—its upper leather was torn— he thrust in his fingers, and said, with a most avaricious grin, ' What have you here ? ' I immediately arose and exclaimed, ' You are not my father; the Wallasena told me you would treat me kindly ; this is not doing so.' He begged pardon and said, ' Do not be frightened, my son ; I will take nothing from you but what you give me freely. You think I am a bad man ; people have been telling you ill things about me. I am now an old man, and have given up such child's work as plundering people.' It became, however, necessary to inquire of Datah Mahomed what were his intentions with regard to myself. I found that I had been deceived at Shoa ; there it was asserted that he lived at Errur and was brother to Bedar, one of the most powerful chiefs of the Adel, instead of which it proved that he was not so highly connected, and that he visited Errur only occasionally. Datah told me that his marriage feast would last seven days, after which he would forward me to Doomi, where we should find Bedar, who would send me either to Tajoorah or to Hurrur, as he saw fit.

" I now perceived that all hope of reaching Hurrur was at an end. Vexed and disappointed at having suffered so much in vain, I was obliged to resign the idea of going there for the following reasons : The Mission treasury was at so low an ebb that I had left Shoa with only three German crowns, and the prospect of meeting on the road Mahomed Ali in charge of the second division of the Embassy and the presents, who could have supplied me with money. The constant demands of Datah Mahomed for tobacco, for cloth, in fact for everything he saw, would become ten times more annoying were I left with him without an interpreter. The Tajoorians, also, one and all, begged me not to remain, saying, 'Think not of your property, but only of your and your servants' lives. Come with us to Tajoorah; we will travel quick, and you shall share our provisions.' At last I consented to this new arrangement, and Datah Mahomed made no objection. This individual, however, did not leave me till he had extorted from me my best mule, all my Tobes (eight in number), and three others, which I borrowed from the caravan people. He departed about midnight, saying that he would take away his mule in the morning.

"At 4 A.M. on the 26th I was disturbed by Datah Mahomed, who took away his mule, and then asked for more cloth, which was resolutely refused. He then begged for my 'Camblee,' which, as it was my only covering, I would not part with, and checked him by desiring him to strip me if he wished it. He then left me and returned in about an hour with a particular friend who had come a long way expressly to see me. I acknowledged the honour, and deeply regretted that I had only words to pay for it, he himself having received my last Tobe. 'However,' I continued, seeing the old man's brow darken, 'I will endeavour to borrow one from the Caffilah people.' Deeni brought me one, which was rejected as inferior. I then said, 'You see my dress—that cloth is better than what I wear—but here; take my turban.' This had the desired effect; the cloth was accepted. At length Datah Mahomed delivered me over to the charge of the Ras el Caffilah in a very impressive manner, and gave me his blessing. We resumed our journey at 2 P.M., when I joined heartily with the caravan people in their ' Praise be to God! we are at length clear of the Bedoos!' About 8 P.M. we halted at Metta.

"At half-past 4 A.M. on the 27th we started; all the people of the Caffilah were warm in their congratulations that I had given up the Hurrur route. At 9 A.M. we halted at Codaitoo: the country bears marks of having been thickly inhabited during the rains, but at present, owing to the want of water, not an individual was to be met with. At Murroo we filled our water-skins, there being no water between that place and Doomi, distant two days' journey. As the Ras el Caffilah had heard that the Bedoos were as numerous as the hairs of his head at Doomi and Keelulhoo, he determined to avoid both and proceed direct to Warrahambili, where water was plentiful and Bedoos were few, owing to the scarcity of grass. This, he said, was partly on my account and partly on his own, as he would be much troubled by the Bedouins of Doomi, many of them being his kinsmen. We continued our march from 3 P.M. till 9 P.M., when we halted at Boonderrah.

"At 4 P.M., on January 28th, we moved forward through the Wady Boonderrah, which was dry at that season; grass, however, was still abundant. From 11 A.M. till 4 P.M., we halted at Geera Dohiba. Then again advancing we traversed, by a very rough road, a deep ravine, called the " Place of Lions." The slaves are now beginning to be much knocked up, many of them during the last march were obliged to be put upon camels. I forgot to mention that one died the day we left Murroo. At 10 P.M. we halted at Hagaioo Geera Dohiba: this was formerly the dwelling-place of Hagaioo, chief of the Woemah (Dankali), but the Eesa Somali having made a successful attack upon him, and swept off all his cattle, he deserted it. During the night the barking of dogs betrayed the vicinity of a Bedoo encampment, and caused us to keep a good look-out. Water being too scarce to make bread, I contented myself with coffee and parched grain.

"At daylight on the 29th we resumed our journey, and passed by an encampment of the Eesa. About noon we reached Warrahambili. Thus far we have done well, but the slaves are now so exhausted that a halt of two days will be necessary to recruit their strength. In this Wady we found an abundance of slightly brackish water, and a hot spring.

"*Sunday, 30th January.*—A Caffilah, travelling from Tajoorah to Shoa, passed by. The people kindly offered to take my letters. Mahomed ibn Boraitoo, one of the principal people in the Caffilah, presented me with a fine sheep and a quantity of milk, which I was glad to accept. There had been a long-standing quarrel between him and our Ras el Caffilah. When the latter heard that I accepted the present he became very angry, and said to my servant, Adam, ' Very well, your master chooses to take things from other people; why did he not ask me if he wanted sheep? We shall see!' Adam interrupted him by saying, ' Be not angry; my master did not ask for the sheep, it was brought to him as a present; it has been slaughtered, and I was just looking for you to distribute it among the people of the Caffilah.' This appeased him; and Adam added, ' If my master hears your words he will be angry, for he wishes to be friends with all people.' I mention the above merely to show how very little excites these savages to anger. The man who gave me the sheep, hearing that I wished to go to Tajoorah, offered to take me there in four days. I told him I would first consult the Ras el Caffilah, who declared it would not be safe for me to proceed from this alone, but that from Dakwaylaka (three marches in advance) he himself would accompany me in. The Ras then presented me with a sheep.

" We resumed our journey at 1 P.M., January 31st, passed several parties of Eesa, and at 8 P.M. halted at Burroo Ruddah.

"On February 1st we marched from 4 A.M. to 11 A.M., when we halted in the Wady Fiahloo, dry at this season. Grass was abundant. At 3 P.M. we resumed our journey. Crossing the plain of Amahdoo some men were observed to the southward, marching towards the Caffilah; the alarm and the order to close up were instantly given; our men threw aside their upper garments and prepared for action, being fully persuaded that it was a party of Eesa coming to attack them. However, on nearer approach we observed several camels with them; two men were sent on to inquire who they were; they proved to be a party of Somalis going to Ousak for grain. At 8 P.M. we halted on the plain of Dakwaylaka.

" At daylight on February the 2nd, the Ras el Caffilah, Deeni, and Mahomed accompaniėd me in advance of the caravan to water our mules at Dakway-laka. Arriving there about 11 A.M. we found the Bedoos watering their cattle. Mahomed unbridled his animal, which rushed towards the trough from which the cattle were drinking; the fair maid who was at the well baling out the water into the trough immediately set up the shrill cry of alarm, and we were compelled to move about a mile up the Wady, when we came to a pool of water black as ink. Thirsty as I was I could not touch the stuff. The Caffilah arrived about half-past 1 P.M., by which time the cattle of the Bedoos had all been driven off to grass, so that the well was at our service. We encamped close to it. Ibrahim recommended that Adam Burroo of the Assoubal tribe, a young Bedoo, and a relation of his should accompany our party. I promised

him ten dollars at Tajoorah.[1] At 3 P.M., having completed my arrangements, and leaving one servant behind
to bring up the luggage, I quitted the Caffilah amidst the
universal blessings of the people. I was accompanied by
Ibrahim, the Ras el Caffilah, Deeni ibn Hamid, my
interpreter, three of my servants, and the young Bedoo,
all mounted on mules. One baggage mule, fastened
behind one of my servants' animals, carried a little flour,
parched grain, and coffee, coffee-pot, frying-pan, and one
suit of clothes for each. Advancing at a rapid pace,
about 5 P.M. we came up with a party consisting of Eesa,
with their camels. One of them instantly collected the
camels, whilst the others hurried towards us in a suspicious way. The Bedoo hastened to meet them, and
we were permitted, owing, I was told, to my firearms,
the appearance of which pleased them not, to proceed
quietly. At 7 P.M., having arrived at a place where
grass was abundant, we turned off the road and halted.

"At 1.30 A.M., on Thursday, 3rd February, as the
moon rose we saddled our mules and pushed forward at
a rapid pace. At 4 A.M. we halted and had a cup of
coffee each, when we again mounted. As the day broke
we came upon an encampment of the Debeneh, who
hearing the clatter of our mules' hoofs, set up the cry of
alarm. The Bedoo pacified them : they had supposed
us to be a party of Eesa. We continued our journey, and
about 10 A.M. we halted for breakfast, which consisted of
coffee and parched grain. At noon we again moved
forward, and at 3 P.M. having arrived at a pool of water
called Murhabr in the Wady Dalabayah, we halted for
about an hour to make some bread. We then continued
through the Wady, passed several Bedoo encampments

---

1 As the youth gave perfect satisfaction, he received, besides
the ten dollars, a Tobe and a European saddle, "to which he had
taken a great fancy."

till a little after dark, when we descended into the plain of Gurgudeli. Here observing several fires, the Bedoo crawled along to reconnoitre, and returned to say they were Debeneh. We gave them a wide berth, and about 8.30 P.M. halted. We were cautioned not to make a fire, but I had a great desire for a cup of coffee after the fatigue of this long march. Accordingly we made a small fire, concealing it with shields.

" At 3 A.M. on Friday, the 4th February, we resumed our journey. After about an hour and a half arriving at a good grazing ground, we halted to feed the mules, and then watered them at Alooli. At 1 P.M. I found the sun so oppressive that I was obliged to halt for two hours. We had struck off to the right of the route pursued by the Embassy, and crossed, not the Salt Lake, but the hills to the southward. The wind blowing very strong considerably retarded our progress, so that we did not arrive at Dahfurri, our halting-place, till sunset. Dahfurri is situated about four miles to the southward of Mhow, the encampment of the Embassy near the Lake, and about 300 yards to the eastward of the road. Here we found a large basin of excellent water, which the Tajoorians informed me was a mere mass of mud when we passed by to Shoa, but that the late rains had cleared away all the impurities. After sunset a gale of wind blew.

" At 1 A.M. on the 5th February, the wind having decreased we started. Passing through the pass of the Rer Eesa, the barking of dogs caused us some little uneasiness, as it betrayed the vicinity of the Bedoo, whether friend or foe we knew not. Ibrahim requested us to keep close order, and to be silent. As day broke we descended into the plain of Warrah Lissun, where we halted and ate the last of the grain. After half an hour's halt we continued our journey. Ibrahim soon declared his inability to keep up with us, so he recommended me to the care of the Bedoo and Deeni, saying he would follow slowly. We arrived at Sagulloo about 11 A.M., and Ibrahim about two hours afterwards. At 3 P.M. we resumed our march, and a little before sunset arrived at Ambaboo.

"The elders had a conference which lasted about a quarter of an hour, when they came forward and welcomed me, directing men to look after my mules. I was led to a house which had been cleaned for my reception. Ibrahim then brought water and a bag of dates, and shortly afterwards some rice and milk. Many villagers called to pay their respects, and remained but a short time as I wanted repose: they would scarcely believe that I had travelled in eighteen days from Shoa, including four days' halt.

"Early on the morning of the 6th February I set out for Tajoorah, where I was received with every demonstration of welcome by both rich and poor. The Sultan gave me his house, and after I had drunk a cup of coffee with him, considerately ordered away all the people who had flocked to see me, as, he remarked, I must be tired after so rapid a journey.

"It may not be amiss to mention here that the British character stands very high at Tajoorah. The people assured me that since the British had taken Aden they had enjoyed peace and security, and that from being beggars they had become princes. As a proof of their sincerity they said with pride, ' Look at our village, you saw it a year and a half ago, you know what it was then, behold what is now ! ' I confessed that it had been much improved."

(From Tajoorah the traveller, after rewarding his attendants, took boat for Zayla, where he was hospitably received by the Hajj Sharmarkay's agent. Suffering severely from fever, on Monday the 14th February he put to sea again and visited Berberah, where he lived in

Sharmarkay's house, and finally he arrived at Aden on Friday the 25th February, 1842. He concludes the narrative of his adventure as follows.)

"It is due to myself that I should offer some explanation for the rough manner in which this report is drawn up. On leaving Shoa the Caffilah people marked with a jealous eye that I seemed to number the slaves and camels, and Deeni reported to me that they had observed my making entries in my note-book. Whenever the Bedoos on the road caught sight of a piece of paper, they were loud in their demands for it.[1] Our marches were so rapid that I was scarcely allowed time sufficient to prepare for the fatigues of the ensuing day, and experience had taught me the necessity of keeping a vigilant watch.[2] Aware that Government must be anxious for information from the 'Mission,' I performed the journey in a shorter space of time than any messenger, however highly paid, has yet done it, and for several days lived on coffee and parched grain. Moreover, on arrival at Aden, I was so weak from severe illness that I could write but at short intervals.

"It will not, I trust, be considered that the alteration in my route was caused by trivial circumstances. It would have been absurd to have remained with the Bedoos without an interpreter : there would have been daily disputes and misunderstandings, and I had already sufficient insight into the character of Datah Mahomed

---

1 In these wild countries every bit of paper written over is considered to be a talisman or charm.

2 A sergeant, a corporal, and a Portuguese cook belonging to Captain Harris's mission were treacherously slain near Tajoorah at night. The murderers were Hamid Saborayto and Mohammed Saborayto, two Dankalis of the Ad Ali clan. In 1842 they seem to have tried a *ruse de guerre* upon M. Rochet, and received from him only too mild a chastisement. The ruffians still live at Juddah (Jubbah ?) near Ambabo.

to perceive that his avarice was insatiable. Supposing I had passed through his hands, there was the chief of Bedar, who, besides expecting much more than I had given to Datah Mahomed, would, it is almost certain, eventually have forwarded me to Tajoorah. Finally, if I can believe the innumerable reports of the people, both at Tajoorah and Zalaya, neither I myself nor my servants would ever have passed through the kingdom of Hurrur. The jealousy of the prince against foreigners is so great that, although he would not injure them within the limits of his own dominions, he would cause them to be waylaid and murdered on the road."

INDEX.

INDEX.

THE END.

A CATALOG OF SELECTED
DOVER BOOKS
IN ALL FIELDS OF INTEREST

A CATALOG OF SELECTED DOVER
BOOKS IN ALL FIELDS OF INTEREST

DRAWINGS OF REMBRANDT, edited by Seymour Slive. Updated Lippmann, Hofstede de Groot edition, with definitive scholarly apparatus. All portraits, biblical sketches, landscapes, nudes. Oriental figures, classical studies, together with selection of work by followers. 550 illustrations. Total of 630pp. 9⅛ × 12¼.
21485-0, 21486-9 Pa., Two-vol. set $25.00

GHOST AND HORROR STORIES OF AMBROSE BIERCE, Ambrose Bierce. 24 tales vividly imagined, strangely prophetic, and decades ahead of their time in technical skill: "The Damned Thing," "An Inhabitant of Carcosa," "The Eyes of the Panther," "Moxon's Master," and 20 more. 199pp. 5⅜ × 8½. 20767-6 Pa. $3.95

ETHICAL WRITINGS OF MAIMONIDES, Maimonides. Most significant ethical works of great medieval sage, newly translated for utmost precision, readability. Laws Concerning Character Traits, Eight Chapters, more. 192pp. 5⅜ × 8½.
24522-5 Pa. $4.50

THE EXPLORATION OF THE COLORADO RIVER AND ITS CANYONS, J. W. Powell. Full text of Powell's 1,000-mile expedition down the fabled Colorado in 1869. Superb account of terrain, geology, vegetation, Indians, famine, mutiny, treacherous rapids, mighty canyons, during exploration of last unknown part of continental U.S. 400pp. 5⅜ × 8½. 20094-9 Pa. $6.95

HISTORY OF PHILOSOPHY, Julián Marías. Clearest one-volume history on the market. Every major philosopher and dozens of others, to Existentialism and later. 505pp. 5⅜ × 8½. 21739-6 Pa. $8.50

ALL ABOUT LIGHTNING, Martin A. Uman. Highly readable non-technical survey of nature and causes of lightning, thunderstorms, ball lightning, St. Elmo's Fire, much more. Illustrated. 192pp. 5⅜ × 8½. 25237-X Pa. $5.95

SAILING ALONE AROUND THE WORLD, Captain Joshua Slocum. First man to sail around the world, alone, in small boat. One of great feats of seamanship told in delightful manner. 67 illustrations. 294pp. 5⅜ × 8½. 20326-3 Pa. $4.95

LETTERS AND NOTES ON THE MANNERS, CUSTOMS AND CONDITIONS OF THE NORTH AMERICAN INDIANS, George Catlin. Classic account of life among Plains Indians: ceremonies, hunt, warfare, etc. 312 plates. 572pp. of text. 6⅛ × 9¼. 22118-0, 22119-9 Pa. Two-vol. set $15.90

ALASKA: The Harriman Expedition, 1899, John Burroughs, John Muir, et al. Informative, engrossing accounts of two-month, 9,000-mile expedition. Native peoples, wildlife, forests, geography, salmon industry, glaciers, more. Profusely illustrated. 240 black-and-white line drawings. 124 black-and-white photographs. 3 maps. Index. 576pp. 5⅜ × 8½. 25109-8 Pa. $11.95

ILLUSTRATED GUIDE TO SHAKER FURNITURE, Robert Meader. All furniture and appurtenances, with much on unknown local styles. 235 photos. 146pp. 9 × 12. 22819-3 Pa. $7.95

WHALE SHIPS AND WHALING: A Pictorial Survey, George Francis Dow. Over 200 vintage engravings, drawings, photographs of barks, brigs, cutters, other vessels. Also harpoons, lances, whaling guns, many other artifacts. Comprehensive text by foremost authority. 207 black-and-white illustrations. 288pp. 6 × 9. 24808-9 Pa. $8.95

THE BERTRAMS, Anthony Trollope. Powerful portrayal of blind self-will and thwarted ambition includes one of Trollope's most heartrending love stories. 497pp. 5⅜ × 8½. 25119-5 Pa. $8.95

ADVENTURES WITH A HAND LENS, Richard Headstrom. Clearly written guide to observing and studying flowers and grasses, fish scales, moth and insect wings, egg cases, buds, feathers, seeds, leaf scars, moss, molds, ferns, common crystals, etc.—all with an ordinary, inexpensive magnifying glass. 209 exact line drawings aid in your discoveries. 220pp. 5⅜ × 8½. 23330-8 Pa. $4.50

RODIN ON ART AND ARTISTS, Auguste Rodin. Great sculptor's candid, wide-ranging comments on meaning of art; great artists; relation of sculpture to poetry, painting, music; philosophy of life, more. 76 superb black-and-white illustrations of Rodin's sculpture, drawings and prints. 119pp. 8⅜ × 11¼. 24487-3 Pa. $6.95

FIFTY CLASSIC FRENCH FILMS, 1912–1982: A Pictorial Record, Anthony Slide. Memorable stills from Grand Illusion, Beauty and the Beast, Hiroshima, Mon Amour, many more. Credits, plot synopses, reviews, etc. 160pp. 8¼ × 11. 25256-6 Pa. $11.95

THE PRINCIPLES OF PSYCHOLOGY, William James. Famous long course complete, unabridged. Stream of thought, time perception, memory, experimental methods; great work decades ahead of its time. 94 figures. 1,391pp. 5⅜ × 8½. 20381-6, 20382-4 Pa., Two-vol. set $19.90

BODIES IN A BOOKSHOP, R. T. Campbell. Challenging mystery of blackmail and murder with ingenious plot and superbly drawn characters. In the best tradition of British suspense fiction. 192pp. 5⅜ × 8½. 24720-1 Pa. $3.95

CALLAS: PORTRAIT OF A PRIMA DONNA, George Jellinek. Renowned commentator on the musical scene chronicles incredible career and life of the most controversial, fascinating, influential operatic personality of our time. 64 black-and-white photographs. 416pp. 5⅜ × 8¼. 25047-4 Pa. $7.95

GEOMETRY, RELATIVITY AND THE FOURTH DIMENSION, Rudolph Rucker. Exposition of fourth dimension, concepts of relativity as Flatland characters continue adventures. Popular, easily followed yet accurate, profound. 141 illustrations. 133pp. 5⅜ × 8½. 23400-2 Pa. $3.50

HOUSEHOLD STORIES BY THE BROTHERS GRIMM, with pictures by Walter Crane. 53 classic stories—Rumpelstiltskin, Rapunzel, Hansel and Gretel, the Fisherman and his Wife, Snow White, Tom Thumb, Sleeping Beauty, Cinderella, and so much more—lavishly illustrated with original 19th century drawings. 114 illustrations. x + 269pp. 5⅜ × 8½. 21080-4 Pa. $4.50

SUNDIALS, Albert Waugh. Far and away the best, most thorough coverage of ideas, mathematics concerned, types, construction, adjusting anywhere. Over 100 illustrations. 230pp. 5⅜ × 8½. 22947-5 Pa. $4.50

PICTURE HISTORY OF THE NORMANDIE: With 190 Illustrations, Frank O. Braynard. Full story of legendary French ocean liner: Art Deco interiors, design innovations, furnishings, celebrities, maiden voyage, tragic fire, much more. Extensive text. 144pp. 8⅜ × 11¾. 25257-4 Pa. $9.95

THE FIRST AMERICAN COOKBOOK: A Facsimile of "American Cookery," 1796, Amelia Simmons. Facsimile of the first American-written cookbook published in the United States contains authentic recipes for colonial favorites—pumpkin pudding, winter squash pudding, spruce beer, Indian slapjacks, and more. Introductory Essay and Glossary of colonial cooking terms. 80pp. 5⅜ × 8½. 24710-4 Pa. $3.50

101 PUZZLES IN THOUGHT AND LOGIC, C. R. Wylie, Jr. Solve murders and robberies, find out which fishermen are liars, how a blind man could possibly identify a color—purely by your own reasoning! 107pp. 5⅜ × 8½. 20367-0 Pa. $2.50

THE BOOK OF WORLD-FAMOUS MUSIC—CLASSICAL, POPULAR AND FOLK, James J. Fuld. Revised and enlarged republication of landmark work in musico-bibliography. Full information about nearly 1,000 songs and compositions including first lines of music and lyrics. New supplement. Index. 800pp. 5⅜ × 8¼. 24857-7 Pa. $14.95

ANTHROPOLOGY AND MODERN LIFE, Franz Boas. Great anthropologist's classic treatise on race and culture. Introduction by Ruth Bunzel. Only inexpensive paperback edition. 255pp. 5⅜ × 8½. 25245-0 Pa. $5.95

THE TALE OF PETER RABBIT, Beatrix Potter. The inimitable Peter's terrifying adventure in Mr. McGregor's garden, with all 27 wonderful, full-color Potter illustrations. 55pp. 4¼ × 5½. (Available in U.S. only) 22827-4 Pa. $1.75

THREE PROPHETIC SCIENCE FICTION NOVELS, H. G. Wells. *When the Sleeper Wakes, A Story of the Days to Come* and *The Time Machine* (full version). 335pp. 5⅜ × 8½. (Available in U.S. only) 20605-X Pa. $5.95

APICIUS COOKERY AND DINING IN IMPERIAL ROME, edited and translated by Joseph Dommers Vehling. Oldest known cookbook in existence offers readers a clear picture of what foods Romans ate, how they prepared them, etc. 49 illustrations. 301pp. 6⅛ × 9¼. 23563-7 Pa. $6.50

SHAKESPEARE LEXICON AND QUOTATION DICTIONARY, Alexander Schmidt. Full definitions, locations, shades of meaning of every word in plays and poems. More than 50,000 exact quotations. 1,485pp. 6½ × 9¼. 22726-X, 22727-8 Pa., Two-vol. set $27.90

THE WORLD'S GREAT SPEECHES, edited by Lewis Copeland and Lawrence W. Lamm. Vast collection of 278 speeches from Greeks to 1970. Powerful and effective models; unique look at history. 842pp. 5⅜ × 8½. 20468-5 Pa. $11.95

THE BLUE FAIRY BOOK, Andrew Lang. The first, most famous collection, with many familiar tales: Little Red Riding Hood, Aladdin and the Wonderful Lamp, Puss in Boots, Sleeping Beauty, Hansel and Gretel, Rumpelstiltskin; 37 in all. 138 illustrations. 390pp. 5⅜ × 8½. 21437-0 Pa. $5.95

THE STORY OF THE CHAMPIONS OF THE ROUND TABLE, Howard Pyle. Sir Launcelot, Sir Tristram and Sir Percival in spirited adventures of love and triumph retold in Pyle's inimitable style. 50 drawings, 31 full-page. xviii + 329pp. 6½ × 9¼. 21883-X Pa. $6.95

AUDUBON AND HIS JOURNALS, Maria Audubon. Unmatched two-volume portrait of the great artist, naturalist and author contains his journals, an excellent biography by his granddaughter, expert annotations by the noted ornithologist, Dr. Elliott Coues, and 37 superb illustrations. Total of 1,200pp. 5⅜ × 8.

Vol. I 25143-8 Pa. $8.95
Vol. II 25144-6 Pa. $8.95

GREAT DINOSAUR HUNTERS AND THEIR DISCOVERIES, Edwin H. Colbert. Fascinating, lavishly illustrated chronicle of dinosaur research, 1820's to 1960. Achievements of Cope, Marsh, Brown, Buckland, Mantell, Huxley, many others. 384pp. 5¼ × 8¼. 24701-5 Pa. $6.95

THE TASTEMAKERS, Russell Lynes. Informal, illustrated social history of American taste 1850's–1950's. First popularized categories Highbrow, Lowbrow, Middlebrow. 129 illustrations. New (1979) afterword. 384pp. 6 × 9.

23993-4 Pa. $6.95

DOUBLE CROSS PURPOSES, Ronald A. Knox. A treasure hunt in the Scottish Highlands, an old map, unidentified corpse, surprise discoveries keep reader guessing in this cleverly intricate tale of financial skullduggery. 2 black-and-white maps. 320pp. 5⅜ × 8½. (Available in U.S. only) 25032-6 Pa. $5.95

AUTHENTIC VICTORIAN DECORATION AND ORNAMENTATION IN FULL COLOR: 46 Plates from "Studies in Design," Christopher Dresser. Superb full-color lithographs reproduced from rare original portfolio of a major Victorian designer. 48pp. 9¼ × 12¼. 25083-0 Pa. $7.95

PRIMITIVE ART, Franz Boas. Remains the best text ever prepared on subject, thoroughly discussing Indian, African, Asian, Australian, and, especially, Northern American primitive art. Over 950 illustrations show ceramics, masks, totem poles, weapons, textiles, paintings, much more. 376pp. 5⅜ × 8. 20025-6 Pa. $6.95

SIDELIGHTS ON RELATIVITY, Albert Einstein. Unabridged republication of two lectures delivered by the great physicist in 1920–21. *Ether and Relativity* and *Geometry and Experience*. Elegant ideas in non-mathematical form, accessible to intelligent layman. vi + 56pp. 5⅜ × 8½. 24511-X Pa. $2.95

THE WIT AND HUMOR OF OSCAR WILDE, edited by Alvin Redman. More than 1,000 ripostes, paradoxes, wisecracks: Work is the curse of the drinking classes, I can resist everything except temptation, etc. 258pp. 5⅜ × 8½. 20602-5 Pa. $4.50

ADVENTURES WITH A MICROSCOPE, Richard Headstrom. 59 adventures with clothing fibers, protozoa, ferns and lichens, roots and leaves, much more. 142 illustrations. 232pp. 5⅜ × 8½. 23471-1 Pa. $3.95

SIR HARRY HOTSPUR OF HUMBLETHWAITE, Anthony Trollope. Incisive, unconventional psychological study of a conflict between a wealthy baronet, his idealistic daughter, and their scapegrace cousin. The 1870 novel in its first inexpensive edition in years. 250pp. 5⅜ × 8½. 24953-0 Pa. $5.95

LASERS AND HOLOGRAPHY, Winston E. Kock. Sound introduction to burgeoning field, expanded (1981) for second edition. Wave patterns, coherence, lasers, diffraction, zone plates, properties of holograms, recent advances. 84 illustrations. 160pp. 5⅜ × 8¼. (Except in United Kingdom) 24041-X Pa. $3.50

INTRODUCTION TO ARTIFICIAL INTELLIGENCE: SECOND, EN-LARGED EDITION, Philip C. Jackson, Jr. Comprehensive survey of artificial intelligence—the study of how machines (computers) can be made to act intelligently. Includes introductory and advanced material. Extensive notes updating the main text. 132 black-and-white illustrations. 512pp. 5⅜ × 8½. 24864-X Pa. $8.95

HISTORY OF INDIAN AND INDONESIAN ART, Ananda K. Coomaraswamy. Over 400 illustrations illuminate classic study of Indian art from earliest Harappa finds to early 20th century. Provides philosophical, religious and social insights. 304pp. 6⅜ × 9⅜. 25005-9 Pa. $8.95

THE GOLEM, Gustav Meyrink. Most famous supernatural novel in modern European literature, set in Ghetto of Old Prague around 1890. Compelling story of mystical experiences, strange transformations, profound terror. 13 black-and-white illustrations. 224pp. 5⅜ × 8½. (Available in U.S. only) 25025-3 Pa. $5.95

ARMADALE, Wilkie Collins. Third great mystery novel by the author of *The Woman in White* and *The Moonstone*. Original magazine version with 40 illustrations. 597pp. 5⅜ × 8½. 23429-0 Pa. $9.95

PICTORIAL ENCYCLOPEDIA OF HISTORIC ARCHITECTURAL PLANS, DETAILS AND ELEMENTS: With 1,880 Line Drawings of Arches, Domes, Doorways, Facades, Gables, Windows, etc., John Theodore Haneman. Sourcebook of inspiration for architects, designers, others. Bibliography. Captions. 141pp. 9 × 12. 24605-1 Pa. $6.95

BENCHLEY LOST AND FOUND, Robert Benchley. Finest humor from early 30's, about pet peeves, child psychologists, post office and others. Mostly unavailable elsewhere. 73 illustrations by Peter Arno and others. 183pp. 5⅜ × 8½. 22410-4 Pa. $3.95

ERTÉ GRAPHICS, Erté. Collection of striking color graphics: *Seasons, Alphabet, Numerals, Aces* and *Precious Stones*. 50 plates, including 4 on covers. 48pp. 9⅜ × 12¼. 23580-7 Pa. $6.95

THE JOURNAL OF HENRY D. THOREAU, edited by Bradford Torrey, F. H. Allen. Complete reprinting of 14 volumes, 1837–61, over two million words; the sourcebooks for *Walden*, etc. Definitive. All original sketches, plus 75 photographs. 1,804pp. 8½ × 12¼. 20312-3, 20313-1 Cloth., Two-vol. set $80.00

CASTLES: THEIR CONSTRUCTION AND HISTORY, Sidney Toy. Traces castle development from ancient roots. Nearly 200 photographs and drawings illustrate moats, keeps, baileys, many other features. Caernarvon, Dover Castles, Hadrian's Wall, Tower of London, dozens more. 256pp. 5⅜ × 8¼.
24898-4 Pa. $5.95

AMERICAN CLIPPER SHIPS: 1833–1858, Octavius T. Howe & Frederick C. Matthews. Fully-illustrated, encyclopedic review of 352 clipper ships from the period of America's greatest maritime supremacy. Introduction. 109 halftones. 5 black-and-white line illustrations. Index. Total of 928pp. 5⅜ × 8½.
25115-2, 25116-0 Pa., Two-vol. set $17.90

TOWARDS A NEW ARCHITECTURE, Le Corbusier. Pioneering manifesto by great architect, near legendary founder of "International School." Technical and aesthetic theories, views on industry, economics, relation of form to function, "mass-production spirit," much more. Profusely illustrated. Unabridged translation of 13th French edition. Introduction by Frederick Etchells. 320pp. 6⅛ × 9¼. (Available in U.S. only)
25023-7 Pa. $8.95

THE BOOK OF KELLS, edited by Blanche Cirker. Inexpensive collection of 32 full-color, full-page plates from the greatest illuminated manuscript of the Middle Ages, painstakingly reproduced from rare facsimile edition. Publisher's Note. Captions. 32pp. 9⅜ × 12¼.
24345-1 Pa. $4.95

BEST SCIENCE FICTION STORIES OF H. G. WELLS, H. G. Wells. Full novel The Invisible Man, plus 17 short stories: "The Crystal Egg," "Aepyornis Island," "The Strange Orchid," etc. 303pp. 5⅜ × 8½. (Available in U.S. only)
21531-8 Pa. $4.95

AMERICAN SAILING SHIPS: Their Plans and History, Charles G. Davis. Photos, construction details of schooners, frigates, clippers, other sailcraft of 18th to early 20th centuries—plus entertaining discourse on design, rigging, nautical lore, much more. 137 black-and-white illustrations. 240pp. 6⅛ × 9¼.
24658-2 Pa. $5.95

ENTERTAINING MATHEMATICAL PUZZLES, Martin Gardner. Selection of author's favorite conundrums involving arithmetic, money, speed, etc., with lively commentary. Complete solutions. 112pp. 5⅜ × 8½.
25211-6 Pa. $2.95

THE WILL TO BELIEVE, HUMAN IMMORTALITY, William James. Two books bound together. Effect of irrational on logical, and arguments for human immortality. 402pp. 5⅜ × 8½.
20291-7 Pa. $7.50

THE HAUNTED MONASTERY and THE CHINESE MAZE MURDERS, Robert Van Gulik. 2 full novels by Van Gulik continue adventures of Judge Dee and his companions. An evil Taoist monastery, seemingly supernatural events; overgrown topiary maze that hides strange crimes. Set in 7th-century China. 27 illustrations. 328pp. 5⅜ × 8½.
23502-5 Pa. $5.95

CELEBRATED CASES OF JUDGE DEE (DEE GOONG AN), translated by Robert Van Gulik. Authentic 18th-century Chinese detective novel; Dee and associates solve three interlocked cases. Led to Van Gulik's own stories with same characters. Extensive introduction. 9 illustrations. 237pp. 5⅜ × 8½.
23337-5 Pa. $4.95

Prices subject to change without notice.

Available at your book dealer or write for free catalog to Dept. GI, Dover Publications, Inc., 31 East 2nd St., Mineola, N.Y. 11501. Dover publishes more than 175 books each year on science, elementary and advanced mathematics, biology, music, art, literary history, social sciences and other areas.